F
on

To r
or

Yo

Michael Quentin Morton grew up in Qatar, Bahrain and Abu Dhabi in the 1950s and 1960s. A barrister using his first-hand knowledge of the region, he has written a number of books and articles on the history of oil exploration in the Arabian Peninsula.

For Gill

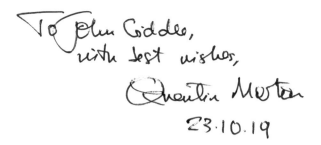

To John Criddle,
with best wishes,
Quentin Morton
23.10.19

Buraimi

The Struggle for Power, Influence and Oil in Arabia

MICHAEL QUENTIN MORTON

I.B. TAURIS

LONDON · NEW YORK

Published in 2013 and reprinted in 2014 by I.B.Tauris & Co Ltd
6 Salem Road, London W2 4BU
175 Fifth Avenue, New York NY 10010
www.ibtauris.com

Distributed in the United States and Canada Exclusively by Palgrave Macmillan
175 Fifth Avenue, New York NY10010

ISBN 978 1 84885 818 3

A full CIP record for this book is available from the British Library
A full CIP record is available from the Library of Congress

Library of Congress Catalog Card Number: available

Printed and bound by CPI Group (UK) Ltd, Croydon CR0 4YY
from camera-ready copy edited and supplied by the author

Contents

Acknowledgements   vii

List of Illustrations   viii

Abbreviations   x

Note to the Reader   xii

Notes on the Main Characters   xiii

Prologue   1

1. Jedda Calling   7

2. A Bend in the Wadi   17

3. The Riyadh Line   26

4. Lanterns in the Dark   34

5. A Tale of Two Brothers   50

6. Squeezing Aramco   63

7. The Stobart Incident   75

8. Borderlands   86

9. Turki and the Tribes   95

10. Taking a Stand   110

11. The Hamasa Blockade   120

12. No Oil Man's Land   133

13. Make it a Red Fire   144

14. The Buraimi Arbitration Tribunal   159

15. Dust in Their Eyes   174

16. Operation Bonaparte   181

17. The Road to Suez   192

18. Rebels and Refugees   205

19. Shaybah Rising   216

Epilogue   231

Maps   239

Glossary   242

References   245

Bibliography   270

Index   277

Acknowledgements

This book is about the Buraimi dispute, or Buraimi affair, as it was known, which propelled a quiet oasis onto the world stage and laid the foundations for the modern states of the United Arab Emirates and Oman.

For the handful of Westerners who knew it in the 1950s, the Buraimi Oasis denoted a group of oases and nine villages situated between the desert and mountains of south-eastern Arabia. Today, they would hardly recognise the area. On the UAE side of the border, six of the villages have been swallowed up by the Al-Ain conurbation, while on the Omani side the pace of development has not been quite so rapid.

I have been especially fortunate to have received help from a few who lived through those times: Peter Clayton, formerly of the Trucial Oman Levies; Michael Sterner, former US ambassador to Abu Dhabi; Julian Walker and the late Sir John Wilton, erstwhile British diplomats. Dr A.T. and Amr al-Otaishan, son and grandson respectively of Turki bin Abdullah al-Otaishan, helped me to see the affair in a different light. For their guidance, assistance and advice, I wish to thank Peter Aitkens, Tim Barger, Arthur P. Clarke, Dr Paul Cornelius, Dr Alan Heward, Nick Lee, Ivor Lucas, Doug Manning, Ron Miller, Julian Paxton, John Vale, Sir Harold Walker and Dr John Wilkinson. My thanks also to Minna Cowper-Coles for advice on the manuscript; John Harper, Linda Burton and the staff at the Chevron Archive, San Francisco; Nicholas Scheetz and Scott S. Taylor of the Georgetown University Library, Washing-ton DC; Peter Housego and Joanne Burman of the BP Archive, Warwick University; Debbie Usher of the Middle East Centre Archive, St Antony's College, Oxford.

Finally my brother Peter Morton and my mother Heather provided sterling support for this project. And to my late father, the geologist and explorer Mike Morton, I shall always be grateful.

List of Illustrations

Abdul Aziz ibn Abdul Rahman Al Saud ('Ibn Saud')   8

Ibn Saud with Casoc representatives   22

Sultan Said bin Taimur   38

Wilfred Thesiger   47

Saud bin Jiluwi   54

Shakhbut bin Sultan Al Nahyan   58

Zayed bin Sultan Al Nahyan   62

Abdullah Suleiman   69

Suleiman bin Hamyar and Imam Ghalib bin Ali al-Hinai   88

Saqr bin Sultan al-Naimi   89

Obaid bin Juma al-Kaabi   90

Rashid bin Hamad al-Shamsi   92

The Buraimi Oasis   98

Turki bin Abdullah al-Otaishan   100

Prince Faisal at a press conference, 11 March 1953   117

The Jimi tower   124

Buraimi *suq* with Sheikh Saqr's fort in the background   127

Yusuf Yasin   135

Major Abdullah bin Nami   146

Sir Hartley Shawcross, QC   163

The ruins of Hamasa   190

Meeting of rulers at Buraimi, December 1955   198

Anthony Eden and John Foster Dulles   200

Colonel Nasser meets King Saud, 9 March 1956   204

A suspected mine smuggler   209

King Fahd, Sheikh Zayed and Sultan Qaboos, 1994   226

Maps

The Arabian Peninsula in 1948   239

Boundary proposals   240

South-eastern Arabia   241

Abbreviations

General

FO   Foreign Office
FRUS   Foreign Relations of the United States (archive material)
GCC   Gulf Co-operation Council
IOR   India Records Office
UAE   United Arab Emirates

Oil Companies

ADMA   Abu Dhabi Marine Areas Limited, which obtained the offshore concession of Abu Dhabi in 1954 and was owned in equal shares by British Petroleum and Total.

APOC   Anglo-Persian Oil Company, which became the Anglo-Iranian Oil Company in 1935 and then British Petroleum (BP) in 1954.

ARAMCO   Arabian American Oil Company, created in 1943 from the California-Arabian Standard Oil Company (Casoc). The Saudi Arabian government acquired a 25 per cent share of the Company in 1973, a 60 per cent share in 1974 and a 100 per cent share in 1980. It was renamed Saudi Arabian Oil Company (or Saudi Aramco) in 1988.

CASOC   California-Arabian Standard Oil Company, formed in 1933 by Standard Oil of California in 1933 to develop the Hasa oil concession. In 1936 Casoc joined forces with the Texas Oil Company to form Caltex.

CFP   Compagnie Française des Pétroles, which in 1991 became Total.

IPC   See overleaf.

SOCAL   Standard Oil of California. It formed the California-Arabian Standard Oil Company (Casoc) to operate the Al-Hasa oil concession. Socal became Chevron in 1984, and merged with Texaco in 2001.

SOCONY   Standard Oil of New York (which merged with the Vacuum Oil Company in 1931 and became Mobil in 1955). Mobil merged with Exxon in 1999.

IPC   Iraq Petroleum Company

The following companies held shares of 23.5 per cent in the Company:
The Anglo-Persian Oil Company; Royal Dutch Shell; CFP; and the Near East Development Corporation (a consortium of five large US oil companies, among them Standard Oil of New York (Socony) and Standard Oil New Jersey (which became Exxon). Calouste Gulbenkian held a 5 per cent share. IPC's assets in Iraq were fully nationalised in 1971.

IPC created subsidiary companies to develop oil concessions outside Iraq. In southern Arabia these were:

ADPC   Abu Dhabi Petroleum Company Limited, formed in 1963. In 1974 the Abu Dhabi National Oil Company acquired a 60 per cent share in ADPC, which later became the Abu Dhabi Company for Onshore Oil Operations.

PCL   Petroleum Concessions Limited, which operated in the Aden Protectorates (today in Yemen) under an exploration licence granted in 1938.

PDO   Petroleum Development (Oman) Limited.

PDQ   Petroleum Development (Qatar) Limited (which became Qatar Petroleum Company in 1953).

PDTC   Petroleum Development (Trucial Coast) Limited (which became ADPC in 1963). The company obtained the first onshore concession for Abu Dhabi in 1939.

QPC   Qatar Petroleum Company, successor to PDQ, nationalised in 1979.

Note to the Reader

I have aimed this book at a general as well as specialist audience, therefore spellings are derived from Western sources rather than any recognised system of transliteration. Many of the names of places and individuals are as they appear in the Foreign Office files: the king of Saudi Arabia, Abdul Aziz ibn Abdur Rahman Al Saud, was commonly referred to as 'Ibn Saud' and so appears as such in the book.

This can lead to inconsistencies, for example, my usage of 'ibn' and 'bin' (both meaning son of) varies according to the sources. I have used the modern spelling 'Otaishan' for the family name of Turki bin Abdullah, although it is spelt 'Utayshan' or 'Atoishan' in various other documents. Where certain place names in Arabic contain the definitive article, such as Al-Buraimi, I have only included it where necessary to make sense of a name (e.g. Al-Ain) or where it was commonly included in the files (e.g. Al-Kharj). For the sake of simplicity, I have not included diacritical marks.

The Gulf is described as the 'Persian' Gulf because it was so described in official documents of the time. It is appreciated that the rise of the Arabian states has led to the term 'Arabian' Gulf being used more often than it used to be, and perhaps it is more diplomatic to call it 'the Gulf' today, as has been done in the later episodes of this book.

Regarding monetary values, I have converted each larger sum into its modern equivalent, indicating in brackets how much it might be worth today. Rupees were converted into sterling based on a fixed exchange rate of 1s. 6d. (7.5 pence) to the rupee for the period 1927–66.[1] Then the Bank of England Inflation Calculator[2] was used (based on the relative cost of goods and services) to calculate the modern value of the sterling amount, taking account of inflation. For riyal calculations, a rate of 1 riyal = $0.27 dollars in 1952[3] was used to convert the sum into dollars. The effect of inflation was then taken into account by using another calculator[4] before converting the amount into sterling.

However, it is acknowledged that this is not an exact science, and there are other ways of making the calculations; therefore, all the figures are approximate.

Notes on the Main Characters

Abdul Aziz ibn Abdul Rahman Al Saud ('Ibn Saud')
Believed to have been born in 1876, Ibn Saud led a series of conquests that culminated in the nation of Saudi Arabia being founded in 1932 with him as king. He died on 9 November 1953, and was succeeded by his son Saud.

Abdullah al-Qaraishi
Ostensibly a clerk and Quran reader, he was in fact a political officer and in charge of Saudi operations on the ground in the Buraimi Oasis between August 1954 and October 1955.

Abdullah bin Nami ('Bin Nami')
Nominally the officer in charge of the Saudi police post, replacing Turki al-Otaishan in August 1954 and carrying on Turki's campaign of winning over the people of the Buraimi Oasis and beyond.

Abdullah bin Salim
Sheikh of the Bani Kaab and nephew of the defiant Obaid bin Juma, Abdullah originally rebelled against the sultan but changed sides, deposed his uncle and assumed leadership of his tribe.

Abdullah Suleiman
Chief finance minister in Ibn Saud's government 1928–52.

Thomas C. Barger
A geologist for the California-Arabian Standard Oil Company (Casoc), he went on to become president of Aramco in 1959 and chief executive officer of the company in 1961.

Dick Bird
Represented the IPC associate company, Petroleum Development (Trucial Coast) Ltd, in the Buraimi Oasis between 1948 and 1951. His knowledge of the tribes of south-eastern Arabia equalled, or possibly exceeded, that of Wilfred Thesiger.

Reader Bullard (from 1943, Sir)
Diplomat, who was based in Jedda between 1923 and 1925 as consul to the Hashemite kingdom and between 1936 and 1939 as minister to Saudi Arabia. In 1955 he was an arbitrator on the Buraimi Tribunal.

Bernard Burrows (from 1955, Sir)
Political resident, Bahrain 1952–8.

Peter Clayton
Captain in the Trucial Oman Levies who supervised the Neutral Zone in Buraimi between August 1954 and October 1955, and attended the arbitration tribunal hearing in Geneva as a witness.

John Foster Dulles
From a family of diplomats, Dulles was secretary of state in the Eisenhower administration of 1953–9.

Anthony Eden (from 1954, Sir)
Served as British foreign secretary for three terms, 1935–8, 1940–5 and 1951–5, when he succeeded Winston Churchill as prime minster. He resigned in January 1957 after the Suez crisis.

Fahd ibn Abdul Aziz Al Saud
Born in 1921, the eighth son of Ibn Saud, Fahd became crown prince upon the death of Faisal and king in 1982 upon the death of Khalid. He died of natural causes in 2005.

Faisal ibn Abdul Aziz Al Saud
Born in 1904, the third son of Ibn Saud, Faisal was appointed minister of foreign affairs in 1932, crown prince in 1953 and king in 1964. He was assassinated in 1975.

Ghalib bin Ali al-Hinai
In May 1954 he became imam of Oman, spiritual leader of the Ibadhi sect.

Edward Henderson
A liaison officer for IPC, he was seconded to the Foreign Office and helped to prepare the UK Memorial for the arbitration proceedings.

Eric Johnson
Colonel in the TOL, he was in charge of the handover arrangements in August 1954 when Major Abdullah bin Nami replaced Emir Turki al-Otaishan. In October 1955, as commanding officer of the force, he was in charge of Operation Bonaparte.

Stephen Longrigg
Having served in Iraq, he joined IPC. He was based in its Land and Liaison Department in Haifa, Palestine, and served as a negotiator for the company. He returned to IPC after World War II as a senior manager. He retired from the company in 1951.

Reginald Manningham-Buller
Attorney-General between 1954 and 1962, he became Lord Chancellor and served as a Law Lord in the House of Lords as Viscount Dilhorne.

Muhammad bin Abdullah al-Khalili
Imam of Oman until his death in 1954.

Muhammad ibn Abdul al-Wahhab
Radical preacher born in about 1702, the founder of Wahhabism. He joined forces with the Al Saud in 1744.

Obaid bin Juma al-Kaabi
Sheikh of the Beni Kaab who declared for the Saudis, was deposed by his nephew Abdullah bin Salim and went to live in Hamasa.

Harry St John ('Jack') Philby
Arrived in the Saudi capital Riyadh as an adviser for the British government during World War I, becoming an adviser to Ibn Saud, converting to Islam and taking an Arab wife.

Rashid bin Hamad al-Shamsi
Sheikh of the Al Bu Shamis tribe with a strong interest in the slave trade, he was the headman of Hamasa village and the Saudis' main supporter in the area.

George Rentz
Head of Aramco's Arabian Research and Translation Division.

Sir Andrew Ryan (knighted in 1925)
British minister (ambassador) in Jedda 1930–6 whose memoir *The Last of the Dragomans* was published in 1951.

Said bin Taimur
Born in 1910, he succeeded to the sultanate of Muscat and Oman in 1932 upon the abdication of his father and reigned until 1970.

Saqr bin Sultan al-Naimi ('The Old Fox')
Sheikh of the Naimi tribe and paramount sheikh of Buraimi village. He was the sultan of Oman's representative in the Buraimi Oasis.

Saud ibn Abdul Aziz Al Saud
Eldest surviving son of Ibn Saud and king who ruled Saudi Arabia from 1953 to 1964.

Saud bin Jiluwi
Son of Abdullah bin Jiluwi, he became emir of the Eastern province upon the death of his father in 1935 and presided over Saudi operations in the Buraimi Oasis in 1952–5. He was known to Aramcons as the 'Big Bin'.

Shakhbut bin Sultan Al Nahyan
A grandson of Zayed the Great, Sheikh Shakhbut was born in 1905. He succeeded to the sheikhdom of Abu Dhabi following the murder of his father and ruled from 1928 to 1966.

Evelyn Shuckburgh
He was appointed private secretary to the British foreign secretary in 1951 and served under Anthony Eden for three years.

Michael Sterner
Employed by Aramco as a government relations representative at Ras Tanura in 1952, Sterner went on to become a diplomat and was US ambassador to the UAE between 1974 and 1976.

Suleiman bin Hamyar al-Nabhan
The leader of the Beni Riyam tribe of Oman. Nominally loyal to the sultan of Oman, he eventually sided with the Omani rebels in 1957.

Sultan bin Zayed Al Nahyan
A son of Zayed the Great, he assassinated his elder brother Sheikh Hamdam in 1922 and thus became sheikh of Abu Dhabi. He was in turn assassinated by another elder brother, Saqr, in 1927. Father of Shakhbut and Zayed.

Talib bin Ali al-Hinai
Brother of the imam of Oman, Ghalib, Talib opposed the sultan in central Oman, leading to the Jebel Akhdar War of 1957.

Turki bin Abdullah al-Otaishan
Born in Buraydah, Saudi Arabia, in 1911. After serving in the army and police, he was appointed emir of Ras Tanura in 1945. In August 1952, he led a column of Saudi guards to Hamasa and raised the Saudi flag over the village. He stayed there for two years. In September 1955 he was appointed to the Dammam Labour Office.

Hafiz Wahba
An Egyptian born in about 1890, he became Saudi ambassador to London in 1929 and continued in that post until 1956, when Saudi Arabia broke off diplomatic relations with Britain over the Suez crisis. He returned to serve a second term in 1963–6.

Yusuf Yasin
A Syrian refugee from Palestine, Yasin became deputy prime minister of Saudi Arabia and was closely involved in border negotiations with the British. He had overall responsibility for Saudi operations in the Buraimi Oasis between 1952 and 1955 and was an arbitrator on the Buraimi Arbitration Tribunal.

Zayed bin Sultan Al Nahyan
Youngest brother of Sheikh Shakhbut, Sheikh Zayed was governor of Abu Dhabi's Eastern province from 1947 and resided in Al-Ain, a village of the Buraimi Oasis. In 1966 he became ruler of Abu Dhabi and in 1971 president of the United Arab Emirates.

'If Calais was imprinted on Queen Mary's heart,
Buraimi is certainly imprinted on mine.'

Roderick Parkes, diplomat
27 April 1966[1]

Prologue
The Arabian Peninsula, 1744–1927

The settlement of Diriyah stood on the dusty plateau of the Nejd, and in AD 1744 a renegade preacher sought refuge there. Abandoned by his escort of horsemen beside a cave, he continued his dusty journey alone on foot with only a fan to spare him from the searing desert heat. On reaching Diriyah, he came to the house of a friend who, although fearful of his ruler's reaction to the presence of the visitor, reluctantly admitted him. Here, amid the palm trees and cracked mud walls, the visitor found a willing audience for his teaching, and soon word reached the ruler that a stranger was preaching to the people of the town.[1]

The ruler, Emir Muhammad ibn Saud, instead of being hostile was receptive to the stranger's preaching. In this the preacher was fortunate, for it had not always been so: Sheikh Muhammad ibn Abdul al-Wahhab was an outcast, having been exiled from his last settlement because of his radical views. Now, with the settled Al Saud tribe as his audience, the charismatic preacher's words struck a chord. The emir saw in his arrival the opportunity to combine his own plans of conquering the Arabian Peninsula with a strong religious message. His tribe accepted the preacher and his status among them was confirmed by his marriage to a number of their women.

This was a marriage of minds but it was the extremity of the preacher's beliefs and the emir's ambition that gave their partnership such potency: the fusion of religion, politics and military force in a single vision of Arabian domination. A radical Muslim preacher who believed that the Quran was literally true, Sheikh Muhammad ibn Abdul al-Wahhab was in fact carrying forward an Islamic tradition that stretched back to the tenth century AD, a puritan desire to go back to basics, stripping religion of all its artefacts, distortions and distractions: nothing, in short, should come between Man and God.

Thus the decoration of mosques, the cult of saints and the smoking of tobacco were banned; and the stoning of adulterous women and destruction of idols were approved. Sheikh Muhammad espoused a doctrine that his followers – Wahhabis as they were known to

outsiders, *Muwahidun* or Unitarians as they preferred to be known –
took to extremes. If you were not with them you were against them,
Muslim or Christian alike, and deserved to be killed. With a promise
of admission to Paradise if they fell in battle – it was said they carried
orders from Sheikh Muhammad to the gatekeeper of heaven to admit
them forthwith – the Wahhabi warrior must have felt invincible
indeed.

With the emir leading his tribes into battle, and Sheikh Muhammad
beside him, the Al Saud presented a formidable fighting force. Driven
by a fervent desire to impose *sharia* law on the rest of the Arabian
Peninsula, they remained in a state of *jihad*, or holy war, for
generations. Their dream of carving out an Islamic kingdom stretching
the length and breadth of the peninsula almost came true: Wahhabi
warriors flooded over the shores of the Persian Gulf, occupied the
Yemen coast, and attacked what is known today as southern Iraq,
including a bloody massacre in the city of Karbala. In 1802 – long after
Sheikh Muhammad's demise – they stripped Mecca of its treasures and
baubles.

For those unfortunates who lay in their path, and for the tribes of
Oman who had already experienced the full glare of Wahhabi
intimidation, it was a humbling experience. Seven hundred Wahhabi
camel-riders under General Salim al-Hariq came out of the desert in
the spring of 1800 and seized a cluster of nine villages known
collectively as the Buraimi Oasis. Being at a crossroads between desert
and coast, mountains and plain, the oasis was an attractive prize since
whoever controlled it might dominate the tribes of south-eastern
Arabia, tax them and reap profit from the lucrative trade in slaves. The
tribes around Buraimi, notably the Naimi and Dhawahir, were fiercely
independent yet hopelessly divided and, when confronted by the wild-
eyed soldiers of God, they were easily overcome. Having captured the
oasis, the Wahhabis proceeded to build their own fort and the oasis
became their headquarters for attacking central Oman.[2]

Even so, there were those who embraced the Wahhabi invasion, the
combination of prayer with plunder appealing to the Qawasim tribe of
Sharjah who brought a maritime dimension to the Wahhabi cause:
from 1804 they were characterised as pirates after a series of attacks on
British ships on the Persian Gulf.[3] Elsewhere, those tribes who resisted
the Wahhabis were attacked and brought to their knees, and their
sheikhs required to pay tributes to their Wahhabi overlords. No one

was immune: even the sultan of Muscat and Oman was forced repeatedly to buy off the invaders and, as if to rub salt in his wounds, a Wahhabi agent came to live in Muscat.

The first Saudi state, as some historians have called this period of Al Saud expansion, ended in 1818 when Diriyah fell to the Ottoman commander Ibrahim Pasha, who made a point of dealing severely with the leaders of the Wahhabi faith. He forced one cleric to dig his own grave, after which the cleric's teeth were extracted and he was made to listen to some 'light music' before being decapitated and tumbled into a pit.[4] Diriyah was destroyed, and the rump of the tribe drifted south to the desert town of Riyadh, which became their base. Their leader, Imam Abdullah ibn Saud, was allowed to go into exile in Egypt. Then, having been invited to Istanbul, he was paraded there for three days before being executed, his head crushed, and his body hung on a post.

Meanwhile, for those Wahhabis left behind in Buraimi, there was no prospect of reinforcement and their leader surrendered himself to the sultan of Muscat and Oman. But the Wahhabi occupation would have repercussions for many years to come. In 1820, Qawasimi pirates were threatening the shipping routes to and from India, and the British East India Company negotiated an agreement, the General Treaty of Peace, with their ruler. In 1835 a Maritime Truce, subsequently renewed and then made permanent in 1853, ended hostile activities on the Gulf. Since all the tribes of the coast agreed to abide by the truce, the lower Gulf region became known as the Trucial Coast, or Trucial Oman, but Britain held back from any further involvement with the Trucial sheikhs, and declined a request from them to establish a protectorate.[5]

The Wahhabis were not finished with Buraimi yet. A second Saudi state sprang up in 1824 with the recapture of Riyadh from Egyptian forces. In 1853 Abdullah ibn Faisal, son of the Wahhabi emir, arrived in Buraimi, extracted a tribute of $12,000 from the sultan of Muscat and Oman, and again forced him to make peace with them the following year. The British were not amused. In 1866 the British Resident in the Persian Gulf, Colonel Lewis Pelly, intervened and extracted a promise from Abdullah ibn Faisal not to attack any Arab tribe that was in alliance with the British, especially those of Oman, so long as a tribute, or *zakat*, was paid.

In 1869 the Wahhabis were finally ejected from Buraimi. The Naimi tribe of Buraimi had enlisted the help of Azzan ibn Qais of

Muscat. Azzan marched on the oasis and defeated the Wahhabis. He told the British political resident:

> God has thus relieved his people from the aggressive Wahhabis. He drove them out in shame and feeling low. We found the people living in those parts under the worst conditions [...] of their despicable tyranny and high-handed cruelty. And we returned to these all that those had robbed or confiscated of their stock and property.[6]

Azzan entered into an alliance with the ruler of Abu Dhabi, Sheikh Zayed bin Khalifa (Zayed the Great), and agreed to pay him a subsidy to protect Buraimi. After installing a garrison under the command of a relative, Azzan returned to Muscat.

When Lt-Col. Samuel Miles, the British political agent in Muscat, visited the oasis in November 1875, he found the Naimi tribe dominant in the villages of Buraimi and Saara. Later reports confirmed that Zayed the Great had bought property in and around Al-Ain, another of the oasis villages, and that he was a 'strong and increasing' influence in the district.[7] Apart from a brief return of the Wahhabis in 1871, the Buraimi tribes heard no more from them for the next 50 years.

In 1891, after the battle of Mulayda, the Al Saud were expelled from Riyadh. But they were soon in the ascendant again. In 1902 their leader's young son, Abdul Aziz ibn Abdul Rahman Al Saud, later known to the British as Ibn Saud, with his cousin Abdullah bin Jiluwi and a small raiding party, stormed the Masmak fort in Riyadh and regained the town. Bin Jiluwi, who would strike terror into the hearts of his opponents in later years, famously left his spear tip embedded in the postern of the fort.

With the Al Saud back in control, an uneasy balance developed in the region. Ever since Palmerston's declaration of 1833 that 'Turkey would be as good an occupier of the road to India as an active Arab sovereign would be', the British had been happy to leave the affairs of the Arabian interior to the Turks. When the Al Saud first made overtures to the British government through the political resident, they were studiously ignored.[8]

There was little doubt about Ibn Saud's ambition. He had set out his plans for southern Arabia early in his reign: 'By God I will explore the country belonging to my father and grandfather from Muscat to

Ja'alan,' he had declared, referring to what he considered to be his ancestral lands in central Oman.[9] Based on the conquests of his ancestors, he also considered that he had a claim to the sheikhdoms of Qatar and the Trucial Coast. When he made approaches to the Trucial sheikhs in 1905, the Persian Gulf Resident, Sir Percy Cox, was quick to pour cold water on the initiative and to keep the sheikhs in line. He warned them that 'the display of any inclination on the part of any of them to give encouragement to, or to intrigue with, Ibn Saood [*sic*] or his Agents will not be regarded by Govt. with complacency.'[10]

Otherwise, to the British, Ibn Saud was just another minor potentate and of little importance in the grand scheme of things: a landlocked ruler who posed no threat to British interests in the Persian Gulf. In time, however, it became apparent that Ibn Saud was a power to be reckoned with, particularly when his warriors arrived on the shores of the Persian Gulf. While British and Turkish officials were meeting in London in 1913 to define the boundary between their respective spheres, the Al Saud snatched the Turkish province of Al-Hasa from under their noses.[11]

Having other preoccupations in Europe, the British did not attempt to intervene militarily, but the need to prevent the Al Saud from assisting Turkey in World War I led the British Government of India (which handled relations with the Arabian sheikhs) to urge an approach to Ibn Saud. The result was a treaty of friendship signed in December 1915. Ibn Saud recognised the independence of the coastal sheikhdoms and was required to gain British approval for any concessions granted to foreigners; he agreed not to 'cede, sell, lease, mortgage or otherwise dispose of any part of his territories to any other foreign power, or to the subjects of any such power, without the consent of the British government whose advice he would follow unreservedly'. In return, Britain recognised Ibn Saud's domain of the Nejd and Al-Hasa and awarded him an annual stipend of £60,000 (£5 million in today's money).[12]

Always the pragmatist, Ibn Saud was able to rein in his ambition for the time being, yet the past glories of the Wahhabis were never far from his mind. In 1922 he finally defeated his arch-rivals, the Al Rashid tribe and, three years later, using ferocious Wahhabi warriors known as the *Ikhwan*, he captured Mecca. When fighting broke out between the tribes of the Dhahira plain and Abu Dhabi in 1925, his cousin Abdullah bin Jiluwi, then emir of Al-Hasa province, sent the

Murrah tribe to raid the Abu Dhabi tribes, followed closely by Saudi tax collectors. In the spring of 1926 the Wahhabis were back in Buraimi, collecting tax from nomadic tribesmen and imposing their strict version of *sharia* law, hanging a criminal in the public market place of Buraimi village.

In 1927 Bertram Thomas, a British civil servant employed as the sultan of Muscat's *wazir*, attempted to visit Buraimi. The sheikhs of the Naimi tribe who were dominant in the area warned him to stay away because his visit would be a 'disturbance' and likely to upset Ibn Saud. Thomas did keep away, but when he visited the following year he received a warm welcome from Sheikh Saqr bin Sultan of the Naimi. Saqr told Thomas that the warning of the previous year had been issued by his mentor, Abu Sindah, and not by the sheikhs themselves. The situation around Buraimi was, nonetheless, confused: Saudi tax collectors had been at work arousing great resentment among the surrounding tribes by gathering *zakat* once more.[13]

In the collection of tax the Wahhabis – or Saudis as they would be known – held the whip hand. Although the nomadic bedouin could either accept the tax regime or move out of the taxman's reach, the settled villagers had no such choice. Nonetheless, the Wahhabi presence was disorganised and sporadic, and in 1927 the tax collectors disappeared from Buraimi once more. The oasis returned to its routine, disturbed only by the occasional slave caravan lumbering on its way to Al-Hasa. 'No news in your country here except happiness, and nothing against it,' one of the Naimi sheikhs cheerfully reported to the sultan of Muscat, giving a nodding acknowledgement of the sultan's rule over them.[14]

Such was the situation in Buraimi when the oil age dawned.

Chapter 1
Jedda Calling
Oil Negotiations, 1933

In those days, from the balcony of the Grand Hotel in Jedda, you could see the white minarets across the rooftops, hear the *muezzin* calling the faithful to prayer, and briefly imagine a romantic picture of Araby. As with other towns in Arabia, the modern age had bypassed Jedda, leaving it firmly entrenched in an earlier time. The narrow alleyways below the balcony were dark and winding, protected from the burning sun by mats and loose boards, while merchants did business from little booths in the *suq*. Street cries filled the air and camels passed by, loaded with freight or pilgrims on their way to the holy places.[1]

Jedda on the Red Sea was the main port on the western coast of Saudi Arabia and the gateway to Mecca and the holy places. In reality, Westerners found its climate unhealthy, the rain and cold of winter replaced by a rising humidity in the spring that presaged the unbearable heat of summer. In 1933 there were no modern amenities to speak of: the recently refurbished Grand Hotel had no running water, no air conditioning and toilets of sand. All the foreign delegations to the Kingdom of Saudi Arabia were housed in the town. The British were the most numerous, followed by the Dutch, who spent most of their time looking after the large number of pilgrims arriving from the Dutch East Indies. The isolation of foreigners, however pressing or welcome their business, was a constant feature of life in the town and much felt by the diplomatic and consular corps.[2]

When T.E. Lawrence visited Jedda during the Great War, he felt the heat of Arabia that came out 'like a drawn sword and struck us speechless'. In the alley of the food market, along the meat and fruit stalls, 'squadrons of flies like particles of dust danced up and down the sun shafts'. The atmosphere, he concluded, 'was like a bath'.[3] Sir Andrew Ryan, British minister in Jedda between 1930 and 1936, described a tumbledown and squalid town that, although picturesque with an air of greatness, looked as though it had never quite recovered from the bombardment it had received from a British warship in the nineteenth century.[4]

There was little Western interest in the Arabian interior, apart from a starry-eyed attachment to the great sand desert, the Rub al-Khali which Bertram Thomas had crossed two years before. But an oil strike on the island of Bahrain in May 1932 had triggered the interest of an American company, Standard Oil of California (Socal), in the oil prospects of the Arabian mainland. Not to be outdone, their rival in the region, the Iraq Petroleum Company (IPC), was also attracted. Now the oilmen gathered in Jedda to discuss with representatives of the kingdom an oil concession for the eastern province of Al-Hasa.[5]

The king of Saudi Arabia, Ibn Saud, was six feet three inches tall and made an impression both by his height and by his air of command. Then in his fifties, he was still a handsome man apart from a blotch across the left eye due to neglected leucoma. 'He has,' an observer once wrote, 'the characteristics of the well-bred Arab, the strongly marked aquiline profile, full-flesh nostrils, prominent lips accentuated by a

Abdul Aziz ibn Abdul Rahman Al Saud, known to the British as Ibn Saud, in middle age. (source: Royal Geographical Society)

pointed beard. His hands are fine with slender fingers [and he has a] slow sweet smile.'[6] Not everyone was taken in by that smile however; as Ryan once remarked, 'it was spoilt by his habit of switching it on and off almost mechanically'.[7]

For those who had dealings with Ibn Saud, it was his apparent spirituality combined with an acute political skill that left a lasting impression. And although a deeply religious man – he took his duties as imam or spiritual leader of his people very seriously – he also took a close interest in foreign news programmes on the radio and avidly read translations of newspaper cuttings sent by his representatives abroad; thus he managed to keep himself up to date with international events. His political judgment was sound and he was rarely wrong: it was only in his later years that it weakened and became clouded by a degree of sentimentality.[8]

Now, in the Jedda of the 1930s, Ibn Saud was at the height of his power but, in the eyes of many foreign diplomats, his hold on power was weak. His throne had been forged by violence and violence threatened to break up his domain: live by the sword, die by the sword. The notion of a kingdom stretching from one shore of the Arabian Peninsula to another was a novelty and, since 1920, hardly a year had gone by without Ibn Saud having to put down an uprising somewhere in his kingdom.[9]

Ostensibly, however, Ibn Saud appeared strong and secure in his tenure. All this talk of oil was most propitious; and payments for an oil concession for Al-Hasa might refill his flagging coffers. His stipend of £60,000 from the British government had long since ended and the Great Depression had crippled his main source of income – taxes on pilgrims travelling to Mecca – as the number of pilgrims dropped from a peak of 127,000 in 1927 to 29,500 in 1932.[10] There was little point in trying to persuade the king to curb his spending. Ibn Saud preferred to indulge his family rather than consider any stringent financial measures. His advisers were constantly scrimping, saving, and looking for new sources of income. The rental payments from an oil concession promised to go some way towards meeting the shortfall.

It was a situation that would have challenged the most competent minister, but the king's advisers were unfazed. The confidential pen-pictures of leading Saudis compiled by British officials in Jedda make interesting reading today. The chief finance minister, Abdullah Suleiman from Aneiza in the Nejd, was described as an able and vigorous man. Born about 1887, he had started as a coffee boy and clerk before rising through the ranks of royal advisers to acquire complete control of all financial matters, and a certain grandeur besides. Ready and energetic in conversation and full of ideas about development, he showed great enthusiasm in the face of much hostility, envy and ill-natured criticism from his brother advisers. He was a keen fisherman and tireless traveller, his other pleasures including tobacco and the bottle.[11]

Yusuf Yasin, a Syrian refugee from Palestine, was the king's confidential secretary, dogged negotiator and procurer of royal concubines. Born in about 1898, he was described as a pompous busybody, although his loyalty to Ibn Saud was never in doubt. He was 'a difficult colleague with the small-mindedness of a Latakian grocer [he came from Latakia in Syria], but not unpleasant if taken with a pinch of salt'.[12]

There were other advisers such as Foreign Minister Fuad Hamza and Hafiz Wahba, the Saudi ambassador to London, who will figure later in our story. Despite their differences, these advisers had something in common: they had emerged from the dying embers of the Ottoman Empire with a strong sense of their Arab identity. Many were of Palestinian, Syrian or Egyptian origin, intelligent, enthusiastic, and they saw in Ibn Saud the opportunity to advance the Arab cause. Although the British underestimated and often denigrated them, one diplomat calling them 'pinch-beck politicians', such men were moving into positions of influence in governments across the Middle East.[13]

Amid this crowd stood an Englishman who, when at royal audiences (majilis), dressed in Arab robes: Harry St John Philby, known variously as 'Jack' or 'Abdullah'. To some, Philby's attempt to ingratiate himself with the king seemed a little absurd. The British minister in Jedda of the late 1930s, Reader Bullard, remembered seeing Philby in the majilis: a Muslim convert who imitated the Arabs by preceding every remark addressed to the king with the words 'God prolong your life!', Philby wore only sandals on his feet when all the other courtiers were in socks and slippers and even the king wore socks with 'Pure Wool. Made in England' on the soles.[14]

Philby had first arrived in Saudi Arabia as a British political officer with a brief to keep Ibn Saud 'on side' during the Great War. He returned to Saudi Arabia after the war as a special adviser to the king. Converting to Islam in 1930 had opened doors and enabled him to follow Bertram Thomas' achievement of crossing the great sand desert, the Rub al-Khali or Empty Quarter. According to one British diplomat, Philby's main purpose in life was to establish that the British were aligned with the forces of darkness. Another referred to him as 'that Muslim renegade'.[15] Yet, in 1932, Philby's star was rising with the Saudis and his links with the ruling family made him attractive to a foreign company wanting to do business in the kingdom.[16]

Socal was an outsider to the Middle Eastern oil business. Based in San Francisco, the company was 'crude-short', meaning that it had limited access to supplies of crude oil. In response to domestic fears that American oil reserves were rapidly depleting, it had taken up the post-war challenge of seeking new sources of oil abroad. In 1920 it had set up a division specifically to look for new oilfields, sending geologists worldwide and spending $50 million in the process.[17]

As a foreign company seeking to operate in Saudi Arabia, Socal faced huge obstacles. It had no experience of Saudi Arabia and was unsupported by an American diplomatic presence in the country. It was unable to gain direct access to Ibn Saud and his advisers, and the lack of modern communications made it impossible to negotiate from a distance. In this situation, Philby was the perfect fixer.

In February 1933 a Socal delegation arrived in Jedda and checked in to the Egyptian Hotel, recently upgraded to a 'government institution principally for high-class pilgrims'.[18] Lloyd Hamilton, an astute property lawyer with no Arabic, soon abandoned the hotel and decamped with his wife to Philby's house at the Beit Baghdadi. This was hardly any better, a rickety old building where the shutters were drawn all day to keep out the flies. Karl Twitchell, a mining engineer assisting Socal, and his wife were old desert hands and found the zinc baths and sand closets of the Egyptian quite tolerable.

IPC was much better placed than its rival, for it already had more oil than it knew what to do with. Since striking oil at Baba Gurgur in 1928, the company had made massive oil discoveries in Iraq. The company's representative in Jedda was Stephen Longrigg, the archetypal English gentleman, tall, debonair, aloof, wearing a Panama hat and sporting a monocle. A member of the company's Land and Liaison Department in Haifa, Longrigg's skill as an Arabic speaker marked him out as an ideal negotiator of oil concession agreements with Arab potentates. He was accompanied by Sulaiman Mudarres, a young Syrian Muslim educated at Oxford, and they lodged in the

Grand Hotel. As Ryan wryly observed, 'we really now need a separate hotel for concession hunters'.[19]

* * * * *

Despite Socal's oil strike in Bahrain, prospecting for oil on the Arabian mainland was still a massive gamble. With hindsight, this seems absurd, since Saudi Arabia today is the largest oil producer in the world. But in 1933 it was an entirely different matter, since no one really knew if there was oil in Arabia, let alone in the eastern province of Al-Hasa. Indeed, before oil flowed to the surface at Bahrain, the consensus of geological opinion had been that there was no commercial oil in Arabia.

Socal had a report from Karl Twitchell, following his visit to the province, stating that he had found oil seepages there. The report was not disclosed to Longrigg, who considered the concession a 'pig in a poke'. The geological theory underpinning Saudi hopes of finding oil was, in his opinion, 'somewhat naïve', and the rationale for taking on the concession appeared to be exceedingly weak.[20]

But there was more to it than that. Socal's discovery in Bahrain threatened IPC's monopoly of oil in the Middle East. In the longer term, if oil was found in large quantities in Arabia, it might undercut prices and undermine IPC's position in Iraq. The company's aim was tactical – it intended to block Socal's ambitions in the region by getting the Hasa concession and sitting on it. IPC executives did not want to explore Al-Hasa province, only to have the right to explore it: this was the 'dead hand of IPC' that would so infuriate Ibn Saud and his advisers.[21]

In one sense, however, IPC's participation suited the Saudis since it brought an element of competition to the proceedings.[22] The Saudis wanted a loan of £100,000 (£6 million today) in gold along with rental and royalty payments. The company replied with an offer of £5,000, which the Saudis rejected out of hand. The Americans countered with a better offer and Longrigg, suffering in the oppressive climate and pining for a boat back to Haifa, telegraphed London for further instructions.

An enervating heat settled over the town. With nothing else to do but wait, the parties shuffled back to their lodgings and made the best of their situation, trying to alleviate the boredom by writing up their notes and composing letters home. Meanwhile, Abdullah Suleiman would travel to Mecca, the headquarters of the Saudi government, and not communicate for days.

Mecca was the ideal retreat for a secretive government, 72 kilometres from Jedda and forbidden to non-Muslims. Ibn Saud kept away from the talks, disliking Jedda for its climate and phalanx of foreign representatives. But there was no doubt that the views of the Saudi delegation were in fact those of the king himself. All conversations were radioed nightly to the king wherever he might be. When Longrigg complained that Suleiman would not answer his questions, he was only expressing a common frustration among the delegates that everything had to be referred back to the king.

The arrival of the boats carrying pilgrims and rising temperatures now added to the oppressive atmosphere of the port. Waking to this backdrop, knowing that another heat-laden day lay ahead, Longrigg was irritable. Apart from the occasional telegram and letters that took days to arrive, he did not know what was happening in London, where his company had its headquarters. His general manager, John Skliros, tried to placate him:

> I appreciate how sick you must be of being kept hanging round with nothing to do in a one-horse place like Jedda. I can only hope you can find some consolation in a contemplation of Arabian government methods when uninstructed by European advice, and also of the manners and customs of rival concession hunters.[23]

Although it represented British oil interests, IPC was in fact an international concern comprising five partners, four of which held shares of 23.75 per cent each. Oil magnate Calouste Gulbenkian held the remaining 5 per cent share in IPC, giving him the nickname 'Mister Five Percent'.[24]

This corporate mélange made it difficult to get quick decisions. Each partner company had to be consulted, the matter discussed and a decision communicated back to Longrigg. In this instance, opinion among the board was 'very divided'. Anglo-Persian was prepared to offer £50,000 (£3 million today) for the Hasa concession but the other partners in the company were undecided: although the American partners were in favour of making the higher bid they could not agree on the amount; the French firm CFP would join only if everyone else did; Shell would have nothing to do with the concession. 'There is no oil in Arabia' was their mantra.[25]

For Longrigg, marooned 5,000 kilometres away in Jedda, the delays only added to his isolation. It was perhaps inevitable that he should confide in his compatriot, Philby. They had much in common – both men had served in the British Administration in Iraq – and he admired Philby for his knowledge. 'Mr Philby is extremely well informed,' he wrote. '[He] knows remarkably well what is going on in oil as well as other matters and appears frank.'[26] Philby was genial companion and Longrigg would often dine with him and, after dinner, talk about his discussions with Abdullah Suleiman while the others played Bridge.

In fact Philby was playing a double game, reporting his after-dinner conversations with Longrigg to the Americans. Unbeknown to Longrigg, Socal had signed up Philby in February to provide Lloyd Hamilton with 'information and advice' during the negotiations. Longrigg went so far as asking Philby to take his place in the negotiations, which must have amused Philby, knowing what he did. He gave nothing away, and expressed his sympathy to Longrigg for his predicament before politely turning him down.[27]

But it was the opinion of Ibn Saud that mattered, and he appeared to encourage the IPC bid. On 15 April, on a rare visit to Jedda, he gave Longrigg the impression that he wanted British-backed IPC to succeed. He spoke of the 'pleasure he would have in giving privileges to a British company,' his words no doubt delivered with his customary charm and trademark smile.[28]

Longrigg soldiered on. On 9 May, he wrote to Skliros:

> A fairly pronounced state of disappointment and irritability exists by this time, which I lack the materials to allay [...] those at present puzzled and (each in their degree) suspicious of our own inaction include the king, his staff, Abdullah Suleiman, Ryan and Philby. Hamilton has now raised his offer.[29]

Then a cable arrived from IPC: Anglo-Persian and the American partners in the company now wanted to make their own offer of £25,000 (£1.5 million today) in rupees for a 75-year concession, an annual payment of £2,000 prior to exploitation and 4 shillings per tonne of oil exported. Longrigg duly communicated the offer to

Abdullah Suleiman, but Suleiman dared not communicate it to the king for fear of 'physical violence'. Ibn Saud wanted payment in gold, not rupees.[30]

On the 14th, Longrigg sent a telegram suggesting that IPC should improve its offer. He waited. On the 23rd, having heard nothing, he wrote again to Skliros: 'Candidly two and a half months virtual idleness in this detestable backwater have made me eager to get on and get out,' he complained to London. 'Which will it be I wonder?' He did not have to wait much longer. The company replied on the same day in a telegram that was terse and to the point: 'Terms are utterly impossible you should return forthwith to London and report.' Longrigg packed his bags and caught the next steamer out of Jedda, no doubt relieved that his ordeal was at an end.[31]

Lloyd Hamilton now moved to close the deal. On 29 May, Ibn Saud signed the oil concession, falling asleep during the ceremony and being nudged awake in order to put his signature to the document.[32] Socal agreed to loans of £30,000 (£1.8 million today) and £20,000 (£1.2 million) in gold to the Saudi Arabian government, along with a first annual rental of £5,000 (£300,000) also in gold and subsequent rental payments in a currency of the company's choosing. A last-minute hitch arose when the US government imposed an embargo on the export of gold from the United States, but the company managed to obtain the gold from London and dispatched it to Jedda. Here Karl Twitchell counted each of the 35,000 gold sovereigns on a table of the Netherlands Bank under the watchful eye of Abdullah Suleiman.

But even when the ink was barely dry on the concession document, new worries began to surface about the extent of Ibn Saud's domain. In July 1933 Karl Twitchell asked Abdullah Suleiman for clarification of the boundaries of the kingdom, a question to which Suleiman did not know the answer. He telegraphed the king: 'How far does the Saudi territory extend to the south of al Ahsa [Al-Hasa]. Does the boundary extend as far as the Hadhramaut? Is the Rub al-Khali included in it? Are there demarcation signs on it?'[33]

Astonishingly, throughout the long, tedious – at times soporific – negotiations no one had thought to question the precise geographical area of the proposed concession. The western area was defined by reference to physical and geographical features but the eastern side was simply defined 'as the eastern portion of our Saudi Arab kingdom, within its frontiers'.[34] It could have been a strip of land on the eastern coast of Arabia, or virtually the whole peninsula. Ibn Saud regarded south-eastern Arabia as his own. But an early Socal map appeared to acknowledge that the south-eastern portion of the Rub al-Khali was within the British sphere of influence, describing it as 'The British Hinterland of Aden'.[35] The truth was that no one was sure where the frontiers lay.

This point was unlikely to have been missed by Lloyd Hamilton, a lawyer and land-lease expert, but this was not a discussion between American lawyers over a piece of well-defined real estate in the suburbs. American geologists were about to set foot in an unfamiliar strange and dangerous land, virtually unknown to the cartographer, and Socal needed the king's support and his guards to protect and guide them. In Ibn Saud's mind, the frontiers of his kingdom took in the territory of his Wahhabi ancestors, including the shores of western Abu Dhabi and the Omani borderlands.

There was nothing to suggest that any imprecision in the agreement was deliberate, but it certainly suited the king's ambition well.

Chapter 2
A Bend in the Wadi
Oil Exploration in the Southern Desert, 1938–48

Somewhere out there in the sleepy south-eastern desert of the Empty Quarter, east of Riyadh and west of Muscat, was a territory rich in oil. The bedouin moved their flocks from one grazing area to another as they followed the rain, caring nothing for what lay beneath the ground apart from water. They owed their allegiance to the strongest leader and had no concept of property ownership in the Western sense. Defining territory on a map was meaningless to them, since the range of their grazing and the sway of their rulers, rather than lawyer's talk or the stroke of a pen, determined the frontiers of this land.[1]

Looking at the landscape, it is not difficult to see why this was so. To the untrained eye there is nothing here: it is a land that avoids clear definition. There are no reference points, no mountains or rivers, valleys, signposts or roads to provide certainty. A dust-laden haze smudges the horizon, each perspective and fold of dune is indistinct and yet seems familiar. The next dune is much the same as the one before, as if you were forever travelling in a circle. The glare of the midday sun is relentless, making this a shadowless land.

The wind is the great shape-shifter of the desert. Despite the apparent stillness the sand is constantly on the move. The wind builds dunes to a height of 250 metres, constantly fine-tuning their shape and size. It carries sand to form smaller deserts well beyond its margins, leaving sand to form a legacy of dunes in its wake. For most of the time you cannot see its movement since the lightest breezes carry grains of sand invisible to the naked eye but then, like a living creature, a dirty-brown sky will consume the sand, sucking it up and rolling it across the desert, scourging the dunes. The wind makes everything here, polishing and shaping the stones, hollowing out the valleys, sculpting the dunes, moving them, building them up and wearing them down again.

Socal had set up an operating company – the California Arabian Standard Oil Company (Casoc) – to develop the Hasa oil concession, and the problem of defining the boundaries of the concession soon became apparent. A Casoc survey party was asked to investigate an apparently well known feature which was the subject of a boundary dispute between the Saudis and the British.[2] Tom Barger, one of the geologists sent into the desert, wrote 'One place, which the British negotiators claimed as an immutable landmark, we found to be some 35 miles [56 kilometres] further north, which is favourable to Saudi Arabia, than shown on the maps used by the English. They promptly lost interest in that site.[3] In an age before satellite navigation, geologists would struggle to overcome misunderstandings caused by vague boundaries and incomplete maps. The maps they used were next to useless. 'Someone,' Barger noted, 'sat in an office, called in a bedouin, asked him the names of the places and then wrote them on a map, scattering them about so as not to leave too many blanks and thus produce a pleasing effect on the eye.'[4]

To avoid any confrontation with the British, the American survey parties kept a low profile. In January 1938 Barger was writing, 'The government thinks it is more secretive for us to travel in one car.'[5] Discussions over the radio were of necessity brief; and progress of the drilling in Dammam was conveyed to the field parties in letters rather than over the airwaves. Secrecy in the desert was a relative concept: there were ears and eyes everywhere. Bedouin watched their progress, read their tracks in the sands and gossiped to their kinsmen and the tribesmen they met – the famous 'bedouin telegraph' at work.

At least the geologists were safe in the field. Armed Saudi guards protected them throughout their journeys to places where few if any Westerners had ventured before. The many nomadic and settled tribes of Saudi Arabia were bound to Ibn Saud through varying degrees of fear and respect, and few dared to oppose his will. For this reason, most acquiesced in these intrusions of the infidel.

The king's writ did not, however, guarantee universal acquiescence. Two ancient settlements, one the town of Layla on the northern fringes of the Rub al-Khali and the other a string of villages leading south to Sulaiyil in Wadi Duwasir, were the main centres of Wahhabi extremism. The explorer Bertram Thomas had been careful to avoid them in his travels, but these places were less formidable when travelling with a detachment of Saudi guards.[6]

In February 1938, when geological work and drilling in Al-Hasa had yet to produce any positive results, Casoc launched an expedition to explore the Rub al-Khali. The expedition that set off for the Liwa Oasis was the first motorised party to penetrate the southern desert; and even bedouin shepherds warned of the dangers, telling the geologists that 'Not even Allah has been there.'[7] They had four vehicles comprising two pick-ups, a sedan and a four-wheeled drive Marmon Harrington station wagon. In scenes that would become familiar to future generations of desert explorers, it was a tedious procession that threaded its way for many kilometres along shallow rolling valleys called *hauta* that lay between long linear dunes called *uruq*. Such was the pattern of their traverses: keeping to the harder sand to avoid the softer dune sand until their luck ran out and their wheels became stuck. This often required the station wagon and a length of stout rope to haul them out. Carrying strips of rubber belting to use as mats under the wheels to improve traction in the sand was also an essential aid. They composed a ditty of the Rub al-Khali: *'shiyl al bultz, wa hatt al bultz, shiyl al bultz, wa hatt al bultz'*, meaning 'remove the belts, put the belts down; remove the belts, put the belts down.' It was about as far as you could get from an everyday journey along a tarmac road.[8]

The purpose of the Casoc expedition was both to map the area and to see if there were any geological structures likely to signify the presence of oil. The key to finding oil lay in the rocks. The word 'petroleum' comes from the Latin 'petra' meaning rock and 'oleum' meaning oil, alluding to its origin. 'Rock oil' is formed in the Earth over millions of years when organic detritus sinks to great subterranean depth to be heated and transformed into oil. The oil rises to the surface until impervious rocks stop it rising any farther; then it becomes trapped in porous rocks known as 'reservoirs'.

Traditionally, geologists had looked for evidence of these underground reservoirs in rocky outcrops and other features such as anticlines and seepages that appeared on the surface. As the pressures of the Earth tilted or folded rock formations, some were exposed at the surface, and it was possible to 'read' these surface rocks in order to predict where oil might be found, but it was by no means a fail-safe method. In the desert, the simple act of finding rocks could be difficult since sand covered most of the terrain.

The search for oil in the desert meant looking for hills that would expose the underlying rocks or finding outcrops of ancient rocks protruding above the sand.

Barger observed:

> All of the oilfields known in the Middle East were associated
> with either oil or gas seepages at the surface or with structures
> that were prominent geographical features. We didn't have the
> time to attempt a minute geological investigation of such a vast
> area, so we narrowed down the search by quizzing our guides
> about the terrain around us.[9]

They crossed the flat plain of the Sabkhat Matti and penetrated the
sands south of the petty sheikhdoms of the lower Gulf, known as the
Trucial Coast. The bedouin telegraph picked up their presence and
conveyed the news quickly to the coast where it was intercepted by
the political agents of the British government. The ruler of Abu
Dhabi, Sheikh Shakhbut bin Sultan Al Nahyan, heard rumours that
Europeans or Americans with Saudi guards had 'almost' come up to
Liwa on three occasions but had been stopped by the sand. In his eyes,
they were trespassers. The British political agent assumed it was Casoc
men, and took it up with the Americans.[10]

The first question a bedouin will ask a visitor is 'What's the news?'
and – once the formality of denying that there is any news is done –
they will proceed to discuss every little scrap of news in great detail.
The arrival of Americans in a motor car was definintely big news in
the desert, but to the watching bedouin they might just as well have
been visitors from another planet, or meteorites crashing in from
space. One bedu herdsman, seeing approaching geologists, tied a white
rag to his rifle and waved it in the air as an act of surrender, thinking
the Americans were camel raiders. The motor vehicles, too, were
objects of fascination although it was the leather upholstery rather
than the mechanical features that attracted the bedouin eye.

While in the desert, Barger and his colleagues heard news of the
first commercial oil strike on the Arabian Peninsula. Casoc had drilled
several wells around the Dammam dome without success and,
although the second well brought in a strong flow of oil, this had soon
turned to water. In 1936 Socal joined forces with the Texas Oil
Company to form Caltex to market Arabian oil in the east. But by
March 1938 it was by no means certain that there was oil in
commercial quantites in Arabia. After spending $15 million with no
serious oil to show for it, the company was considering ending its

drilling operations in Saudi Arabia. But when a deeper well was drilled, oil was struck in a new formation in rocks of the Jurassic age. This well, No. 7, achieved a flow rate of 3,690 barrels of oil by the third day, a major discovery by the standards of the time.[11]

* * * * *

By 1939 Ibn Saud had an entourage the size of a small army. Travelling to Dhahran on the way to open the first oil terminal at Ras Tanura, on the eastern coast, there was no modesty about his procession: a long caravan of black cars stretching into the distance with oil company trucks placed at intervals to pull out those unfortunates who got stuck in the *sabkha*.

A city of 350 white tents sprang up to the east of Jebel Dhahran and American families watched from the hillside as two thousand Arabs lined up facing west towards Mecca, saying their evening prayers, with Ibn Saud at the fore. Then cooking pots large enough to contain the whole carcass of a sheep came out, and the glow of many fires lit up the night.[12]

Two days later the procession moved on to Ras Tanura where flags fluttered in a light breeze and onlookers gathered to welcome the king. A smiling Ibn Saud wore a dark gown over a white *thobe* and a red *ghutra*, held in place by a double gold cord. A little man followed him holding a white umbrella over his head, keeping off the sun.[13] With the first oil shipment about to leave the country, Ibn Saud had plenty to smile about. As he opened the valve that allowed the first Saudi oil to flow through a pipeline into a waiting tanker, he was opening the door to momentous changes. There was money to modernise, the Saudis were growing closer to the Americans, other newly rich oil states were developing their economies as fast as they could, and the kingdom was not short of oil. But Saudi society was resistant to change: as the twentieth century rolled on, the country remained firmly tied to its past.

The Casoc geologists had tried to bridge the cultural gap by wearing beards and Arab robes and being as inconspicuous and inoffensive as possible. In time, oil company employees would shave off their beards but they were still forbidden from getting married in Saudi Arabia. Although Christian services were allowed, they could only take place behind closed doors. The main Christian faiths had

Ibn Saud (centre seated) with representatives of the California Arabian Standard Oil Company (Casoc), which operated the Hasa oil concession in the 1930s. Yusuf Yasin stands immediately behind Ibn Saud. (source: the Chevron Archive, copyrighted by Chevron Corporation and used with permission)

priests or ministers who, with the knowledge of the higher echelons of Saudi officialdom, were allowed into the country on visas describing them as 'special teachers'.[14] The government banned imports of whisky, beer and wine but for men who refined crude oil, distilling bathtub gin and Scotch, known locally as 'the white' and 'the brown', was not difficult.[15]

Saudi society remained closed and secretive despite the new wealth. Slavery endured, and there was no question about its legitimacy within the kingdom: it was part of the fabric of life, patronised by the Saudi royal family itself. Although Westerners were tolerated, they found the boundary wall between public hospitality and private society impenetrable. Western perceptions were largely fashioned by glossy oil company magazines and the accounts of a few intrepid travellers.

Whatever lay beyond this wall was guesswork – a world of 'unhurried dignity, a correctness of speech and manner, and a respectful treatment of rich and poor alike', perhaps. Wahhabi values predominated: an unbeliever, however cultured, well mannered or wealthy, was an infidel and therefore an outsider.[16]

At the heart of the Saudi state was the religious body known as the *ulema*, a legacy from the time of Sheikh Muhammad ibn Abdul al-Wahhab and his eighteenth-century pact with Emir Muhammad ibn Saud. It was understood that the ruler was responsible for ensuring that *sharia* law was strictly enforced, with the backing of the religious police, and that he should act in consultation with the clerics of the *ulema*. The government was framed by a strict religious code and ruled over a people who were devout by nature.

For those on the other side of the divide, it could be daunting. When a Casoc party next ventured into the Rub al-Khali in the 1939–40 season, its members found themselves up against the silent hostility of religious fanatics. The survey team mapped the northern reaches of the desert, an area that included Layla, a town 500 kilometres south of Riyadh, lying under the Aflaj Ridge. Old mud forts, reputed to be from ancient times, surrounded Layla. West and south-west of the town were the clear blue *ains,* or wells, so-called because the inland Arabs did not have a word for lake. One was 85 feet deep, a quarter of a mile wide and three-quarters long. A network of canals spread out from these wells, some disappearing into the desert. These were marked by lines of stone well shafts that had been exposed by drifting sand, poking up like the chimneys of an abandoned village.

Philby had come to Layla in 1917. When he arrived on the outskirts of the town, a group of women gathering grass for their cattle were so bewildered by the appearance of an infidel that they dropped their bundles and fled. In an attempt to reassure them, one of Philby's escorts caught up with the women but they fell to their knees, begging for mercy. Eventually, suitably reassured, they returned to pick up their bundles. The escort told Philby: 'they have never seen the likes of you before, and their teachers tell them that your people eat up the men and ravish the women wherever they go.'[17]

The town was out of bounds to the survey party until March 1940 when Ibn Saud finally gave team leader Tom Barger permission to enter. Taking no chances, the party was accorded 15 guards led by a relative of Ibn Saud and Ibn Saud's chief tax collector from Al-Hasa,

Muhammad bin Mansur, who had already achieved notoriety as the man who had slit the throats of Ajman hostages during the *Ikhwan* Revolt.[18] The tax collectors performed an important role in collecting religious dues from the settled and nomadic tribes of the desert. In future they would play an vital role in advancing Ibn Saud's territorial claims over the south eastern desert. For the time being they were necessary protection: the name of Ibn Saud was respected in these parts, and the presence of his tax collectors was a valuable, if not cast-iron, guarantee of safe passage for the infidels.

There were no dramatic incidents to report, only the sullen looks of the townspeople who kept their distance as the infidels set up camp on the outskirts of town. When Barger and his men were invited to dinner with the governor of the town, they trapsed in Arab dress through dark, silent streets and found the governor away 'on business'. It was a calculated snub, compounded by the conduct of his son who was there to greet them but unable to stay for the meal. So they ate alone.

Such incidents were minor inconveniences, but the threat from Wahhabi zealots remained. The survey party stayed away from the more fanatical villages of Sulaiyil and the south, reaching Ain Hisy and going no farther. Three days later, they were back at Layla, where they stopped only for water before returning to Dhahran.

* * * * *

The great caravan city of Yamama was located at the head of the Wadi Sahba and in its day – more than 1,500 years ago – it was reputed to be the richest city in Arabia as the caravans used the Wadi as the route to the interior beyond the Tuwaiq Mountains. Wadis were of interest to the geologists because they carved a course through the sand and exposed the underlying rocks. But Wadi Sahba caught the geologist's eye for a different reason. Originating in the Tuwaiqs and heading due east, the Wadi ran almost in a straight line until reaching Haradh where it bent south for a distance, continued eastwards and disappeared into the sands. This bend in the wadi was a puzzle: there was no clue on the surface as to its cause.

One of the geologists, Ernie Berg, set about mapping the surrounding jebels and noticed that their summits sloped away from the centre at Ain Haradh in a pattern that indicated that the underground rock structures might have been uplifted, which would explain why the Wadi Sahba had changed direction. This uplift, an anticline, was a possible indicator of oil. The geologists' interest grew a few months later when they found that rocks at its centre were from the Eocene age.

With the Japanese attack on Pearl Harbor in December 1941, exploration came to a halt. The company rolled up its survey maps and dispersed its survey teams, concentrating on closing down wells, keeping basic operations going and plotting escape routes across the desert to Aden in the event of a German victory in North Africa. Yet, apart from a futile Italian air raid on the oil installations of Bahrain and Al-Hasa, the threat of enemy action came to nothing.

In 1944 Casoc became the American Arabian Oil Company (Aramco) and, by the end of the War, the company was ready to recommence its operations. A well was finally drilled at Haradh in 1948. It proved to be a massive strike, the first discovery in the supergiant oilfield that became known as Ghawar.

The bend in the Wadi had revealed the largest oilfield in the world.[19]

Chapter 3
The Riyadh Line
Frontier Negotiations, 1933–9

In May 1933 Anglo-Persian managers, hearing news of Socal's success in winning the Hasa concession, hurried to get an oil concession for neighbouring Qatar sewn up. Two years later, after much haggling, the sheikh of Qatar was persuaded to put his signature to a concession agreement for a period of 75 years in return for 400,000 rupees (£1.8 million today) on signature and 150,000 rupees (£700,000 today) per annum with royalties. Anglo-Persian transferred the concession to the IPC subsidiary, Petroleum Development (Qatar), later to become the Qatar Petroleum Company.

The boundary between Qatar and Saudi Arabia was uncertain, however. In 1922, at a conference at Uqair on the Arabian coast, the British High Commissioner in Iraq, Sir Percy Cox, had tried to settle the issue by arbitrarily drawing a line on a map at the base of the Qatar peninsula. But the interests of the oil companies now demanded a more exact approach. In June 1933 the British political agent for the Persian Gulf, Trenchard Fowle, wrote to the Colonial Office: 'In view of the grant of the Hasa oil concession to the Standard Oil Company of California and of the negotiations entered into by the Anglo-Persian Oil Company for an oil concession in Qatar, the early determination of the boundaries is desirable.'[1]

In fact, there was already a formal agreement in existence. In the dying days of the Ottoman Empire, the British government had settled with the Turks their respective spheres of influence in Arabia. First, in 1913, officials had drawn in blue ink a line due south from the Gulf of Uqair to parallel 20°N in the Rub al-Khali, calling it the Blue Line. In the following year they had drawn a second line from the south-western corner of the peninsula to intersect the Blue Line in the Rub al-Khali, calling it the Violet Line. The Foreign Office view was that Ibn Saud, as successor in title to the Turks, was bound by that treaty. Therefore Saudi territory on the south and eastern side of the peninsula, and the border with Qatar, was defined by the Blue Line.

In April 1934, in response to an enquiry initiated by Socal, the Foreign Office informed the American Embassy in London that the Blue Line was the boundary with Saudi Arabia and that Ibn Saud had inherited this boundary from the Turks. Four days later, Sir Andrew Ryan, conveyed the same message to the Saudi Arabian government. Deputy Foreign Minister Fuad Hamza protested that there had been many changes since 1914 and rejected the Blue Line as the boundary. When the British chargé d'affaires in Jedda informed Ibn Saud, he was not impressed. He did not accept the Blue Line as binding upon him, relying instead on older ancestral claims – the conquests of his Wahhabi forefathers – to stake a claim for territory to the east of it. He denied ever having been a Turkish subject.[2]

Ibn Saud considered Qatar as his own territory. If there was any doubt in the matter, a Saudi official in Al-Hasa was soon telegraphing Abdullah Suleiman to dispel it. Regarding the possibility of the Americans purchasing an oil concession from the sheikh of Qatar, he reported that 'the conditions and the area included in them are of the utmost importance to [...] the Saudi government, because you know that the district of Qatar and its bedouin come under our rule. We collect taxes from them every year.'[3]

On 20 June, Hamza provided the British with a more detailed argument, claiming that because the British had already recognised Ibn Saud's hegemony over the bedouin tribes of the northern part of Arabia, the same must apply in the south. 'All tribes living between the coastal towns of Qatar and the coast of Oman and the Hadhramaut belong to the Saudi Arab Kingdom, are entirely submissive to the laws of the country, pay *zakat* and are obedient to the calls of government in time of war [*jihad*],' he claimed.[4]

It was a sweeping declaration, and the main difficulty for the British was in trying to get a more precise statement of the Saudi government's territorial claims. Ibn Saud considered that any discussion about frontiers was a matter between him and the local sheikhs, and nothing to do with the British. Faced with this complete rejection of the Blue Line, some on the British side began to question the strength of their own case. In July 1934 Ryan admitted in a memorandum that he could not 'personally believe in the undoubted validity of the Blue Line'.[5] The following month, the Foreign Office received legal advice on the matter, the conclusions of which were not encouraging. 'I do not think we would win before a tribunal,' was the legal adviser's view of the strength of a legal argument based on the Blue Line.[6]

When Fuad Hamza came to London in September 1934, little progress was made. Hamza had not received any definite instructions from the king, and he stuck to the position that the boundary should be determined by tribal areas, notably those of the Murrah and Manasir tribes. The Foreign Office replied that the Murrah might be considered loyal subjects of Ibn Saud but not the Manasir who were mostly subjects of the sheikh of Abu Dhabi, Shakhbut bin Sultan Al Nahyan.[7]

And so the arguments went to and fro. For Ryan, it was another opportunity to witness the Saudi ministers at work. British diplomats might well have regarded Fuad Hamza as another one of Ibn Saud's 'pinch-beck' advisers and Ryan summed him up as a 'bumptious young man', adding:

> He has two personalities, that of the Fuad who is personally imbued with the sentiments of Arab nationalism and that of the Fuad who serves Ibn Saud, without enjoying his master's entire confidence and without sharing all his master's views, because he sees in him the best present embodiment of the Arab idea and perhaps the best provider of a career.[8]

The king often kept his advisers at arm's length. The distance between them was a common obstacle faced by foreign diplomats when dealing with the Saudis, particularly when they tried to divine the king's mind. It also allowed the king to disown his advisers' public statements when it suited him, as he did when Hamza's boundary proposals later became an embarrassment.[9]

Among the shifting sands of Saudi politics there were a few constants, such as the king's territorial ambitions, his sentimental attachment to the glorious past and an incremental approach to border negotiations. This was based on an old bedouin tactic: having captured one well, you moved on to the next. But, as one British diplomat complained: 'If the Saudi government always claimed as a Murrah well the next well beyond the last well we had conceded, there would be no reason why they should not eventually claim Muscat town.'[10]

Indeed, this is what seemed to be happening. The frontier line slipped farther eastwards across the map as the British made various proposals, beginning with a Green Line, followed by a refinement known as the Brown Line and then a Yellow Line – all lost on one diplomat who was reputedly colour blind.[11] Another diplomat remarked: 'All these lines had one thing in common: they gave more and more territory to Ibn Saud [...] surely the time has now come for this bargaining to cease?' He likened the negotiations to haggling over a Persian carpet.[12]

In fact these concessions made little impression on the Saudis, who appeared to interpret them as a sign of weakness to be exploited by making even greater demands. On 3 April 1935 Hamza handed Ryan a memorandum setting out the Saudi proposal. It advanced a new boundary line with Qatar and the Trucial Coast, which became known as the Red Line, or the 'Hamza Line'. Based on a list of 161 wells that the Saudis claimed were owned by the Murrah tribe, the Line embraced the area around Bunaiyin and a string of wells to the east towards a place called Sufuq. It also took in Jebel Nakhsh in Qatar, and a place called Khawr al-Udayd on the coast, at the eastern foot of the Qatar peninsula.

The British mulled it over. Although they accepted in principle that the Murrah tribe were loyal to the king, and that their territory should go to Saudi Arabia, it was difficult to establish the geographical limits of their 'territory', an alien concept in the bedouin mind. Talk of creating a desert zone, similar to the Neutral Zones of Kuwait, where the bedouin could roam at will, came to nothing.[13] After more research, the Foreign Office discovered that the range of the tribe's grazing, or *diyar,* ran from the southern end of the Sabkhat Matti in a south-easterly direction, taking in a considerable segment of the Rub al-Khali. When the parties returned to the negotiating table later in the year, the British indicated that they were prepared to take this into account. The result was the Riyadh Line, or Ryan Line, so-named because it was first proposed to the Saudis at Riyadh by Sir Andrew Ryan.

The Riyadh Line conceded the Bunaiyin Well to Saudi Arabia, reduced Saudi claims on Qatar, retained Khawr al-Udayd for Abu Dhabi, and rebuffed Saudi claims on Oman and the Eastern Aden Protectorate. Ibn Saud rejected it out of hand. He insisted on having Jebel Nakhsh – presumably because it was part of the promising Jebel Dukhan oil structure – and Khawr al-Udayd because of its access to the sea. The talks ended in deadlock and were not resumed for over a year.

In March 1937 the political agent, Lt-Col. Percy Loch, was instructed to investigate the correct location of the Sufuq well, which was then thought to be within Abu Dhabi territory. He arranged for a party to set out from the coast on camels, locate the well, mark the spot with white sheets laid on the sand and light a fire at a prearranged time when the political agent would be passing over in an aircraft.[14] This was duly accomplished and the co-ordinates reported back to the new British minister in Saudi Arabia, George Rendell. At this point, a ghastly error was revealed: the Sufuq well was only 20 kilometres from the coast, much farther north than had been previously supposed. Rendell had to reopen negotiations with Sheikh Yusuf Yasin on the basis that the Saudis would *gain* territory. For the British this might have been hard to swallow but they had no option but to adjust the Riyadh Line in the Saudis' favour.

Now a wider picture emerged, as the need to resist a growing Italian influence on the Red Sea urged British officials to seek an accommodation with Ibn Saud. The boundary negotiations were taking place against a developing British policy of appeasement, as epitomised by Prime Minister Neville Chamberlain's famous phrase of 'peace for our time'.[15] Foreign Office officials saw little merit in defending the interests of the Persian Gulf sheikhs when richer prizes, such as Ibn Saud's support over Palestine, might be gained. On 18 February 1938 Foreign Secretary Anthony Eden wrote 'In view of difficult situation resulting from developments in Palestine [the government] desire to see whether anything further can be done with a view to securing Ibn Saud's goodwill.'[16] With a war looming in Europe, the war ministries were anxious to enlist Ibn Saud's co-operation, considering the Persian Gulf to be strategically important, the 'Suez Canal of the Air' as they called it.[17]

And yet, if concessions were to be made, what territory might be given away? On the face of it, the Rub al-Khali was an empty desert and easily conceded, but Bullard had already received reports of a Casoc oil strike around Jebel Dhahran and of Socal wishing to extend its concession.[18] One possibility was to make further concessions to the Saudis on the Qatar border, such as Jebel Nakhsh.

However, IPC was anxious to protect its own oil concession and flatly rejected the idea. So the Foreign Office turned its attention to Khawr al-Udayd as a possible bargaining counter in the debate over Palestine.

Khawr al-Udayd was a picturesque but otherwise unremarkable inlet. The sea pierced the coastline here, sending a strong current surging through a narrow channel which then curved and opened up to create the impression of an inland sea. The first geophysicists to survey the inlet in the 1950s would find these fierce currents tricky, especially when the tide was going out, making it difficult to shoot a seismic line.[19] On the slopes to the south of the inland sea were the gravel remains of an ancient river that once ran from the mountains of Yemen and joined the outwash of the Tigris and Euphrates at this place. It was once known as a bolt-hole for pirates. Here, in the nineteenth century, the lighter pirate boats could hide from the ships of the British Royal Navy. Now it was a more peaceful scene: winter fishermen dried their fish and pitched their camps on the beach, using their sails as tents.[20]

To the British, the Saudi claim for Khawr al-Udayd seemed illogical. The inlet was useless as a port because the adjoining sea was too shallow for commercial or military shipping to anchor near the shore.[21] In fact, the Saudis were probably motivated more by a fear of being encircled by British protégés than by anything else: a Saudi Khawr al-Udayd might drive a territorial wedge between Qatar and Abu Dhabi.[22] Perhaps, as one British official surmised, they wanted it for reasons 'of prestige exacerbated by poverty and smell of oil.' A 'window on the Gulf' it was called.

The Foreign Office was keen to do a deal, but the history was against them. In 1869–80 it had been settled by the Qubaisat tribe, who ran pirate ships from its sheltered waters. When the Turks occupied Qatar in 1871, the *khawr* had come under the Ottoman sphere of influence, frustrating British military action against the tribe. However, in 1872 the Government of India decided to recognise it as belonging to the sheikh of Abu Dhabi, a device that would enable the British navy to suppress the pirates under the 1853 Perpetual Maritime Truce. In 1906 Sir Percy (then Major) Cox had written to Shakhbut's grandfather Zayed the Great) confirming the decision: 'The government [...] recognise that the place is in your territory [...] '[23]

Thus the opposing white sand dunes and pink cliffs of the *khawr* now marked the coastal boundary between Qatar and Abu Dhabi. To cede it to Saudi Arabia would mean having to go against the wishes of Sheikh Shakhbut of Abu Dhabi. Although it had long been a tenet of British foreign policy that agreements would not be made against the interests of the Trucial Coast rulers, now their sensitivities were considered expendable.

Yet behind the scenes – and unbeknown to Sheikh Shakhbut – Abu Dhabi had an important ally in London. The India Office (to which the Government of India reported) opposed the Foreign Office: it would not countenance any further concessions, especially for some dubious deal elsewhere in the Middle East and was protective of the Gulf. Through its agents and officers, the Indian Political Service (the diplomatic corps of the Government of India) had acquired a vast knowledge and experience of Gulf affairs. As the 1930s progressed, however, these bodies found themselves increasingly isolated from the mainstream of government thinking.[24]

For the meantime, instead of being a dispute between Britain and Saudi Arabia, the issue became an inter-departmental struggle, a greater battle inside Whitehall about control of the Persian Gulf.[25] Traditionally, the Gulf had been ruled as part of India, its security considered necessary for the defence of the Raj. But as India became increasingly 'Indianised', the Foreign Office sought to have the India Office's responsibilities transferred to itself. The argument was not settled until 1947 when India became independent and the Government of India and India Office ceased to exist. Members of the Indian Political Service were gradually replaced in Gulf posts by members of the Foreign Service. Yet some of the terminology of the Raj lived on: archaic titles like 'political resident' and 'political agent' survived for over two decades to describe the political officers who effectively ran affairs in the Gulf on behalf of the British government.

For the time being, the India Office battled on. They rejected Ibn Saud's claim to his ancestral lands and stuck firmly to the legality of the Blue Line.[26] Having reached stalemate, the proposal to cede Khawr al-Udayd to Ibn Saud was referred to the Committee of Imperial Defence which resolved, on 19 July 1938, that:

> The Foreign Office and India Office should be authorised to take up the question of the cession by the sheikh of Abu Dhabi of a strip of territory in the Persian Gulf known as the Khor-el-Odeid [sic]; and that, should compensation in the form of a cash payment prove necessary, the expenditure of a sum tentatively estimated at £25,000 [£1.4 million today] for this purpose should be provisionally authorised.[27]

The new foreign secretary, Lord Halifax, waded into the argument by adding that an even larger sum would be necessary to secure Sheikh Shakhbut's agreement. The Foreign Office advised the India Office that, if Shakhbut proved obdurate, he should be informed that the British government would insist on its advice being followed. The India Office would not give way, however, and the departments reached an impasse. 'Why not let sleeping dogs lie?' asked the political resident quite reasonably.[28] When arbitration was suggested as a way out the India Office rejected the idea. At this juncture, World War II intervened and discussions were put on hold.

As far as the lower Gulf was concerned, it was not a moment too soon. If the events of the 1930s had demonstrated anything, it was that the Foreign Office was ready to sacrifice Khawr al-Udayd for British interests elsewhere. Through the decade officials had moved away from a resolute stand on the Blue Line towards accepting – to a limited degree – the idea of determining territory by tribal ranges and allegiances. This set a difficult precedent for the future, allowing Ibn Saud to put forward far-reaching claims which would be difficult to refute: the Sufuq wells debacle had already demonstrated how little was known about the local geography. The tribal issues would not go away; indeed they were set to burst into life after World War II. The Saudis, with the help of American lawyers, would realise that effective occupation was the key to establishing a claim to vacant territory in international law: 'possession is nine-tenths of the law'. Occupation was the strongest claim of all.[29]

For the time being, at the end of the 1930s, Ibn Saud's claim had ground to a halt. The sultan of Muscat and Oman had escaped scrutiny, but the rulers of Qatar and Abu Dhabi were clearly in his sights. These rulers knew only too well that they could not afford to cede any territory, either for prestige or for practical reasons, to him. They were British protégés: they depended on Great Britain for their survival. Ibn Saud would not dare to make a direct move against their territories while the British were backing them – at least not yet. And so these rulers looked on, with a rising apprehension but without any real fear, trusting in British protection and relying on international diplomacy to run its course. But when the war ended and the oil companies began opening up the southern desert to oil exploration, the arguments about frontiers would take a new and dangerous turn.

Chapter 4
Lanterns in the Dark
Muscat and Oman, 1915–53

Unlike the Kingdom of Saudi Arabia, which was united under the sword of Ibn Saud, south-eastern Arabia was a patchwork of territories and tribes owing allegiance to different rulers. If an oil company was to make any progress here, it had first to unravel the complexities of an enigmatic land.[1]

Ancient Arab geographers described the territory lying to the south-east of Al-Hasa as Oman, a land extending far beyond the Oman that exists today. It stretched from the Hajar Mountains in the east to the vast featureless salt flat known as the Sabkhat Matti in the west. Historically, the Sabkhat Matti formed the geographical boundary between Al-Hasa and Oman.[2] The *sabkha* formed a natural demarcation because, in contrast to the undulating desert, its surface is as 'smooth as a dance floor'.[3]

The people of the Omani coast, cut off from the rest of Arabia by the Rub al-Khali and the Hajar Mountains, tended to look seaward for a living. Trade routes had taken Omanis to Pakistan and China for more than a thousand years. The seventeenth-century Omani empire encompassed most of the southern Arabian littoral, Zanzibar and Mombasa on the east African coast. An astonishing mix of languages packed the *suqs* of Muscat and Muttrah, reflecting many different aspects of the country's colourful past. At the end of the nineteenth century, a British agent recorded 14 different languages in use there.[4]

Muscat had been a centre of the slave trade, but slaves who managed to escape and find refuge under the flags of Britain or France became automatically free. British and French men-of-war had freed many slaves in Muscat. During periods of acute rivalry between the two nations, these communities of freed slaves staunchly supported the flag to which they owed their freedom and, from time to time, there were fights between them. But it was not all bad news for, as Sir Percy Cox noted, 'Altogether the slave communities were a merry crowd, and a frequent source of interest. For instance the British freed [slaves] had their own band which on state occasions such as the king's birthday, would come and discourse sweet music at the British Agency.'[5]

In 1915 a harsher music was heard in Muscat. Tribes of the interior under the leadership of Imam Salim bin Rashid al-Kharusi occupied the Batinah plain north of Muscat and attacked the town but were repulsed by a British-Indian force. Although the sultan of Muscat, Taimur bin Faisal, regained control of Muscat, the imam kept hold of the interior and in 1920 both parties signed the Treaty of Sib.[6] The Treaty was not published at the time (and not released for 30 years) and was the subject of much speculation in the Arab world over succeeding years. In fact, it was a thing of smoke and mirrors, achieving the apparently impossible by allowing the tribes to believe that they were independent of the sultan while enabling the British to reassure the sultan that he retained sovereignty over them.[7] It made no mention of the imam and did not define any of the sultan's (or imam's) boundaries. The sultan's title, 'of Muscat and Oman', was a convenient fiction since his de facto rule barely extended beyond Muscat and the coast.[8]

It was impossible to define the sultan's territory by geography alone. Both sultan and imam ruled by virtue of the allegiance of a particular tribe or section of a tribe. Tribal dynamics were complicated. As well as the split between tribes loyal to the sultan or imam, there were other tribal divisions running through the country: the split between the Hinawi faction and the Ghafiri; the split between the settled and nomadic tribes. Then there were the waverers, nomadic tribes like the Duru, which tended to be less fastidious in their allegiances.[9] But if a tribe's allegiance changed, the territory they inhabited would travel with them. Thus, the map of Oman was constantly changing, giving true expression to the saying that the boundaries of the desert were drawn in men's hearts.

But it was possible to make some broad assumptions. By the late 1940s, Imam Muhammad bin Abdullah al-Khalili was based in Nizwa and his influence extended to Jebel Akhdar. He was the spiritual leader of the Ibadhis, a religious sect that had split from mainstream Islam. The Ibadhi tribes populated the western Hajar Mountains and parts of the plain, and were generally inclined against the Sunni tribes. This was significant for the Buraimi area, where most of the Sunni tribesmen had an affinity with the Wahhabis.

Indeed, it was a potentially volatile mix. The conservative Ibadhi tribes could be pragmatic in their alliances, siding with the Sunni tribes when it suited them, and occasionally conspiring with them against the sultan. For his part, the sultan needed to keep their respect in order to retain an influence over the interior of Oman. But, although the idea may have appealed to his natural conservatism, he failed to win them over.[10]

The dichotomy of power between the sultan and imam was most troublesome for the Anglo-Persian Oil Company. The D'Arcy Exploration Company, the exploration arm of Anglo-Persian, obtained a two-year licence to prospect in 1925. The agreement ominously stated that certain parts of the territory were 'not at present safe for its operations', a reference to the unstable internal situation.[11]

The company duly sent a survey party to Muscat. It was led by Captain G. J. Eccles and included D'Arcy Exploration geologists, George Lees and K. Washington Gray, with 'Haji' Williamson as their guide.[12]

In November 1925 the party was able to penetrate the mountain country on camels, reaching Yanqul on the western side of the mountain range. The ruling sheikh had invited them for political rather than philanthropic reasons: his tribe was loyal to the sultan and under threat from forces of the imam. An imamate force had recently set out for Buraimi to investigate reports of Saudi tax collectors visiting there, effectively ruling out one of the most interesting geological areas, the Dhahira plain, to the geologists.

On climbing a nearby scarp, Lees and Gray gazed westwards towards the Buraimi Oasis in the far distance, across the Dhahira plain. Barred from going any farther, Lees aptly summarised the difficulties that lay ahead: 'Systematic exploration of the Arabian Peninsula, or indeed its fringes, is greatly hampered by formidable natural barriers and by the still more serious obstacles caused by the independent spirit of its inhabitants.'[13]

It would be another 30 years before geologists would roam freely on the Dhahira plain.

* * * * *

In 1932 Sultan Taimur of Muscat and Oman, then in his mid-forties, abdicated to enjoy a comfortable retirement in India, leaving his son, the 21-year-old Said, to manage the debts he had left behind. 'Now Said in jail, I free,' Sultan Taimur chortled as he enjoyed his new life in Bombay.[14] The Treasury was empty and the only significant state income came from customs dues and the Canning Award, compensation awarded for the loss of Zanzibar in the nineteenth century.

Sultan Said made it his first priority to balance the budget, which he did by the end of the 1930s. Yet his hands were still tied: without a substantial income of his own, he could not break free from British control. He dreamed of the day when oil would be found in his domain. 'Just think what I can do for my people when we have oil' he once told an American oilman, Wendell Phillips, when oil wealth was just a gleam in the sultan's eye.[15]

On a world tour in 1938, Sultan Said, a plump, dark-skinned, 27-year-old with a neat moustache – it was only later in his reign that he retained a thick bushy beard – alighted from a train at Washington DC. He wore a brown robe with gold trim, white undershirt, jewelled turban and *khanjar*. His arrival aroused great interest. While reporters unkindly nicknamed him 'Sultan Muskrat', he received an official welcome that would have graced King George VI. In Muscat, the American press speculated, the young sultan had a $225,000-a-year salary, a harem with many wives and a Ford car that he drove up and down the barren country's sole 30-mile highway.[16]

This image of a racy young potentate enjoying the trappings of wealth was wide of the mark. When it was all over, Sultan Said returned to Muscat where dark mountains towered over rickety houses, trapping and magnifying the heat, reputed to be 'the hottest city in the world'. A popular story told of a European being prepared for burial who was wrapped in a thick blanket because the fires of hell would be cold after the heat of Muscat.[17]

The wooden gates of the town creaked shut each evening at dusk. Those walking the streets after dark had to carry a lantern at arm's length and constantly announce themselves to avoid the risk of being shot as strangers. There was no development to speak of: if a house burnt down it had to be rebuilt with exactly the same style and materials as before. It was illegal to wear glasses, ride a bicycle or own a radio. Western clothes, dancing and smoking were banned and the ban was enforced with public floggings. Women were not permitted to attend school and were unable to appear in public unless they wore

A young Sultan Said bin Taimur visits Washington DC, 7 March 1938.
(source: US government archives courtesy of Critical Past)

black *abeyas*. Oman's missions abroad were closed, virtually no foreigners were allowed into the country and the few students who had
gone abroad to study were denied employment when they tried to
come home.[18]

There was no means of transport other than dhows plying the
coast, camels in caravans trekking along the coastal plain or through
the mountain passes and the desert, and the occasional hard-pressed
donkey. Motor cars were virtually non-existent. Oil company
representative Dick Bird described the reaction when he drove his car
to Ibri in central Oman: 'The car aroused great interest among the
local inhabitants, some 500 of whom spent the entire night watching it
to see if it breathed, slept, partook of nourishment or even took to the
air.'[19]

Sultan Said was an admirer of the British way of life and, in his
palace in Salalah, the tinkling of teacups was never far away. Foreign
visitors were served tea in silver teapots, with cakes on plates covered
with lace squares trimmed with glass beads.[20] These visitors – who

numbered few – might describe Sultan Said as a shy, charming man. Others would describe a strong-willed and selfish man, the charm and outward diffidence concealing an old-fashioned tyrant. Sultan Said commanded respect but little affection among his relatives, and he treated his servants cruelly. There was a suspicion that he put on his mild manner for the benefit of Westerners, and some said that he was cleverer than he appeared to be. Indeed, the fact that he remained on the throne for almost 40 years attested to his shrewdness.

The British felt they were in a bind. 'Responsibility without power' was a common complaint among British officials who were unhappy about their position in the region. 'Our difficulties derive from our having special responsibilities without having executive powers,' wrote one diplomat in the late 1950s. 'We can persuade, advise, cajole but we cannot command.'[21] This was most certainly true of Bahrain by then, less so of the Trucial Coast. Sultan Said fell somewhere between the two extremes. In external affairs, he was content for the British to take the lead. Over internal matters, he retained complete control. On more than one occasion, this almost led to his downfall as he struggled to suppress internal unrest and had to rely on British military assistance to save his throne.

These states – if they could be called such – were neither colonies nor protectorates. The Gulf sheikhdoms were tied to the British by anti-piracy treaties, and Oman had enjoyed a special relationship with Great Britain since signing a treaty of friendship in 1800. Despite the sultan's assertion that his rule extended inland, his jurisdiction was limited to Muscat, a strip of land running up the Batinah coast and the small enclave of Gwadar on the Asiatic coast. The real seat of his power was Salalah, the capital of Dhofar province, some thousand kilometres to the south.

Apart from the palace guards who formed the Muscat Infantry (later the Muscat Regiment) and loyal tribesmen, there was no body of troops to protect the oil survey parties in the Omani interior. In the 1950s, the sultan extended his troops with the Batinah Force and the Hugf Militia (later the Muscat and Oman Field Force), an oil company-funded force especially developed to protect survey parties, but in the 1930s, security arrangements were poor.[22]

And so, while Socal geologists were enjoying the protection of Ibn Saud's guards, IPC was contemplating a survey of Oman in rather more trying circumstances. In contrast to Saudi Arabia where the name of Ibn Saud struck fear into men's hearts, in Oman the name of Sultan Said bin Taimur brought a range of responses from loyalty, indifference or contempt. It soon became clear to company officials that they were dealing with a most complex situation in the search for oil: an emasculated sultan, an ailing imam and an assortment of sheikhs.

Among these sheikhs was Saqr bin Sultan al-Naimi, paramount sheikh on the Omani side of the Buraimi Oasis. Known as the 'Old Fox', Saqr lived in a crumbling mud fort in the village where reputedly he hoarded silver rupees in Kuwaiti chests behind its walls. Few could match Saqr's tenacity. Quite young when his father died, he and his brother Muhammad had been raised by a slave called Abu Sindah, who became de facto ruler of Buraimi in the process. When Saqr learnt that Abu Sindah was planning to murder him, he stepped forward and fired the first shot, followed by family and friends who joined in a lethal fusillade. Later, when Saqr's popular brother died, it was rumoured that a jealous Saqr had poisoned him.[23]

Saqr was a cruel man, unloved by his people. Once, a British political officer came across three sightless tribesmen, their eyeballs completely white, whom Saqr had blinded with red hot nails because he suspected them of disloyalty.[24] On another occasion, a prisoner was discovered in a pit, some forty feet deep, in Saqr's fort where he had been incarcerated for eight months.[25]

In 1937 IPC obtained a 75-year concession for Oman through its associate, Petroleum Development (Oman and Dhofar) Ltd (PDO).[26] Next year company geologists Henry Hotchkiss and Lester Thompson travelled to Buraimi with the blessing of Sultan Said. Here they found an entourage of more than 100 armed tribesmen and several important sheikhs waiting for them, including Sheikh Saqr. On the face of it, all was well: Saqr was loyal to the sultan and effectively in charge of an area stretching from Buraimi village to the town of Dhank, where he had a *wali*. He appeared to welcome the arrival of the survey party with open arms, having assured the sultan that he would co-operate, telling him 'This place is yours.'[27] But Sheikh Saqr, small and stout in appearance and devious in his ways, saw this as a God-given opportunity for a first class hold-up.

Alarmed at the prospect of so many tribesmen accompanying them into the interior, Hotchkiss and Thompson persuaded the sheikhs to split the group in two. One group stayed in Buraimi, while the geologists set off for the coast with a smaller group, travelling on camels with a sheikh called Gosum and a few tribesmen. Sheikh Saqr had thoughtfully offered them three guides for the journey. Meanwhile, unbeknown to the geologists, Saqr had sent out a messenger in advance to warn the villagers of Hail that the survey party was on its way – the idea being that they should prime their muskets and prepare an ambush of the hapless geologists.[28]

On the second day, the party's caravan came to a fork in the road. Saqr's guides insisted that they take the right fork but Sheikh Gosum said they should take the left. The guides became irate and, for a moment, the geologists feared that they would have to use their guns to settle the argument. Eventually the guides rode off down the right fork leaving the caravan to take the left. When the villagers learnt of the caravan's change of direction, they reset their ambush in a narrow wadi farther up the left hand track.

When confronted by the villagers, the geologists decided to negotiate rather than turn back to Buraimi. After some discussion, they persuaded the ambushers into agreeing to a conference that night in the town of Wasuth, knowing that its inhabitants were friendly to the survey party and hostile to the ambushers. On their arrival, the ambushers were overwhelmed. The geologists' first thought was to seize the ringleader and the three guides and take them to Muscat for punishment, but they relented and released them with a mild reprimand.

This was to be the way of things in Oman, an unpredictable mixture of suspicion and hospitality, a bullet dispatched from behind the rocks to deter a straying intruder or the slaughter of the last goat in honour of an esteemed guest. The tribesmen were naturally curious and alarmed by the appearance of the westerners. But, as the geologists contemplated the interior they saw troubles ahead. Surely the company liaison officers would help them find a way through, travelling from area to area, negotiating their safe passage with the sheikhs?

Dick Bird was the company's representative in the Buraimi Oasis after the World War II. He had served in Bahrain and Muscat with the Indian Political Service and had now acquired the dubious distinction of being the only European to live for months at a time in the oasis. In those days it was an achievement, cut off for weeks from his colleagues in Sharjah and Dubai, struggling in primitive conditions and living among those who were suspicious of his presence. He was knowledgeable about the tribes and fluent in the local dialect, which greatly eased his dealings with the local sheikhs. He would repair to England in the hotter months and return to Buraimi in the autumn.[29]

A colleague observed:

> Dick seemed to know everyone [in Buraimi], and after a break of seven or eight months was carrying on the bedouin gossip where he had dropped it off at the end of the last season. He had a disarming and pleasant way and, after greeting the head of the house, would fold up his long legs to settle down and chat with an easy familiarity, for this is exactly what the bedouin expected. They had excellent memories, they expected you to remember all you had heard about them. They, likewise, have disconcertingly exact memories of all you have said in the past.[30]

The sheikhs kept a close watch on his comings and goings. As Bird himself noted, one sheikh invested him with superhuman powers 'to steal a sort of super penetrative glance at their sands and locate the presence of oil or otherwise in one second'.[31] Sheikh Saqr once suggested that the geologists might examine a small hill to the south of Buraimi village only to insist that he should keep any rocks they found, being convinced that they were valuable.[32]

* * * * *

That Sheikh Saqr was able to create such confusion said much about the lack of any central authority in Oman. The need to define the survey area begged a resolution of Oman's territorial boundaries and, of course, the question of chieftainship.

The British explorer Wilfred Thesiger summed it up thus:

> Jealous and often hostile sheikhs [in northern Oman] rely upon the uncertain support of the bedu to maintain their position [...] None of these sheikhs is prepared to acknowledge a paramount power nor is any of them able to enforce his authority over the bedu; indeed none of them would venture to try lest by doing so he should alienate their support.[33]

One wonders how different things would have been with a strong ruler in charge. Neither sultan nor imam had much control in the north, over the three 'Omani' villages of the Buraimi Oasis or the Dhahira plain, these being the areas that interested the oil company the most. Sultan Said had a historical claim to three villages of the oasis but had let his influence slip. He was not a desert sheikh, did not understand the bedouin, did not make any effort to get to know them and never visited them. His mean and cavalier treatment of tribal visitors was legendary and deterred the wavering tribes. For many of these tribes, the allure of charismatic Ibn Saud was a powerful one, not easily resisted.[34]

The Buraimi Oasis was of particular interest to the Saudis because of the slave trade. It was significant that the staunchest Saudi supporter in the oasis, Sheikh Rashid bin Hamad al-Shamsi, was an active trader in slaves. His village, Hamasa, was the principal depot for slaves taken from the Trucial Coast and the sultanate of Muscat. These slaves were transported to Hamasa where they were sold to slave traders who then transported them to Saudi Arabia. Despite British attempts to suppress the slave trade, it was thriving. As late as 1949, Thesiger counted a party of 43 slaves being driven out of the village 'like cattle'.[35]

For the oil company, however, the oasis was the gateway to the Dhahira plain and the south, where the real oil prospects lay. In March 1948 IPC geologists on board a De Havilland Dove took a reconnaissance flight over the interior of Oman. They spotted a jebel that Thesiger had passed on his travels 14 months before, Fahud, lying to the south of the Dhahira plain. Amid much excitement, Chief Geologist F.E. Wellings declared that Fahud was an 'absolute natural' with all the classic hallmarks of an oil-bearing anticline. They took some 250 photographs which were later unscrambled after developing and printing in Beirut. 'If we can only get in on the ground, we have aerial anticlines and stratigraphy galore to work on' the company journal breezed.[36]

Bird recognised that directly paying the sheikhs was the only practical way of gaining access to the interior. With a colleague, he paid a visit to Sheikh Saqr at his fort in Buraimi village. After much knocking, a small shutter in the thick wooden door opened and part of Saqr's face appeared. The sheikh let his visitors in, leading them to a small dark room where he sat on a palm mat and waited for them to speak. They explained the company's proposal and found him surprisingly receptive. But there was a catch: Saqr wanted his own oil concession.[37]

It was in a sheikh's interest to be assertive in his dealings with the oil company. As J.G. Lorimer had noted in his *Gazetteer*:

> The position of an Arab sheikh was not that of an absolute or arbitrary monarch; he ruled by influence over subjects who voluntarily accepted his dominion and his subjects and subordinate allies possessed a large degree of local freedom and even rights that he could not with safety invade.[38]

In order to maintain his standing among his people, a sheikh had to demonstrate a certain prowess which, in the case of the oil company, meant being a tough bargainer. That he might be able to squeeze more money out of the oilmen than he could out of the sultan was a good reason for his entering into direct negotiations with them.

In the winter of 1948/49 Bird returned to the Dhahira region to find that the sultan had distributed money to the local sheikhs, thus overturning the agreements Bird had reached with them. But at least his company could now pursue its plans to enter the Dhahira plain. Of particular interest was Wadi Jizzi, a mountain pass that linked the Batinah coast with Buraimi, which might be useful for transporting oil and materials in the future. In February 1949 Bird led a small party, which included the author's father, Mike Morton, but the convoy met armed resistance as it struggled across the mountain pass to Buraimi.[39]

Presently the sultan agreed that the oil company could negotiate directly with the local sheikhs, but this turned out to be a disaster. As part of the agreement for an oil concession the sheikhs were required to accept the sultan's sovereignty, which they adamantly refused to do. They also failed to grasp the concept of royalties, instead demanding more cash up front. Angry with the sultan and anxious for a better deal, they could not agree the terms of an oil concession.[40]

Given these obstacles, and the fact that the more promising rock formations lay to the south, it was predictable that the oilmen would stall in their attempts to open up northern Oman. The oil company adopted a 'wait and see' policy and the dust settled once more on the Dhahira plain: there was no sign of geologists anywhere.

* * * * *

In the late 1940s Wilfred Thesiger was wandering about the southern desert disguised as a Syrian bedouin. But although he may have looked the part, enough to deceive a passing traveller, his large feet were like a calling card, his footprints so distinctive that his bedouin companions could easily track his progress in the sand.[41]

Thesiger had arrived in southern Arabia in 1945 with a brief to find the breeding grounds of the locusts that were plaguing East Africa. He went on to complete two camel-borne crossings of the Empty Quarter in the company of a few bedouin. He was tall, thin, gaunt, dressed in bedouin clothes and known affectionately by his companions as 'Mubarak bin London'. Yet he was in many ways the archetypal Englishman, the son of a diplomat, educated at Eton and with an Army career that included service with the SAS in the North African desert during World War II.

Many viewed him with suspicion. Wandering through the Saudi part of the Empty Quarter without seeking Ibn Saud's permission was sure to win him no friends in Riyadh. Sultan Said revoked his visa, although this little troubled Thesiger since, as he pointed out, he had never been granted a visa in the first place. The imam of Oman's hostility to all Europeans forced Thesiger to travel in disguise through the lands where the Imam's white flag flew. The ambassador in Jedda, Alan Trott, was worried that Thesiger might prove to be another Muslim renegade like Philby.[42] But Bernard Burrows, then in the Eastern Department of the Foreign Office in London, reassured him: 'I do not think you need be afraid of Thesiger turning into another Philby. They seem to me to be temperamentally very different and while Thesiger has a strong attachment to the bedouin and their ways, I do not think he would have the least ambition to become a hanger-on of an Arab court.'[43]

Then there were the oilmen. In November 1947, while preparing for an expedition to the desert, a party of IPC geologists met Thesiger in Aden. At this time the great explorer was about to embark on his second crossing of the great sands, a 'mad scheme in the desert' according to one geologist.[44] Thesiger's natural instinct made him wary of the oil industry. A profound empathy with the bedouin led him to fear the impact of oil on their nomadic way of life. Most of all, he feared that the tribesmen, attracted by the high wages the oil companies could offer, would be drawn to the oilfields and would settle permanently in camps nearby.[45]

Thesiger's bedu companions knew little of these things, for the oil camps then were few and far between. They took everything with good humour, possessing an unerring belief in the overriding will of God, which equipped them well for the hardships they encountered. But Thesiger emerged from the desert forever changed. 'I went there with a belief in my own racial superiority, but in their tents I felt like an uncouth, inarticulate barbarian, an intruder from a shoddy and materialistic world,' he wrote.[46]

There is a strange paradox at the heart of Thesiger's Arabian travels. In seeking to record the bedouin way of life, he was in a small way helping to bring it to an end. It was inevitable that news of his travels would spread by books and lectures and expose this wilderness to a wider audience. His travels would also yield practical details that would assist the oil companies. His maps, intelligence about the tribes and routes through the sands were all matters of interest to the Iraq Petroleum Company, and were used by them to good effect.

On one occasion, while travelling through the Omani desert, Thesiger had noted two jebels in an area that would become of prime interest to the company. 'Both of them were dome-shaped', he later wrote, 'and I thought regretfully that their formation was of the sort which geologists associate with oil.'[47] In the 1950s the first IPC geologists to land on the southern Omani coast were well schooled in Thesiger's travels, having studied his various publications in the *Quarterly Journal of the Geographical Society* and the *Journal of the Royal Asiatic Society*. A man who could travel through the desert and mingle with the bedouin was a valuable source of information indeed.

Thesiger's sympathies were with the bedouin yet he was rooted in the West. He had made it his business to move through both worlds, as easily as changing his clothes, but was in danger of belonging to neither. 'When I was among my own people,' he wrote, 'a shadowy figure was always at my side watching them with critical intolerant eyes.'[48] On 5 April 1948 he arrived in the Buraimi Oasis and received a cool reception from Dick Bird, who wanted Thesiger off his patch. 'Wilfred Thesiger to put it mildly is most unwelcome to me in these parts,' he wrote to Noel Jackson. Nothing could dispel the suspicion among local tribesmen that Thesiger was connected with the government or the [oil] company. 'It is an extremely delicate problem this penetration of Oman and no bride was ever more bashful of the advances of the other party.'[49]

The explorer Wilfred Thesiger with his travelling companions, February 1947.
(source: Pitt Rivers Museum, University of Oxford 2004.130.6827.1)

Thesiger, wishing not to be associated with the oil company, stayed with Sheikh Zayed of Abu Dhabi rather than lodge with Bird. Although distracted for a month or so by hunting for wild goats on Jebel Hafit, he persisted with his plan to visit Jebel Akhdar to collect wild plants and complete his travels of Arabia, 'otherwise his book would not be complete.'[50]

At the heart of Bird's concern about Thesiger – and what made Thesiger such a risk to oil negotiations – was the way he appealed directly to the bedouin and openly derided Western ideas and oil companies. He concluded: 'Thesiger is, then, potentially dangerous.'[51]

But Bird recognised that Thesiger might be of some value to the government or IPC. Thesiger had demonstrated his knowledge of both the tribes and the oil possibilities of Oman. Indeed, Bird thought, he knew more about the oil prospects of Oman than he let on. His expertise might be useful when it came to boundary disputes and oil exploration. How, it might be asked, could Thesiger be persuaded to assist an oil company? Surely he would not compromise his principles, therefore asking him would be a waste of time?

It sounded far-fetched, but Bird persisted. He suggested to his manager in Bahrain that IPC might consider employing him in some capacity. 'I believe Mr Thesiger would accept some form of remuneration for work which would involve travel to remote parts by camel' he wrote.[52] The company saw some merit in the idea, made a proposal and, surprisingly, Thesiger agreed. Caught between the financial reality of mounting another expedition and his own conscience, his scruples melted away. On his return to London, he came to an arrangement with the company, which both parties were anxious not to advertise. In May 1949 Stephen Longrigg – now a senior manager with IPC based in London – was writing a memo describing Thesiger 'as one who acts for us as an advance agent for exploring the wilder areas'.[53]

By early 1950 the company was sponsoring Thesiger's latest expedition to central Oman, although Longrigg played down the arrangement by suggesting that it was simply a case of helping a cash-strapped explorer.[54] The grant of money was no more than a contribution towards his expenses for any information he might bring back for them from the wilderness. Even so, it was a remarkable turn of events for an explorer who had been so critical of the oilmen in the past.

Thesiger was helpful to the British government too. On 12 April 1950, having shaken the sand from his boots after his latest expedition, he called in on the Foreign Office in London to advise officials about Saudi territorial claims. The tribal situation was so volatile that penetration by the oil company was a 'catalyst for rebellion', he told them, recommending that central Oman be left alone while the Omani villages of the Buraimi Oasis should be annexed by Abu Dhabi.[55] But it was Bird, not Thesiger, who carried the day. IPC followed Bird's advice in drawing up plans for an expedition into central Oman from the south.

In time, Bird would mellow towards the great explorer. 'Thesiger's claim to fame,' he wrote in 1953, 'was earned by virtue of some first-class exploration work which he could not have undertaken without a very intimate knowledge of tribal affiliations and also without his extreme "toughness" and intrepidity and, finally, without the genuine affection a lot of people bore him.'[56]

Thesiger spent as much time walking on eggshells as he did on sand. At the end of his second crossing of the Rub al-Khali, he returned to London and gave a lecture to members of the Royal Geographical

Society. The Saudi chargé d'affaires was sitting in a place of honour in the audience. Thesiger, unabashed, gave an account of his travels which included a story about his incarceration by the Saudis in the town of Sulaiyil. At any other time, a diplomatic row might have blown up but, as a British official noted, the chargé did not understand a word of English and the incident passed quietly away.[57]

Chapter 5
A Tale of Two Brothers
Abu Dhabi, 1928–55

When IPC returned to the Buraimi Oasis after World War II they
were looking for a strong leader on the Abu Dhabi side of the border,
a leader who might steer them through the quicksands of tribal
politics. In Sheikh Zayed bin Sultan Al Nahyan they found such a
man. He had come to the oil company's notice through his skill as a
guide, assisting survey parties to explore the interior from the late
1930s. In 1947 he was appointed governor of Abu Dhabi's eastern
province and set up his headquarters in a mud-walled fort in the village
of Muwaiqi, one of the six villages on the Abu Dhabi side of the oasis.
His elder brother Hazza, also an influential figure among the tribes,
was appointed governor of the western province.[1]

Wilfred Thesiger first met Zayed when the sheikh was embroiled in
the tribal disputes of the 1940s. He found him squatting on the
ground, picking stones out of his toes with a stick and surrounded by
tribesmen. 'He was a powerfully built man of about 30 with a brown
beard. He had a strong intelligent face, with steady observant eyes and
his manner was quiet but masterful. He wore a dagger and cartridge
belt; his rifle lay on the sand beside him.' His bedu companions were
full of praise for him: 'Zayed is a bedu. He knows about camels, can
ride like one of us and knows how to fight.'[2]

More significantly, Zayed opposed any move by the Saudis to
extend their influence in the area. He knew his country and people
well and his reputation for fair dealing extended well beyond the
boundaries of his governorship into central Oman. He was a man of
power and influence who could be trusted to work with the oil
company towards opening up the country for oil exploration. Yet he
never tried to upstage his elder brother, as Martin Buckmaster, a
political officer based in Dubai, described: 'He has never tried to
exploit the almost universal popularity he enjoys among townsmen
and bedouin – a popularity that extends far beyond Abu Dhabi territory – at the expense of his brother.'[3]

Zayed's brother Shakhbut was the ruler of Abu Dhabi. In contrast to Zayed, Shakhbut was like Sultan Said bin Taimur: a Canute-like figure trying to stare down a rising tide of expectation. He had been born into the traditional mould of a desert sheikh, unshakeable in his faith, deeply conservative and resistant to the modern age. The people of Abu Dhabi would see Shakhbut and his retainers leaving his palace on the island to go hunting with their Salukis (hunting dogs) and falcons in the desert and await their return at the end of spring. The arrival of mangoes and the passage of hoopoes heralded the hot weather that would soon wrap everyone in a blanket of humidity for the summer.[4]

These were diehard bedouins with no particular desire to change their ways. The Bani Yas tribe had established itself in the eighteenth century in the Liwa Oasis, making a living from trading in dates and camels and moving in the summer months to the coast to fish and gather pearls. In 1761 some Bani Yas tribesmen discovered a well with potable water on the salt-encrusted island of Abu Dhabi ('Father of the Gazelle') and settled there. A narrow channel, fordable at one place at low tide, divided the island from the mainland, and was guarded by a single, mud-walled fort.

As we have seen, the lower Gulf was known as the Pirate Coast in the nineteenth century. Wahhabi pirates operating out of Ras al-Khaima and creeks along the coast threatened the shipping lanes. From 1820 the British entered into a series of treaties and maritime truces with the coastal sheikhs, which afforded them naval protection against piracy and gave the region its name, the Trucial Coast. Gun-running continued into the twentieth century, as well as a few unscrupulous captains who carried on dumping their pilgrim boatloads on the barren shore. What these captains failed to mention was that Mecca was on the other side of the peninsula, and that death was almost certain if they tried to cross the desert to get there.[5]

The Wahhabi influence failed to sway the Bani Yas, who remained a bedouin people without the fanaticism of the Wahhabis. Despite a brief period of piracy in the 1830s, they settled down to peaceful relations with the British and occasional land wars with their neighbours. In 1870 Zayed the Great, leader of the Al Bu Falah section of the tribe, helped to stop the Wahhabis from returning to Buraimi, and since then the rulers of Abu Dhabi and Oman had enjoyed cordial relations. The tribes of Abu Dhabi experienced a settled period under

Zayed the Great, a situation that was to change dramatically after his death in 1909.

To understand the relationship between the brothers Zayed and Shakhbut one has to go back in time, to the events of the 1920s. Following a spate of internecine murders, their mother Sheikha Salaamah told her sons: 'The killing has to stop. You four must get together and decide which of your generation should become Ruler and all of you, all of you, must give that person your unquestioning loyalty and service.'[6]

They decided that Shakhbut should rule. By the late 1940s he was based on Abu Dhabi Island while his younger brothers Hazza and Zayed dealt with the tribal affairs of the interior. Thus it happened that when the oil company started to explore the interior, Sheikh Zayed was waiting to meet them.

Nevertheless, the legacy of murder would endure for many years. Two sons of an assassinated sheikh went to live in Dubai and remained a source of dissent. Later, when the Saudis were looking for disaffected members of the family, they did not have to look far to find them.[7] It also had a debilitating effect on Al Bu Falah authority over the tribes around the Liwa Oasis. The Saudis would allege with some justification that the Al Bu Falah were a dynasty of petty squabbling sheikhs incapable of providing stable government.[8] Sheikh Shakhbut's outstanding characteristic – parsimony – and his apparent apathy towards asserting his authority in the area only added to the ruling family's worries.

* * * * *

In the late 1920s, the coast of the lower Gulf was a shop without many goods. The Dubai *suq* was busy enough, with traders bringing pearls for merchants to haggle over and sell on, the best ones travelling to the markets of India and beyond. Fish was plentiful, and trading boats came southwards from Basra with fruit and vegetables fresh from the Euphrates basin. Inland, dates, camels, sheep and goats were the staple trade of the tribesmen. Nevertheless, in the main, the land was wretchedly poor.

The village of Abu Dhabi was a collection of *barrasti* dwellings situated on a flat barren island, isolated and rarely visited by steamers, an occasional British ship bringing in a dispatch box for the ruling sheikh. The ruler's relatives may have been a little curious to know what was inside this dispatch box, money and jewels maybe, but any speculation was soon dispelled when a safe belonging to one of the assassinated sheikhs was forced open and found to contain only a single rupee.[9]

The authority of the Al Bu Falah sheikhs having been damaged by their squabbling, the British in 1934 sent a secret mission into the desert in order to assess the loyalties of the tribes of the interior, primarily in and around the Liwa Oasis. The Manasir tribe was loyal to Ibn Saud, it was reported, having paid Abdullah bin Jiluwi's tax collectors *zakat* at the rate of one Maria Theresa dollar per camel. The Bani Yas tribe was loyal to Shakhbut, but his influence was waning.[10]

Ibn Saud regarded the Persian Gulf states as part of a greater Arabia. Once he had consolidated his rule in Riyadh he cast an acquisitive eye towards the territory of his Trucial Coast neighbours but, as we have seen, the British warned the Trucial sheikhs against closer ties. In 1927, Ibn entered the Treaty of Jedda with Great Britain by which he pledged under Article Six 'to maintain friendly and peaceful relations with [...] the sheikhs of Qatar and the [Trucial] Oman coast who are in special relations with Her Britannic Majesty's government.'[11] Although the treaty did not delineate the boundaries of these sheikhdoms, the Foreign Office would later rely on Article Six as evidence of Ibn Saud's acceptance of them.[12]

Ibn Saud had other ideas. His ambition to swallow up the little sheikhdoms of the lower Gulf remained undimmed, and he retained a particular dislike of Sheikh Shakhbut. On 28 August 1935 a Damascus newspaper *Al Shahab* reported Fuad Hamza as saying, 'The small emirates which you see on the coasts of Arabia will not stand before the hurricane as their existence is contrary to the law of nature.'[13] Perhaps there was an element of posturing in Hamza's remarks, since at the time he was engaged in discussing the south-eastern boundary of the kingdom with the British, but the thrust of Saudi aspirations was plain.

The Trucial Coast sheikhs began sending money presents to Ibn Saud and the emir of Al-Hasa, Abdullah bin Jiluwi, an unwise move because it simply bolstered Ibn Saud's claim to their territory. Indeed, many years later, the Saudis would use these presents as evidence to support their claim. Sheikh Shakhbut went even further: he would not deal with those who had committed offences on his own territory for fear of displeasing Ibn Saud. Instead, he would send them to Bin Jiluwi whose reputation for inflicting severe punishment was well known. Offenders, a British official noted ominously, 'do not run away to Saudi Arabia.'[14]

Abdullah bin Jiluwi's cruel reputation ran the length and breadth of the Arabian Peninsula. A cousin of Ibn Saud, he had played a crucial role in the capture of Riyadh in 1902, and as we have seen, leaving his calling card – a spear tip – embedded in the postern of the Masmak fort. A story told about Abdullah was of a man who came to his *majilis* and said that there was a sack of rice on its way to Uqair. Abdullah asked him how he knew it was a sack of rice and the man replied that he had kicked it with his toe. Abdullah ordered his men to take the man outside and cut off his toe as a lesson not to interfere with other people's property.[15]

When he died in 1938 his son Saud succeeded him and continued his father's reign of fear – indeed, Saud was reputed to be harsher than his father.

Saud bin Jiluwi, governor of Al-Hasa province.
(source: the T.C. Barger Collection)

The British described him in unflattering terms:

> Born in about 1900 [...] repulsive in appearance owing to a
> super-squint. Reported from Bahrain to take an even stronger
> line with the bedouin than his father did, and that much of his
> father's work in the last four years of his life was, in fact, done
> by the son.[16]

To Aramcons, Saud and his brother Abdul Muhsin, who ran
Dammam and the Dhahran district, were known as the 'Big and Little
Bin' respectively.[17] When people spoke of Bin Jiluwi in hushed tones,
it was obvious that they were referring to the Big Bin. In later years he
took to dyeing his beard black, giving him a sinister appearance which
was in tune with his popular reputation. His loyalty to Ibn Saud was
unshakeable, as was his faith in the Wahhabi creed. As emir of Al-Hasa
province he took a close interest in the Omani borderlands, and in the
wayward tribes of southern Arabia.

* * * * *

Today, Abu Dhabi is part of the United Arab Emirates, which is
described as one of the world's richer countries, but in the 1930s the
area was one of its poorest. The decline of the pearl trade hit Sheikh
Shakhbut and his family hard, as it had many tribes in the area. When
cultured pearls from Japan destroyed the market for natural ones,
many in Abu Dhabi were so poor that they could not afford to buy
wood for a fire and had to eat their food raw.[18]

Shakhbut was eager to find a better water supply for Abu Dhabi
village. He had heard about water wells being drilled in Bahrain and
thought the same might be done on Abu Dhabi Island where water
was taken from shallow pits and very brackish except after an
occasional heavy rainfall. He agreed enthusiastically to the political
officer's suggestion that a water survey be carried out.

In 1934 an Anglo-Persian geologist, Peter Cox, arrived on board the
sloop HMS *Lupin* ready to undertake the survey.[19] However, upon
viewing the coastal plain from the ship's crow's nest, he realised that a
more extensive survey would be needed. In 1935 he returned with Haji
Williamson as his guide. 'There had been good rains recently,' wrote
Cox, 'so the water problem was not immediately pressing.'

Even so, they were surprised to find a lukewarm Shakhbut waiting for them. While Cox carried out a restricted survey of the coast, it was evident that Shakhbut was no longer interested in water but in oil. Shakhbut asked Haji Williamson if he thought the British would be displeased if he allowed the Americans to search for oil in his territory. It was apparent that he was aware of what oil companies had paid to his fellow sheikhs for prospecting rights elsewhere. The haggling went on until, on 5 January 1936 Shakhbut granted a two-year option on a down payment of 7,000 rupees and 3,000 rupees a month.[20]

The first survey began later in the year. It was a story of storms and aggravation: 'We landed from the Gulf mail steamer at Dubai after a day and night lying to and waiting until one of the most violent storms of thunder and rain we had ever experienced had blown itself out,' wrote IPC geologist T.F. ('Jock') Williamson (no relation to Haji Williamson). 'During the first few months in Dubai we were advised never to leave the house without an armed escort, as we were the first Europeans to live in the town and it was considered desirable to accustom the local populace gradually to our presence.'[21]

The party would travel inland with the sheikh and his followers who used each occasion as an excuse for hunting. Williamson continued:

> With our two cars, we had the sheikh's and at least one other filled with his men, six or eight to a car, each with his saddle bag of belongings and his rifle. Room had also to be found for cooking pots and one or two hawks, while on one occasion a large Saluki was also squeezed in. Our routes followed camel trails, the only tracks of any kind which existed and, as most of the country was sand, the cars were very often stuck.[22]

After covering the desert between Dubai and the Hajar Mountains, they reached Abu Dhabi Island to find that a four-day holiday was about to start. They spent the next few days doing no work but visiting local notables instead, drinking countless cups of coffee.

The party went on to the Buraimi Oasis and studied the most prominent geological feature of the region, Jebel Hafit. Otherwise, everything pointed to future difficulties for the oil explorers: sand, sand and more sand. Jebels Hafit and Dhana and a few coastal outcrops – those features that enabled the geologists to read the rocks – were the only exposed features in Abu Dhabi. It would be a few years before the oil company could rely on the new science of geophysics, with its seismic techniques, rather than geology to identify the rock structures deep underground.

Such problems lay in the future. The survey party returned to Iran and disbanded. IPC, through its associated company, Petroleum Development (Trucial Coast) Limited (PDTC), obtained a 75-year concession for Abu Dhabi on 11 January 1939.

* * * * *

In 1946 the Persian Gulf scene began to change. The headquarters of British political activity in the Gulf, the Political Residency, had been transferred from Bushire to Bahrain two years before, reflecting the growing importance of the Arabian coast to British interests. After the independence of India in 1947, responsibility for political arrangements in the Gulf passed from India to the Foreign Office.[23]

Although many members of the Indian Civil Service were retained, the Eastern Department of the Foreign Office brought a new and wider perspective to British diplomacy in south-eastern Arabia. Decisions were more likely to be influenced by world opinion and United Nations' resolutions about her role in Gulf affairs, as opposed to the old days of the India Office when the Gulf was regarded as a 'British lake'.[24]

Not much had changed in Abu Dhabi, however. Since the decline of the pearl trade, Shakhbut and his family had relied on the concession payments from the oil company and a meagre income from their date gardens around the Buraimi Oasis. Shakhbut had used the proceeds from the oil concession to extend his fort of coral rocks, the first – and for many years the only – major construction project on the island.[25]

But there were stirrings in the sheikhdom. As PDTC began drilling for oil at Ras Sadr in 1950, opportunities for local employment increased. The drilling rig and survey parties required guards for their own protection, which Shakhbut supplied. Manasir tribesmen from the Liwa Oasis were travelling to Al-Hasa and Qatar to find work in the oilfields. Some found permanent jobs while others stayed for a couple of years, enough time to save money to get married, and to buy date palms or camels.[26] Seismic parties roamed the desert and oil exploration began offshore. Having gained the offshore concession in March 1953, Abu Dhabi Marine Areas Ltd (ADMA) brought Commander Jacques Cousteau and his research ship *Calypso* to the Persian Gulf to carry out a gravity survey of the sea bed. The expectation of oil discoveries, amplified by garish stories emerging from Saudi Arabia, heightened the sense that the old way of life was about to change.

The story of Abu Dhabi now crystallises into the tale of the two brothers, Shakhbut and Zayed; certainly, after the death of Sheikh Hazza in 1958, they were the most prominent sheikhs in the territory. Shakhbut was a shy, intelligent man, with a mind 'like a computer', who could remember the names of everyone who lived in his sheikhdom.[27] His natural caution, and a desire to safeguard his people and their ways, found expression in a frugal lifestyle and conservative mindset. Westerners could mistake these characteristics as mere foibles,

Sheikh Shakhbut bin Sultan Al Nahyan outside his fort, Qasr al-Hosn.
(source: the BP Archive)

and there were some whimsical stories about him. He distrusted banks, it was said; the state treasury consisted of bank notes kept in a shoe box under his bed or, depending on which version of the story was told, jerry cans in the courtyard. These notes were occasionally counted by Shakhbut and nibbled by rats; with a dutiful harem and the occasional *shamal*, they were reputed to be his main distraction.[28]

Shakhbut was the type of ruler, others said, who preferred to keep oil where it belonged – in the ground. Yet, from the late 1930s when Saudi oil wealth became ostentatious, a sheikh such as Shakhbut might have felt justified in this approach. Vulgar extravagance and greedy materialism clashed with the simplicity of the bedouin life. In many respects Shakhbut was no different from many of his contemporaries, a desert tribesman grappling with the onset of the twentieth century. In Shakhbut, however, the qualities of bedouin stoicism combined with a natural curiosity about the modern world. He was by no means uninterested in change: when Jacques Cousteau arrived on the scene, Shakhbut insisted on visiting *Calypso*, accompanied by 20 of his followers, asking many questions and showing a keen interest in the equipment.[29]

Oil was still a pipe dream. Back on dry land, Shakhbut would use his mother's *majilis* room for meetings. It was hung with wall mirrors that reflected the images of the sheikhs, guards and tribesmen who sat on either side of the room, creating a bewildering array of reflections fading into the far distance. 'We've waited a long time for news of oil in Abu Dhabi,' Shakhbut told a visitor in 1955, some 19 years after the first survey. 'It's a long time to wait.' His brother Khaled nodded sagely, echoing Shakhbut's words. 'A long time to wait,' he said, the mirrors reflecting his nods into infinity. A moment of silence and then Shakhbut added: 'It is the will of Allah.'[30]

The early oilmen soon discovered that, despite the sheikha's plea, family disagreements were never far below the surface. Shakhbut promised that oil company trucks could pass freely between the mainland and the island. But this was thwarted by his younger son Sultan who controlled the crossing, a narrow stretch of water that could be safely forded at low tide, later replaced by a stone causeway. If Sultan was away or asleep, his followers refused to let anyone past, causing great confusion. 'Chitty systems, messages by the clerk etc have been tried and are useless,' wrote the exasperated ADMA representative, Tim Hillyard.[31]

The effects on the local economy were dire: supplies of goats and chickens almost dried up and prices increased twenty-fold. The British political officer, who was not burdened by having to run trucks and supplies in and out of the island, considered the whole problem a storm in a teacup. Meanwhile, Sultan offered 'rather contemptuously' to go into exile in Bombay or anywhere else but only on the proviso that Shakhbut should pay his fare. Described as dashing and slightly wild, Sultan had impossible ambitions.[32]

Shakhbut's elder son, Said, was a worry too. Headstrong, spoilt, with a fondness for liquor, he once demanded a large sum of money from his father and, when he did not get it, promptly disappeared, sparking rumours that he was planning a coup. He was eventually found marooned on the track to Buraimi village, his car having run out of water and petrol after he had forgotten to replenish it in his haste to get away. 'Today,' wrote Hillyard, 'he is back here and sulking.'[33] In 1953, when Said was stationed with a detachment of soldiers at Markhiya in the Abu Dhabi desert, he caused much trouble, especially when drunk. On one occasion, in a fit of temper, he countermanded the commandant's orders, deprived the men of their arms, and allowed his own followers to pick quarrels with and browbeat them.[34]

There was little indication of the momentous changes to come, and the rhythm of life was unchanged. Susan Hillyard, wife of Tim, told a story about a man who arrived from the Buraimi Oasis on camel carrying firewood to exchange for dried fish. At the fort guarding the crossing to Abu Dhabi Island, the rider greeted the guard in the customary manner:

> 'Peace upon you.'
> 'And upon you be peace. What is the news?'
> 'There is no news. By God, Al Yard's [Hillyard's] lorry is stuck in the *sabkha*.'
> 'In God's name what a mess!'
> 'What is to be done? It is the will of God. At least there are no camels involved.'[35]

For the British, Sheikh Zayed was a man with whom they could do business. Unlike Shakhbut, Zayed seemed to be receptive to progress. But, although he would despair at his brother's conservatism and lack of interest in development, Zayed held back from plotting against him and never tried to exploit his popularity against him. In 1954, when Shakhbut threatened to resign, Zayed and his brothers begged him not to do so. It showed 'a degree of family loyalty little short of incredible,' the political officer, Martin Buckmaster, observed. It also reflected the power of the oath that Sheikha Salaamah had extracted from her sons in 1928.

* *****

Water is close to the bedu spirit. No two wells are exactly alike: some are salty, others harsh and bitter, some sulphurous, others sweet as the purest rainwater. Martin Buckmaster noted all these qualities on a tour of the western desert of Abu Dhabi. 'The water of Markhiya,' he observed, 'contains a particularly pleasing blend of salts.'[37]

For the bedouin, each well had a special character, which was reflected in the names they gave them, such as Mother of the Guns, Milk, the Bride, the Spout, the Red Face, the Watchman, the Digger, Father of Salt, the Navel, the Leaning One, Mother of Dryness, Father of Sorrow and the Cricket. Others were named after the man who built them, the word Bada' (meaning 'to begin') being placed before them: Bada' Khamis, Bada' bin Suwaid and so on.

The wells in the open desert were free and owned by no man. Those around Liwa and the Batin were considered to be owned by the villagers. Certain tribes gravitated towards certain wells. If a tribe was grazing around one of these wells, they would claim the right to refuse water to tribes they were not on good terms with. The digger of the well might have written his name on the inside of the well but he could not call it his own.[38]

For dwellers of the desert, a water well has a powerful effect for it can both determine the rise (and if it runs dry, the fall) of a settlement and trade routes. It has instilled in the Arab mind a love of greenery and streams, the oasis being the most potent symbol of all. There is a strong fascination about finding water beneath a bleak and desiccated land, and it was significant that Shakhbut's early interest was in drilling for water, not oil. Zayed's passion was water, too. The villages of the Buraimi Oasis, including Zayed's village of Al-Ain, were linked by desert tracks and ancient *aflaj*, which Zayed set about repairing and extending on the Abu Dhabi side.

There is a fable-like quality to some of the stories about Sheikh
Zayed. In one, he sets about securing free water supplies for the poor
farmers of Al-Ain. He summons the rich farmers of the district and
asks them to grant free irrigation rights to all-comers. When they turn
down his proposal, Zayed allows the poor farmers to use his own
family's wells, and bans the rich farmers from using a new *falaj* he has
built. These farmers have little option but to comply; thus free water
becomes available to all.[39]

Today, along the Al-Ain highway, lies one of Zayed's most
endearing legacies, a ribbon of trees, bushes and shrubs, a green lifeline
stretching into the desert. It is proof that it is possible to meet the
challenges of progress while remaining true to one's roots.

Sheikh Zayed bin Sultan Al Nahyan (on the right) at a dance in Al-Ain in the 1960s.
(source: the BP Archive)

Chapter 6
Squeezing Aramco
US–Saudi Relations, 1939–52

On 26 March 1939, a Japanese mission led by diplomat Tomoyoshi Yokoyama arrived in Riyadh and spent several weeks negotiating an oil concession.[1] Ibn Saud may have welcomed this foreign interest in the oil prospects of his kingdom but the mission did not succeed. The king and his advisers were simply repeating the tactics they had used in 1933, playing one side off against the other in order to raise the bidding. Some of the players from that time, such as Stephen Longrigg and Lloyd Hamilton, shuffled back on to centre stage to negotiate with the Saudis for the concession.

The Americans carried no political baggage, an advantage in the eyes of a king who had spent years trying to avoid the imperial clutches of Great Britain. 'Americans get oil out of the ground and stay out of politics' was how Ibn Saud once put it, and in the 1930s there was more than a grain of truth in his view.[2] They had a proven track record of oil exploration in Al-Hasa and had conducted their operations with discretion.

There was little surprise therefore when the Saudi Arabian government accepted Socal's bid. In a supplementary agreement, it extended the company's concession area from 830,000 square kilometres to 1.14 million square kilometres – about a sixth of the area of the United States. In return, £140,000 (£7.5 million today) in gold was paid to the Saudi government, the rental fee was increased to £25,000 a year and £100,000 was promised if a new oilfield was discovered, and royalties remained unchanged.[3]

Yet Socal officials felt disadvantaged by the lack of diplomatic support in the kingdom. Although the USA and Saudi Arabia had established diplomatic relations in November 1933, there was no US minister in Jedda. A Socal representative, Francis Loomis, wrote to the State Department in April 1939 asking for a permanent diplomatic presence in the country. Eventually the State Department acceded to his request and on 1 May 1942 the first American legation in Jedda was established in an old building just inside the city wall. The building had no electric power, which had to be supplied by a generator in the oil company office next door.[4]

There were other pressures bringing the two nations closer together. Ibn Saud's financial needs were growing apace while his income from pilgrims had dropped drastically with the outbreak of war.[5] Socal was unable to meet the king's demands for advances against oil revenues and, in desperation, they asked Washington to lend Ibn Saud $6m in return for Saudi Arabian oil of equal value. On 18 July, President Roosevelt gave his answer: 'Will you tell the British I hope they can take care of the king of Saudi Arabia. This is a little far afield for us.'[6]

But, with America involved in the war, everything changed: fuel scares hit the United States and during 1943 New York was down to two days' supply of fuel oil, Boston two and a half and Providence to three.[7] With its domestic oil reserves rapidly diminishing, the country faced the prospect of becoming a net importer of oil. Washington began casting a fresh eye over the oil potential of the Middle East.[8] In 1943 Everette Lee DeGolyer, a 57-year-old geologist, was dispatched to assess the oil potential of the region. Small, stout and energetic, DeGolyer hitched rides on military transport aircraft to get to the Persian Gulf and visited all the major oilfields. His findings were ground-breaking. Having predicted that the centre of world oil production would continue to shift to the Persian Gulf, he observed:

> When one considers the great oil discoveries which have resulted from the meagre exploration thus far accomplished in the Middle East, the substantial number of known prospects not yet drilled, and the great areas still practically unexplored, the conclusion is inescapable that reserves of great magnitude remain to be discovered.[9]

Strategically, too, the kingdom was proving important to the American war effort. The Persian Gulf was a link in the air route between the United States and the Far East, and a key staging post in the supply route to the hard-pressed Russians. German advances towards the Caucasus and in northern Africa threatened the British position across the Middle East. The need to mollify the king and secure American oil interests in Saudi Arabia were paramount.[10]

Where they had once accepted that Saudi Arabia was within the British sphere of influence, the Americans were now willing to challenge the status quo. Since Roosevelt's rejection of their proposal, Socal executives had been working quietly in the background, lobbying the State Department to back their cause. As part of their strategy, the oilmen played on fears of British influence in the kingdom which at worst, they claimed, might lead to the company losing the Saudi Arabian oil concession. At a meeting on 2 December 1942, the oilmen voiced concerns that their oil concession might be cancelled and given over to British interests.[11] Roosevelt himself expressed a concern that the British might be using their Lend-Lease payments as leverage 'to horn in on Saudi Arabian oil reserves.'[12]

And so, in February 1943 President Roosevelt issued an executive order declaring 'Saudi Arabia is vital to the defence of the United States' and authorised financial aid to the kingdom in the form of Lend-Lease.[13] Anglo-American rivalry would now be fought out in subsidies. It was a battle that suited the Saudis' situation perfectly, but one that the British could not hope to win, since they were unable to match the spending power of the Americans and thus could not satisfy the insistent demands of Ibn Saud's growing family and a venal administration.

* * * * *

The war years thus saw a noticeable decline of British influence in the kingdom and a corresponding rise in the fortunes of the Americans. The latter still had differences with Ibn Saud, mainly over Palestine, but these were papered over. After an amicable meeting in February 1945 with Ibn Saud on the Great Bitter Lake in Egypt, President Roosevelt wrote to the king assuring him that he would not assist the Jews against the Arabs in Palestine and would not harm the Arab people. He also promised that the United States government would not change its policy on Palestine without prior consultation with Arabs and Jews.[14]

It came to nothing. A week after writing the letter, on 12 April, Roosevelt was dead of a brain haemorrhage. Harry Truman, the new president, was left to pick up the pieces. 'I felt like the moon, the stars and all the planets had fallen on me,' he told reporters.[15] In contrast to the patrician style of Roosevelt, Truman was more down to earth and

tried to make a virtue of simplicity in his first days in office. But
Jewish leaders in the United States were soon putting pressure on him
to commit American power and forces in support of Jewish aspirations
in Palestine, and Truman was acutely aware of the need to win over
the Jewish electorate in the United States.[16] When the British
withdrew from Palestine, the Jews proclaimed the independent state of
Israel on 14 May 1948. The Truman administration recognised the
state the same day.[17]

In theory, all this should have set Saudi Arabia against the United
States, since Ibn Saud was implacably opposed to the creation of a
Jewish state. In fact it made little difference to the overall tenor of US-
Saudi relations, and the United States was already heavily committed
to supporting the Saudis. Their relationship seemed to bring progress
and prosperity. By the end of World War II, Americans were drilling
water wells around Riyadh and advising on agricultural schemes.
There were hardly any other Westerners in sight, apart from Italian
prisoners-of-war drafted in to work on the Dhahran camp and the new
oil pipeline running from Dhahran to the Mediterranean coast, to be
known as Tapline. Meanwhile the Saudi sheikhs were making use of
their oil wealth, shunning sterling goods and adopting the 'baubles of
American civilization – Coca-Cola, Cadillacs and the rest', as the
British ambassador observed.[18]

For Aramco (as Casoc had been known since 1944), the discovery
of oil had brought new challenges. Having got the oil out of the
ground, they were faced with the problem of getting it to the market.
When two large oil companies, Standard New Jersey and Socony, both
of which had a sound distribution network in Europe but lacked oil
resources, expressed an interest in buying into Aramco, the biggest
deal in the history of the US oil business loomed. But red tape, a red
line to be exact, stood in the way.

Standard New Jersey and Socony-Vacuum were partners in the Iraq
Petroleum Company. They were bound by the Red Line Agreement,
which derived its name from a red line drawn on a map that restricted
the company's operations to the territory of the former Ottoman
Empire. The Agreement contained a clause – the famous 'self-denying
clause' – that prevented any of the participating companies from
operating within the red line without the consent of the other
partners.[19] This effectively prevented the American partners in IPC
from joining Aramco in Saudi Arabia without their partners' consent;

it was, in other words, a legal straitjacket. For those companies struggling to break free, the Red Line Agreement was, in the words of the president of Standard Oil New Jersey, Walter Teagle, 'a damn bad move!'[20]

When CFP and Gulbenkian refused to release them from the Red Line Agreement, the American companies considered their next move. Their lawyers had devised the notion of 'supervening illegality', a legal device to secure their clients' escape: it made use of the fact that the British government had deemed France and Gulbenkian enemies of state during World War II, which – the Americans now claimed – had nullified the Red Line Agreement.[21]

For Aramco, the risks were breathtaking, for there was a real danger that the IPC partners might turn the tables and all demand to join Aramco. This raised the prospect of British firms becoming stakeholders in Aramco, a nightmare scenario for Ibn Saud. The Americans bought off the British firms with lucrative oil deals and argued with the French partners and Gulbenkian until they settled out of court and were free to join Aramco. In 1948, they bought a 40 per cent interest in the company for a reported asking price of $250m. Aramco now had the capacity to develop the concession fully and sell Arabian oil in Europe, the biggest market in the world outside North America.[22]

All this was excellent news for Ibn Saud. An increase in oil production bringing money, jobs and investment to the kingdom was most welcome. To the American government also, the Aramco deal was opportune. If the Middle East supplied European needs, Latin America oil supplies could be used to meet US domestic needs and reduce the drain on US reserves. Arabian oil could – and would – also provide ample fuel for the US Navy in the Middle East. As for the accusation that the administration was mixing politics with business, the Department of State shrugged, 'it's just a business deal.'[23]

US foreign policy, after lagging behind for years, was at last catching up with the needs of American commerce. The Truman Doctrine of 1947 aimed at containing the spread of communism by supporting free peoples 'who are resisting attempted subjugation by armed minorities or by outside pressures.'[24] In 1950, in a letter to Ibn Saud, President Truman affirmed America's interest 'in the preservation of the independence and territorial integrity of Saudi Arabia. No threat to your kingdom could occur which would not be a matter of immediate concern to the United States.'[25] Whether this amounted to a guarantee of US support for the Saudis in their territorial dispute with Great Britain remained to be seen.

* * * *

Ibn Saud's weakness was not greed but generosity. The expanding house of Saud needed as much money it could get because, despite the oil wealth, it was nearly bankrupt. A large part of the national income supported Saud family members in a life of luxury. The chief recreation of the Al Saud men was matrimony and producing children, and in this they were remarkably active. As Muslims, they were allowed as many wives as they wished, so long as they never exceeded four at any one time. They could divorce by simply renouncing a wife three times. There were certain constraints, such as the cost of maintaining four wives at any one time and the fact that they were entitled to be kept at the same standard of living as each other.

Such constraints were meaningless in the gold-plated world of the Al Saud. Ibn Saud fathered 40 or more sons, his eldest son Saud would go on to have 53 sons, and it was estimated that the Al Saud numbered about 1,000 by the late 1940s.[26] Ibn Saud never begrudged his wives and children their fair share of his largesse but, as the Saudi families grew, Finance Minister Abdullah Suleiman's task of balancing the books became increasingly difficult. The British ambassador once remarked that in Saudi Arabia there was no high finance in the European sense and that Suleiman's methods were 'stocking finance.'[27]

Sheikh Suleiman kept the king's treasury in a proverbial tin trunk. When money came in from taxes, it went into the trunk until the king decided to spend it. When the money ran out, Suleiman would borrow from abroad and, when that money ran out, Suleiman would make himself scarce.

In some ways, Suleiman stood apart from the crowd of royal advisers. Dutch consul Daniel van der Meulen observed:

> He was a man who knew no fatigue [...] He was endowed with the Arab gift of accommodating himself to all circumstances of life but he was not strong enough to withstand two enemies which unexpectedly came his way; money and whisky. And a Wahhabi he certainly was not.[28]

Aramco was an easy source of income for the Saudis, and the company had already advanced large sums of money, advances and loans, to the Saudi Arabian government. But the oilmen were experiencing an increasingly anti-American undertone in their dealings with Saudi Arabia. They complained to American officals of 'ceaseless Saudi Arabian nibbling' at company operations wherever money was involved. The Saudis demanded that the company postpone invoices, pay 'protection fees' to support their army, shut down company communication centres, pay sterling royalties at discount rates, pay other fees and duties. These were not circumstances that the negotiators of the first oil concession had envisaged. Saudi Arabia was in 'financial anarchy'.[29]

Abdullah Suleiman was now pressing Aramco to either exploit their concession area to the hilt or give up blocs so that they could be sold on to the highest bidder. As we have seen, the Saudis had defined

Abdullah Suleiman, Ras Tanura 1939.
(source: the T.C. Barger Collection)

the concessionary area in the original agreement 'as the eastern portion of our Saudi Arab kingdom, within its frontiers.'[30] Under the terms of a revised agreement made in 1948, Aramco was obliged to carry out a detailed and ongoing survey of the country and surrender its rights to 85,000 square kilometres every three years. They were required under their contract to use 'due diligence', and it made good business sense to survey these blocs in order to find the bad acreage before giving it up. They were, paradoxically, mapping the areas where the oil was not going to be found.[31]

Meanwhile, the Saudis squeezed Aramco for a greater share of the oil revenues. In Venezuela, Standard New Jersey had entered into a 50-50 deal with government. The Venezuelans, keen to spread the news, translated their documents into Arabic and, during a tour of the Middle East, found Ibn Saud receptive to their message. Abdullah Suleiman hired an American tax expert, and in November 1950, Ibn Saud was ready to pass an income tax decree that would take half of Aramco's profits immediately and possibly a bigger slice later. Although Aramco argued with Suleiman, protesting that the decree violated their 1933 agreement, the Saudis would not back down.

Events moved towards a conclusion. One day in May 1951 Suleiman, now aged 60, received Aramco's executive vice-president, Fred A. Davies, at his home. Over small earthenware cups of tea and thick coffee, they signed an agreement to share the company's profits equally. These profits had amounted to $180 million ($1.4 billion today) before royalties in the previous year – for Ibn Saud a take of $90 million. The good news was that Aramco was expecting an operating profit of $200 million in 1951. For Suleiman, it was the highlight of his career with Ibn Saud.[32]

The 50-50 agreement (as it was known) dismayed the British government and oil company officials. The Anglo-Iranian Oil Company (formerly Anglo-Persian) had been trying to persuade the Iranian government to accept much lower royalties. Now, with the signing of the Saudi agreement, the Iranians were unlikely to settle for anything less than a 50-50 deal. IPC, in the process of concluding lengthy negotiations with the Iraqis on a new oil agreement, faced the same predicament.

In the long term, 50-50 agreements can be seen as marking a major shift of power from consumer to producer nations, opening the door for state take-overs of oil production and paving the way for the creation of the Organization of Petroleum Exporting Countries (OPEC) in the 1960s. For the Aramcons, in the short term, it was not such a bad deal, since their company could offset the impact with tax breaks in the USA. But for the British there was no such salve.[33]

In September 1951, the first Aramco exploration field party left Dhahran to begin work on the northern and western areas of the Rub al-Khali. About 35 Americans and 200 Saudis, including guards, staffed the party, which continued its work until June 1952. The autumn departure of field parties for the southern desert became an annual event in Dhahran, making good the company's promise to explore all parts of the concession in order to decide what parts to relinquish.[34]

* * * * *

All correspondence from the Saudi government to Aramco was in Arabic, so everything had to be translated. In order to process this work, Aramco had established an Arabian Research and Translation Division (later shortened to the Arabian Research Division, or ARD). At its height, there were some 50 translators working for it, plus typists and other necessary staff. In the late 1940s, as the Saudi government's interest in defining the south-eastern boundaries grew, the division began to research the history and tribes of Arabia. Originally based in Jedda, it moved to an air-conditioned office-block in Dammam in 1953 in a short-lived attempt to get closer to the Arab population.[35]

The division was headed by Dr George Rentz, an American historian and scholar of Arabic who had first arrived in Jedda as a translator in 1944 at the invitation of Karl Twitchell. A stocky man with a full head of brown hair, Rentz was in his forties at this time and highly regarded for his encyclopaedic knowledge of the tribes, of the genealogy and personalities of the royal family.[36] Most important, he was well versed in the history of Wahhabism, having completed a Ph.D thesis for the University of Berkeley entitled 'Muhammad B. 'Abd al-Wahhab (1703/4-1792) and the Beginnings of Unitarian Empire in Arabia'.

The division's work dove-tailed into Aramco's plans and Saudi ambitions. The oilmen wanted to plan their operations with certainty, to know that they were within their legal rights in surveying an area or drilling in a particular place. Ibn Saud wanted to regain the lands of his ancestors. Any evidence that could be used to support these claims would be most valuable to both parties.

Thus Rentz and his colleagues went on to compile a record of Arabia that was quite unlike anything written before. The British had published various guides, such the Indian Army's Handbook of Arabia and Lorimer's *Gazetteer of the Persian Gulf, Oman and Central Arabia*, mostly for the use of military and political officers. John Gordon Lorimer had been an official of the Indian Civil Service on the North West Frontier. In November 1903 he was given six months in which to compile a Gulf handbook and spent the next ten years working on the project. Assisted by a small team of equally dedicated researchers, he studied government archives in Bombay and Calcutta and carried out field trips and surveys in the Gulf.

The result was a collection of historical documentation running to six volumes. Based on local sources and having a vast amount of information, the *Gazetteer* contained some outspoken comments. Take the pen portrait of the sheikh of Sharjah:

> In private life the sheikh was weak, miserly and uxorious; in public business he was apathetic and seemed incapable of exertion. He alienated his subjects and former bedouin adherents by indifference to their grievances and requests; and he forfeited the respect of the other Trucial sheikhs by his general insignificance, both as a man and as a ruler.[37]

According to Lorimer, British wisdom reigned supreme and rulers and their subjects were to blame for any conflicts.

The division aimed to redress the balance. It sought new sources of Arabian history, relying on Arabic-speaking scholars and political reporters to talk to local people, visit settlements, to monitor the Arabic language press and compile dossiers on prominent individuals. It employed a number of 'relators', bedouins used for their knowledge of the history, tribes and customs of Arabia. Under the direction of Dr Rentz, it produced numerous research papers, translations and two major geographical and historical reports. In January 1950 it published *The Eastern Reaches of Al Hasa Province* which included a study of the collection of *zakat* in the region. Actual tax rates were enumerated in the book: the *zakat* on five healthy camels not used for menial tasks such as hauling water was a medium sized goat, for example.[38]

Anxious to discover the extent of the division's research, Edward Henderson, the liaison officer working for PDTC, bribed a Saudi official to give him an Arabic copy of *The Eastern Reaches*, which he arranged to be translated into English. In 1952, on a visit to Dhahran, Henderson stayed with George Rentz and saw a copy of the book on his bookshelf. 'He refused to allow me to read it,' noted Henderson, who kept quiet about his earlier acquisition.[39]

In the same year, the division published its second book, *Oman and the Southern Shore of the Gulf*, a tactical blunder because it confirmed the extent of Aramco's knowledge about the tribes of the area. Although the book was withdrawn before general circulation, a copy was seen by Foreign Office officials, confirming what IPC already knew: that the British government was ill prepared to meet the challenge to come.[40] There followed an upsurge in data-gathering on the British side, including a fact-finding visit by Martin Buckmaster to the Liwa. In this respect, the British held an advantage since Rentz and his colleagues were not able to visit the area in question; indeed, it was not until 1969 that Rentz visited the Buraimi Oasis for the first time.[41]

In time, the research carried out by members of the division would furnish the *Saudi Memorial*, which was the foundation of the Saudi Arabian case in arbitration proceedings over their boundaries with Abu Dhabi and Oman. Certainly their work was of great scholarship but it would bring accusations of partisanship from the British, who saw the memorial as an Aramco-inspired attempt to win the territorial argument for the Saudis on the basis of flawed research.

At the centre of the Saudi territorial claim was the collection and distribution of *zakat*. It might not have been designed for the modern age but, when identified by Rentz and his colleagues as a useful tool for establishing sovereignty in international law, *zakat* became a central feature of their claim.[42] If a tribe had paid *zakat* to his tax collectors, then Ibn Saud might establish his government's exercise of jurisdiction and, therefore, sovereignty over the tribe's grazing area. Thus the tax receipts of the last hundred years were of great interest to the Saudis and the Arabian Research Division.[43]

In the classical sense, *zakat* was an act of religious worship and was not valid unless the tax was paid with this intention. Since the Saudis belonged to a theocratic regime they considered it their duty to send out tax collectors and the payment of *zakat* could easily become an act of political submission. But Ibn Saud's interest in the collection of *zakat* had waned. Collections in settled areas had virtually ceased after 1927 and only revived in and around Buraimi when it became clear that it might assist the Saudi territorial claim.[44]

What did they tax? There were no 'owners' of the desert in the traditional sense. In the towns, *zakat* was imposed on palms and crops. In the desert where there were no fixed settlements, *zakat* was applied exclusively to camels which ranged across their *diyar*. As a consequence, the extent of sovereignty was less easily defined. Boundaries were hazy and – if a tribe switched their allegiance to another sheikh – moveable.

But changing allegiance was not an easy thing to do. There was another side to the tax collectors, and the tribes ignored them at their peril. In 1927 Bertram Thomas summarised how *zakat* was used to influence them: 'Payment of *zakat* to Ibn Saud is a kind of insurance against the raider [...] In reality it is not Ibn Saud himself whom they desire to propitiate but his viceroy Bin Jiluwi, governor of Hofuf, whose activities extend to the eastern marches.'[45]

Zakat was not just an abstract concept designed to confound the British: it was the cornerstone of Saudi territorial claims in south-eastern Arabia: it could be used to prove sovereignty over vast stretches of barren desert. And the purpose of this? The king might be weak, losing his powers and prone to lapse into vague ramblings about his 'ancestral rights', but his advisers who were squeezing Aramco, and the Aramco executives themselves had a powerful motive for probing the outer reaches of the company's concession area: the search for oil.

It was time to test the boundaries.

Chapter 7
The Stobart Incident
Oil Exploration and Diplomacy, 1949–51

In the late 1940s the oilmen began to rely more on new scientific methods and less on what the early prospectors would have called a 'nose' for oil. From the geologist's hammer to the most sophisticated technology of the day, geologists and geophysicists used every item at their disposal to look for oil. Aeroplanes and photographic analysis enabled geologists to survey much greater areas than before and, as we have seen, adventurers like Jacques Cousteau were employed to make maps of the surface of the seabed. Equipment for mapping sub-surface strata was now being used in the mainstream of oil exploration. There was the gravimeter, once described as looking like a portable ice-cream freezer, which measured variation in the Earth's gravity field caused by underground structures; the magnetometer which did the same using the Earth's magnetic field; and the seismograph which relied on small detonations in the ground to record reflected sound waves from the different rock layers on a long roll of paper. All these techniques enabled oil prospectors to build up a more detailed picture of what lay hundreds of metres beneath their feet.[1]

As geologists put together the geological history of the Middle East, a fascinating picture emerged: the petroleum of the Arabian Peninsula had begun its life in the ancient Tethys Sea, an abundant tropical ocean that stretched across the region. Over millions of years, when the sea was quiet, vast layers of shale were deposited in the Earth, trapping organic matter which heat and pressure turned into petroleum. When the sea was more disturbed, fossil shells or sphere-shaped grains called oolites were sifted to form great potential reservoirs. To complicate the picture, Arabia split from Africa along the Red Sea and was squeezed against Asia causing the Hajar and Zagros Mountains, among others, to form. But areas of the Arabian Peninsula, with their large gentle folds, formed ideal traps for the accumulation of oil.

By the end of 1939 the oil companies had at last struck oil on the peninsula. The Americans had found oil the year before at Dammam in the Jurassic rocks of Al-Hasa, which its geologists called the Arab Zone. The IPC subsidiary, Petroleum Development (Qatar) Limited (PDQ), had struck oil at Jebel Dukhan in Qatar in the same rock formation. Although the IPC geologists called this structure the Zekrit Zone, the first name stuck. The rocks of the Arab Zone contained oil that had been deposited between 145 and 155 million years before and were at a much deeper level than had been drilled before in the Middle East. As more discoveries were made, the Arab Zone promised to be the most productive series of oil reservoirs in the world.[2]

Evidence pointed to the possibility of large oil deposits hidden under the southern desert and beyond. As Aramco field parties accompanied by Saudi guards pushed farther south and east into the desert, the risk of clashing with their rival, IPC, which operated the oil concessions in the territories along the southern periphery of the Rub al-Khali, grew.

In 1949 surveys around Abqaiq showed a likelihood of oil in the Rub al-Khali. Aramco geologists also reported the likelihood of gas and oil deposits around Jebel Hafit, near the Buraimi Oasis, in territory claimed by the sultan of Oman and the sheikh of Abu Dhabi.[3] Aramco sought Ibn Saud's advice about how to proceed in these politically sensitive areas. The king's response was suitably vague: 'You tell me the areas that interest you,' he would say, 'and I will tell you if it is mine and if you can develop it.'[4] Keen as the Aramco geologists were to explore fully their concessionary area, they were no wiser about where the frontiers lay. As one Aramco geologist once told his IPC counterpart, 'we go where our Saudi guards take us'.[5]

It began on 13 December 1948 when an Aramco survey aircraft flew over the islands lying between Qatar and Abu Dhabi, part of the disputed area of the 1935 Anglo-Saudi discussions.[6] Early next year, men working in the field for PDQ were intrigued to find new roads suddenly appearing in the desert, having been scraped in the sand. It was clear that Aramco had created these roads: wherever Aramco operatives worked in the desert, they made these drag-roads for speed of movement and to save their vehicles from the lumps and bumps of the rough ground. One of these roads, reaching well into PDQ's concession area, connected Selwah with Khawr al-Udayd.[7]

There were other worrying signs. In March 1949 Jimmy Derham, a PDQ surveyor, was working at the southern end of his company's concession area in Qatar when he came upon two Aramco employees travelling by car from Selwah who told him that the road was an 'access' road. Derham reported this and the fact that Aramco had built two trig points inside his company's concession area to his superiors, and his report was forwarded to the headquarters of their parent company, IPC, in London.[8]

In another time IPC executives might have shrugged off these incursions, but with potentially valuable oilfields at stake they were too serious to be ignored. Indeed, there were more to come: IPC personnel working for subsidiary companies were increasingly alarmed by the growing number of reports of Aramco incursions into their concession areas.[9]

On 15 March 1949 chief geologist of IPC, Norval Baker, was making one of his regular tours of the Persian Gulf when he arrived at Sharjah, then a decrepit coastal town with a crumbling palace where public floggings were carried out at the front door. A large, jovial American, Baker was a highly experienced geologist who recognised the oil potential of south-eastern Arabia.

As he waited at the airstrip for his onward flight, Baker learnt that an Aramco aircraft with geologists on board had quietly departed that very morning for the western boundary of PDO's concession area, the Oman mountain front. It set his alarm bells ringing, since it was more evidence that Aramco's ambitions stretched beyond the Empty Quarter and into Oman. He asked his managing director whether IPC should remain within its boundaries or 'as Aramco apparently are doing, disregard frontiers.'[10]

Baker was under no illusion about this intrusion and the scraped road which had been reported by the surveyor Jimmy Derham. He recognised the danger posed to his company's concessions by the ongoing boundary dispute, which had to be resolved. 'Results of recent seismic and surface geological surveys with various structures crossing boundaries prompt us to point out the need for an early definition of these boundaries.'[11]

Aramco activities were not restricted to the Qatar border. On 3 April, a driver returning to Dubai from Abu Dhabi reported seeing a convoy of five vehicles in the area with a party comprising six Americans, four Arab drivers and four or five Arab guards.[12] They were riding in two station wagons, two trucks and one large truck with a crane and extra large tyres for travelling through the sand. A party set off to contact the convoy but the Americans had gone, having reached Ras Sadr before turning back and leaving the area by the same route. It later transpired that George Rentz, head of Aramco's Arabian Research Division, had accompanied the party.[13]

For Sheikh Shakhbut and the oilmen, it was a disquieting situation and soon there was no doubt about Aramco's intention. More reports came in: Aramco had set up a camp opposite Ghaghah Island just below Khawr al-Udayd, where a section of the Bani Yas loyal to Sheikh Shakhbut, the Qubaisat, had a fishing village.

On 18 April, Sheikh Shakhbut made a complaint to British political officer Patrick Stobart about these incursions:

> I have to inform you that I have heard that some Americans of the oil company in Saudi Arabia have quietly penetrated my territory and set up their camp on the coast 32 kilometres south-east of Khor al Udaid [sic] near Ghaghah Island. They reached as far as Jebel Dhanna and Mughira. On 4 April these people entered my territory eastwards up to Abu Khiraiban.
>
>   This is a strange thing and an encroachment upon my rights in my territory. I have, therefore, deputed my brother Hazza bin Sultan to consult you on this matter.[14]

On 19 April, a flight with IPC officials on board followed the scraped road reported by Jimmy Derham and continued south. They came upon an unidentified geophysical party working on the coast to the south of Khawr al-Udayd. Beacons had been erected on a nearby headland, Ras al-Hamra, well-worn roads could be seen and nearby islands had been marked with cairns.[15]

On 21 April, Stobart set out to investigate. A convoy of five PDTC vehicles led by Sheikh Hazza and Stobart with an IPC representative, two agency guards, five of Shakhbut's armed men, four drivers and a cook, left Abu Dhabi. It crossed the Sabkhat Matti towards Khawr al-Udayd.[16]

At one point, seeing a strange drilling rig and tents on the skyline, they stopped and sent one vehicle ahead. It was an Aramco field party. Stobart and Hazza spent a few minutes talking to the Aramco men while their convoy waited on the other side of a sand dune. But this was just a fly camp – the main Aramco base was some 50 kilometres to the north-west. So Stobart and Hazza set off for this camp, leaving their convoy behind.

Though the country between the rig and main camp was rough and scrubby, the journey took little over an hour on a wide and smooth Aramco dragged road. When they arrived at the camp, the guards took Stobart to see Don Holm, the senior Aramco geologist in charge, a slim man whose office was in an air-conditioned caravan. Polite conversation ensued. Holm told them that the Saudi government had given his company permission to work in the area.

There was a triangulation camp about three kilometres north of the rig. An airstrip had been laid out beside the main camp for bringing in personnel, urgent rations and equipment. Heavy materials and drinking water had been brought by land from Dhahran. They were shown a map of Aramco operations and could see that there were, or had been, camps over a wide area stretching from Khawr al-Udayd to Dhafrah (Zafrah) in the south-east. Also in the camp was a member of Robert Ray, the geophysical company charged with carrying out seismic work for Aramco. During their discussion, Holm asked Stobart about entering Oman. It was left to Stobart to draw his own conclusions about Aramco's intentions in the region.

Stobart and Hazza then went to visit Emir Hayif who was in charge of the Saudi guards at the camp. After the initial shock of receiving such unexpected visitors, the emir recovered sufficiently to tell them that he and his men merely went where the Americans told them to go. He said that he was just a servant of Ibn Saud and that the matter should be settled at government level.

Stobart and Hazza returned to their convoy and decided to return to Abu Dhabi in the morning. Later, Stobart sat down to write Holm a note advising him to withdraw his personnel from the area:

> I should like before leaving to refer to the most delicate position at present in connection with the action taken by the Arabian American Oil Company in this area. His Majesty's government has always recognised that the territory of the ruler of Abu Dhabi extends up to Khawr al-Udayd. The ruler will, of course consider the presence of your party at certain points north of Safaq [Sufuq] as aggression, especially since the party has been accompanied by Saudi Arabian soldiers.
>
> It is my duty, from the point of safeguarding peace, to advise you to take steps for the withdrawal of parties operating in the areas whose possession has not yet been agreed upon, in order

to preclude the occurrence of any incident which might take place by (between) Saudi and Abu Dhabi subjects.

I thank you very much for your kind reception.[17]

The following day, before the convoy's departure, Stobart set off with the two agency guards to inspect the triangulation camp and deliver his letter. Here he found 12 tents and 12 vehicles, about six Americans and a 'few dozen' labourers and drivers. Three Saudi guards allowed him in and he was introduced to the American in charge. Suddenly a Saudi guard appeared and pointed a rifle at Stobart, telling him not to leave. After a tense conversation, the guard agreed to release Stobart but kept the two Abu Dhabi guards – who had been disarmed – under guard in the camp.

An Aramco party presently arrived from the main camp. A heated argument ensued, with the Saudi guards shouting that the Abu Dhabi guards had come with their rifles loaded. As a Saudi guard made to knock one of them down with his rifle butt, the emir intervened and a fragile peace was restored. But the emir seemed wary of his own men and swung between two extremes: once saying the matter was easily settled and then, after one of his men whispered in his ear, saying that it could only be settled by the emir of Al-Hasa province, Saud bin Jiluwi.

The emir retired for a private discussion with his men. This lasted two hours during which time the British and Americans talked among themselves. In an interesting aside, one of the Aramco surveyors admitted that he had a company map that clearly showed that they were in territory marked Trucial Oman. But when the emir returned, they were all smiles. The Abu Dhabi guards were released and the convoy made its way back to the coast. Stobart duly made his report to the political resident in Bahrain.

The British government could not ignore the Stobart Incident, as it became known, and urgently sought the views of IPC. At this moment, a familiar figure stepped forward. Stephen Longrigg had come a long way since representing IPC at Jedda in 1933. In World War II he had achieved the rank of brigadier and served on the general headquarters staff in Cairo before being appointed chief administrator (military governor) of Eritrea. He now found himself back with IPC as a senior manager based in London and it was in this capacity that he responded on behalf of the company.

Longrigg warned of the threat that Aramco field parties accompanied by Saudi guards posed to IPC's operations in Oman and the Trucial Coast. Ibn Saud's prestige was enormous in these areas and the border tribes would find it hard to resist the incursions. They were susceptible to Saudi influence and the allure of Saudi silver, so much so that there was a real danger that their territories would pass to Ibn Saud without a shot being fired. The US State Department would probably give their tacit support to this state of affairs, he concluded.[18]

This was almost true. Longrigg was right about the threat that Saudi Arabia posed to the Omani tribes and British oil interests, but he misread the State Department's stance. The Americans had a foot in both camps. Although American oil interests were mainly identified with those of Saudi Arabia and Aramco, American companies also held a 23.5 per cent share in IPC, with the remaining shares being held by British, Dutch and French interests.[19]

And so in July 1949 we have the bizarre situation of an American geologist suggesting that IPC might raise an army to resist Saudi/Aramco incursions. Norval Baker had come to IPC in 1935 from one of its American partners, Standard Oil of New Jersey, the same company that bought a share of Aramco in 1948. He noted:

> In summary, there are no geological grounds on which we can abandon the area. It is highly prospective and if it can only be held by raising an army the value of the area justifies that action for at least a period of time to permit essential examination.[20]

Some voices urged caution. Thesiger had already warned the Foreign Office that any landing on the southern Omani coast might be dangerous and be resisted by the tribes. Yet discussions were already under way for the creation of the military force provisionally named the Hugf militia to protect any future survey in southern Oman, financed by IPC. In 1951 the British government established a small military force known as the Trucial Oman Levies to protect the Gulf sheikhdoms and suppress banditry and the slave trade.

For the time being, Baker advised, the company should cultivate the 'so-called unapproachable tribes, through any means or channel which might win them over', once the results of the company's first test well at Ras Sadr were known.[21] The well proved to be dry but this did not deter IPC, which switched its attention to western Abu Dhabi.

Meanwhile, the diplomatic wheels creaked into action. The Saudis protested about Stobart's actions, denying that the Aramco party had ever been in Abu Dhabi territory. The British government rejected the protest and lodged a counter-claim. The Saudi government agreed to discuss the matter but on their terms. The British refused, pressing the Saudis to specify the extent of their territorial claim before negotiations could begin. It was the 1930s all over again.

Indeed, the parallels were unsettling. It will be recalled that in 1934 a Foreign Office legal adviser had questioned Britain's stance in international law. Now, in August 1949, a Foreign Office report entitled 'Frontier Negotiations with Saudi Arabia' repeated that advice: since occupation was the determining factor in international law, and a large part of the disputed area was unoccupied, the issue could only be resolved by occupation or agreement. The advice warned that arguing the territorial claim on the basis of the Blue and Violet Lines was purely a 'matter of tactics' and not based on sound legal principles.[22] If the Foreign Office appreciated the importance of this advice, they did not show it, relying instead upon the Blue Line as a backstop in the hope of negotiating a tactical compromise with Ibn Saud.

They were soon disappointed. On 14 October 1949 the Saudi Arabian government gave their answer. Their claim encompassed a large segment of south-eastern Arabia and pushed Shakhbut's realm into a small pocket around and to the east of Abu Dhabi Island, depriving Abu Dhabi of the Liwa Oasis. Sheikh Abdullah of Qatar also lost territory, a 25-mile wide strip of territory along the base of the Qatar peninsula.

The audacity of the claim was breathtaking enough, but then the Saudis went on to declare the tribes around the Buraimi Oasis to be independent. The British government was not in treaty relations with the sheikhs for the areas lying south and east of a point 24° 25' North, 55° 36' East; therefore, the Saudis argued, they were free to negotiate directly with Saudi Arabia. In other words, the Omani borderlands and the oasis were included in the claim, and for the first time the territorial dispute had a name: the Buraimi dispute.

In November 1949 the British rejected the claim entirely, falling back on the Blue Line and Article Six of the Treaty of Jedda of 1927 by which Ibn Saud had pledged friendly relations with the Trucial sheikhs.[23] The Saudis countered by expanding their claim. The arguments – and counter-arguments – began to fly between Jedda and

London. When the Saudis erected a series of plaques in the king's name, cementing them into concrete *rijims* on certain islands in the Gulf and ignoring Foreign Office protests, British sappers appeared on the scene and dynamited all of them.[24]

The part that *zakat* would play in the dispute now became apparent. The Saudis challenged Sheikh Shakhbut's title to the Liwa Oasis and other areas, claiming that Saudi tax collectors had been gathering *zakat* from the local tribes ever since Ibn Saud had acquired Al-Hasa in 1913. The British retorted that the onus was on the Saudis to prove their title to these areas. Since Ibn Saud was a successor to the Ottomans he had inherited their agreements including the Blue and Violet Lines which had defined the extent of Ottoman influence. In British eyes, Ibn Saud's claim failed. Payment of *zakat* did not establish sovereign rights in international law. In any event, it did not necessarily denote allegiance, since tribesmen usually paid *zakat* for reasons of expediency rather than loyalty.[25]

The stance of the US State Department in the boundary dispute was strictly neutral. American interests fell both sides of the fence, in south-eastern Arabia through American oil companies owning a part share in IPC subsidiary companies and in Saudi Arabia through Aramco. American diplomats faced a dilemma if they tried to interfere: 'Our own policy is one of strict neutrality in these matters as important American interests in Bahrain, Saudi Arabia and the Trucial sheikhdoms would be adversely affected if we became involved.'[26]

Aramco was nevertheless pressing the State Department to support the Saudi claim. On 25 April 1950 members of the Near Eastern Department (a section of the State Department) met with Aramco officials and Judge O. Manly Hudson, a jurist specialising in international law. Hudson said that Rentz's investigations into taxes and tribal allegiance made a 'strong basis' for Saudi Arabian claims since Abu Dhabi was 'a skeleton of a government and little more'.[27]

But this view was challenged a few weeks later by the American ambassador in Jedda, J. Rives Childs, who reminded his colleagues that the British disputed Rentz's work to a large extent, and that the Saudi government was as much a skeleton as Abu Dhabi's in the disputed area, which was mostly deserted.[28] Childs identified two issues at stake: the special British position in the Gulf and the validity of claims based on taxation and tribal allegiance. He suggested a compromise that would preserve the first and allow an examination of the second.

Although American diplomats did not always march in step with Aramco and the Saudis, any difference of opinion was restrained. The US consul in Dhahran from 1949 to 1952, Parker T. Hart, told an interesting story in this regard.[29] One day, conversing with Saud bin Jiluwi, he asked 'By the way, I've been going around the area. Does Saudi Arabia have any jurisdiction in Buraimi?'

Bin Jiluwi simply and emphatically said: 'No.'

Hart was aware that Bin Jiluwi was closer than anybody in Riyadh to the background of the dispute, and probably knew it better than the king – and a lot better than Sheikh Yasin, who had told Aramco 'Buraimi is ours.' He reported his conversation to the Department of State and stood by it when consulted by Aramco. 'The discrepancy embarrassed Aramco and embarrassed, I think, the Saudis, but I never heard complaint from Bin Jiluwi that I had misquoted him,' said Hart.

Years later, when Hart was director of Near East affairs, the Saudi foreign minister, Prince Faisal ibn Abdul Aziz Al Saud, made a visit to Washington in the final days of the Truman Administration. The prince took Hart aside and said, 'You are not with us on this problem of Buraimi.'

'No. I'm not, because I don't think it is correct,' Hart replied.

In July 1950 the parties agreed to set up a frontier commission to examine the loyalty of the tribes in disputed areas. Both sides would abstain from putting any pressure on, or making inducements to, the tribes. In September, they agreed that there should be no undue influence on the commission and that the status quo before October 1949 should be respected. This became known as the Status Quo Agreement. In 1951 it was settled that the commission should start its work in the autumn, and the parties agreed to suspend oil and military operations in the disputed areas while the commission carried out its work.[30]

But the frontier commission never materialised, and the disagreements rumbled on. A conference opened at Dammam on 28 January 1952 between Saudi Arabia and Great Britain (representing Qatar and Abu Dhabi). The discussions were confined to the land boundaries between Saudi Arabia and Qatar and the western approaches of Abu Dhabi, and did not include the boundaries of the Buraimi Oasis and Oman. The Saudi delegation stuck to their 1949 claim, and declined to explain why it was so much greater than their Red Line proposal of 1935, which they now disowned, contending that it had been made by

Fuad Hamza without Ibn Saud's permission. Sir Rupert Hay, political resident for the Persian Gulf, leading the British delegation, closed the final session with an offer to use the Red Line as a basis for future discussions. Despite Saudi reservations about the Red Line, Prince Faisal agreed to take the proposal back to Ibn Saud.[31]

On 14 February the Dammam conference broke up without agreement being reached, and was never reconvened.

Chapter 8
Borderlands
Oman and Abu Dhabi, 1948–52

In 1949 the Saudis claimed the right to negotiate directly with the Omani sheikhs. The claim had some force since Dick Bird had done a similar thing the year before; nevertheless it presented a serious challenge to the sultan of Oman's authority. Although Ibn Saud was already influential in the area, there was a new and compelling factor at work – he had more money than anyone else.

Ibn Saud, in true bedouin style, was anxious to demonstrate his largesse. The Saudis now applied this to winning the hearts and minds of the sheikhs and tribes of the borderlands. In their eyes, this was unremarkable, nothing more than sharing a little wealth between friends. It was certainly the prerogative of an Arab ruler to distribute largesse among his own people. Even Sultan Said was not averse to spending money, albeit in more modest amounts than Ibn Saud, as circumstances required. He had demonstrated this when he bought back the Omani sheikhs after Bird's little spree. But the Saudis would take the practice to new and unprecedented heights.[1]

For the British, this was more than a simple matter of custom or cultural interpretation. Whether they considered it bribery or generosity, they had good reason to be concerned. The position of a sheikh could be precarious at the best of times: he held power for as long as he commanded the respect of his people. Some, like the parsimonious Shakhbut, kept going because they had the support of family members, whose interests were best served by avoiding internecine strife. Others were not so lucky. Apart from a few exceptions, such as Sheikh Rashid of Hamasa who had made his money from the slave trade, most were of modest means and struggled to retain their tribes' loyalty against rival factions and ambitious relatives.

Thus the appearance of a Saudi official bearing money and making extravagant promises was a temptation for many of the borderland sheikhs. It is possible that some of those who accepted Saudi money did so with an eye on the future, believing that Ibn Saud would inevitably become their overlord, while others took it for personal gain. But it is likely that most were hedging their bets, ready to swing behind whoever emerged as the strongest leader.

Another aspect of the Saudi campaign was a revival of their interest in collecting *zakat* in the region. In 1950 Ibn Saud's tax collectors were back, led by Muhammad bin Mansur, the emir who had accompanied the Casoc expedition to the southern desert in the 1939/40 season. He arrived in the Liwa Oasis with a small party of tax collectors. Finding an Abu Dhabi man who – allegedly – had been collecting *zakat* from Saudi tribes in Qatar, they beat him and robbed him of his camel. The incident led to a British protest and a Saudi counter-protest, the latter asserting that their tax collectors were simply exercising their historic prerogative to collect *zakat* in the area, based on Ibn Saud's conquest of Al-Hasa in 1913.[2]

Tax collectors might have been an obvious threat to the status quo but the lure of money was an insidious one. In November, a stranger visited the Buraimi Oasis 'and all stations south', travelling under two different names, using one for the general public and other for the Omani sheikhs. Dick Bird was intrigued:

> He carries a letter purported to be signed by one Abdullah Karim, an alleged Saudi official, introducing himself to the sheikhs of Oman [...] This Ruritanian character states that he is an emissary of Ibn Saud, and an American oil company, and holds forth on the lavishness of the American concession payments.[3]

Things were stirring in the mountains of central Oman, too. Suleiman bin Hamyar al Nabhan was the ruler of the Bani Riyam tribe. He was not an especially charismatic man. He was of medium height with a thick beard and wore the customary *khanjar* in his belt, and had a reputation for duplicity. In 1950 he had promised Wilfred Thesiger access to his mountain if he would help him. For the explorer, it was an impossible request: he declined, abruptly ending his journey and turning back, subsequently reporting the conversation to the British political agent in Sharjah.

Later, through an intermediary, Suleiman asked the political resident in Bahrain for permission to enter into negotiations for an oil

Suleiman bin Hamyar (left) with the imam of Oman, Ghalib bin Ali al-Hinai.
(source: *Warlords of Oman* by P.S. Allfree, published by Robert Hale)

concession with IPC, claiming that he was entitled to make his own agreements. For an Omani sheikh this claim was nothing new, but Suleiman went farther than the others by styling himself as 'King', ending letters headed with a seal that read 'The Kingdom of Nabhan, Suleiman bin Hamyar al-Nabhan'.[4]

He had much to say about his 'kingdom'. Once, in an interview to a newspaper in Bahrain, he told a reporter he was proud that his country was the only one untrodden by the feet of foreigners.

> It is just like Lebanon, in winter snows, and in summer flowing rivers and springs and ripe fruit. Verily it is a paradise of the world [...] In some places oil flows on the surface of the earth and the bedouin are accustomed to kindle their fires from it.[5]

It was a fantasy, much as Suleiman's ambition to rule as an independent sovereign would turn out to be. Yet the British could not ignore Suleiman completely, for his Bani Riyam tribe numbered some 11,000 men who controlled a high plateau and a strategic pass through the Hajar Mountains.

In 1951 Suleiman travelled to Riyadh on a passport describing him as an Omani subject without any reference to the sultan of Muscat and Oman. But he upset Ibn Saud by promoting himself as an independent ruler and received a lukewarm welcome. The irony of the situation, that Ibn Saud was promoting the independence of local rulers as part of his strategy, appeared to be lost on both parties. The king of Nabhan returned to Oman, disappointed but undeterred, declaring that the Treaty of Sib gave Omanis complete independence.[6]

As we have seen, the British and Saudis had agreed to suspend oil and military operations in the disputed areas and not to influence the tribes while the frontier commission went about its work. The Saudis, having embarked on a campaign of luring sheikhs to Riyadh with gifts of money and promises of support, were little troubled.

Sheikh Saqr bin Sultan al-Naimi, the paramount sheikh on the Omani side, held a pivotal role. But the Old Fox was equivocal. On one occasion, when a troop of Trucial Oman levies was hunting a notorious bandit, Bin Qitami, they called on Sheikh Saqr at his fort in Buraimi. Saqr was much embarrassed because he was at the time entertaining Saudi slave traders, and refused to assist the levies.[12]

Sheikh Saqr bin Sultan al-Nami (1956).
(source: the William E. Mulligan Collection at Georgetown University, with permission from Saudi Aramco)

The other Omani sheikhs responded in varying degrees. Some visited Riyadh to declare their loyalty to Ibn Saud. Muhammad bin Salimin, a sheikh of the Al Bu Shamis tribe, arrived in the latter part of 1950 and discussed oil prospecting with the Saudis. 'The people of Oman are followers of the Arabian Reformation,' Muhammad declared. 'They wish to have the rule of the king in Oman and to have him install a deputy in Oman.'[7] Ibn Saud gave him 8,000 riyals (£12,000 today) and promised to protect his tribe from being attacked.

This was good business so far as the sheikh was concerned: the most he had ever been able to extract from the sultan of Oman was a miserly 35 rupees (£75) a month for protecting a mountain pass.[8] Muhammad returned to his tribe, which controlled areas to the west and south-west of Buraimi. But he had second thoughts about his conversion and, for the moment, stayed loyal to the sultan of Oman.[9]

The ruling sheikh of the Beni Kaab was the strong-minded and forthright Obaid bin Juma al-Kaabi. 'Sheikh Obaid [...] had a good presence,' wrote Edward Henderson, the IPC representative, 'and clearly had leadership; a pleasing personality, he was popular with his tribesmen.'[10]

Sheikh Obaid bin Juma al-Kaabi (1956).
(source: the William E. Mulligan Collection at Georgetown University, with permission from Saudi Aramco)

Sheikh Obaid's tribal territory lay to the east and north-east of the Buraimi Oasis. He was nominally under the paramountcy of Sheikh Saqr bin Sultan al-Naimi of Buraimi but his loyalty was changeable. He visited Ibn Saud in Riyadh, leaving his sheikdom as an Omani and returning as a Saudi. The Saudis would later produce a letter from Obaid to Saud bin Jiluwi signifying his loyalty to Ibn Saud: 'We are your subjects and our territories are yours,' he had written.[11]

In February 1952 the British political officer in Sharjah, John Wilton, visited the Buraimi Oasis with a brief to assess the tribes' allegiances and their attitudes towards reopening oil negotiations.

Wilton was a traditional diplomat, remembered years later as the 'one with the fly whisk'.[13] He travelled across the desert by Land Rover – there were no proper roads at this time. He observed:

> It was a relatively short and easy journey from Sharjah to Buraimi; you set out in the afternoon and arrived at the only major obstacle, the sand dunes, in the evening. You camped for the night and set out at dawn (with your tyre pressures lowered) while the sands were still cool and if you were lucky damp with dew, and scuttled across the mile or so of firm sand, when you had the tedious task of pumping your tyres up.[14]

Wilton found the sheikhs, with a few exceptions, resentful of Saudi claims, which they saw as inspired by Aramco. They had received no help or support from the Saudis during years of hardship and were hoping that IPC would succeed in their search for oil in their territories. Sheikh Zayed of Abu Dhabi had encouraged this attitude and, generally, the sheikhs found him easier to deal with than the distant Saud bin Jiluwi and the irregular Saudi emissaries. Zayed lived in nearby Al-Ain, and was the focus of British support in the area.

The most notable exception was Sheikh Rashid bin Hamad of the section of the Al Bu Shamis tribe that lived in the village of Hamasa. A small man with a pointed beard, Sheikh Rashid was also involved in the slave trade for which, according to Dick Bird, 'he was notorious and generally hated.'[15] He was pro-Saudi and made no bones about admitting that it was Saudi money that determined his attitude. In order to survive, he told Wilton, he would look to the highest bidder.

The people of Hamasa appeared to be loyal to Ibn Saud. A few Nejdi slave traders lived in the village, operating a lucrative business

Sheikh Rashid bin Hamad al-Shamsi of Hamasa (1956).
(source: the William E. Mulligan Collection at Georgetown University, with
permission from Saudi Aramco)

for the Saudi Arabian market. Sheikh Rashid himself travelled to
Riyadh in the summer of 1951, and wrote to Ibn Saud declaring that
'we, our towns and our lands belong to you.'[16] On his return to
Hamasa, Rashid hoisted a Saudi flag over his fort and started issuing
his followers with passes written on notepaper that exempted them
from paying Saudi quarantine and visa fees. In these he described
himself as 'Ruler of Hamasa'.[17] Yet despite his proclamation of loyalty
to Ibn Saud, Sheikh Rashid continued to accept regular payments from
the sultan of Oman.

Sheikh Rashid told Wilton that Ibn Saud had a *markaz* in Buraimi.
A surprised Wilton, thinking that perhaps Saudi soldiers had crept into
the oasis and constructed a makeshift stronghold overnight, asked
what he meant by this. Rashid replied that the ruins of a fort built in
the 1850s during the last Wahhabi occupation by Turki bin Ahmad al-
Sudairi were still visible to the south of Hamasa. Wilton asked if Ibn
Saud had any representative, exercised any of the functions of government, or taxed the people in the area. Rashid said he did not. Wilton
returned to Sharjah, shortly followed by Saudi claims that his visit had
'aroused the anger of the people of Buraimi.'[18]

So there it was: the only real evidence of a Saudi presence in the village was a handful of Saudi merchants engaged in the slave trade and a crumbling fort known to the locals as the Castle of the Najdis (the Sudairi fort). During his 14-month posting to Sharjah, Wilton made several visits to the Buraimi Oasis and found no other signs of the Saudis there, apart from their influence over Sheikh Rashid bin Hamad. The remoteness of Saudi Arabia from the oasis was real enough: in contrast to the relatively short journey from Sharjah, it was a major logistical challenge to travel from, say, the Aramco base in Dhahran to the oasis. The journey was entirely dependent on four-wheel drive trucks with winches to negotiate across the sands and the Sabkhat Matti.

Wilton's report was a routine matter in the eyes of Foreign Office officials, who considered such visits to the inland sheikhs as part of his administrative duties. But the Saudis' reaction told another story. The Saudi government believed that the purpose of Wilton's visit was to bring the sheikhs of the Buraimi Oasis into the British orbit of the Trucial sheikhdoms, thus prejudicing any decision about the owner-ship of the Buraimi area. According to the Saudis, the sheikhs recognised the sovereignty of Ibn Saud, who rejected the authority of any Trucial sheikhs in the oasis. In short, Wilton had no right to be there at all. The British government was requested to put an end to activity in the oasis and to keep British officials out of the area.[19]

The British government refuted the claim. Officials pointed out that the London and Dammam agreements did not restrict British administrative officials in the execution of their routine duties, which had been the purpose of Wilton's visit.[20]

In the general scheme of things, the Wilton incident seemed a minor diplomatic skirmish. In fact, it had a profound effect on Saudi thinking: it hardened attitudes and triggered a determination among Ibn Saud's advisers to resort to other measures to break the deadlock over the frontier dispute. Their first move was to dispatch a party of men in two vehicles for Buraimi. The party arrived at the PDTC camp at Tarif, in western Abu Dhabi, and was turned back by a detachment of the Trucial Oman Levies.[21]

If the Saudis were waiting for a pretext for intervention, they did not have to wait long. On 5 August 1952 Sheikh Rashid slipped out of Hamasa and set off for Riyadh once more, travelling with an identity certificate that described him as a subject of Muscat and Oman. Then, towards the end of the month, the Saudi emir of Ras Tanura, Turki bin Abdullah al-Otaishan, mysteriously disappeared. Outside the Saudi inner circle, no one knew what his intentions were or where he had gone. On 23 August news reached the British Foreign Office that Turki was heading south-east but again there was no definite information about the exact purpose of his journey.[22]

Rumours were circulating among the Aramcons: a young Aramco employee by the name of Michael Sterner, who was working in Ras Tanura as a government relations representative, heard that Turki had gone to raise a Saudi banner over the Buraimi Oasis.[23]

By now it was the height of summer, the desert was burning hot and even mad dogs were resting in the midday shade, but this slumbering world would soon be stirred by an unfamiliar sound, the grumble of engines, as a Saudi motorised column under Turki, with Sheikh Rashid at his side, made its way across the desert towards the oasis.

The Wahhabis, after an absence of 25 years, were back.

Chapter 9
Turki and the Tribes
The Buraimi Oasis, Oman and Abu Dhabi, 1952–3

There is a curious story about Turki bin Abdullah al-Otaishan's trek to the Buraimi Oasis, told by a German doctor. Herbert Pritzke was with Rommel's Afrika Korps during World War II, captured by the British and held in a POW camp in Egypt. Escaping into the desert, he spent the next few years travelling among assassin squads of the Muslim Brotherhood, with drug smugglers, to the front line of the Arab-Jewish war in Palestine and to the Cairo underworld in the last days of King Farouk. In 1949, he accepted the post of doctor in charge of Hofuf hospital in Saudi Arabia.[1]

Now, in the summer of 1952, Pritzke was at the end of his contract with the Saudi Health Office and contemplating his next move. One of Emir Saud bin Jiluwi's personal slaves, distinctive in a blue gown, came running across the square below him. The slave informed him and a colleague that they were to report to the emir immediately. Realising that a summons from the emir was not to be taken lightly, they sprang into action. Taking a case of medical instruments, they arrived at the palace in a dripping sweat to find the emir waiting for them in his *majlis* room. The emir told the two doctors that they were to set off with a bedouin escort in order to treat some people who had been injured in a road traffic accident 'somewhere outside the town'.

A car picked them up outside the palace and drove them to the south gate of the town where they took possession of two trucks. They went to a garage to fill up tins of petrol and water skins which they loaded onto the vehicles and then set off. They navigated through the outskirts, through date plantations and past stinking refuse pits full of dead animals in various stages of decay, to the next town where they rested a while. When the doctor asked where they were going, he was told 'a bit behind Selwah', at the base of the Qatar peninsula.

In fact, they were to travel much farther than that. Their journey was difficult and the conditions treacherous: the desert was vast, they got lost, one of their vehicles broke down and they were overcome by a sandstorm. After a day and night of driving, they came over a dune to find a long flat depression in which eight vehicles were parked in a square. There were a dozen long tents with open sides pitched around a scooped-out waterhole, with bundles of rifles in leather cases tied to the tent poles.

The leader of this party was Turki bin Abdullah al-Otaishan. Quite what Turki, a subordinate of Saud bin Jiluwi, was doing hundreds of kilometres from Ras Tanura in the middle of a desert was not immediately apparent to the sand-blown and somewhat puzzled German doctor.

Turki greeted him and his companion warmly, shaking them by the hand with the customary *marhaba*. He then presented three sheikhs from the Buraimi Oasis who were travelling with his party. Pritzke guessed that they had recently been guests of Ibn Saud in Riyadh for they were wearing brand new black mantles with gold-laced borders, inlaid daggers, gold wristwatches with green enamelled monograms, embroidered silk headcloths and new sandals.

There followed an awkward conversation about Buraimi. Turki asked the doctor if he thought annexing the oasis would be to Saudi Arabia's advantage. Pritzke had been in Arabia long enough to know the form. He gave a textbook answer, telling Turki that union with the powerful kingdom could only bring the benefits of peace, freedom and prosperity to the inhabitants of Buraimi. 'Well spoken!' declared Turki. 'The people of the oasis have always felt that they belong to our house and that they stand loyally by us in the struggle against the British colonisers and are resolved to shake off the rule of the puppet government of Oman.'

And yet Turki's progress on the path of liberation had not been entirely peaceful. The injuries from a 'road traffic accident' turned out to be gunshot wounds from a skirmish with bedouins. Indeed, while the doctor was treating them, a group of bedouin raiders invaded the camp and hand-to-hand fighting ensued, with the doctor himself killing one of the attackers in self-defence before they were repulsed.

When at last the party settled down for the evening meal, the campfire was lit. The guards sat under the stars, singing, their bearded faces lit up by the flickering flames. A blood-red moon was rising on the horizon. The doctor and his party said their farewells and left Turki and his men to press on to the oasis the next day.

Pritzke's account is the only one we have of Emir Turki's journey through the sands. It reads much like a *Boy's Own* story of derring-do, especially his description of the battle with the bedouin. There is no corroboration of his account in the files of British political officers at the time of this incident. Any bedouin resistance to the Saudis would have come from the Manasir, and would surely have weakened a Saudi claim to the territory. One would have expected such news to have quickly reached the Trucial Coast and for the British to have made the most of it for propaganda purposes. But there was no such report and, for this reason, Pritzke's story remains a curious one.

* * * * *

Sixty years ago barrastis leaned around the Buraimi Oasis, their interiors dark and dusty, the mud watch-towers cracked and broken, people shuffling along sandy tracks, a few tyre marks in the sand, women dressed in black carrying pitchers or firewood and men with donkeys, camels or a few goats in tow. The oasis was bordered on the west and north by heavy dunes virtually impassable to motor transport and on the east and south by foothills and scrub.[2]

Sheikh Zayed's village, Al-Ain, was a small settlement of mud-walled and barrasti huts nestled against the backdrop of Jebel Hafit. The few Englishmen who had been there described a scene of pastoral simplicity: early morning smoke rising from fires, cocks crowing and donkeys braying. In one part, a small fort with weathered brown towers and curtain walls looked over the village, and palms skirted it. As a visiting political officer once observed, 'had it not been for the small group of Land Rovers parked in the courtyard of the guesthouse below, we might have been living in the eighth, or eighteenth century'.[3]

The nine villages of the oasis each had their own plantations of date palms and lime trees fed by water running by gravity along underground channels, *aflaj*, some of which were as much as 11 kilometres from the foot of Jebel Hafit. In the gardens of Al-Ain, date palms interspersed with alfalfa (lucerne) grew in the gardens. There were man-made irrigation channels on the surface, built in grids across the plantations. Mud sluices would be broken and built up again every day or two in order to allow water to flow freely to every part of the gardens. According to the IPC liaison officer, Edward Henderson, the mornings were still, 'the only sounds a few birds, some parakeets and the creaking of the rope at a well worked by oxen'.[4]

An idyllic scene, no doubt, but the region was hardly an earthly paradise. Abu Dhabi a fishing village of barrasti huts with population of some 3,000 people, Sharjah a crumbling town of 7,000 and a silting creek and Dubai a bustling community of some 30,000 were the main settlements of the Trucial Coast. None of these towns had regular water supplies, roads, electricity, telephones or other conveniences of Western civilisation. The largest British community in Dubai then numbered 12 as compared with some 30,000 today, most of whom have never known any close contact with a citizen of Dubai, and know the city only for its shopping malls, housing compounds and traffic jams.[5]

Tribal affairs were unsettled in parts of the interior. Political officers and oil company survey parties travelled with escorts. Progress was slow and difficult. As Wilton had found, the quickest way for

The Buraimi Oasis. (source: the BP Archive)

Westerners to travel overland between Dubai and Al-Ain was by Land Rover, a journey lasting just under eight hours. To climb Jebel Hafit (height 1,200 metres) would take at least a day. There were no hospitals or medical facilities available in the oasis, the nearest hospital being the recently completed Al Maktoum in Dubai with only 12 beds. Although water was supplied along the *aflaj*, those on the Omani side were faltering while Sheikh Zayed did his best to ensure a steady flow to the villages on the Abu Dhabi side.

The villages dotted about the north, west and south of the oasis – Al-Ain, Hili, Jimi, Murtiridh, Muwaiqi and Qattarrah – remained under the control of Sheikh Zayed, acting for his brother Shakhbut. The villages of Hamasa, Buraimi and Saara in the east-central part of the oasis forming a tongue of land surrounded on three sides by Abu Dhabi territory were, in the British mind at least, under the rule of the sultan of Muscat and Oman. But this was by no means fact: there were no formal borders in those days, only a time-honoured understanding between the sheikhs of the area where their respective territories lay. It was on the shifting allegiances of these sheikhs and their tribes that the national boundaries might be drawn.

* * * * *

Turki bin Abdullah al-Otaishan travelled through the Abu Dhabi desert at the hottest time of year. We can only imagine how a bedouin tending his goats on the outskirts of the oasis might have seen the convoy's approach: a column of trucks carrying 40 armed men lumbering across the sands, flying the green flags of Saudi Arabia, trailing dust in its wake.

Turki was 'a man about 40 years old though short [...] a man of stature in both the physical and personal sense, with a sense of humour and good manners.' After a career in the police and army, in 1945 he had been appointed emir of Ras Tanura, on the eastern coast of Saudi Arabia, at the age of 34. He was a charming and generous host in the best traditions of the Arab, qualities that would serve him well in the coming months.[6]

Since Aramco's oil terminal was at Ras Tanura, their officials had regular discussions with Turki on a range of issues arising from the company's operations in the area. The Aramcons found him alert and capable, handling the matters the company brought to him promptly

Turki bin Abdullah al-Otaishan. (source: the Otaishan Family Collection)

and fairly. They preferred dealing with him than with some other officials: he had an immediate presence when he entered the *majilis*, and seemed well informed about foreign affairs.[7]

Turki came to Hamasa with a fine sense of history. Familiar with the achievements of his famous namesake, Turki al-Sudairi, who had built the Wahhabi fort in Hamasa in the 1850s, he was acutely aware of the background to the Saudi claim for the Buraimi Oasis: the collection of *zakat* in and around the villages, the nineteenth-century Wahhabi occupations and close links between some of the Buraimi sheikhs and Ibn Saud. In Turki's mind this was no invasion: he had been *invited* to Hamasa, his mission to befriend the population and provide assistance to them in the form of food and financial support, which they lacked from the sultan of Oman. In some respects a worthy humanitarian task, it was likely to be interpreted differently by the British and their allies in the context of inter-tribal relations of south-eastern Arabia.[8]

According to the British, three of the nine villages making up the Buraimi Oasis held allegiance to Oman and six to Abu Dhabi – but the Saudis naturally viewed them differently. On his arrival, Turki announced that Emir Saud bin Jiluwi had appointed him as emir to rule over the northern Omani tribes. He brought letters from Emir Saud addressed to all the borderland sheikhs as far south as Dhank stating that, owing to repeated requests made by his subjects in Oman to appoint a *tarifa*, or representative, to be with them, he had been appointed to that office.[9]

Turki set up his base in Sheikh Rashid's village of Hamasa, a logical choice in view of Rashid's close ties with Ibn Saud, and the close affinity between the Al Bu Shamis and Naim tribes of the Buraimi Oasis. But the leaders of those tribes were rivals, and the decision to stay in Hamasa was a tactical error. It snubbed the leader of the Naim tribe, Sheikh Saqr, the Old Fox, causing him severe loss of face.[10] Saqr remained a staunch supporter of Sultan Said bin Taimur. Indeed, he wrote to the sultan urging him to take action to expel the Saudis: 'Their arrival at Hamasa has upset us [...] If you wish [to have] this place you must show reaction as quickly as possible and do what is necessary to expel them from this country.'[11]

There were others, too, who were unimpressed by Turki's arrival. For example, the imam of Oman, Muhammad bin Abdullah al-Khalili, wrote to Ibn Saud in protest: 'Your statement that in view of repeated requests from your subjects in Oman to appoint a representative has astonished us because we do not know that you have subjects in Oman.'[12]

The day following Turki's arrival, 31 August, was the occasion of the *Eid al Adha* feast. Turki invited the local people to join him in Hamasa for a meal, providing a magnificent spread for those who attended. Tribesmen came from far and wide to enjoy his hospitality. Turki quickly settled in, allowing his men to take up houses in Hamasa and sending his cars to Dubai for repairs and supplies. He promised to open a school, bring in a doctor and to distribute money and food in even greater quantities.

All the while, Sheikh Saqr stood aloof, his feelings a mixture of envy and anger, while tribesmen – including some of his own – flocked to Hamasa to enjoy Turki's hospitality. Saqr, never popular among his own people at the best of times, would struggle to resist his people's drift towards the banquets of Hamasa.

Sheikh Zayed, for his part, responded to Turki's occupation with typical firmness, recognising the threat that his influence posed to villages on both sides of the Oman/Abu Dhabi divide. As governor of Abu Dhabi's eastern province, Zayed was the centre of resistance to the Saudis. He worked closely with the British political agent, keeping his people on side through his personal influence and popularity, and punishing those who strayed. Later in the year he made a camel tour of Liwa with his brother Hazza in order to strengthen loyalties and stiffen resistance to the Saudis among those who lived on the western approaches of the sheikhdom.

At first the British delayed their diplomatic response to Turki's arrival on the pretext of checking the terms of the Status Quo Agreement in order to establish whether there had been a breach of its terms. It was not until 15 September that Whitehall, on behalf of the sultan of Oman, protested and demanded the Saudis' immediate withdrawal. The Saudis refused. A column of 33 men of the Trucial Oman Levies, five Land Rovers, a three-ton truck and an Army ground-control unit was dispatched to Al-Ain where Zayed provided them with a base in his three-storey tower at Murabba. In the sky, RAF Vampire jets were seen, their engines roaring as they patrolled above Hamasa, dropping leaflets that fell on the *barrasti* roofs and desert tracks below. The flights, according to one report, left the villagers in 'obvious terror'. Meanwhile, Sheikh Shakhbut and Sultan Said sent small forces to reinforce strategic points around the oasis.[13]

For Sultan Said, the presence of Turki and his men in what he regarded as his village was a grave provocation. At first the Foreign Office sympathised, expressing the hope that the sultan would take all necessary steps to assert his authority in the Buraimi Oasis and, if Turki or his followers did not withdraw, take action to 'place them outside [his] borders and prevent their return'.[14] But the sultan's troops were only to fire if fired upon and he was not to expect any military support from the British. Nonetheless the British representative to Muscat, Consul-General Leslie Chauncy, found the sultan in a belligerent mood, threatening to bombard Hamasa if Sheikh Rashid and his followers did not submit to his authority.[15]

The imam, offended by Turki's letter of introduction, was in no mood for compromise either. He wrote to all tribal leaders warning them against foreigners, especially Nejdis and Americans.[16] He began assembling a force at Dariz, on the western side of the Hajar Mountains, while the sultan did the same on the eastern side, both with the aim of marching on Hamasa. On 28 September, Chauncy reported that the sultan's plans were being implemented. The sultan expected to have about 2,500 picked men at Sohar and 1,000 with

Ahmad Ibrahim [minister of the interior]. Their first act would be to cut Hamasa's water supply and invite parley.[17]

This sabre rattling was all very well, but there were larger issues at stake. The Saudis had appealed to the United States to intervene diplomatically on their behalf, threatening to take the matter to the UN Security Council if Britain used force to expel Turki from Hamasa. Dean Acheson, the US secretary of state, suggested a stand-still agreement, the mutual withdrawal of armed forces and a resumption of Anglo-Saudi talks over the border issue. The British had good reason to reject this proposal – they agreed with their protégés that Turki al-Otaishan and his followers had no right whatsoever to be in Hamasa. However, the Foreign Office did not wish to offend the Americans and agreed to put Acheson's proposal to Ibn Saud.

But when the British chargé d'affaires, Derek Riches, arrived in Riyadh he found a defiant Ibn Saud.[18] The king was angry about the low-flying aircraft over Hamasa and the arrival of the Trucial Oman Levies in the oasis, and was unwilling to compromise. He would not agree to a mutual withdrawal of forces: what was Buraimi if not his own territory? Relying on Truman's 1950 letter, he appealed to the Americans to intervene. The State Department, wishing to protect their interests in the kingdom, now swung behind the king and expressed their 'serious concern' about the crisis, urging the British to make concessions.[19] No matter that the British ambassador, George Pelham, in a conversation with his American counterpart had branded the Saudis' action as 'imperialism', it was a time for cool heads and measured decisions. Pelham hammered out a standstill of forces with the Saudis while each side considered their next move.[20]

It was, in effect, a victory for the Saudis: Ibn Saud's face was saved and Turki and his followers were allowed to stay in Hamasa, but the sultan and imam were still bristling for a fight. By 10 October, the situation in Oman was tense. The imam had declared *jihad* against the Saudis, and some 400 of his loyal tribesmen had gathered at Dariz while another 800 men, loyal to the sultan, were at Sohar. Meanwhile, the British had received an unconfirmed report that the Saudis were concentrating 80 vehicles and 700 troops at Al-Kharj, south of Riyadh, part of which had reached Ain Haradh. 'Everything must be done to prevent a clash between the Saudis and the forces of the sultan,' the Foreign Office told Chauncy. They continued: 'Our prospects of settling these disputes peacefully may be ruined by irresponsible behaviour on the part of the sultan's tribesmen. I rely on you to make this quite clear to him.'[21]

On 15 October, Chauncy climbed into his Land Rover and headed for Sohar. As there were no proper roads, Chauncy drove along the shore, along tracks and through palm groves, arriving just in time to stop the sultan's army before it marched on Buraimi. The sultan was not pleased to call off his campaign, and left Chauncy to tell the tribesmen himself. Chauncy stepped up, delivered the message and the men dispersed. A similar message was sent across the mountains to Dariz where the imam's men were waiting, and they too disbanded.

War had been avoided but a golden opportunity had been lost. As Dick Bird noted a few months later 'It was a great pity from the provincial point of view that the Omanis were restrained. It has had a very grave effect throughout the Gulf and Oman area.'[22] The sultan felt it more than anyone, since he had lost face in the eyes of his tribesmen, especially among those who owed their allegiance to the imam. The British government appeared weak and indecisive – in fact no one in Oman could understand why they had backed down. The tribesmen of the Dhahira plain, who certainly had no understanding of international affairs or standstill agreements and looked to the British to expel the Saudis by force, were confused. Bird met some of their sheikhs in Muscat a few months later and the first thing they told him was: 'When are the British government going to throw out Turki?'[23]

The sultan made no secret of his disappointment. By the time the British and Saudis signed the Standstill Agreement on 26 October, his disposition had still not improved. He disapproved of some clauses in the Agreement and complained that he had not been properly consulted. He also claimed that the Saudis would not observe the Agreement and feared that he would lose much territory in any arbitration. 'The sultan is most depressed,' wrote Chauncy in mid-November. 'He is a pathetic figure and I cannot help sympathising with him and share some of his misgivings.'[24]

The aim of avoiding a war in the region had been achieved but at a cost: the British now found themselves committed to supporting Sultan Said and Sheikh Saqr in the Buraimi Oasis. By persuading the sultan to back down, they had weakened the status quo in the Oman borderlands and strengthened the Saudi cause. If the spread of Saudi influence was to be further resisted, Britain would have to come off the fence and bolster her protégés as best she could.

Without military action, the flow of people into Hamasa continued apace. Sheikh Obaid bin Juma of the Beni Kaab appeared in the village and was delighted by his reception: he was royally entertained and sent off to Riyadh with his nephew to receive generous gifts of money. Men of the Bani Qitab and Khawatir tribes from the north came for a free meal and money, and the waverers came too: Muhammad bin Salimin, the sheikh who had set the ball rolling by visiting Riyadh in 1950, then switched sides and declared his support for Sultan Said, now arrived to declare his allegiance to Ibn Saud and was duly dispatched to Riyadh to receive his reward. Some 250 members of Suleiman bin Hamyar's tribe went over to Turki. Eventually Suleiman himself succumbed, but only after Turki had sent an invitation and a car to collect him. Suleiman, forever the showman, then used the car on his ostentatious tour of the Trucial Coast, proclaiming himself to one-and-all as the king of Nabhan.

* * * * *

A cannon boomed out its greeting to Suleiman on his tour of Sharjah, briefly distracting the political officer, Michael Weir, from his desk. A dedicated Arabist, Weir had been appointed to his post earlier in the year, and was trying to write a report on the situation in Abu Dhabi where Shakhbut's position was weakening.

It was 6 December 1952. Weir had heard that a large section of the population was about to decamp and leave Abu Dhabi Island. Sheikh Ali of Qatar had promised tribal leaders houses and a monthly stipend to move to his domain. But the main reason for the impending exodus appeared to be Shakhbut's refusal to give them a loan at the start of the pearling season, something they had always received in the past. 'The situation could easily be settled by a present of three or four thousand rupees [£5,000–7,000 today],' Weir wrote. This was not an argument that made an impression on the frugal Shakhbut.

Sheikh Shakhbut had recently returned from medical treatment in India looking frail and anaemic, and maintained a 'generally unhelpful attitude' towards the frontier problem. His approach was simple enough: he agreed that the most effective remedy would be to expel the Saudis from Hamasa by force. What was the use of bribing his people to stay in Abu Dhabi when Turki or Sheikh Ali [the ruler of Qatar] could always pay double? In his opinion, the prevailing motive of the bedu was greed. Thus, if the Saudis stayed in Hamasa, all the tribes would eventually go over to them. His solution was to throw the whole problem into the lap of the British government, the *daulah*.

Shakhbut had a point. In the bedouin mind, the use of force was the true measure of power: Ibn Saud had the reputation of a strong and forceful leader, the British appeared supine. If the British appeared to be doing nothing, there was a real danger that the bedouin might assume that the Saudis were in Hamasa with their tacit consent and go over to Turki en masse.

The real concern for the British was the western approaches to the Liwa Oasis. This was the Achilles' heel of the defensive arrangements around the Buraimi Oasis: Turki had travelled through the area unchallenged on his way to Hamasa, and it was still poorly defended and vulnerable to attack. Nor was this an idle concern, for there were rumours that Ibn Saud's tax collectors were planning to return to the Liwa in February or March.

Sheikh Hazza, Shakhbut's brother and governor of the western province, was popular among the tribes but he was short of resources: money, troops, equipment and transport. Weir had made various suggestions, such as setting up a string of levy posts in the desert to the west of Buraimi along the track likely used by the Saudis, appointing new *walis* and paying them extra money to entertain and impress the surrounding bedu, to which Shakhbut reluctantly agreed. But when Weir suggested that he might show his face in the area by taking a hunting trip, Shakhbut showed little enthusiasm. 'He might well agree to go at our expense,' Weir noted wearily.[25] This episode did nothing to quieten British concern about Shakhbut's leadership, but they kept it to themselves for now.

* * * * *

Sheikh Saqr's loyalties remained variable. The southern flank of his territory, and his position in Dhank was susceptible to Saudi influence. Sheikh Rashid bin Hamad had visited Dhank and stirred up pro-Saudi feelings. But Saqr was strangely reluctant to visit the town, preferring instead to stay in Buraimi and look after his money chests. Outwardly, he still supported the sultan.[26]

It was vital for the British that he should do so. If anyone doubted Saqr's influence on the outcome of the dispute, they only had to look at the *aflaj* that supplied Hamasa with water to know that he held the whip hand. Buraimi and Hamasa were almost a single entity, supplied by one water channel that passed through Buraimi on its way to Hamasa. It flowed directly beneath Saqr's fort and, by cutting off the water supply, Saqr could easily destroy the gardens of Rashid bin Hamad. Saqr also controlled access to Hamasa from the north and east. The two sheikhs were old rivals and it seemed inevitable that Saqr would seek to destroy him. But – as became apparent over the coming months – Saqr showed an alarming tendency to veer towards the Saudi camp.[27]

On 12 November 1952, fifty of Saqr's tribesmen arrived at his fort in Buraimi and, despite Saqr's entreaties, insisted on riding over to visit Turki. Any doubt about their intentions were dispelled when the men returned next day, no doubt invigorated by Turki's generosity and feelings of goodwill towards Ibn Saud, and urged Saqr to join them. If he did not, they warned, Turki would establish a post in Saqr's second town of Dhank.[28]

At this point, Michael Weir decided to take matters into his own hands. He jumped into his Land Rover and dashed over to Buraimi, arriving at 10 p.m. to find a startled Saqr dressed only in his nightshirt. At first, Saqr resisted Weir's plea to travel to Muscat, claiming it was too dangerous to leave Buraimi. But Weir was adamant, and would not back down. 'We had to drag him,' he wrote.[29]

They drove to Muscat, a hard journey of 17 hours over rough tracks, past Ibn Saud's watchful spies in the mountains, reaching the sultan's palace in mid-afternoon. No doubt Saqr presented a feeble creature at the sultan's gate, yet the sultan duly played his part, mollifying the wayward sheikh and reassuring him of his support. Saqr in turn reaffirmed his allegiance. The customary platitudes were then exchanged and Saqr climbed back into the Land Rover for the return journey to Buraimi, his relationship with the sultan apparently confirmed, but the doubts persisted.[30]

Elsewhere, tribal loyalties were mixed. The Bani Kaab might have acknowledged the sultan's rule in the past but they now regarded themselves as semi-independent, as did the bedouin section of the Al Bu Shamis. Sheikh Obaid bin Juma took a firmer line; he declared his independence, pronouncing his sheikhdom as 'the Imarat [State] of Mahadha' and planting a notice that read 'All Cars Stop' alongside the track that ran by his stone tower. He banned Sheikh Zayed from

passing through, informing him so in a letter which he signed 'emir of
the Bani Kaab and his relatives, of Mahadha in the Kingdom of Saudi
Arabia.' Bearing in mind that Mahadha lay some 30 kilometres north-
east of Buraimi, well within the sultan's territory, this was an
astonishing claim.[31]

Obaid's nephew, the thin, almost stick-like, Sheikh Abdullah bin
Salim, took matters a stage further. He approached an outpost of the
Trucial Oman Levies at Khurnus, in Wadi al-Qaur, just as the levies
were preparing their breakfast. The outpost, one of several dotted
about the area, had been set up to prevent tribal warring, banditry and
slave smuggling along one of the main trade-routes through the
mountains. In other circumstances, the arrival of a bearded young
sheikh, small, sprightly and slightly nervous, might not have stirred
the levies but the 50 tribesmen who accompanied him were a different
proposition. The tribesmen surrounded the outpost and, with a couple
of sangars in the surrounding hills they had taken the night before,
they had control of the valley. They duly hoisted the Saudi flag over
the track that led through the Wadi. But the revolt was soon over: a
TOL sergeant was allowed to leave in a taxi and he went back to
Sharjah to raise the alarm. The following day, a TOL convoy arrived
and, after a brief parley with Sheikh Abdullah, peacefully reoccupied
the post. The sheikh promptly disappeared.[32]

That evening, Weir was travelling from Buraimi towards Wadi al-
Qaur when he came upon Obaid's tower and found the 'All Cars Stop'
notice. About 12 tribesmen gathered round his Land Rover and told
him that they would allow no traffic to pass at night. It was already
dark, but they would allow Weir through 'as a favour'. In future,
however, they would detain until dawn anyone arriving after sunset.
They produced Obaid's edict for Weir's inspection, a grimy piece of
paper headed 'Imarat [State] of Mahadha'. It contained several words
that, in Weir's opinion, were unknown to Obaid and must have been
written with Saudi assistance. Indeed, it later transpired that Sheikh
Abdullah had visited Turki in Hamasa ten days earlier and received a
quantity of dates, coffee and rice and an unknown sum of money.

'Nor is it conceivable that anything other than a Saudi bribe could
have induced Obaid and Abdullah to act in collusion,' wrote Weir,
alluding to the strained relations between uncle and nephew.[33] It was
not long before Abdullah was back on the scene and changing sides.
On returning to his home village of Sharm, he raised the sultan's red

flag and, when the sultan appeared to give him little encouragement, the British stepped in and supported him against Obaid.

Obaid remained ensconced in his fort at Mahadha, his dreams of an independent state in tatters, his tower a crumbling symbol of his prestige. The only vehicle ever detained there overnight belonged to Sheikh Saqr, a present from the sultan, while night taxis were allowed to pass through unhindered. In March, Weir drove to the tower expecting to be stopped and detained for the night but instead found Obaid's men in hospitable mood: they invited him to join them for dinner. By now there were only five of them in residence, the remainder being on strike over low wages.[34]

Like an insect with a short life-span, the state of Mahadha had sprung into life, fluttered and died. All that remained was a sad green banner hanging upside-down from the branch of a tree. On close inspection it was found to be a waterproof tablecloth of Saudi Arabian origin. Printed on one side were two crossed swords in the centre, palm trees, a camel at each corner and the Arabic words, 'Long Live the Saudi Arabian Kingdom'. A tablecloth hardly heralded a revolution, and it was later reported that an identical tablecloth had been seen hanging up for sale in the fancy goods shop of the Manama *suq*.[35]

Chapter 10
Taking a Stand
International Diplomacy, 1952–3

In December 1952 British Foreign Secretary Anthony Eden, in a paper to the cabinet, spelt out the situation then current in the Gulf:

> Ibn Saud was once utterly dependent on us for money, arms and international protection. Today he obtains all these benefits from his new friends in the United States. Ibn Saud is in no way beholden to us, and it is our influence alone that stands in the way of his absorption of his less powerful neighbours.[1]

This was something of a reality check. In Whitehall the Buraimi dispute had been as much about British prestige as oil. Emerging from the debris of World War II and the loss of India in 1947, many British politicians did not accept their country's decline as inevitable, and still imagined a future as a global superpower. The fact that the Americans were in the ascendancy did not necessarily conflict with this ambition. Strategically, Whitehall welcomed an American presence in the Middle East: 'A potential aggressor might hesitate to interfere where both American and British interests are involved,' a cabinet paper noted. 'There will be no interest in challenging the American claim to a strategic interest in the Middle East oil.'[2]

But it was not quite so simple. It was true that both governments wanted the same thing, to foster stability and develop the oil resources in the region. But there remained a deep-seated insecurity among the British that the Americans aimed to replace them in the world. In 1943 President Franklin Roosevelt had pestered Churchill about Britain's colonial possessions so much that Churchill exclaimed 'Mr President, I believe you are trying to do away with the British Empire.'[3] Suspicion about American intentions in the Middle East had been reinforced by events in Saudi Arabia and the American rise to pre-eminence in the kingdom; the Americans were *arrivistes* in a world that had been dominated by the British.[4]

However, Washington saw value in having a British presence in the Middle East, especially in the Persian Gulf. As Secretary of State John Foster Dulles once put it, 'wherever Britain had evacuated territories since the war they had left a vacuum which was eventually filled by Russian influence.'[5] Although a British ban on the import of dollar oil into the sterling area of the Middle East ran contrary to American free trade policy, the Americans showed willingness to compromise: American companies entered into dollar-sharing agreements with the British government, promising to re-invest profits in the sterling area.[6]

At the heart of the special relationship between Britain and the United States was another, that between the United States and Saudi Arabia. British diplomats visiting Riyadh struggled to understand why the Americans gave their unqualified support to Ibn Saud. The political resident in Bahrain, Bernard Burrows, noted:

> It seems to us a pity that the Americans sometimes seemed willing to go to such lengths in seeking to please Ibn Saud when this might in certain cases increase our difficulties, particularly in the Persian Gulf, and get in the way of Anglo-American objectives in the Persian Gulf.[7]

In American eyes, the growing importance of oil in World War II had seen a corresponding rise in Saudi Arabia's stock. Post-war, through the Marshall Plan, the Americans sought to regenerate Europe and resist the march of communism which posed a severe threat to their interests in the Middle East. The uninterrupted supply of Saudi oil was vital to these plans, as was having an airbase in Dhahran. And here lay the key to the American stance during the Buraimi dispute: the Americans wanted to preserve their interests in Saudi Arabia without threatening British hegemony in the Persian Gulf.

With Eisenhower's election as president, the first test on the boundary issue came in May 1953. On a visit to the kingdom, the new secretary of state, John Foster Dulles, was asked by Crown Prince Saud if President Truman's letter of 1950 meant that the United States would protect Saudi Arabia from British aggression over Buraimi. Dulles replied that the dispute was not about aggression but about boundaries, therefore the question did not arise in this case.[8] The diplomatic tightrope was being tugged in opposite directions from Riyadh and Whitehall, but Dulles took it all in his stride.

He was certainly well prepared and well connected: his grandfather, John Foster, had been secretary of state to President Harrison and his uncle, Robert Lansing, secretary of state to President Woodrow Wilson. In January 1953, a month before his 65th birthday, Dulles emulated their achievements by becoming secretary of state in Eisenhower's administration. He was didactic as well as intense and had an eye for detail, but came with a reputation of being 'dull'.[9]

Not entirely dull, however, as Dulles made a series of anti-colonialist remarks that unsettled Whitehall. In the next few weeks, there was a distinctive shift in the emphasis of US foreign policy: communism was seen as the greatest threat to stability in the Middle East and Washington aimed to distance itself from colonialist powers such as Britain and France. In the Buraimi dispute, this meant a perceptible sympathy among members of the administration towards the Saudi Arabian case. Perhaps this was not surprising in view of the influence that Aramco held in the kingdom. Indeed, the company knew a lot more about Saudi Arabia than the US government and had acted as a de facto representative of the Saudi Arabian government in Washington for many years.[10] It was well placed to shape Washington's view of events in Arabia. Dulles' brother Allen was director of the CIA. The company supplied the CIA with information about the Buraimi dispute, and shared a common outlook with the Bureau of Near Eastern Affairs in the State Department. In one report, for instance, referring to information supplied by Terry Duce, Aramco vice president, Allen Dulles wrote: 'In view of Duce's business connections, this report may be somewhat prejudiced, but on the whole we have found him an able reporter.'[11]

Washington had commissioned its own research into the Buraimi dispute. This concluded that, since the Saudis had not occupied the oasis after 1869, their claim was a weak one. But its view changed as the dispute went on. Richard Young, an American attorney working for Aramco, dismissed the research, claiming that officials had been swayed by British propaganda.[12] A few years later Eisenhower was claiming that American public opinion was on Ibn Saud's side, telling British prime minister Sir Anthony Eden that 'people in general [...] tended to think that the whole Arabian Peninsula belonged, or ought to belong, to [the then] King Saud.'[13] He was not alone in his sympathy for the Saudi Arabian cause, which was echoed by other members of the administration.[14]

By now Ibn Saud was an old man, sick and weary, his hair and beard dyed, his hands stiff and wrinkled, his face set and his gaze 'weak and lustreless.'[15] Consul Daniel van der Meulen, making his last visit to the king, was saddened by the apparent decline he saw since their last meeting eight years previously. The king lived in the Badi Palace with a row of gleaming Cadillacs parked outside and bedouins squatting inside on the floor. He seemed tired and uninterested. Although he said he recognised van der Meulen, he sounded unconvincing and took little interest in conversation. 'The unfailing spring had failed [...] The audience chamber was no longer a place of inspiration for his people. The voice that used to resound there no longer raised an echo in men's hearts. Before long it would be stilled.'[16]

This was the Lion of the Desert, the man reputed to have had 200 wives, now reduced to potions to restore his sexual prowess. He was crippled by arthritis in both knees and could not walk up or down the stairs. Yet his emotions were still strong and nothing was likely to quicken the king's pulse more than thoughts of losing his 'ancestral rights' to Buraimi and of the British stealing his oil. Ibn Saud was an old man wishing to settle his legacy, telling the British ambassador 18 months before he died that he wished to leave the kingdom in 'proper order.'[17]

It was his attitude towards Buraimi that left British diplomats angry and frustrated. On 17 September 1952, barely two weeks after Turki's arrival in the oasis, they had a 45-minute audience with Ibn Saud in his *majilis*. The tired king, speaking on a querulous note, told them:

> Buraimi was his country and he would never give up the land of his ancestors and grandfathers before him. If force was used – well, his head could be cut off. He could take the matter (here he stumbled a bit and looked at Yusuf) to the United Nations. He then suddenly reverted to his natural manner and said that it was preferable to settle matters directly as between old friends.[18]

Relations between Ibn Saud and the British had been conducted on a personal basis in the past, but the two men shaping British foreign policy, Prime Minister Winston Churchill and Foreign Secretary (later Prime Minister) Anthony Eden, were unlikely to be swayed by sentiment alone.

Michael Weir told a story about Churchill that would have struck fear into Gulf sheikhs if they had heard it. Churchill was sitting at the bottom of some stairs after a banquet when the sheikh of Bahrain approached him. The sheikh said that he hoped Britain would support Bahrain's ancestral claim to territory opposite Qatar. 'Tell him,' Churchill replied, 'that we try never to desert our friends.' The great man paused and then added, 'unless we have to'. It was perhaps fortunate that Weir, who was accompanying the sheikh, refrained from translating this last remark.[19]

The Buraimi dispute developed as Churchill's forceful character was waning and Eden's star was rising. It was in the complexity of Eden's character that the direction of policy towards Ibn Saud began to take shape. Eden had first served as foreign secretary in 1935 until he resigned in 1938 after a disagreement with Prime Minster Chamberlain over appeasement of the Nazis. During the war years he again served as foreign secretary and was present at major conferences, such as Yalta and Potsdam, at which the post-war future of Europe was settled. With the election of a Conservative government in 1951, he returned once more to the Foreign Office and waited with rising impatience for Churchill to retire.

No one was as experienced as Eden in the international sphere. His career might have lacked the human breadth of Churchill's or Eisenhower's, having seldom strayed beyond the polished corridors of Westminster and Whitehall but, as *Time* magazine observed:

> When Dwight Eisenhower was an army major in the Philippines, Khrushchev an obscure bureaucrat, Nehru a revolutionary in jail and Mao Tse-tung an outlaw in the Shensi hills, the youthful Mr Eden was parleying at the summit with Hitler, Mussolini and Stalin.[20]

On a personal level, Eden was cultured and elegant with film star looks but in public he lacked the common touch and was a poor speaker. In private he suffered rapid mood-swings, being rude to his secretaries only to regain his composure a few moments later. All this might have been insignificant in other circumstances but Eden's dislike towards those such as Ibn Saud and Colonel Gamel Nasser of Egypt coloured his decision-making, and deserves further consideration in the context of the Buraimi dispute.

Otherwise, Eden's opposition to Nasser is puzzling. Eden had pro-Arab sympathies, read Oriental Studies at Oxford, was an Arabic speaker and, unlike Churchill, did not support the Zionist cause. Why, then, should he detest the Arab World's most prominent leader? In his mind, the parallels between Nasser, Hitler and Mussolini, were too obvious to ignore. He wrote to Eisenhower: 'It would be as ineffective to show weakness to Nasser now in order to placate him as it was to show weakness to Mussolini.'[21]

Eden's view of the Saudis was no less restrained: Saudi money was corrupting the Middle East, and the Saudis were co-operating with the Communists against Western interests, using Aramco money for that purpose. He remarked: 'American, that is Aramco, money was being spent on a lavish scale to abet communism in the Middle East.'[22] He saw Saudi influence as pernicious, undermining British-backed regimes in Jordan and Iraq. He was severe; indeed Bernard Burrows doubted that the Saudis ever felt so hostile towards the British as Eden did towards them.[23]

* * * * *

On the question of settling the southern Arabian boundaries, British attitudes could be ambivalent. Had not officials at the Foreign Office been willing to give up Khawr al-Udayd in the 1930s? Then, as we have seen, the India Office had resisted them. Now, with India having gained its independence in 1947 and the India Office no more, there were no leathery imperialists to stand up for the interests of the Gulf sheikhs. In Anthony Eden, however, the ghosts of the India Office lived on. Since his first priority was to ensure Ibn Saud did not get away with any territorial gain from his actions in Hamasa, Eden proved to be the counterweight to any resurgent idea of doing a deal with Ibn Saud.

If the people of the Buraimi Oasis thought that Whitehall had abandoned them after Turki's arrival in August 1952, they were mistaken. The ink was barely dry on the Standstill Agreement when Eden circulated a paper to cabinet members in which he argued that arbitration was the best option. Using military force would bring clashes with Saudi forces, and trying to match Ibn Saud's largesse would be futile. 'Our chances under arbitration are fair,' he wrote. An arbitration tribunal could determine the case on the historical facts rather than on the present situation, which had been distorted by Saudi payments to the tribes.[24] The cabinet agreed and, in November, a Note was delivered to the Saudi Arabian government.

Anticipating a final Saudi rejection of the British proposal, Eden set out the options to the cabinet in another paper on 19 December 1952. He called for a 'stiffening measure' in the Persian Gulf. British prestige was at stake: the continuing Saudi presence in Hamasa threatened the Trucial States and events in Iran, where the government had nationalised the oil industry, had been a 'stunning blow' to British standing in the Arab world. Until 1947, the British had depended on the Indian Army and Ibn Saud's goodwill to protect the Trucial Coast. Now British India was gone and Saudi Arabia had become more wealthy and powerful. 'Thus, for the first time in the history of the Persian Gulf', Eden advised, 'our relations with Saudi Arabia become a matter of first importance.' The cabinet approved sending reinforcements to the Persian Gulf. The result was Operation Boxer, in which 12 armoured cars, a squadron of Vampire jets and three warships were to be dispatched and arrive in Sharjah by the end of March.[25]

When the final Saudi rejection came, Operation Boxer was put into effect. It was hardly a declaration of war, but a provocation nonetheless, to which the Saudis acted sharply. They resorted to a propaganda campaign against the British. It began on 6 March when selected government documents about the dispute were published in Jedda. Five days later, Saudi foreign minister Prince Faisal held a press conference in New York, described by Eden as 'tendentious'. The Saudi line was that they had no quarrel with other Arab rulers in the region, and it was solely British intervention that had caused the dispute. There was nothing of substance to refer to arbitration because Buraimi was Saudi territory and any doubts could be dispelled by a plebiscite. They claimed that the real threat to peace came from British actions, not Saudi, and hinted at an appeal to the United Nations.[26]

More disturbing for the British was news that 38 Saudi tax collectors, including the chief tax collector for Al-Hasa, Muhammad bin Mansur, had crossed into Abu Dhabi territory and were going to the Buraimi Oasis to raise *zakat*. On 12 March they arrived at Tarif on the western coast of Abu Dhabi, where a detachment of the Trucial Oman Levies was stationed. After making threats against the levies, the Saudis withdrew and made their way overland to Hamasa by

New York, 11 March 1953: Saudi foreign minister, Prince Faisal ibn Abdul Aziz Al Saud, with members of the Saudi Arabian delegation to the United Nations holds a press conference in response to British proposals to blockade Hamasa.
(source: Corbis Images)

another route. Muhammad bin Mansur then set about his work, travelling as far as 50 kilometres south of Hamasa to collect *zakat*.[27] When the British protested, the Saudis claimed their tax collectors were carrying out their customary duties in the area, a claim that conveniently ignored the fact that that no *zakat* had been collected in these southern parts before.

Four days later, Eden presented another paper to the cabinet in which he stated that more forceful action was required. He wrote:

> We cannot wait on events. So long as Turki remains in Buraimi, Saudi intrigue will continue and so will the threat to our position in the Trucial States and to the sultan of Muscat in Central Oman. The Saudi reply to our Note of 5 January will inevitably be unfavourable.[28]

The cabinet declared the existing agreements void, ordered a blockade around Turki's force in Hamasa and levy posts to be established at key points around the village and to the west. Washington was to be told two days beforehand, the Saudis on the day it began, 2 April 1953.

Churchill tried to sweeten the pill by sending a personal note to Ibn Saud, who replied the following day. The king agreed that the two countries should not fall out over Buraimi and invited Churchill to suggest ways in which the dispute might be resolved.[29] At subsequent meetings, it appeared that the Saudis had in principle agreed to arbitration. The Foreign Office, anxious to help save Ibn Saud's face, urged more conciliatory measures, including neutral supervision and the withdrawal of some British troops, but Churchill was defiant.

On 12 April Eden underwent an operation on his biliary tract at the London Clinic that went badly wrong. Despite being recommended three expert surgeons, Eden had chosen a 60-year-old Mr John Basil Hume, a general surgeon who had removed Eden's appendix some years before. But Hume became so agitated that the operation had to be delayed for nearly an hour while he regained his composure. A second operation, to correct the mistakes of the first, followed in Boston during which Eden came within a whisker of death. The view, now generally accepted, is that the knife slipped during the first operation, accidentally cutting the common bile duct that carries bile from the liver to the small bowel.[30]

Churchill, who had been handling foreign affairs in Eden's absence, refused to make any further concessions to the Saudis. 'Let us sit resolute and phlegmatic on this high ground and see what happens' he wrote to Selwyn Lloyd.[31] He soon relented, agreeing that British forces could be withdrawn if Turki departed from Hamasa. Yet despite this and a personal appeal from Eisenhower to Ibn Saud – 'You and I are both old soldiers and I believe that we shall understand each other fully' – the Saudis refused to back down over Turki.[32]

While Eden was on the operating table in Boston, Churchill suffered a severe stroke and he too came close to death. The matter was hushed up and, with the agreement of the British press, nothing appeared in the newspapers about the seriousness of his condition.[33] If Eden been well at the time, it is possible that Churchill would have retired allowing Eden to become prime minster. Instead, Churchill soldiered on for almost two more years and Eden's frustration grew.

Their incapacity served only to perpetuate the stalemate. On 13 July 1953, with Churchill and Eden still recuperating, the cabinet met and discussed, among other things, the Buraimi dispute. The meeting made little progress. There was talk about the 'large incomes of the little chiefs [sheikhs]', a reference to protecting the interests of the rulers of southern Arabia, and to the risk of damaging relations with Washington over a relatively minor dispute. The cabinet decided to send another message to the Saudi Arabian government to the effect that 'Turki must go' but to no avail since the Saudis again stood firm.[34]

Meanwhile, back at Riyadh, the tedious audiences went on. At one such meeting, a whimsical Ibn Saud asked the British ambassador, 'What is your name?' The ambassador, alluding to a remark that Churchill had once made that Ibn Saud had been a friend of the British during the darkest nights of World War II, replied 'the friend of the darkest nights'.[35] The king, taking dark nights to mean a time of peace and tranquillity, expressed the wish that the dark nights might come again so that he might prove his friendship – but those dark nights still seemed far away.

Chapter 11
The Hamasa Blockade
The Buraimi Oasis, 1953–4

There was something unreal about the early days of Turki's occupation. While the diplomatic tug of war went on in London and Riyadh, and Turki entertained a stream of visitors in Hamasa, little in the wider oasis suggested that anything was amiss: a green flag fluttering from a distant flagpole, a Land Rover in a wadi, a levy standing guard.

Images of oil, sand and Beau Geste forts briefly captured public imagination in the West, and the dispute even inspired an episode of the popular British radio comedy programme *The Goon Show*.[1] Noel Monks, a reporter from the *Daily Mail*, visited Al-Ain and returned to Sharjah on the first flight from the oasis, an airstrip having been made by uprooting a few bushes the evening before. But the political officer travelling with him was disappointed that Monks was more interested in 'human interest' stories than any political issues.[2]

It was also reported that the British Embassy in Washington had received a request from an American travel agency for an up-to-date list of the best hotels in the oasis.[3] And *Time* magazine reported with some jollity in April 1953:

> So far, not a shot has been fired. In bleak, besieged Buraimi, Turki still holds out; he has 800 bags of rice, enough for many meals. Around him circles a busy band of British. Happiest of all are the local sheikhs. They figure that all this excitement means oil. One of them has already decided how to spend his first oil royalty check – on a fancy new airplane.[4]

With the influx of visitors, Hamasa acquired a festive air. This was no liberation of an oppressed people: there were no troop carriers trailing dust and fumes across the desert, no tanks lurking in the shade of date plantations. The slave trade was flourishing, despite the ring of levy posts around Hamasa. The sheikhs who had declared for Ibn Saud were enjoying a new prosperity as they received regular payments from the Saudis. On one estimate, £10,000 (£230,000 today) a month was being paid to various sheikhs in salaries and pensions.[5]

Turki married two local girls, one from the Al Bu Shamis tribe and the other from the Awamir. It was an astute move, since the two tribes had been at odds with each other before Turki's arrival and his marriages now brought them together. He also encouraged his younger men – lonely and far from home – to take local wives, thus forging even closer links with the villagers.[6]

Turki moved into a new house built for him on south-western corner of the village overlooking the wadi. Levy officers knew this house as Bait Turki, and a smaller house built for Turki's assistant, Aqil, as Bait Aqil. Turki stationed men in a watchtower some 50 metres south of the Hamasa–Buraimi border (such as it was) and in various other houses in the western outskirts of the village.[7]

The most controversial aspect of the Saudis' stay in Hamasa was the provision of gifts to the local population. Their explanation of this generosity – that it was simply an expression of the wealth and prestige of Ibn Said – was dismissed by Whitehall as 'bribery'. But there was nothing the British could do to stop it. As levy officers watched through binoculars from a safe distance, they saw tribesmen coming to the village to pay their *salaams* to Turki and enjoy free lunches of mutton and rice. Few, if any, of them could have given much thought to the administrative arrangements, which must have seemed a small price to pay for a meal and a gift.

There was a certain calculation in all of this. Turki asked each tribesman to sign a visitors' book with a signature, mark or thumbprint, declaring his loyalty to Ibn Saud. Thus feasted and clutching a certificate of Saudi nationality, the distended tribesman would wend his way home. By the end of October, 900 certificates had been issued. For every present he gave, Turki took a receipt and even required some tribesmen to give an undertaking to fly the Saudi flag on returning to their villages. Although the tribesmen did not know it at the time, these apparently harmless pieces of paper would be kept and produced three years later in order to support the Saudis' legal claim to the oasis.[8]

Once this custom had been established there was little the levies could do to stop it. Sheikh Rashid looked after his own followers in Hamasa, while Muhammad Salih, the richest Persian merchant in the village, acted as Turki's local agent on the outside. He distributed monthly payments to the bedouin tribes living near the village as well as to Bani Kaab refugees who came into the village to collect their cash.[9]

Most of the intelligence reaching the levy officers came from interrogating travellers and from snippets picked up by local spies, most notably those loyal to Sheikh Zayed. Certainly news of Turki's generosity had spread widely: the levies intercepted a courier carrying a number of messages to Turki from villages outside the oasis, most of which were requests for money. For his part, Turki had his own intelligence sources, paying Adeni soldiers in the TOL to report to him on their activities.

As the months slipped by, Saudi influence began to spread more widely. Reports came in that the imam was now leaning towards the Saudis. Even Philby was heard off-stage threatening to break free from the confines of Riyadh and get in on the act, proposing to visit Suleiman bin Hamyar in his mountain fastness. No wonder British officials were alarmed – 'a propaganda circus that we must try to prevent', wrote one.[10]

Yet, in the see-saw world of tribal politics, not everything had gone the Saudis' way. The action of the levies in quelling the Bani Kaab revolt at Mahadha had been a useful reminder to the wavering tribes that the British meant business. Sheikh Zayed had also shown his resolve. When two youths from Qattarah village in Abu Dhabi territory had visited Riyadh and raised a Saudi flag on their return, passing themselves off as Saudi citizens, Zayed promptly expelled them, ordering them never to return.

Tribesmen of the Murrah tribe – old allies of Ibn Saud – rode their camels across the desert to keep Turki's men supplied, enabling Turki to maintain his generous levels of hospitality. But in time these began to decline: the cash presents were reduced or refused and the good old days of a free meal served to all-comers were fast becoming a distant memory. Now it was only lunch – if you were lucky.[11]

The Saudis brought Syrian doctors into Hamasa but these, according to Michael Weir, failed to impress. One of their patients, a subject of Sheikh Saqr, complained of a fever and died shortly after they had given him an injection. Weir reported that, because these doctors appeared to lack medical skills, gossip-mongers in the oasis were saying they were not proper doctors but a pair of '*Hasawi* quacks' imported for propaganda purposes.[12]

The blockade announced on 2 April 1953 brought a keen edge to the dispute. It aimed to prevent the flow of visitors who came to Hamasa to sign declarations of allegiance in exchange for money and a meal, and to reduce the supplies that Turki was using to entertain his guests. At this point there were five levy posts at intervals around Hamasa, almost surrounding the village, and night ambush positions on the northern side. The average strength of each post was an NCO and nine men. The posts were within sight of each other by day and at night the intervals between the posts were policed by armed patrols. It was, in the words of Michael Weir, 'about as foolproof as it is possible to make it.' Apart from small-scale smuggling from the *suq*, and the women of Sheikh Zayed's villages supplying Turki with rice, receiving a few rupees and some cooked rice in return, no supplies reached the village and vehicles and camels were unable to get through.[13]

On 5 May, however, a supply caravan of 24 camels with 47 bags of rice approached Hamasa across the sands from Dubai. They laid up until nightfall and then made for Hamasa through the date gardens of Buraimi, avoiding the levy posts by breaking down the irrigation ditches and meeting up with Turki and 30 armed men. A second caravan, of 'about 12 beasts', also heading for Hamasa, was intercepted after being shadowed by the RAF.[14]

The efficacy of the blockade depended on the calibre of the men manning the posts. The Trucial Oman Levies had originally been formed to protect the sheikhdoms and control bedouin raiders and Nejdi slave traders. But it was a relatively small force and, when Turki arrived at Hamasa, it was unable to take effective action. Therefore Aden Protectorate levies were brought in to hold the situation until the TOL could be brought up to strength. Two hundred ex-levies were provided but these included men who had been dismissed from the service or otherwise found unsuitable to be recruited. This deeply flawed decision would have tragic consequences when Major Otto Thwaites and an officer were murdered by three of their own men.[15]

For the Trucial Oman Levies, Turki's arrival brought a fundamental shift of emphasis. Having been set up as a peace-keeping gendarmerie, they were now to be a military force, designed to shore up the gaping holes in the defences. In November 1953 a directive was issued to the levy commander 'to prevent arms, ammunition, supplies and reinforcements from entering the Trucial States and to blockade the Saudis in Hamasa'. Over the summer, arguments had rumbled on

The Jimi tower, which was manned by TOL guards during the blockade of Hamasa.
(source: the BP Archive)

in London between the Foreign Office and War Office over funding
the levies. Meanwhile, the force was expanded to cover the blockade,
replacing the Aden Protectorate Levies in the process, and to meet its
other commitments across the Trucial States. Their duties now
included manning outposts in western Abu Dhabi and protecting
PDTC seismic crews who were working up to the Qatar border.[16]

The blockade occupied the levies more than anything else. Long
periods of dull routine were punctuated by shocking outbreaks of
violence. On 19 June 1953 a caravan of 17 men approached Hamasa at
8 a.m., refused to stop when challenged, and fired on a sentry. There
followed an exchange of fire between the villagers on one side and a
TOL post and Muscati *asakirs* on the other, during which one of the
asakirs was killed by a sniper from the top of the village tower.[17] The
camels and men got into the village unscathed. However, as a result of
the incident, the Muscatis 'suddenly woke from their months' long
lethargy and there was some fear [...] that they might attempt reprisals

on the villagers'.[18] Three weeks later, a number of Muscatis entered Hamasa and shot dead the first man they saw. The victim was a slave who was believed to have occasionally acted as *muezzin*, and was sitting at the door of the mosque at the time of the killing.[19]

In September 1953 a party of armed tribesmen trying to enter Hamasa were challenged by a levy patrol. The tribesmen refused to stop and opened fire on the levies. A firefight ensued as tribesmen in the village joined in the mêlée. Later in the day, a patrol went to stop a man heading for Hamasa. On the levies' approach, the man turned and fired at the patrol. More rifles opened up from the direction of Hamasa, and the man was hit. A force of about 100 men, some wearing uniforms, advanced from Hamasa on the levy post at Jimi in a threatening manner. The defenders of the post, who numbered only seven, returned fire. As a British press statement helpfully explained:

> In both incidents, everything possible was done to avoid opening fire, the disparity in the numbers involved shows, indeed, how careful the security forces were to avoid needless provocation and that their action was undertaken solely in self-defence.[20]

What the British saw as 'self-defence', the Saudis saw as 'aggression'. Lodging a Note with the Foreign Office protesting against the levy actions, the Saudis claimed that 'at least several people were killed.' A Saudi press statement spoke of 'cruel actions' and the 'killing of weak and innocent inhabitants.'[21] The Saudi Arabian delegation to the United Nations said that British forces had attacked Saudi civilians with machine-guns and tanks in 'acts of aggression'.[22]

Meanwhile a great deal was happening to the east of the oasis. Since the failure of his independent state, Sheikh Obaid had been quiet. But then his pickets at Mahadha burst into life, firing on passing levies and disrupting Sheikh Zayed's camel traffic, causing Zayed to complain to the political agent in Dubai about Obaid's 'enormities'.[23]

Obaid's nephew, Sheikh Abdullah bin Salim, was now firmly committed to the sultan's cause. He seized Mahadha with the help of a levy force and thus deposed Obaid as paramount sheikh of his tribe. Obaid threw in his lot with Turki, going to live in Hamasa with a few loyal retainers. By October 1953 the area was settled again but Obaid remained a threat, using Saudi gold to undermine Abdullah's position among his tribe and retaining his hold over many villages to the south and east.[24]

Indeed, Sheikh Obaid would remain a thorn in the side of his enemies for many months to come. A levy post was established at Kahil, a short distance from Mahadha, but Obaid's attacks and feuding continued. In the spring of 1954 he deprived Sheikh Abdullah of more villages. For a time Abdullah's position looked precarious but, although both Zayed and Abdullah had come up with workable schemes for removing Obaid once and for all, the British held back. The same caution that had restrained them in Hamasa now crept into their dealings with Obaid. In May 1954 the political agent, Christopher Pirie-Gordon, noted that 'Obaid continues to do great damage to our position.'[25]

* * * * *

The oasis was still tense. The rationing system which was meant to ensure that the Hamasa villagers received their essential supplies from the Buraimi *suq* was failing. Saqr controlled the *suq* and, in his desire to make a profit, he had allowed the villagers to buy as much as they wanted, instead of rationing them. The effect was disastrous for the blockade, undermining all the work that the levies were doing to prevent supply caravans getting through.[26]

Pirie-Gordon visited Buraimi and questioned Sheikh Saqr about the rationing system. But the Old Fox was evasive: he was unable to give an estimate of the population of Hamasa and therefore could not say how many people he had been rationing. When it was put to him that people from Hamasa could buy as much as they could afford, Saqr denied this, contending that his control of the blockade was perfect, and blamed the levies for any laxity.[27] The British rejected the obvious solution – of using levy troops to complete the Buraimi side of the blockade – for fear of provoking the Saudis into taking counter-measures. And so it went on, the situation in the oasis deteriorating all the while. To add to their discomfiture, there were signs that all was not well with their ally.

Sheikh Zayed was thoroughly demoralised and running out of patience. Until now, Pirie-Gordon had been able to soothe him with bland statements about negotiations taking place elsewhere, but that particular excuse was wearing thin. 'Zayed is convinced that for reasons of our own we are no longer interested,' he reported to the political resident in Bahrain.[28]

It was hardly surprising. A year before, Zayed had taken matters into his own hands when he attacked and captured a Saudi-backed post at Mazyad at the southern end of Jebel Hafit. It was an important action, securing the southern flank of the Buraimi Oasis and checking Saudi expansion into Oman. The Saudis condemned it as an 'aggressive military action' and even the political resident in Bahrain disapproved, considering Zayed's achievement to be 'ill-advised'. Whichever way Sheikh Zayed turned, it seemed, he could not win.[29]

Something had to be done. Pirie-Gordon had 'sharp words' with Sheikh Saqr and the rationing system was tightened up. Under the old system, the Hamasa villagers had been allowed to visit the *suq* on Wednesdays in order to buy enough provisions for themselves. Pirie-Gordon now persuaded Saqr to cancel two Wednesdays and let only ten men buy goods for the village on the third Wednesday. After that,

Buraimi *suq* with Sheikh Saqr's fort in the background.
(source: Julian Walker)

the same ten men would come over fortnightly to receive ration cards. The only goods allowed were coffee, sugar, flour and rice, and the arrangements would be supervised by a member of the British Agency staff.[30]

But Turki would have none of it. He rejected the new system, claiming that the villagers had enough food to last for 40 years. A camel and several sheep and goats were slaughtered every day at sunset and a free meal given to all comers, it was said. The good times were back. Many tents appeared outside Bait Turki to house the increased number of visitors taking up residence in Hamasa. 50 tribesmen from Sunaina were rewarded with cash payments averaging 50 rupees a head and, at the beginning of May, another 60 arrived. When a British negotiator visited Turki in order to secure the release of two British NCOs who had mistakenly strayed into Hamasa, he was astonished to find a feast sufficient for 120 people under way.[31]

Now it was Sheikh Saqr's turn to complain about the blockade. With supplies being smuggled into Hamasa, villagers could buy goods from their own *suq* rather than going to the Buraimi *suq*, thus depriving Saqr of his profit. Zayed, too, was unhappy about the lax blockade. As a result, two levy posts were moved and a new one was built only a few hundred yards from Turki's house. Levy posts now encircled the village. The levies kept their distance, occasionally returning fire as one or two restless tribesmen took pot-shots at them or tried to break the blockade.

And then a new tactic emerged. The Hamasa villagers began returning to the Buraimi *suq* but, instead of asking for food for 300 – the number of people who the British reckoned were living in the village – they demanded food for 3,000. It was by any standard an outrageous estimate, and their demands were refused. The villagers traipsed empty-handed back to Hamasa. Nonetheless, medical requests were met and medicines were sent to Turki's doctor four days later.[32]

Yet Turki still claimed that the British were starving the villagers by rationing their food and depriving them of medical supplies. The Saudis through Yusuf Yasin pressed their case with the International Red Cross with the result that a representative was appointed to visit and report on the situation in Hamasa. The British, fearing a propaganda show, briefly considered blocking the visit but relented when they realised that such an action might only confirm the worst suspicions of the Arab world. Besides, it was pointed out, the visit would give them a good opportunity to get inside Hamasa and see what conditions were really like.[33]

On 6 July, the Red Cross representative, Pierre de Cocatrix, duly arrived in Buraimi and was met by political officer Julian Walker, along with interpreter Ali Bustani and Captain Criddle of the Trucial Oman Levies. Shortly after 10 a.m., they all piled into Criddle's Land Rover and drove down the wadi leading to Hamasa. About 70 metres beyond Sheikh Saqr's post they met the Syrian doctor from Hamasa, by appointment. Dr Naamani was a tall, gangling man with an aesthetic face and rimless spectacles. He spoke good French. They transferred to Turki's car, an eggshell blue Mercury with weak springs and a tendency not to start, driven by an assistant.[34]

They were driven into Hamasa where a festive crowd of about 400 men, women and children was gathered, comprising Sheikh Rashid bin Hamad and four other sheikhs of the Al Bu Shamis tribe, 20 bodyguards and an array of Duru, Baluchis, Persians and Naimis. The Shamsi sheikhs received the party and, after introductions, suggested that they called on Turki.

At this moment, a crowd of women and children encircled the car and began to shout loudly, 'We are hungry. We went food. We do not want *Ingleez*. We want our King Saud. God save the king.' However, as Julian Walker noted, 'nearly all the crowd was laughing or smiling, and no one looked undernourished.'

An old slave approached de Cocatrix, complaining that the *Ingleez* had killed his son, and showed him an old scar on his knee caused by a levy bullet. Three women came on the left side of the car and cried that they had lost their cattle and been forced to move from their houses because of the *Ingleez* machine guns. To drive home the point, Sheikh Hamad added, 'Look now what *Ingleez* have done to our village and poor subjects.'

They drove on to Turki's house, the horn sounding as they approached, and stopped at Turki's back door. Dr Namani explained that no one had been able to use the front door for fear of being shot from the levy post that stood opposite. Turki appeared with a retinue of Saudi guards in attendance, all of whom carried modern rifles, some of British make. He wore a white silk summer *thobe*, a half silver, half golden sword and presented a formal air. He gave a speech of welcome to de Cocatrix, saying that the Saudis had always been friends with the British and wanted to continue to be so. 'He could not understand what had come between us,' noted Walker. The visitors were bundled through the crowd into Turki's house, where they went upstairs for coffee with a gathering of sheikhs. One of the sheikhs, seemingly bemused by the presence of de Cocatrix, observed 'We are puzzled to see a man from Switzerland, the country of snow and flowers, coming to Hamasa. Our village is situated in the corner of the World.'

After the formalities were over, Dr Namani offered to show the party around the village and meet men who they 'would not believe could exist.' They visited members of the Awamir tribe, true bedouins of the Rub al-Khali, in their settlement of a dozen *barrastis* and tents scattered among the dunes. The sheikh and his relatives, 'like students in a school', began to recite a familiar refrain: 'Ya sahib, we belong to the Saudis, we are hungry, we want food, we love His Majesty our King Saud, we do not want Christians.'

The doctor tried to pass off the Awamir as inhabitants of the village saying that they had lived there for two years. However, he soon admitted that they were in fact bedu who had been forced to settle there because their animals could not graze due to lack of rain that winter. 'They therefore stayed in Hamasa doing nothing while Turki fed them and paid them money.'

The party drove past the front of Turki's house. The opposing levy post was quiet and a large crowd, feeling unthreatened, followed the car still chanting 'we are hungry, we want food, we don't want the *Ingleez*, we love King Saud,' while women surrounded the car screeching and waving in the air their babies who, having proper cause to screech, screeched also. Many curious eyes examined the visitors, and boys tried to ride on the bumper of the car.

The car accelerated away and headed towards the north of the village, passing a building which, the doctor claimed, had been abandoned because of gunfire from the levies. This part of the village was deserted. De Cocatrix was shown four *barrastis* that had been closed up, and one that appeared to belong to an Adeni. 'They were all extremely neat and clean, which was surprising as two of them were occupied by goats,' wrote Walker.

Returning to the car the doctor pointed to a cluster of browning date palms, saying 'look, they even take the water, the very water from us, draining it off into little side channels.' Although a lack of rain might have caused this, a comparison between the Buraimi and Hamasa trees (which were fed by the same *falaj*) appeared to support the doctor's claim that Sheikh Saqr had been diverting some of the water supply from the village. The party drove on to the *suq*, scattering a small herd of goats before them, and visited a shop which was selling herbs. The other shops were closed, including a coffee shop where the walls were pasted with unfaded pages from recent English magazines. The shops, the doctor told them, had been forced to close by lack of supplies but, as a sceptical Ali Bustani noted, the shops of the two merchants supplying Turki were not shown to the party. They came across more houses with their doors closed, some also occupied by goats.

The doctor showed them bullet holes made by the levies who, he told them, fired on the village 'night and day'. He pointed to blocked up windows and doors, saying how people had to use the internal doors and passages between the houses to avoid the levies' gunfire. They visited the dispensary where the doctor kept two pet gazelles which, Walker noted, were 'as yet undevoured by the starving mob.' There was a paraffin refrigerator packed with drugs donated by the British but no fuel to keep it running. On the way back to Turki's house they saw pits dug as shelters against levy bullets, and heard complaints that the villagers were unable to bury their dead because the cemetery was regularly fired upon from the levy posts.

They returned to Bait Turki for lunch. 'Turki must have been in a quandary' wrote Walker. On the one hand, he was bound by the requirements of Arab hospitality to provide a feast. On the other, he needed to maintain the fiction of a village starved by the blockade. He received them at the gate, leading them through the courtyard past bubbling cauldrons filled with stewing meat and, inside, a pot of cooked rice. There was a big pile of palm firewood in the corner of a room, enough for six months of cooking. Turki was 'hospitable and talkative.' He said 'For the first time I am opening the gate of my house. I was compelled to keep it closed for the past 18 months because of bullets.'

They went up to his office where they found his clerks busy writing reports and arranging papers. Then they sat down to lunch which – by Arabian standards – was a modest feast comprising rice topped with two goats, dates, mangoes, limes and watermelons, but no tinned fruit. 'However, we were given to understand that we would be given as much to eat as we wanted, even if the village had to be scoured to discover the means to satisfy our hunger.'

After lunch, a discussion began. They talked about the blockade: Turki refused the British offer to provide enough rations for 300 people and produced a list of 2,400 people living in Hamasa, a figure challenged by the interpreter, Ali Bustani, who claimed it was more like 600. Sheikh Rashid, never one to mince his words, retorted that he would eat all the dates from his plantations, the pith of the stones and the palm trunks, before he would accept rations from the British.

At this moment, Emir Turki resumed a formal air. He produced some notes and began to outline a catalogue of complaints, saying that there had been 441 acts of aggression against Saudi subjects living from Nizwa to Dubai, including: causing abortions and scaring camels and donkeys in the Ibri area with low flying jets; flying four large aircraft low over Hamasa; blocking all supplies from the north and east for three months in 1953; evicting Obaid and his men from the TOL post and Mahadha (Turki produced two paper ultimatums and the remains of mortar shells used in the 'battle'); wounding and killing 41 people; terrorizing the villagers of Hamasa with Very lights; a major driving to within a few yards of Turki's house and then retreating, firing a sten gun; last, the confiscation and sale of goods valued at 150,000 rupees by Major MacDonald of the TOL in the Buraimi *suq*.

In the face of these aggravations, Dr Namani added, the Saudi side had not fired a single shot in the last 18 months. 'M. de Cocatrix appears to have swallowed this remarkable statement,' observed Walker who nevertheless was confident that the real villagers would get adequate food and that Dr Cocatrix's report would 'puncture' Turki's propaganda. The meeting broke up and the party returned to Buraimi, de Cocatrix returning to Geneva to prepare his report and Walker to Dubai to resume his duties.

Meanwhile, Saudi efforts to break the blockade became more determined, leading to armed exchanges and the inevitable exchange of protests. By the end of the month, four blockade runners had been killed, two captured and one camel killed.

All eyes were on the diplomats to come up with a solution but, for those on the ground, there was no end in sight.

Chapter 12
No Oil Man's Land
Oil and Diplomacy, 1953–4

In public, all sides were anxious to downplay the oil issue. 'If questioned about oil you should deny that we are actuated by a desire for more oil,' the Foreign Office advised the consul-general in Muscat.[1] Fifteen months later Aramco's Arabian Research Division was advising on a film about the history of Saudi Arabia entitled *Island of Allah*. During a rough-cut screening, Dr Rentz objected to a scene in which the Aramco geologist Max Steineke says 'Truly, the Arabian Peninsula is the island of the Arab. It is floating on oil.' Rentz felt that it might prejudice Aramco's stance in negotiations with the Saudis who were pressing the company to raise oil production.[2]

In the meantime there had come, at last, some good news for IPC. 'Recently there have been indications that our efforts might be rewarded by the discovery of a field in western Abu Dhabi' IPC Chairman Stephen Gibson informed the Foreign Office.[3] The British ambassador in Jedda was anxious to keep the news quiet:

> Is it too much to ask that our oil company should (a) let it be known discreetly that they have not found anything and (b) suspend work in the whole area pending Saudi agreement to arbitration on terms satisfactory to us? In any event I hope that everything possible will be done to ensure that the Saudis obtain no hint that traces of oil have been found.[4]

It was impossible to keep things quiet, however. Aramco had heard already rumours of an oil strike in Abu Dhabi. Sheikha Salaamah, in her excitement at the 'discovery', had taken a bottle of crude oil to show to her son Zayed in Buraimi. 'So it is virtually certain the Saudis already know about it,' wrote an exasperated Bernard Burrows, the British political resident in Bahrain. The secret was out.[5]

But it was a false dawn. Although the well in question, Murban No. 1, had struck traces of light oil and gas at a depth of about 10,000 feet, promise turned to disappointment. The well proved to be a puzzle for the geologists because they were unable to identify the strata from which the oil had come: a later examination of the well cuttings would eventually reveal the answer.[6] Drilling ended abruptly at a depth of below 12,500 feet when the well suddenly blew out with high-pressure sulphurous gas, killing a petroleum engineer and brittling the drill string. The well was cemented over and abandoned.

The results of the post-mortem showed that the oil show had in fact come from a Cretaceous rock interval known as the Upper Thamama. This would prove to be an important finding, since most of the previous oil strikes in eastern Arabia had been in the Jurassic Arab Zone limestones. IPC continued with its drilling programme elsewhere, heading off to western Abu Dhabi to sink an oil well at a place called Gezira.[7]

By now there were no illusions about the petroleum prospects of the Buraimi Oasis. As early as June 1954 Terry Duce of Aramco was telling the British petroleum attaché in Washington that 'so far as Aramco knew, there was no oil in or near it'.[8] Geologists suspected that big oilfields lay to the west and south-east of the oasis. 'Buraimi is floating on a sea of oil' might have been a popular catchphrase of the day but it was misconceived: the importance of Buraimi was in its strategic location rather than its prospects in oil.

Encouraged by developments in Iran where joint working was being proposed, Eden suggested a consortium of British and American oil companies for eastern Arabia. Stephen Gibson expressed the hope that IPC might obtain an oil concession for the disputed territory even if parts of it went to Ibn Saud. Wishing not to offend their competitors he added a proviso 'with the agreement of Aramco'. He did not, however, wish to go so far as joining Aramco in a consortium, seeing this 'as detrimental to IPC interests all over the Gulf.'[9]

The Foreign Office, as part of a future arbitration agreement, agreed that British oil companies should be allowed into the disputed areas, including any that might go to Ibn Saud. The State Department initially supported this proposal. In a rare moment of accord, Saudi adviser Yusuf Yasin met the British ambassador George Pelham and appeared to support the creation of an oil consortium .[10]

When this news reached Aramco executives, however, they protested loudly, claiming that the British were trying to usurp their legitimate rights. 'Aramco was not prepared to surrender any rights under Aramco's concession,' declared Executive Vice-President Fred Davies. For Aramco there was to be no compromise: if Ibn Saud gained more territory from arbitration, then Aramco's concession area would expand to match it. Aramco's main concern was for the boundaries to be settled and, with this in mind, the company sought to persuade Dulles to support the Saudis in seeking arbitration of the dispute.[11]

At the heart of this controversy were the shadowy manoeuvrings of Yusuf Yasin, who had filled the vacuum left by the death of deputy foreign minister Fuad Hamza in 1951. Yasin's support for an oil consortium surprised the British, who were well accustomed to his antipathy towards them. On the Buraimi dispute, Sheikh Yasin remained dogmatic. 'The question of Buraimi was a matter between the Saudi Arabian government and the people of Buraimi and no one else' was his standard line. Without the controlling hand of Ibn Saud at the helm, Yasin was capable of mischief.[12]

Sheikh Yusuf Yasin, Saudi deputy foreign minister. (source: Gerald de Gaury)

His motivation was plain. Pelham once remarked: 'I am sure that Yusuf Yasin, the Arab nationalist, would gain great satisfaction in attempting to out-imperialise the imperialist.'[13] Daniel van der Meulen was also unimpressed: 'Sheikh Yusuf Yasin seemed to us Europeans moody and morose and fanatically anti-Western. For us he was hard to deal with.'[14] American ambassador George Wadsworth considered that, by holding secret talks with the British over an oil concession, Yasin was seeking to play one side off against the other.[15]

The Saudi ambassador to London, Hafiz Wahba, was an entirely different character. An Egyptian born in about 1890, Wahba had once been deported from India for anti-British activities. In *Leading Personalities* he was described thus:

> He has shown himself well-disposed in London, and has been distinctly helpful [...] Neither taciturn nor talkative, he appeals by his sense of humour and looks anything but a Wahhabi [...] Likes the theatre too, and [is] alleged to have a passion for night clubs to which he gave full rein in New York in 1938.[16]

Those British officials who met Wahba liked him, even when relations between the two governments were tense. Well mannered in his dealings with them, Wahba once apologised for his government's stance against Britain.[17]

These qualities only aroused suspicion among his Saudi peers, and even Ibn Saud playfully referred to him as being 'in the British camp'. Wahba's position in Riyadh was not convincing. He was circumspect in discussions with Sheikh Yasin, giving the impression that he either wanted to distance himself from his government's case or was too timid to speak his mind with others present, or maybe both. British diplomats doubted the extent of his influence in the royal *diwan*.[18]

With Sheikh Yasin scheming in the background, it was difficult to get a direct answer from the Saudi regime. Pelham saw some merit in Wahba's suggestion that the negotiations should be conducted directly with the king, above the heads of his advisers, but recognised that the king's current state of health made this difficult. In his audiences the king was querulous, proclaiming his ancient friendship with Britain and yet tending to refer any discussion back to his advisers, in whom he had complete trust. Pelham wrote: 'I fear that as soon as my back is turned the advisers get busy with Turki's exaggerated reports with which they rouse his ire, swamp him with their own ideas of a solution and obliterate any effect I may have had on him at the moment.' Crown Prince Saud appeared to be friendly but would never commit himself, giving vague answers and referring any queries to Sheikh Yasin.[19]

In September 1953, however, there appeared to be a breakthrough. Hafiz Wahba agreed that Turki could be withdrawn if a joint police force of equal numbers from either side was set up to supervise Hamasa.[20] But the discussions soon became bogged down: should the police force be placed inside or outside the oasis; should the arbitration cover only Buraimi or include the whole area of the dispute? The British demanded that the police post should be outside the oasis; that arbitration should include all the disputed areas except central Oman and that oil operations should continue. And so the arguments went on.[21]

At the beginning of October 1953, tanned and smiling but still looking frail, Anthony Eden returned to his post. He was in a truculent mood: one of his first acts was to ask why Turki was still in residence. While his officials were discussing the options if the Saudis did not remove Turki, options which included using violence or even kidnapping Turki, Eden complained that his officials had not already removed Turki and demanded violent action soon. 'We persuaded him against doing this while we need so much US help in Egypt and Persia' wrote his private secretary, Evelyn Shuckburgh.[22]

On 9 November 1953 Ibn Saud passed away. In their minds the British had rehearsed many possible scenarios following his death: a coup d'état by members of the Al Saud, or possibly tribal warfare leading to the break-up of the kingdom. In the event, the status quo prevailed. Crown Prince Saud assumed the throne, despite worries that his brother Faisal might oppose him. Twenty years before, in a departure from the desert custom of choosing a ruler by consensus, Ibn Saud had designated Saud heir to the throne and later persuaded Faisal to swear that he would not oppose him.[23]

In some ways, Saud resembled his father in appearance and physique. He suffered from eye troubles and had inherited Ibn Saud's magnetic smile.[24] But he was untutored in the ways of international diplomacy and, despite a newly formed Council of Ministers, tended to rely on a small coterie of advisers.[25] A capacity for squandering his country's wealth would quickly emerge as the defining feature of his reign, extravagance and waste the by-words for his profligate regime. On the question of frontiers, Saud was more difficult than his father, Hafiz Wahba advised the British ambassador. He 'genuinely wanted a settlement, but feared that there were many who would regard any concession as a sign of weakness'.[26]

The new king found himself in an awkward predicament. The Saudis had put their faith in Truman's 1950 letter as evidence of Washington's support for their cause, and been rebuffed; they had asked the Americans to mediate the dispute, the Americans had declined; they had asked the Americans to back a plebiscite in the Buraimi Oasis, but the Americans had again declined to do so.[27]

Crown Prince Faisal as foreign minister led the Saudis on the international stage. British diplomats held a grudging respect for the quiet, shrewd and hard working Crown Prince. In *Leading Personalities,* it was noted that Faisal was 'intelligent and has at least had more opportunity than most of his brothers of cultivating his intelligence and powers of observation [...] in the comparatively civilised surroundings of Mecca and has travelled in Europe.'[28] Faisal had settled down since the wild days of his youth. There was an obduracy in his character and an eye for detail that impressed – and sometimes exasperated – those who had dealings with him. Hawk-like was an apt if somewhat clichéd description of his appearance and disposition. He was an astringent figure who came to dominate Saudi foreign policy, first as foreign minister and later as monarch, for the next 20 years.[29]

However, there was little more that Faisal could do in this situation. Saudi forces were not strong enough to take on Britain in open conflict and, with the Americans pushing for arbitration, the Saudis were running out of options. 'There is no difference between a useless friend and a harmless enemy' an embittered Faisal told the Americans.[30] He went on to make threatening noises, cancelling an agreement with them for technical assistance. This, in the American mind, raised the spectre of wider retribution: the Saudis might cancel the Aramco oil concession or the US lease on the airbase at Dhahran. But Washington held its nerve, still seeing some benefit in maintaining the British position in the Gulf, and continued to urge that the two sides go to arbitration.[31]

Faisal was fond of proverbs. He once said: 'A drowning man may clutch at a snake – even a poisonous one – if it is the only chance he has to prevent his going under for the last time!'[32] The Americans interpreted this as being a threat that the Saudis might seek Soviet help but, in reality, this was unlikely. The Saudis, a conservative regime intent on building up an Islamic state united under a king, had little in common with Egypt or Syria whose nationalist urges swayed them towards the communist sphere. Although the Al Saud would become more involved with Egypt as the 1950s went on, their survival depended on the oil wealth continuing to flow. Like it or not, they were anchored to the Americans.

* * * * *

By late 1953 the British were growing uneasy about the activities of Dr Rentz and Aramco's Arabian Research Division. It was apparent that the division was engaged in a vast amount of work preparing the Saudi claim for the Buraimi Oasis. Based in an office in the Aramco building close to that of the chief Aramco representative in Jedda, Rentz himself was friendly to visitors but tight-lipped about the division's activities, raising the suspicions of the British ambassador, George Pelham:

> Rentz's main task is probably to gather and prepare all the historical evidence, particularly that connected with the tribes, which might support the Saudi case. In this he has a very able assistant, Homer Mueller, a leading member of his research team and a more than competent Arabist who has made a special study of the tribes in southern Arabia [...] I do not know what evidence Rentz's department may have collected, but even allowing for tactical bravado I must confess I have been impressed by the confidence which Rentz and Mueller have always shown in the justification which history and present day conditions give to the Saudi claim.[33]

Here was the cause of a profound mistrust between British officials and Aramco, its closeness to the Saudi Arabian government. 'Perhaps the most objectionable of these activities has been the legal, historical and topographical advice which Aramco has furnished in connection with frontier disputes', Pelham complained.[34]

But Aramco shared an interest in these disputes with the Saudi Arabian government, although not to the same degree. As Aramco's

William Mulligan disarmingly put it, the Arabian Research Division was simply helping the Saudis put their case in the same way that the British were helping Abu Dhabi and Oman put theirs.[35]

The rivalry between the British establishment and American oil interests was an old one, dating back to the early struggles over oil concessions for Iraq and Bahrain.[36] The Foreign Office was suspicious of Aramco. The head of the Eastern Department, Derek Riches, remarked that the company had a 'rather evil' personality of its own, quite different from its constituent companies which he found to be more helpful and understanding towards British interests.[37] This outspoken comment probably said more about British insecurity than about the nature of Aramco, but Riches' suspicion did have some foundation. As we have seen, executives of Casoc, the forerunner of Aramco, had played on fears of the imperialist bogeyman to unsettle the US administration during the war years. It was certainly in Aramco's interests to promote a pro-Saudi line in their discussions with State Department officials about the current dispute.[38]

The decline in British influence in the kingdom was all too evident now. British diplomats battled on with their audiences with King Saud – he would pay the usual courtesies, smile sweetly, make reference to the Buraimi 'atrocities' and refer the discussion to his advisers.[39] In the ambassador's opinion, these discussions were often a waste of time, for 'as is always the case when arguing with the Saudis, talk went on for hours, with Yusuf [Yasin] going back and back again into all the old grievances under which he imagines he labours.'[40]

At times, Saud seemed to struggle with even the basic details. When the new British ambassador visited the royal palace at Riyadh on 13 May 1954, the king called for a map and asked where Khawr al-Udayd and Buraimi were. Sheikh Yasin made measurements with a jewelled paper-knife. The ambassador's suggestion that the Saudis might withdraw from Buraimi was met with a burst of derisive laughter.[41]

There was a dangerous edge to all of this. Since IPC had refused to suspend oil operations in the disputed areas, King Saud demanded that Aramco mount an expedition to explore them. It was a risky move because the British might well be provoked into an armed response. Aramco went through the motions, arranging for a survey party of 12 Americans with Saudi guards working near Nibak, below the base of the Qatar peninsula, to strike east towards the coast below Khawr al-Udayd, with instructions to show their faces but not to drill. The company saw it as a face-saving operation, telling their diplomats that the survey was simply a device to mollify King Saud.[42] The State Department was somewhat puzzled by Aramco's stance, and ordered an investigation. In fact, the situation probably reflected a degree of vacillation on King Saud's part with Aramco caught in the middle.[43]

Whatever the explanation, it was a risky enterprise. 'We are expecting a party of Saudi Arabians with some American members of the "Aramco" Oil Company, to make an incursion into Abu Dhabi territory any day now – about 100 strong' wrote Shuckburgh.[44] Diplomats held their breath as, on 31 May, the survey party entered Abu Dhabi territory just south of Khawr al-Udayd. The party continued through the areas known as the Mjann and the Aqal, territory of the Qubaisat section of the Bani Yas tribe, who owed their allegiance to Sheikh Shakhbut of Abu Dhabi.[45]

Bernard Burrows hastily made plans to send a levy force into the area, surround the survey party and immobilise them by shooting out their tyres. But Churchill would have none of it. Shuckburgh noted: 'All plans have been made to eject them by force, but on Monday [...] the PM [Churchill] sent down an order that firearms are not to be used except in self-defence.' This prompted Burrows to remark that 'nothing can be done except a purely formal protest by a district officer which will probably be ignored.'[46] Instructions were duly formulated and a cipher telegram dispatched to the Trucial Coast.

The telegram arrived at night at the Cable and Wireless station in Sharjah. A messenger took the cipher to the political agency in Dubai, driving in the dark along dirt tracks to the creek, where he was rowed across the water to the agency jetty. He then clambered over the compound fence and woke a slumbering guard. Together, messenger and guard tapped on political officer Julian Walker's window. 'Prime Minster says you should on no account fire on the Americans except in self-defence,' read the telegram. The political agent, abruptly woken, exclaimed 'Damn it, this spoils everything!'[47]

On 5 June an RAF aircraft dropped a note on the survey party stating that it was 'committing trespass on territory of Abu Dhabi' and requesting its immediate withdrawal. The party replied that it was operating in the area with the knowledge and consent of the Saudi Arabian government.[48] 'The party left the disputed zone on 9 June at the conclusion of the field season,' an Aramco official noted drily.[49] Whitehall breathed a collective sigh of relief.

* * * * *

On 26 June 1954 a Stratocruiser airliner named Canopus descended through the clouds and touched down at Washington National airport, taxiing to the place where Vice-President Richard Nixon and Secretary of State John Foster Dulles were waiting. A fair-sized crowd had gathered around and polite applause broke out when Churchill appeared at the top of the stairs, looking in better health than he had for several weeks.[50]

After he and Eden had shaken hands with their hosts, they went to the microphones. Churchill, in a reference to his American mother, spoke about coming from his fatherland to his mother's land. Eden spoke about avoiding misunderstandings among the English-speaking family. At a later meeting, Eden was able to reassure the Americans that Britain and Saudi Arabia were moving towards an agreement on arbitration, referring to the negotiations over Buraimi that were drawing to a close in Riyadh.[51]

On 29 July Eden confirmed to the House of Commons that the government had indeed reached agreement with Saudi Arabia over the terms of arbitration. The arbitration tribunal would consist of five members – one nominated by the British, one by the Saudis and three from neutral countries agreed by both parties.

The Arbitration Agreement, as it was known, was a mixed bag of compromises but, on the central issue of Turki's presence in Hamasa, Eden got his way. Turki and his men would withdraw from Hamasa and the Trucial Oman Levies would withdraw from the remaining Buraimi villages. The blockade was lifted, and replaced by neutral zone around the oasis, the so-called Buraimi Zone, defined by a circle 25 kilometres in diameter. This zone was to be patrolled jointly by police detachments of 15 men from each side acting as an peace-keeping force and to prevent any violence erupting in the oasis.[52]

For Turki, it would mark the end of a two-year stay in the village of Hamasa, where he had charmed, suborned and married his way into the local life, and a return to his duties as emir of Ras Tanura. For oil operations, the disputed territory was to be separated into two parts divided by another neutral zone. Aramco would work in the southern part, and IPC in the north with a 'no go' area in between – this became known unofficially as 'No Oil Man's Land'.[53] Britain and Saudi Arabia had six months in which to prepare written submissions and testimonials for the arbitration proceedings that were to be held in Geneva. At last, it seemed, the parties were serious about reaching a settlement of the Buraimi dispute.

As agreed, oil operations ceased in No Oil Man's Land. The days passed much as before in the desert: the breeze sculpting the dunes, sweeping up and depositing grains of sand, building up one dune and eroding another, carrying on its primordial routine, undisturbed by the footfall of man.

Chapter 13
Make it a Red Fire
The Buraimi Oasis and Oman, 1954–5

In July 1954 Captain Peter Clayton of the Trucial Oman Levies was asked by his headquarters to provide a list of the best local tribesmen among the soldiers of his squadron. No reason was given for the request, and Clayton complied without question. His squadron had been deployed in desert outposts for the last six months, and most of the less able men had been weeded out. When they returned to their base in Sharjah, Clayton was put in command of the 15-strong TOL detachment of the Anglo-Saudi Peacekeeping Force under the Arbitration Agreement. They arrived in the Buraimi Oasis on 8 August, a few days before the Saudi contingent came to replace Turki.[1]

Clayton was, like some other officers in the levies, a regular officer in the British Army who had volunteered to join the force. Initially recruited for the Indian Army, an Arabic speaker with knowledge of Arab tribal structures and experience of mobile desert operations, Clayton was well equipped for the role that awaited him. At his first meeting with Sheikh Zayed in Al-Ain, Zayed exclaimed: 'Praise God, we now have someone who speaks Arabic!' This was enough to encourage Clayton to ask Zayed for a flagpole, a red flag (the common flag of Abu Dhabi and Oman in the oasis) and approval of a site he had selected for the joint police camp. This was about one kilometre from Sheikh Zayed's fort at Al-Ain on a gravel plain by the track from Al-Ain to Jebel Hafit, to be known to villagers and soldiers alike as Markaz al-Sarouj. To radio operators on the TOL radio net it went by the name Post 4 with 'Two Alpha Lima' as its call sign.

Meanwhile the incoming Saudi party, led by Major Abdullah bin Nami and comprising four vehicles and 13 men, was struggling across the sands to reach the oasis. They arrived at Nakhla in western Abu Dhabi on 7 August and made contact with a TOL detachment led by Major Eric Johnson who was to show them the remainder of the route. But Bin Nami (as the British called him) wanted to use the track that ran past Dubai and, using his own guides, dispatched a column of vehicles at midnight. They were soon stuck in the sand. The British, anxious to deny the Saudis any opportunity to make a triumphal progress through Abu Dhabi territory, now guided the Saudi column, making sure they avoided any towns or villages on their way. In this respect, their tactics worked.[2]

The party reached Maghaira on the morning of the 8th and spent the day repairing its vehicles. Major Johnson tried to persuade Bin Nami to rest his party for the night, but Bin Nami was unwilling to do so because he was under strict instructions to reach Buraimi by the 9th. The result was a chaotic nocturnal trek, with Johnson reaching the oasis with Bin Nami and only two vehicles. The stragglers arrived two days later, no doubt relieved to glimpse the greenery of the oasis after their long journey through the desert.

Major Abdullah bin Nami presented an impressive figure, impecc-ably dressed in white robes and, on formal occasions, wearing a sheathed sword at his side. The British knew him from his training at the British Military Mission in Taif, Saudi Arabia. 'He is no fool and is not, in my opinion, trying to pull any fast ones,' wrote Clayton on first acquaintance.[3] Although he regularly met and occasionally shared a meal with Bin Nami, Clayton was always careful in his dealings with him. In the event, opinions of Bin Nami were soon changing. Within a few weeks of his arrival, Bernard Burrows was writing that 'whatever his ultimate purpose, Bin Nami is at the present stage making an ostentatious if misleading show of abiding by the rules'.[4]

He arrived with his clerk and Quran reader to the detachment, Abdullah al-Qaraishi. Clayton recognised him from an incident the year before and Sheikh Zayed remembered him from the Dammam conference of 1952. Clayton noted:

> This man is well educated, speaks good French and quite a lot of English, though he tries to hide the latter [...] His briefing is obviously different from Bin Nami's – and so far his behaviour has been that of 'political commissar' attached to the Saudi contingent.[5]

Indeed, Abdullah al-Qaraishi was in charge and Bin Nami was his subordinate: the former was the fixer, the distributor of money, known as the 'Fat Man' among the local people. In time, Clayton cultivated Abdullah by occasionally inviting him to share refreshments

Major Abdullah bin Nami (centre) with two of his men at the Buraimi Oasis.
Initially, relations between Bin Nami and the British were cordial, but they soon
deteriorated. (source: Peter Clayton)

in his hut, which the Saudi was happy to accept. Clayton later claimed
that the arrangement enabled him to gain Abdullah's confidence and
glean details of the goings-on in the Saudi camp and of his relations
with Bin Nami.[6]

The British idea was that, in order to convey a clean break with the
past and to avoid giving the impression that Turki was handing over a
governorship to Bin Nami, the two Saudi parties – incoming and
outgoing – would not make contact with each other. But this finer
point of protocol was of no interest to Bin Nami, who on arrival
headed straight for Turki's house and stayed there for three days and
nights – the traditional period of bedouin hospitality.

That afternoon, Clayton was sent into the village to request that
Turki and his followers leave without delay. Being unsure of the
reception he might find, Clayton approached with stealth, driving

along a wadi bed through the *suq* area and arriving at the entrance to Bait Turki unobserved. The entrance door and its armed guard were on his right hand side so he was able swiftly to get out of the driving seat on that side, say 'salaam alekum' to the guard before he could bring up his rifle, and enter the courtyard. There he found Turki and Bin Nami. He greeted them and, after the usual exchange of courtesies, made his request. There was no immediate response – in fact he would have to repeat it several times over the next three days.[7]

These formal exchanges were occasionally punctuated by episodes of gamesmanship between the two commanders. For instance, both sides were required by the Agreement to set up a joint police camp five kilometres south of Hamasa. On the evening of 9 August, Clayton went with Bin Nami to the site of the camp at Markaz al-Sarouj. Clayton had already marked the spot with the red flag and flagpole supplied by Sheikh Zayed. The Saudis could only manage a short flagpole, but they soon replaced it with a proper flagpole and a Saudi flag that flew higher than Zayed's flag. Not long afterwards, Sheikh Zayed produced an even taller flagpole which was erected at night. The Saudis, Clayton was pleased to note, could not outdo this flagpole.[8]

That was not quite the end of the matter. A few months later a convoy of Muscati supply trucks and troop carriers saw the same red flag flying from a distance, headed for it and – not seeing the Saudi flag on its shorter pole – drove into the Saudi camp by mistake. Bin Nami and Clayton were able to negotiate the convoy's release, but the Saudis were quick to turn the event into a major diplomatic incident. The Saudi radio sets were humming that night with messages flying to and from Dammam.[9]

Three days after Bin Nami's arrival, Turki, having given the last of his feasts and presents, left Hamasa before dawn. His convoy was believed to number 80 people, mostly made up by the wives and children collected by Turki's men during their two-year occupation and returning members of Bin Nami's party. Turki also took Obaid's son and cousin with him but declined to take Sheikh Rashid bin Hamad. As for his own wives, Turki took the Shamsi one with him and left the Awamir one behind, amicably divorcing her.[10]

Turki had declined a British offer of transport and an escort, preferring to use his own vehicles despite the fact that they were unsuitable for desert travel. The convoy struggled on in the August heat through

Abu Dhabi territory on its way towards Al-Hasa. Next day, when there was no news of Turki's progress, the RAF was asked to fly a reconnaissance over the track but the aircraft suffered mechanical failure and the reconnaissance was not completed by nightfall. It was not until the morning of the 15th that the convoy was spotted east of Maghaira. The heat and conditions had taken their toll: Turki was suffering from heat exhaustion and his broken-down Mercury saloon and the rest of his convoy were scattered over 130 kilometres of desert. They were rescued, the trucks recovered and they all continued on their way, crossing into Saudi Arabia on the night of 15/16 August.

On his arrival in Riyadh, Turki was warmly received by King Saud. When told that he could have anything he asked, Turki replied that all he wanted was for God to grant the king long life and happiness. He was appointed as deputy governor of the Eastern Province under Saud bin Jiluwi, with responsibility for labour relations. The Saudis considered his tenure in Hamasa to have been a great success. Judging by the determination of the British government to remove him, they were right.[11]

* * * * *

Shortly after Turki's departure there was an outbreak of banditry, with attacks on caravans and cars travelling along the coast road to Buraimi and the Batinah coast resulting in the deaths of eight people. After local sheikhs threatened to retaliate, the British agreed to set up new levy posts near the trouble spots, and the bandits disappeared, much to the relief of local inhabitants.[12]

Turki had left Hamasa assuring everyone that he would be back in three months' time. He certainly remained popular there, and rumours of his imminent return were a regular feature of life in the oasis. The British naturally saw the matter in a different light: Turki's withdrawal was considered a small victory and a serious loss of face for the Saudis in the eyes of local tribesmen. The travails that Turki had experienced in the desert on his way back to Riyadh were unfortunate, but remained a source of some amusement among the less charitable in the oasis.[13]

Peter Clayton settled down to life in the joint police camp, which was pitched some 200 metres west of the tents where 15 Saudi policemen reposed. Intriguingly, the Saudi detachment included four wireless operators who, for such a small post, seemed to be hard worked, generating much more traffic than their operation might justify.[14] The true nature of their activities, when it emerged, was shocking: the emir of Al-Hasa, Saud bin Jiluwi, was supervising a covert operation to win over – with money and arms – the Omani tribes through a stream of communications with the Saudi post.[15]

The enterprise was conducted on a massive scale. Yusuf Yasin, as minister in charge of activities in the oasis, completed the Saudi chain of command, and even King Saud was implicated. In a series of messages, the king urged Bin Nami to press on with his work. 'We will send you therefore the necessary amount of arms and ammunition to be distributed in a secret way among the inhabitants who support us', read one. 'Encourage the tribes, give them [money], promise them, ask them to be careful to defend themselves and raise their morale.'[16] Sheikh Rashid was the link between the Saudis and tribesmen. He volunteered to approach the tribes of the Dhahira and beyond, which he set about with gusto in the autumn.[17]

At the time, all this was unknown to the British who had their suspicions but no firm evidence. However, some abuses of the Arbitration Agreement were blatant and Clayton's early optimism was soon replaced by a hardened cynicism. He wrote:

> Turki went out and Abdullah al-Qaraishi has come in his place and is living in Aqil's house like the good old days; the money comes in more easily than it did before and in greater quantity; Saudi aircraft come and go at will [...] Turki was cooped up in Hamasa but Bin Nami goes where he pleases.[18]

Meanwhile, the slave trade thrived. In April 1955 Sheikh Zayed reported that a pair of well-known slave traders was preparing to take a group of slaves out to Saudi Arabia: it was believed that Bin Nami himself had bought one of the female slaves and was sending her back to his home in Saudi Arabia.[19]

Bin Nami brought a renewed vigour and a fresh mind to the Saudi campaign. He quickly realised how valuable a prize Sheikh Saqr of Buraimi might be. He recognised the mistake that had been made by favouring Rashid bin Hamad over the Old Fox. On 20 August, less than two weeks after his arrival, he was cabling Saud bin Jiluwi about Sheikh Saqr, saying 'no one has tried to win him over and persuade him so far.' Bin Nami reckoned that, with the change of personnel and a generous cash offer, Saqr might change sides and declare for the Saudis.[20] It was a shrewd assessment.

Sheikh Saqr was spending 1,360 rupees (£2,250 today) to maintain his armed retainers, so Bin Nami asked Bin Jiluwi for funds to match or exceed this amount, to be paid in a secret way. Bin Jiluwi, having gained the approval of King Saud, agreed that 10,000 rupees (£16,500 today) should be sent, immediately followed by an allowance of 3,000 rupees a month to be paid through an intermediary. 'You must be extremely careful not to write him a signed letter,' he wrote to Bin Nami.[21] The money was duly paid to Saqr, whose monthly allowance was raised to 5,000 rupees in October.

It fell to Saqr to demonstrate his gratitude. He raised the green flag of Saudi Arabia over his fort and travelled to his town of Dhank to further the Saudi cause. 'Listen!' he told the townspeople 'I, and all my property, and what I am talking about, belongs first to God and then to Al Saud'. Quite what the people made of this sudden declaration of loyalty to Ibn Saud is not recorded in the official report.[22]

The Saudis now had the three most influential sheikhs of the oasis on their side. While Sheikh Obaid lived in Hamasa he still managed to influence events beyond the village. The establishment of the three new levy posts north and east of Buraimi might have restricted his movements, but in league with Sheikh Rashid he was able to distribute *baksheesh* on a far greater scale than Turki had ever done, about 350 rupees for each recruit to the Saudi cause. 'Obaid remains and will remain a considerable nuisance,' Bernard Burrows observed, echoing the words of Pirie-Gordon a few months before.[23]

Regarding Oman, the Saudis' strategy was simple: if they could demonstrate that tribes beyond Buraimi were loyal to King Saud, the arbitration tribunal might take this into account in its deliberations – and if a pro-Saudi rebellion were raised in those areas, the arbitration process might be by-passed completely.[24] Sheikhs Rashid, Obaid and their tribesmen formed the vanguard of this strategy.

In early October they brought a force of about 150 men to attack the Bani Ghaith, a tribe that was loyal to the sultan of Muscat and Oman. They captured the villages of Hail and Kitna in Wadi Jizzi, occupied the village of Wasit and even threatened the Bani Ghaith stronghold of Rabia. At this juncture, the tide began to turn against them. The *wali* of Sohar, acting in concert with Abdullah bin Salim, repelled the invaders and, by the end of the month, Obaid's men had been cleared from the area.[25]

In November 1954 Obaid and his allies launched another attack, this time on a new levy post at Sbaat at the mouth of Wadi Jizzi, but they were repulsed. Rattled by this and other setbacks, Obaid abandoned his base at Khatwa, leaving his nephew Abdullah bin Salim as undisputed leader of the Beni Kaab. Sheikh Saqr, who had always had a keen eye for the way of things, sensed a shift in the balance of power and stopped flying the Saudi flag from his battlements.[26]

Obaid's next step was a desperate one. He planned to assassinate his nephew, Abdullah bin Salim, and the Saudis gave him their tacit support. Bin Jiluwi cabled Bin Nami:

> In reply to your [cable] 379 referring to the assassination [of] Abdullah and his companions; tell the people mentioned that we have no orders to give them in this matter; and that we have no objection if they wish to revenge their sheikhs who were killed nor do we forbid them to take this course. So do not give them any orders or dissuade them. Be careful about this. God keep you. This is by order of H.M.[27]

Clearly, the Saudi high command was prepared to acquiesce in an assassination attempt – but the plot was never carried out.

The main concern of the British now was the amount of firearms and ammunition being smuggled into Oman from Saudi Arabia. If they had been able to intercept the Saudis' secret signals, they would have been shocked by the scale of the operation: arrangements were being made for arms to be delivered in barrels of paraffin to the coast near Dubai, then carried by camel to the south of the Neutral Zone or to the Wadi Jizzi, while other shipments were being carried by camel across the desert from Al-Hasa – and certainly some of the shipments were getting through.[28]

At the oasis, meanwhile, the game of cat-and-mouse carried on. When the Saudis asked for clearance for a supply flight, the British agreed that aircraft could land outside the Neutral Zone at a place called Kahil, where they could keep an eye on any cargo being unloaded. As the flight approached Buraimi, Bin Nami's men signalled the pilot to land at Kahil as agreed, but the aircraft got 'lost' and landed at Buraimi where a cargo of food and secret arms was unloaded away from prying eyes. Bin Nami confirmed in a secret message to Bin Jiluwi that the open signal to land at Kahil was a decoy, and that he had intended all along that the aircraft should land inside the Zone.[29]

* * * * *

While Sheikh Shakhbut watched events from the relative safety of his palace some 150 kilometres away, Sheikh Zayed was Britain's main ally in resisting the spread of Saudi influence around the oasis. But in September 1954 Shakhbut came under the spotlight when he visited his dangerously ill mother at Al-Ain. The Saudis protested strongly, claiming a breach of the Arbitration Agreement, even though Shakhbut's visits to Al-Ain had been a normal part of life before Turki's arrival. Bin Nami sent a note demanding Shakhbut's withdrawal, but Shakhbut was determined to stay, regarding Bin Nami's demand a grave insult. Shakhbut's supporters were delighted to see him, this being Shakhbut's first visit since Turki's arrival, and they celebrated with feasting.[30]

Pirie-Gordon travelled from Dubai in an attempt to persuade Shakhbut to return to his palace in Abu Dhabi. Shakhbut arrived at their meeting flanked by Zayed and Hazza and seemed on the whole in reasonably good humour but clearly bitter about the Saudi demand. After listening to the request to leave Al-Ain, Shakhbut calmly replied that, if he went back too quickly, everyone would think he was obeying Saudi orders. Eventually, after being reminded that oil company directors were waiting for him back in Abu Dhabi, Shakhbut agreed to depart after a few more days. Zayed sent a counter-protest to Bin Nami and Shakhbut's face was saved.[31]

Perhaps this incident stoked the Saudis' determination to undermine Shakhbut's rule. Not long after Shakhbut had returned to Abu Dhabi, his son Sultan uncovered a Saudi-backed plot against him. Like many of the past troubles in the sheikhdom, it had its roots in the assassinations of the 1920s.

Dhiyab bin Saqr, son of one of the sheikhs who had been assassinated in the 1920s, was living in exile in Dubai. In the autumn of 1954 Dhiyab visited Riyadh with his brother and returned with a large amount of money – possibly as much as 100,000 rupees (£165,000 today). They contacted a local sheikh with the aim of raising a rebellion among the tribes of Abu Dhabi, but Shakhbut heard of the plot and took immediate action. He put armed guards on the causeway leading from the mainland to Abu Dhabi Island and at various points around the town. A curfew was imposed on all land transport and vessels during the hours of darkness. A request was sent to the Political Agency in Dubai for 200 rifles, and the British complied. Fortifications were to be built to guard the entrance to the town, and a number of Shakhbut's tribesmen joined the labour gangs. By Shakhbut's standards, it was a major spending spree and much appreciated by his people.[32]

* * * * *

In January 1955 the arbitration tribunal held its first session at Nice in France. The British, thinking the hearing was to deal with administrative matters only, did not send a delegation to attend but the Saudis had a full team including American lawyer Richard Young, their agent Dr Abdul Rahman Azzam and their representative on the tribunal, Sheikh Yusuf Yasin. It was left to the ex-ambassador to Saudi Arabia, Sir Reader Bullard as the British member of the tribunal, to defend his country's interests.[33]

After the tribunal had agreed on its official title, the Buraimi Arbitration Tribunal, Yasin pressed for neutral supervision of the oasis, alleging that the British had committed numerous breaches of the Arbitration Agreement. Bullard opposed the proposal but held back from making counter-allegations against the Saudis, fearing these might strengthen the case for neutral supervision. At one point Bullard, being concerned that he and Sheikh Yasin were acting as advocates rather than the impartial arbitrators they were meant to be, invited Yasin to retire with him, hoping that the Chairman would 'impose himself on the two other neutrals'. When they returned after some 20 minutes, they found the tribunal members 'all smiles, having accepted a Saudi proposal that each side could arrange up to five flights a month into the oasis.'[34] Bullard was horrified.

The Saudis had an ulterior motive: they planned to use the flights to fly more arms and ammunition directly into the Saudi police post without risk of British detection. In the meantime, all the British could do was catalogue Saudi breaches of the Arbitration Agreement, make their protests, prepare their case and appease their protégés. The next hearing at Geneva in September seemed a long way off.

There was better news from southern Oman. IPC (through its associate company Petroleum Development (Oman) Ltd) had at last found a way to penetrate the interior of Oman and reach the object of their petroleum dreams – Jebel Fahud – without going anywhere near the Buraimi Oasis, approaching it from Duqm in the south. The location of a well site was fixed after intensive field work and meetings in London. Finally, in January 1955, after a boozy lunch at the Fahud oil camp, Chief Geologist F.E. Wellings walked across the desert and light-heartedly marked the spot by urinating on the ground. But – as later events would show – he missed the oilfield by a few hundred metres, and it proved to be the most expensive pee in the history of the oil business. 'If only F.E.'s bladder had held out a few seconds longer!' lamented one observer.[35]

For the time being, however, IPC's star was in the ascendant.

* * * * *

In the same month that Wellings sprinkled the desert, heavy rain fell on the Buraimi Oasis followed by a violent hailstorm which peppered the roofs of the *barrasti* huts of the levy police post. From Hamasa it was reported that a hailstone the size of the cricket ball had hit a camel on the head.[36]

There was no local radio station in those days of course; indeed there were no radio sets in the Buraimi villages. Yet for those in Dubai and Sharjah who could get to a radio, these were interesting times as the shrill voices of Cairo and Damascus Radios dominated the airwaves and condemned imperialism across the Middle East.[37] Nasser's populist, anti-colonialist, anti-Zionist message washed over vast swathes of the Middle East and struck a deep chord with the common Arab. In southern Arabia, its impact was most keenly felt in the oil camps. Many of the camp bosses were of Syrian or Lebanese origin and susceptible to Nasser's propaganda. In one incident Mike Morton, who was working in the Oman desert at the time, found his camp boss lecturing the local workforce and bedouins on their responsibilities as Arab nationalists.[38]

For the British, Cairo Radio was a malign influence, but the lack of available radio sets meant its influence in this part of the world was probably limited. Even so, the imamate tribes of central Oman were ripe for persuasion and it was not long before the Egyptians became involved in another way. In February 1955 an aircraft conveying supplies to the Saudi police post brought an Egyptian army officer to the oasis. Lt-Col. Ali Khashabi then made his way overland to Imam Ghalib of Oman, returning a few weeks later with letters from the imam and Suleiman bin Hamyar addressed to King Saud. And in language reminiscent of Cairo Radio, Bin Jiluwi wrote to Bin Nami 'We have no purpose from this except to work for the unity of Muslims and expel the Imperialist from the Muslims' lands.'[39]

Occasionally, however, Buraimi was a theatre of the absurd. In April 1955 Captain Clayton reported that Saudi drivers had taken to the habit of driving on the right-hand side of the road when approaching Zayed's vehicles which followed the British practice of driving on the left. When Bin Nami had arrived, it was agreed that, since local drivers had been brought up to drive on the left, the Saudis would observe this convention as well. But it did not work, and when Clayton reminded Bin Nami of their agreement, Bin Nami denied all knowledge of it. As a compromise, Bin Nami agreed that his drivers, whether they passed on the right-hand side or not, would 'steer clear of any other traffic'.[40]

One day, Major Bill Little of the levies was lighting a primus stove when he accidentally set light to his barrasti hut, destroying the hut, radio equipment and one of Sheikh Zayed's Land Rovers. The major was left with nothing to wear but his underpants. Bin Nami, when he heard of the fire, offered the use of a tent, bed, bedding and radio, all of which were politely refused.[41]

On a more serious note, Saudi payments continued unchecked. In March, Abdullah al-Qaraishi, made a clumsy attempt to bribe Sheikh Zayed. Speaking 'Muslim to Muslim', he advised Zayed to make overtures to Saud bin Jiluwi before the end of the arbitration proceedings, which in his view were bound to go against Abu Dhabi. If Zayed did make these overtures, his position in Buraimi would be assured and the proceeds from any oil strike in the area would be shared equally between him and Saudi Arabia. 'He [Abdullah al-Qaraishi] did not wish to see Zayed suffering three great losses: one, the esteem of the Arabs, two, the esteem of Islam and three, the loss of [his] country, which three [he] should surely lose if he did not go over to the Saudis.'[42] Zayed declined the offer.

Sheikh Saqr received another pay rise from the Saudis in March 1955, taking his monthly allowance to 7,000 rupees (£11,600 today). In

April, he finally committed himself to the Saudi cause when he supplied a statement saying that he was a Saudi subject. The same procedure was repeated with other bribed sheikhs, all done with an eye on the arbitration proceedings. In May, King Saud issued instructions that Sheikh Saqr should go beyond Buraimi, meet Sheikh Rashid bin Hamad and Bin Nami in secret 'and make it a red fire'.[43]

The Saudis poured more money and arms into the oasis. Realising that supply by air was a simpler method of smuggling than by land, ammunition was flown into the oasis in sacks of rice. One secret Saudi communication cheerfully announced a shipment as if it were a grocery round: 'You are receiving 20 bags of rice, one case cardamom, one case tea, inside all of which are concealed 10,000 rounds of ammunition.'[44]

The overland routes were still being used. In one incident, Saudi gun-runners approached a bedouin camp in an attempt to smuggle arms into the Neutral Zone. The sheikh of the camp later told the story about how he had been alerted to their approach and sent his wife and son over a sand dune armed with sticks and a milking bowl. He instructed them to parade around the nearby dunes holding the sticks like rifles and the boy to wear the bowl on his head as though it were a helmet. When the gun-runners arrived at the camp, the sheikh told them that there were soldiers patrolling the area and therefore, for their own safety, they had better leave the guns with him and make good their escape. The gun-runners did not tarry.[45]

The sheikh, being loyal to Sheikh Zayed, made a report to the levies. Next day Zayed and Captain Clayton visited and found him sitting on a carpet which concealed the haul. There were 21 rifles of British World War I vintage and 2,000 rounds of ammunition. Crude attempts had been made to remove the original Saudi crest of a palm tree and crossed swords from the rifles but they were still visible. The haul was kept in TOL custody for later use as evidence against the Saudis in the arbitration proceedings.[46] It was reported that the gun-runners had come by dhow from Dammam, landing at Dubai and making their way to Buraimi overland.

In June 1955 the bedouin arrived en masse. They came out of the desert and camped in and around Buraimi, creating a carnival-like atmosphere as they merrily signed the usual declarations of loyalty to Saudi Arabia to receive free meals and a few bags of rice. Bin Nami reported that 'the arrival of the tribes at the oasis has impressed our

enemies very much. The people imagined that there is a certain move
or recruitment or preparation for a general war against [...] Zayed and
the collaborators of the British.' However, he cautioned, 'Please note
that the sheikhs of these people deserve more than what is allocated to
them and we will do for them everything possible which will ensure
our interests.'[47]

King Saud responded: 'Pay these people and treat them very well.'[48]
And yet, despite these blandishments, Muhammad bin Salimin, who
had switched sides several times, switched again, declaring his
allegiance to the sultan of Oman. Bin Nami was astonished: 'One
cannot tell when the people of Oman are telling lies or speaking the
truth.'[49]

Despite Bin Jiluwi's plans, the 'red fire' came to nothing. The
Omani tribes stayed loyal to Sultan Said and Sheikh Saqr did not
answer the call to arms. All across the area, sheikhs had realised that
they could take their money from the Saudis without having to do
much in return – a win-win situation for them.

But the Saudis were determined to succeed. They were flying more
of the disaffected from Hamasa to Riyadh, where they could be feted,
and bringing extra officials into their police post on the return flights.
By July, it was reported to the Foreign Office that the Saudi police
post had grown to 18 members in residence compared with 15 as
stipulated by the Agreement.[50]

Hamasa was in a deceptively tranquil state. Abdullah al-Qaraishi
had married a Hamasa girl and was living in the village, apparently to
be close to his mother-in-law. Rumours reached British ears that Major
Bin Nami was trying to buy land in Hamasa: Captain Clayton
reported that the major and a number of his men had gone into the
village to see if they could buy plots with a view to building houses for
themselves. Ironically, they were unable to make a purchase because
there was no land for sale – Turki's party had already bought up all the
available plots.[51] Meanwhile the villagers carried on with their lives in
the traditional way.

The struggle went on around them. While daily routines were
being performed, the precariousness of the situation was easy to forget.
But that changed on the afternoon of 8 July when a fire broke out in
the village, starting near Bait Turki and spreading quickly to nearby
houses. A strong westerly wind fanned the flames and a dense pall of
black smoke filled the sky. About 100 houses were gutted and two

women were reported dead. Sheikh Rashid fled the scene to stay with
Sheikh Saqr in Buraimi while the Saudis, perhaps fearing a reaction to
their presence, kept a low profile. Some of the villagers deserted the
village. 'Since the fire,' a TOL officer reported, 'there has been a steady
dribble out of Hamasa – throughout last night there was a steady pad-
pad of camels etc going south.'[52]

The British put together a relief convoy in Sharjah that carried
1,500 blankets, 500 sleeping mats, clothing and material for 50 *barrasti*,
but it was prevented from entering the village. There was talk of a
Saudi relief convoy coming from Dammam but nothing ever arrived.
The rejected British supplies were used in December to help hundreds
of people in Dubai made homeless by a fire there.[53]

In August, Abdullah al-Qaraishi's attempts to win over Sheikh
Zayed grew increasingly bold. An emissary offered Zayed a new car
and 40,000 rupees, which Zayed refused. Then Abdullah made Zayed
an astounding offer of 400 million rupees (£663m today) from the
proceeds of any oil strike in the disputed areas. At the end of the
month, shortly before Zayed departed for Geneva, a Saudi emissary
offered him a gift of three pistols. On each occasion Zayed stood
firm.[54]

Even as the tribunal was gathering, the Saudis were ignoring British
protests with impunity. More worryingly for the British, evidence was
emerging that the Saudis and Egyptians were working to undermine
the sultan's rule in central Oman in order to establish an independent
state under the imam. The Foreign Office received a report that two
Egyptians had arrived at the oasis by air and travelled to Nizwa in
central Oman with 100 rifles and three *lakhs* of rupees (£500,000 today)
to raise an army for the imamate cause.[55]

On 9 September, another Saudi aircraft landed in Buraimi without
clearance, again in breach of the Arbitration Agreement. To make
matters worse, Turki's former assistant in Hamasa, Aqil, was on board
and, as would later transpire, brought with him 100,000 rupees
(£165,000 today) for the imam of Oman.

For the British, it was an alarming turn of events, since Aqil's
arrival in the oasis suggested an unwelcome return to the days of
Turki's occupation. They duly protested; the Saudis acknowledged the
protest and agreed, without any counter-protest, to withdraw Aqil as
soon as they could.[56] There was one important difference now, of
course: the tribunal hearing was about to begin.

Chapter 14
The Buraimi Arbitration Tribunal
Geneva, September 1955

One night in August 1954, shortly after Bin Nami's arrival in the oasis, Sheikh Zayed and a few of his companions were swimming in a pool while the rest of his men sat around on the bank. As Zayed swam, a pale blue American limousine with its headlights blazing appeared on the track that ran alongside the pool, heading towards the police post at Hamasa. The car drove past but then stopped and turned around, approaching the pool and shining its lights directly at Zayed. He shouted to the driver to put them out. Zayed's men recognised one of the men in the car as 'The Fat Man', otherwise known as Abdullah al-Qaraishi, the clerk in charge of Saudi operations at Hamasa.[1]

What happened next was a matter of dispute. According to Zayed, the car stopped for a few moments and then turned away; there was no conversation between the occupants of the car and Zayed or the tribesmen gathered on the bank. The Saudi told it differently. According to his version, Zayed said 'Come on in, get in the water' whereupon he took off his clothes and went into the water. Zayed waved his retainer away and struck up a conversation: 'How are you, how is your government and how is everything?' The Saudi replied 'By the grace of God, everything is good.' Then they talked about the situation in Hamasa and, according to Abdullah, Zayed expressed the wish to be free of British control. Then they moved on to discuss the terms by which Zayed might come over to the Saudi side. The meeting ended on amicable terms, with Abdullah promising to be in touch, and then departing.[2]

It now seems inconceivable that Sheikh Zayed, after everything that had happened in the past, would have betrayed his brothers' trust and sold out to the Saudis. Abdullah's claim was one of many made during the arbitration hearing. 'Abdullah al-Qaraishi is a notorious liar,' Zayed told the tribunal. But Abdullah's allegations were not so easily dismissed, and he would prove to be a clever and plausible witness.

The long-awaited hearing was held in the building which leading counsel for the British side, Sir Hartley Shawcross QC, described as the 'old and rather shabby town hall.'[3] Yet those approaching the building for the first time could not fail to be impressed by its solid stone construction, part of which dated from the fifteenth century. It was a far cry from the flimsy *barrastis* and crumbling mud-brick towers of the Buraimi Oasis.

For the sheikhs this must have seemed a strange transition, having been uprooted from their desert wilderness and whisked to Europe. They had passed through Rome on 1 September 'a bit bewildered by the length and speed of their journey, [but] quite happy' the British ambassador wrote. 'The only thing that seems to have troubled them was that they could not discover where north was, with the consequence, as Hazza told me, they said their prayers towards America instead of Mecca.'[4]

Captain Peter Clayton, himself a witness before the tribunal, looked after the sheikhs during their stay in Geneva. There were four of them: Sheikhs Zayed and Hazza from Abu Dhabi, and Sheikhs Sultan bin Surur and Mana bin Muhammad of the Dhawahir tribe. They had been instructed to appear in their robes with their daggers in order to bring out the nationalist sympathies of tribunal members. However, they attracted much attention on their strolls through the city. A visit to the circus proved to be unwise when they were invited to participate in the ring. They avoided any high profile excursions after that, as Clayton and his assistant Ali Bustani kept a closer guard on their charges. There was something of the spy novel in their situation since, having been warned by 'other sources' to watch out for possible motor car accidents involving the sheikhs, Clayton and Bustani had to walk on the outside of pavements to protect them.[5]

The delegations came to Geneva with serious intent. They arrived with boxes of evidence and the bound memorials that summarised their cases and included key documents. The *Saudi Memorial* prepared by Dr Rentz and his colleagues comprised three volumes and that of the British prepared by Edward Henderson and others two volumes, with maps submitted by both sides. They were formidable examples of scholarship and research, containing a vast amount of information about the geography of the area, the tribes, tax registers, the legal arguments and history of the dispute. They were true memorials, monuments in their own right, living on both as evidence of the respective claims and as works of meticulous scholarship, valuable long after the arbitration proceedings were over. Indeed, they are the one reason why we know so much about the region today.

* * * * *

The British delegation booked in at the Hotel Beau Rivage and used a sitting room as an office with a cipher officer on hand to transmit long encoded telegrams to London. The Saudis were lodged in the Hotel des Bergues. The British member of the tribunal Sir Reader Bullard stayed with the president of the tribunal in the Hotel de l'Ecu.[6]

At the time of the hearing, Bullard was the director of the Institute of (formerly Colonial) Commonwealth Studies. He was the son of a London docker who had joined the Levant Consular Service in 1906 and had become a specialist in Arab, Turkish and Persian affairs before ending his diplomatic career in 1945 as British ambassador in Tehran. More pertinent to his work on the Buraimi tribunal was the fact that he had served as British minister to Saudi Arabia. Between 1936 and 1939, when he had been based in Jedda, he had become acquainted with Ibn Saud and his ministers, including Sheikh Yusuf Yasin. Now, some 16 years later, this acquaintance was to be revived as Sheikh Yasin took his place as the Saudi representative on the Buraimi Arbitration Tribunal.[7]

Bullard was short and stocky, with a craggy face and deep set eyes. He gave an immediate impression of rugged solidity. He was 69 years old when the tribunal began its deliberations and, although his standing was high in the Middle East, not everyone on the British side approved of him as their choice on the tribunal. 'I had heard that the Abu Dhabi people had expressed a strong hope that our arbitrator would not be an old man' Bernard Burrows wrote to Evelyn Shuck-burgh, Eden's private secretary at the Foreign Office, who laughed it off. 'I thought the Arabs respected grey hair!' he replied.[8]

However, apart from some anxiety about Bullard's age, there seemed to be nothing to worry about. Bullard ticked all the boxes – an ex-diplomat with a wide experience of the Middle East, respected in the Arab world, fair-minded and reliable. Even so, Burrows remained doubtful that he was the right man. In March 1955 he was again voicing his doubts about Bullard, finding his attitude 'disturbing'. At a conference in Beirut, Bullard had told an anthropologist who was doing some research along the Trucial Coast that, as an arbitrator, he would have to be strictly impartial and could not take sides. This seemed a harmless remark – one would have expected an arbitrator to make fair decisions – but it alarmed Burrows. He thought that Bullard should be Britain's advocate on the tribunal, fearing that, if the British position was not 'forcefully argued' in the tribunal's deliberations, the decision would go against them.[9]

At the heart of the British side was a distinct nervousness about the strength of their case. As far back as January 1954, Martin Buckmaster, the British political officer in Abu Dhabi, had warned: 'There is, I think, a distinct risk that the arbitration tribunal will refuse to consider the Buraimi circle *in vacuo* and lend a sympathetic ear to a Saudi request for a corridor from Buraimi to the Rub al-Khali, based on the allegiance of the intervening tribes – Duru, Naimi, Al Bu Shamis etc'. He was not alone in harbouring doubts.[10]

Officials in the Foreign Office looked to Bullard as their advocate on the tribunal. 'The idea that Sir Reader Bullard, KCB, KCMG, CIE, would not favour our case seems odd to me' wrote one official in the margin of Burrows' letter.[11] But this was a grave misconception about the role of an arbitrator, a role that Bullard understood perfectly well. He had no intention of being the British government's stooge on the tribunal. 'I could recall several instances in the history of arbitration where the British member of the tribunal voted against the case put forward by his own government, and I realised that it might fall to me to do so,' he later wrote.[12]

The Saudi representative on the tribunal was Yusuf Yasin. He was actively involved in the Buraimi dispute, being deputy foreign minister, in charge of the Saudi operation in Hamasa and, ultimately, boss of one of the key witnesses, Abdullah al-Qaraishi. But he had no qualms about representing his country on the tribunal. He had already demonstrated his loyalty to the Saudi cause, commendable in a politician, perhaps, but not in an arbitrator on an international tribunal – for him, the distinction between the two roles seemed non-existent.[13] The puzzle is that, faced with his presence on the tribunal, the British did not object to his appointment at an early stage.

One explanation is the British were so confident of their case that they did not feel it necessary to object but this seems implausible. Perhaps they said nothing because they wanted an escape hatch, a pretext for collapsing the tribunal if the proceedings went against them. Whatever the explanation, officials kept quiet and put their faith in Bullard to play Sheikh Yasin at his own game. As we have seen, Bullard had other ideas with the result that a wide gap formed between his expectations and those of the British delegation. This would have a crucial impact on the proceedings.

On the British side, Sir Hartley Shawcross presented the case for the United Kingdom on behalf of the sheikh of Abu Dhabi and the sultan of Oman. Professor Sir Humphrey Waldock, an expert in international law, assisted him. Shawcross was respected as one of the finest advocates of his generation. A dapper dresser with dark wavy hair, he spoke with a grave yet melodious voice in the courtroom. He was already well known on the international stage for his role as lead prosecuting counsel at the Nuremburg trials. He had also been Attorney General in the post-war Labour government. He had remained active in the court room, prosecuting high-profile traitors, spies and murderers. In one trial, a witness famously answered him in cross-examination: 'You're trying to trick me into telling the truth.'[14]

Sir Hartley Shawcross, QC.
(source: Yale Joel, Time & Life Pictures/Getty Images)

When the British were considering their team for Geneva, the name of Wilfred Thesiger cropped up. At first blush, he appeared well qualified to assist the British delegation, since his knowledge of southeastern Arabia and its tribes was unique. But there were grave doubts about whether he could be relied upon to support the British case for the sultan of Muscat and Oman. It was said that Thesiger was an advocate of the happy savage theory and believed that the tribes should be allowed to wander freely. Since he thought that oil development should be banned, Thesiger might 'give us more trouble than help' wrote Shuckburgh. In his place, Edward Henderson of IPC was chosen to assist in preparing the *UK Memorial*, and was duly seconded to the Foreign Office.[15]

The oil companies stayed in the background. IPC paid Shawcross's legal fees 'which were more generous than those normally paid by the British government', and an IPC legal adviser, Robin Dunn, acted as junior counsel.[16] Aramco had funded the research on the Saudi side, and now retained the services of Richard Young, one of the lawyers who had worked on the *Saudi Memorial*, to represent Saudi Arabia. Young was described as 'highly intelligent and a likeable person with a quick mind'.[17]

Captain Clayton had been warned to be wary of Saudi representatives trying to pump him for information in apparently harmless conversation and, sure enough, at a drinks reception held by the British delegation at their hotel, he was approached by Richard Young, who introduced himself and engaged in the customary small talk. They were soon joined by George Rentz and Yusuf Yasin, who surrounded and cornered him. Their questions had an edge, aiming to discover the depth of Clayton's knowledge of and involvement in the Buraimi affair but Clayton, affecting the appearance of the innocent soldier, gave little away before he was rescued by Robin Dunn who had been keeping an eye on him.[18]

On the Saudi side, lawyer Dr Abdul Rahman Azzam, led the delegation. An Egyptian nationalist known for his strong pan-Arab views, Azzam was the first secretary-general of the Arab League, a body created in 1945 to co-ordinate the political aims of Arab countries, until 1952. He went on to represent the interests of Saudi Arabia in the Buraimi dispute well into the 1960s. Once described as a 'King Saud's trusted trouble-shooter', he was a suave political operator who moved easily through the diplomatic world.[19]

Professor Manley O. Hudson of Harvard Law School completed the Saudi legal team. Hudson was a Bemis Professor of International Law at Harvard University, and a judge at the Permanent Court of International Justice. In 1944 he had set down principles of international law that were later incorporated in the United Nations charter. He had already been closely involved in Aramco boundary discussions with US State Department officials.

Charles de Visscher, a Belgian judge on the International Court of Justice in The Hague, was the tribunal chairman. In addition to Bullard and Yasin, there were two other members, Pakistani lawyer Dr Mahmoud Hasan and Cuban jurist Senor Ernesto di Dihigo.

Looking at the tribunal from the floor of the court room, Bullard was on the left nearest the witness box. Beside him sat di Dihigo, with the chairman in the centre, Hasan and Yusuf Yasin next in line. The British team sat to the left in the well of the court and the Saudi team to the right. Each delegation provided a verbatim translator, a Lebanese lecturer and an Egyptian school teacher respectively.[20]

The start of proceedings was delayed when Dr Hasan did not arrive. Urgent messages located him in Dacca, Pakistan – he had apparently just returned from a pilgrimage to Mecca. But, in his reply, Hasan indicated that he wanted two weeks' notice and could not attend the tribunal until October. Foreign Office legal adviser John Simpson noted:

> It cannot be ruled out that Hasan's absence has been arranged by the Saudis, still less that they will arrange for him to stay away. We must therefore consider what we can do to retrieve the situation if as a result of Hasan's continuing absence we are not allowed even to have our evidence placed on record.[21]

Not that the British delegation were too concerned at this stage. The delay gave them valuable breathing space, allowing officials to work up the case against Saudi Arabia more thoroughly and to have discussions with the Abu Dhabi sheikhs. 'This expedition to Geneva has for the first time enabled me to get the points of view of Sir Hartley Shawcross and Professor Waldock as to our prospects of success in this arbitration', Simpson noted.

The *Saudi Memorial* left no room for doubt that the 'self-determination of peoples' was their strong argument. In Simpson's view, it was imperative to counter Saudi attempts to manufacture evidence of the wishes of the local population to belong to Saudi Arabia. 'A defeat at this session, or even an unsatisfactory result, could be disastrous.'[22]

Both sides based their claims on precedent. The Saudi Arabian government maintained that the inhabitants of Buraimi had become Wahhabis at the beginning of the nineteenth century, paid taxes to the rulers of the Nejd and recognised Saudi sovereignty. It admitted that continuity of rule was broken by Egypt's occupation of the Nejd in the early decades of the century, and by the demise of the Saudi dynasty towards its end, but asserted that its rule had been effective in the 1850s and 1860s and again in the last 50 years. It demanded that the inhabitants be allowed to express their feelings through a plebiscite which they believed would be in its favour.

The British government based its case on the Anglo-Turkish conventions of 1913 and 1914. It also relied on the fact that the rulers of Abu Dhabi and Muscat had carried out many administrative acts in the disputed territory without challenge. It pointed out that the current Saudi territorial claim amounted to a massive extension of their 1935 claim. It rejected the idea of a plebiscite because of the effect that Saudi bribery would have had on the fairness of the result. However, it accepted that the dispute should be settled because the two governments had been close and friendly in the past and must surely be close and friendly in the future.

The British planned to strike at the weakest point in the Saudi case, their use of 'bribery'. Although the hearing at Geneva was a preliminary one (the final hearing was planned for the following year), they planned to use it to launch a pre-emptive attack. At this stage they had not uncovered the full extent of Saudi activity in and around the oasis. Nonetheless, they reckoned there was enough evidence to demolish the Saudi case before it reached the final hearing.

Thus on 5 September Shawcross informed the tribunal (still lacking the Pakistani representative) that the United Kingdom would be making grave allegations against the Saudis. Dr Azzam did not admit the allegations of bribery, simply admitting that the Saudis might have been too 'generous'. He made unspecified allegations of 'British murder and use of force in Oman'. This was, according to Shawcross, like defending oneself by accusing the police.[23] On that note, the tribunal adjourned to await the arrival of the Pakistani member.[24]

Dr Hasan arrived on 10 September. At a press conference, he denied showing any discourtesy. There might have been some confusion about dates, he said, but he was shocked at the suggestion that he had gone to Mecca for anything other than religious reasons. He had only seen the king once, at a great dinner for foreigners when there were some 600 other guests present. No one could possibly bribe him, he claimed.[25]

Shawcross opened the case for the United Kingdom at 10 a.m. on Sunday, 11 September. The main charges against the Saudis, he told the tribunal, were of attempting to subvert local sheikhs and notables by systematic and wholesale bribery. There were other complaints about the size, location and activities of the Saudi police detachment and gun-running, all alleged breaches of the Arbitration Agreement.

The first witnesses were called in the afternoon. Sheikhs Zayed and Hazza gave evidence of Saudi attempts to bribe them and Clayton told the tribunal about Saudi bribery and gun running. At the request of the Saudi delegation, their cross-examination was held over until the following day. At 5 p.m. the proceedings were suspended for a few minutes to allow the Muslims present to turn towards Mecca and pray, and then continued until 7.20 p.m.[26]

When the proceedings resumed on the afternoon of the 12th, the Saudis complained about a report in the previous day's *Times* newspaper which, the Saudis claimed, must have been based on information supplied by the British delegation. This the British denied but they were highly embarrassed by a map accompanying the report that appeared to show Saudi Arabia having access to the sea at Khawr al-Udayd – a territorial gain that the Saudis, ironically, would have been happy to accept. The rest of the day was taken up with the cross-examination of Sheikhs Zayed and Hazza, the full evidence of the two Dhawahir sheikhs, and the cross-examination of Clayton. The Saudi team made little impression on the witnesses, all of whom appeared unshaken by cross-examination.[27]

Next day Abdullah al-Qaraishi took the stand. Flatly contradicting the testimony of the British witnesses on the issue of bribery, he appeared to be a credible witness until he let slip the fact that he had been briefed by Sheikh Yasin. Sheikh Yasin, he explained, had met him at the airport two days before because he was shocked by the accusations of Saudi bribery and wanted an account from his subordinate. On this evidence, Yasin had a pair of clean hands.

On the British side, this was considered an absurd suggestion –
Abdullah al-Qaraishi would never have dared to bribe the local
population of Hamasa without the prior knowledge and approval of
his paymasters and Yasin in particular. They concluded that the real
reason for Yasin's meeting with his minion at the airport was to coach
him before he gave evidence to the tribunal.[28]

At this moment, the Saudi case began to teeter. Yasin openly
admitted that he was the minister responsible for affairs in Buraimi
and accepted responsibility for the acts of Abdullah al-Qaraishi. At one
point, he caused astonishment by passing a note to the Saudi
representative, Dr Azzam, during the proceedings. Yasin appeared to
be directing the Saudi Arabian case while acting as a judge upon it. The
president of the tribunal hinted that the proceedings might have to be
aborted. Although the proceedings continued, the British were now
confident of a favourable outcome. In their view, Sheikh Yusuf's
conduct simply confirmed to tribunal members what the British had
been saying all along: that the Saudis had no concept of international
standards of probity and partiality.[29]

Shawcross made the most of it, writing afterwards that 'The
evidence of the only witness called by the Saudis was most discredited
by cross-examination [...] I think a British judge would have found the
charges made by us were substantially established.' But even Shawcross recognised that this was not an English criminal court dealing
with criminal charges, and that an international tribunal would
approach the matter in a different way. On a purely judicial basis the
British case might seem watertight but in the anodyne world of
international tribunals there was another influence at work: the spirit
of compromise.[30]

Bernard Burrows summed it up well:

> I cannot help feeling that when the arbitrators are finally
> presented with the two cases they will find the evidence so
> complicated, so conflicting and so inconclusive that they will
> take decisions on very broad lines, probably with the general
> object of making a compromise between the two positions.[31]

Even Shawcross felt that it would be difficult to persuade a tribunal to
make a finding of bribery and corruption against a Sovereign State.
Tribunals had a tendency to shrink from such findings because they

wished to maintain amicable relations with the parties, allowing an arbitration to run its full course.[32]

This was where Sir Reader Bullard, with his vast experience and forceful presence, was meant to make a difference. But Bullard's conduct on the tribunal was causing concern among the British delegation. The Foreign Office legal adviser, John Simpson, was in despair:

> I have regretfully come to the conclusion that I must make a firm recommendation that, unless it is to be assumed that this tribunal is to break down anyway, Bullard ought to be replaced before we go much further.[33]

One concern was Bullard's understanding of the procedure and issues in the case. Simpson wrote:

> Our star witness, as you know, has been Sheikh Zayed. He finds everything very strange as he has only once before been in Europe. We all realised that giving evidence would be a nerve-racking experience for Zayed and had evolved a plan to make it as easy as possible for him. Bullard, with wholly unnecessary and ill-timed questions as to why the witness had not taken the oath in the Quran, shook Zayed very much at the outset of his examination in chief. Counsel were incandescent with rage over this incident.[34]

In the eyes of the British delegation, Bullard had also acted unwisely in his relations with Dr Hasan. He had travelled with Hasan to Oxford in order to help get his son a job with a firm of chartered accountants. Any fraternising with Hasan was clearly dangerous since any help given to Hasan in England might compromise the British case. Yet Bullard seemed blind to the repercussions: 'We have not been able to get him to see this,' remarked Simpson.[35]

Outwardly, Shawcross remained confident of winning the case but doubts were creeping in. The evidence of his witnesses, once solid, seemed shaky. Captain Clayton's evidence had been mostly hearsay, he noted, and the sheikhs' evidence was not always impressive, owing to their nervousness and unfamiliarity with the procedure.[36]

The parties made their closing speeches on the 15th and the tribunal retired to deliberate. As both sides sat around waiting for a decision, word came out that the tribunal wanted the parties to meet in the presence of Bullard and Sheikh Yasin in order to discuss arrangements for land access by the Saudis to the Buraimi Oasis. This was a worrying turn for the British, who saw land access as a major concession to the Saudis: in practice, it meant more opportunities for the Saudis to bring in arms and money into the oasis. The British delegation immediately tried to block the move by dispatching a letter to the tribunal, drawing attention to Yasin's improper conduct.

Events were now moving towards an ill-fated conclusion. Shawcross recalled:

> Later in the day, Sir Reader asked urgently to see the UK delegation, which up to this time had kept reasonably aloof from him. He stated that the president had indicated that he and the other 'neutral' members of the commission [...] had decided that the bribery charges were not established and he expressed surprise that the UK had ever brought such charges since (in his view) they could not be proved. He also thought the charge of gun running was not proved. He considered the evidence of Captain Clayton was to be discredited because he was a 'political officer'. He thought neutral supervision should be set up over the air service provided by both sides.[37]

Bullard reminded his colleagues that he had twice complained to the president about Sheikh Yasin's conduct, without avail. And then he delivered his bombshell: he was thinking of resigning from the tribunal because of Yasin's conduct.

The British were in a corner. The failure of the bribery allegations would leave them susceptible to accusations of colonialism by trying to suppress the natural right of Arabs to determine their own destinies. The delegation could battle on with the arbitration but the fact that the tribunal had decided against them on such a fundamental issue did not bode well. Paradoxically, Bullard's offer to resign gave them hope. If Bullard resigned because of Yasin's interference with the tribunal's deliberations, the British could derail the proceedings before the tribunal delivered its verdict.

Thus it happened that, with the tacit approval of the British delegation, Bullard resigned. Shawcross helped him to compose a statement in which he took issue with Sheikh Yasin's impossible position on the tribunal. The statement was released to the press with a rider that the resignation did not put an end to the arbitration process – the delegation hoped that it would have the opposite effect.

And so it did. When the tribunal reconvened on 16 September Dr Visscher announced that in the absence of the UK member no further proceedings were possible and no decision could be given. He remarked that all had known Sheikh Yasin's position from the outset but nevertheless he 'appeared to feel' sympathy for Bullard.[38]

Shawcross replied that this was 'the most distasteful case he had ever been in.' He went on: Bullard's resignation had been entirely right and Sheikh Yasin, being minister in charge of Saudi operations at Buraimi, had been wrong to sit on the tribunal. Yasin would have to go. Although the tribunal could not make a decision in its present form, the arbitration process was not over. The British government would consult its client rulers and consider its position.[39]

But Dr Azzam would have none of it. He expressed surprise at Bullard's resignation, and could not understand his reasoning. It had been perfectly obvious to everyone from the start what Yasin's role had been. Had not the sheikh negotiated with the British about the frontier for the past 25 years? The Saudi Arabians had wanted a plebiscite, but the British had insisted on arbitration. Azzam suspected that the British did not wish to continue with the arbitration: they had tried to divert it with their accusations of bribery, launched a press campaign and prepared the ground to sabotage the proceedings. The Saudi Arabians, he assured the tribunal, would do anything for a peaceful settlement.[40]

Shawcross denied the Saudi claims. He reminded the tribunal that the charge of bribery had first been made on 28 May and the Saudis had not replied to it. The president then suspended the proceedings and urged the parties to continue with arbitration in 'a new spirit' at a later date. On this note, the Geneva hearing ended.[41] Since the tribunal was no longer properly constituted and could not continue its work, it could not deliver its decision on the bribery allegations.

For the British, this seemed a good outcome. 'I think it can be said that we have emerged unscathed from an awkward predicament,' wrote Evelyn Shuckburgh.[42] Taking the blame for breaking the proceedings was a small price to pay, and the disagreeable consequences of an adverse finding had been avoided. All that remained was to win the propaganda battle in the wider world.[43]

In theory, the parties were free to select new members to form a reconstituted tribunal to determine the boundaries, but the chances of that happening looked increasingly remote. Sheikh Yasin gave a press conference and reiterated the allegation that Sir Reader Bullard had resigned on the orders of the British government in order to force the suspension of the tribunal. He was astonished that, at this late stage, anyone should have objected to his presence on the tribunal. He refused to resign.[44]

Thus the Saudis, no doubt aware of the tribunal's favourable deliberations, continued to support arbitration. They closed their eyes to the fuss caused by the British accusations of bribery, sticking to the line that giving gifts to local notables was traditional and that their only crime was in being over-generous. As the Saudi ambassador to London put it, 'no Saudi, not even the king, knows what a million is, so that if they said to someone we will give you £30 million, it meant merely 'we'll give you 30 big piles of money.'[45]

The British considered their options. Under the Arbitration Agreement they could appoint a new arbitrator in Bullard's place or, in default, the International Court could appoint one. But despite their public declaration of support for the arbitration process, they did not really have their hearts in it any more. If the arbitration went ahead, there was a good chance that they would lose since Shawcross and the officials had no faith in the tribunal delivering a fair verdict. They were 'staggered by its incompetence and resistance to the truth'.[46]

In Shawcross's view, the British government could treat the whole proceedings as vitiated by Sheikh Yasin's conduct. It could say that the Saudis had engaged in a policy of wholesale bribery and could denounce the Arbitration Agreement. Any test of local opinion such as a plebiscite was now worthless and would only reflect the amount of money the Saudis had spent in the area rather than the true wishes of the people.[47]

Meanwhile, suspicion over Dr Hasan's late appearance refused to go away. Ever since the confused, rambling press conference at Geneva when he had confirmed visiting Mecca, the British had suspected Saudi skulduggery in securing his absence from the opening session of the arbitration. Hasan was adamant that he had done nothing wrong.

So the British set a trap. Someone, mysteriously described as 'a friend of the Foreign Office ostensibly acting as an oil company representative', talked to Hasan.[48] During their conversation, which was recorded, Hasan admitted accepting loans of £100 and £500 from the Saudi Arabian government in January 1955, well after his appointment as a member of the tribunal. A transcript of this conversation was shown to the tribunal chairman who, as a result, resigned on 24 September. The Cuban member also resigned, leaving the tribunal in tatters.[49]

The Saudis quickly reaffirmed their commitment to the arbitration process, but the British were weary of the idea. Deep within Whitehall a different drum would soon be sounding.[50] The government would play for time, pay lip service to the arbitration and secretly consider plans for more drastic action. There was no immediate hurry to make a decision: they had 60 days in which to appoint a new British arbitrator while the tribunal remained suspended.[51]

The first snow had begun to show on the mountains above Geneva as the parties departed. In the sinking light of an autumnal sun, Mont Blanc stood out and the Jura range, spreading its shadow over Cointrin airport, was flecked in white, hinting at the onset of winter.[52] Foreign ministers of the leading nations would soon be gathering in the city for a conference at the end of the month. The 'spirit of Geneva' still lived on in the international mind but, for the parties to the Buraimi dispute, it had died somewhere along the way.

The official line in late September 1955 was that the British government supported the Arbitration Agreement and was working towards the appointment of a new arbitrator. The unofficial line was that the Saudis had well earned their come-uppance. The Buraimi dispute, far from being over, was about to enter its most dangerous stage.

Chapter 15
Dust in Their Eyes
London, September–October 1955

From a vague, angst-ridden desire to settle the score to a cold, calcu-lated plan, the idea of forcibly taking the oasis now began to formulate in the British mind. In Whitehall, widespread disillusion had set in after the collapse of the tribunal. The view that the Saudis could not be trusted to play the game without cheating prevailed.

On 21 September 1955 Evelyn Shuckburgh wrote 'I am beginning to think we should denounce the Arbitration Agreement and resort to methods of straight force. They are crooks of the deepest dye.'[1] Bernard Burrows, who had backed the use of military force in 1954, added his voice to the argument. 'From a strictly legal point of view', he wrote, 'there would be many advantages in denunciation of the agreement and exchange of Notes followed by an immediate military occupation of the oasis and strategic points in [the] western part of the disputed area.'[2]

Superficially, military action seemed simple enough. The Saudi police detachment might present an awkward problem if they managed to flee and take refuge in Hamasa but they were few in number, certainly fewer than Turki's original party. They were unlikely to offer serious resistance to a well planned and swiftly executed operation. The one possible land route for reinforcements from Saudi Arabia could be easily blocked, and the Buraimi airstrip could be rendered unserviceable.[3]

There was a good chance that military action would bring wider benefits too, such as the collapse of Saudi loyalties in the area, leaving south-eastern Arabia, with all its promise of oil, under British influence. A British display of strength would help to make up minds, especially among the tribesmen of central Oman. It would create a bandwagon of support for the long-suffering Sultan Said and his Abu Dhabi allies, and open up the possibility of taking action against the imam. It was too early to talk about a united Oman, perhaps, but the other outcomes seemed attainable.[4]

There were risks, however. The Saudis were in Buraimi with the full agreement of the British government under an international agreement. They sat amicably alongside a British-officered force of 15 men. 'If there were to be some resistance and some of them got shot it would not look good,' admitted Shuckburgh.[5] In these circumstances, in the post-colonial world, opinion might easily turn in favour of the Saudis. They might take Britain before the United Nations Security Council and appeal to the International Court of Justice. However, Britain had friends on the Security Council and could use its influence to make sure that the matters did not go that far. The attitude of the United States would be decisive in this regard.[6]

If the Saudis got their own way in Buraimi, where would it end? As the foreign secretary, Harold Macmillan, told his cabinet colleagues:

> The consequences of this on our position in the Persian Gulf and throughout the Middle East would be very grave [...] If we were to allow the Saudis to impose a major defeat on us – and the loss of Buraimi would be that – the whole of our position might easily slip away.[7]

Talk of military action chimed well with Eden's political views. The weakness of Labour foreign policy had been one of the main planks of Conservative campaign in the 1955 general election. In a personal statement, he said: 'We must be firm and resolute. Weakness can lead only to war or to subjugation without a struggle. Because of this we and our allies have to be militarily strong.'[8]

Eden longed to pursue an independent foreign policy free of Washington's hand. On 4 October, he informed the cabinet:

> Our interests in the Middle East were greater than those of the US because of our dependence on Middle Eastern oil and our experience in the area was greater than theirs. We should not, therefore, allow ourselves to be restricted overmuch by reluctance to act without full American concurrence and support. We should form our own policy in the light of our interests in the area.[9]

As the notion of expelling the Saudis from Hamasa took hold, the debate moved on: how could it be done without attracting international condemnation? The answer was simple: put the blame on the Saudis for the breakdown of the arbitration process and make the charge stick. There was plenty of material available, but among all the bribes, lies and trickery, the issue of Saudi 'loans' to the Pakistani arbitrator, Dr Muhammad Hasan, seemed to stand out.[10]

It will be recalled that the British, through a 'friend', had recorded a conversation in which Hasan admitted accepting two loans from the Saudis. This, combined with Bullard's observation that Dr Hasan and Sheikh Yasin had tried to swing the neutral members of the tribunal in the Saudis' favour seemed incontrovertible proof of the Saudis' attempts to influence the tribunal. News that Saudis had bribed the people of Buraimi was hardly a surprise, but the revelation that they had bribed a judge was – literally – a show-stopper.

There was a catch, however. The circumstances in which the British had obtained the evidence made it difficult to publish it without raising awkward questions.[11] Attorney-General Reginald Manningham-Buller, deemed 'a rather difficult character' by one official, joined the discussions. He saw all cabinet papers, although he did not attend cabinet meetings unless invited. It was said that some-times, out of sheer cussedness, he would deliberately sit down and write a contrary opinion, if he had not been consulted about an issue.[12]

As Manningham-Buller pointed out, the secret recording of the conversation with Dr Hasan was not quite the trump card it had first seemed to be.[13] Dr Hasan might easily deny the claims of corruption by saying that he had repaid the loans. The British government would have to disclose the source of their information, which would raise a swarm of difficult questions about how Hasan had been tricked into making the admissions. Hasan was a Pakistani citizen and, although the Pakistan government had not appointed him to the tribunal, there was a risk of offending them by making this disclosure. The Pakistanis were an important part of the anti-Soviet strategy, a link in a ring of alliances that aimed to contain the spread of communism.

* * * * *

The unreal calm that had settled over relations between Britain and Saudi Arabia after the breakdown of the arbitration proceedings was abruptly shattered on 4 October 1955 when the Foreign Office issued a statement explaining Bullard's decision to resign from the tribunal.[14]

By the genteel standards of international diplomacy, it was an extr-aordinary document. It denounced the Saudis' 'deliberate, systematic and persistent policy of large-scale bribery calculated to subvert the people in the disputed areas.' The Saudis had attempted to promote a coup d'état in Abu Dhabi, bribe Sheikh Zayed, and had extended their methods to the tribunal itself. 'Finally, confirmation was secured of Her Majesty government's suspicion that attempts had been made by the Saudis to tamper with the impartiality of the tribunal behind the president's back.' Within these words, the bribing of Dr Hasan was carefully wrapped, and his name was never publicly revealed.

By some strange process, the Buraimi dispute had reversed the tradi-tional roles in the Anglo-Saudi relationship; now it was the Saudis' turn to lecture the miscreant. On 6 October, Shuckburgh recorded:

> The Saudi Arabian ambassador [Hafiz Wahba] called this morning. He said that he was speaking without instructions but on his own behalf to say how bitterly he regretted the statement which the Foreign Office had put out about Buraimi. This statement had come out of the blue so far as he was concerned and it was not the sort of action he had learned to expect from the British. It was more like Egyptian radio propaganda. I said the difference was that our statement was true.[15]

Behind closed doors, the British had decided to abandon the arbitration proceedings. But nothing was done at this stage to officially close the door: the public façade was maintained by supporting the proceedings and reassuring the Americans. On 29 September, Shuck-burgh had held discussions with the State Department in which he explained the difficulties that had arisen over Buraimi and warned that Britain might have to let the Arbitration Agreement die and declare their own frontier. He said nothing about the possibility of military action to reclaim Hamasa.[16]

With the Saudi ambassador, Shuckburgh was more disingenuous. 'I am afraid that we shall have to indulge in some deception if we want to prevent the Saudis jumping to the true conclusion that we are about to denounce the arbitration method' he wrote. When Hafiz Wahba kept asking what the British intended to do next, Shuckburgh fobbed him off with various excuses such as 'we are thinking about it', 'we are taking legal advice', and 'it may take a little time to get our thoughts clear.'[17] What he dared not say was that the British mind was already made up. Later, when the truth came out, the Saudis would accuse the British of throwing dust in their eyes, and in this regard they were correct.[18]

Wahba would have been horrified to learn the truth. As he talked soft words of reprimand to Shuckburgh, officials of the Foreign Office were secretly discussing borders. Upon the re-occupation of Hamasa, the British government would unilaterally declare a new frontier. Where might the frontier line be drawn? Officials dusted off the 1935 Riyadh Line but considered it too vague and too close to a promising well-site, Gezira B. A new line was devised to bisect the area of suspended oil operations, No Oil Man's Land. The fact that it might cede a large part of Sheikh Shakhbut's territory to the Saudis seemed of little consequence to those poring over maps in Whitehall.[19]

The same old arguments about Khawr al-Udayd began to surface again: should the Saudis be offered their window on the Gulf as a sop to their wider territorial ambitions? Neither Shell, which owned a concession off the coast of Qatar, nor BP, which co-owned the offshore Abu Dhabi concession, raised any opposition. But IPC was not so compliant.

On 18 October, Dick Bird – now a manager with the company – phoned the Foreign Office and expressed strong objections to Khawr al-Udayd or any part of the Liwa area being given up.[20] Bernard Burrows partly supported this view. 'It is clearly desirable that our line should not concede Saudi Arabians access to the sea in the Khawr al-Udayd area. The Ruler of Abu Dhabi would bitterly resent such a concession at his expense, and it would aggravate our difficulties of reconciling him to loss of a large part of Liwa.'[21]

Not for the first time, the debate threatened to descend into a confusion of frontier lines. There was the '1952' line, the '1954' line and all the coloured lines of the 1930s. The arguments criss-crossed between British government departments until the Defence Committee decided to make a stand on the Riyadh Line of 1935, as modified in 1937, thus blocking Saudi access to the sea at Khawr al-Udayd and keeping Liwa in Abu Dhabi.[22]

By now, the wheels were in motion. Harold Macmillan wrote a memorandum for the cabinet: 'arbitration having failed, I doubt whether we can safely entrust the matter to any other form of international decision or negotiation, especially as in the meantime the processes of Saudi corruption in the area would continue unchecked'. The only safe course, he concluded, was to rely upon a position of strength on the ground. He recommended that the Arbitration Agreement should be renounced and the Trucial Oman Levies be authorised to use force to reoccupy most of the disputed areas.[23]

On 18 October 1955 the cabinet considered his advice. As expected, Manningham-Buller sounded a note of caution. A decision to end the arbitration process might lead to legal action against the United Kingdom, he warned. Therefore, it was important that the cabinet's reasons should be expressed as fully and precisely as possible. 'We should have more chance of succeeding in establishing repudiation [by Saudi Arabia] if we alleged and proved that the Pakistani member of the tribunal had been bribed.' He felt that the other evidence of Saudi bribery and misbehaviour was not enough to prove that they had by their conduct repudiated the Agreement.[24]

So far as the cabinet was concerned, this was yesterday's news. Earlier in the meeting, members had considered a report from the Middle East Oil Committee. Britain's oil interests were now playing an ever-increasing part in her Middle Eastern policy. British companies owned investments in the Middle East valued at £600 million (£13 billion today). The UK economy was dependent on oil imports from the Middle East and would become increasingly so. Both the Egyptians and Saudi Arabians had been working to undermine British interests in the Middle East, and the USSR was also a threat to Western influence in the region.

The report spelt out the situation in stark terms:

> Middle East oil is vital to our economy. This is not a matter of priorities as between one area of the world and another in the Cold War, but an essential need. We are vulnerable in this area, which is at present slipping away from us because of the indigenous forces of nationalism, and because our enemies are making a greater effort than we are.[25]

The report's message had set the scene and Eden was in no mood to take hostages. Alerted to the attorney-general's stance by his advisers, he quickly sidelined the legal issue: it was agreed that the attorney-general should continue his discussion with officials elsewhere.

The cabinet proceeded with its business and approved Macmillan's recommendations:

> (a) We should now inform first the United States government and immediately afterwards the Saudi government that the Saudis' actions have rendered a judicial settlement of this problem impossible and that, to protect the interests of the rulers whom we represent, we are resuming our freedom of action in the disputed areas and breaking off arbitration;
> (b) We should then unilaterally declare what we regard as a fair frontier though at the same time saying that we would be prepared to make minor rectifications by agreement;
> (c) We should support the ruler of Abu Dhabi in reoccupying the disputed area and removing the Saudi police from Buraimi;
> (d) We should declare a frontier and be prepared to defend it by force, if necessary;
> (e) We should give the sultan of Muscat the necessary help in resuming control of Hamasa.[26]

The following day, the Defence Committee discussed the means of carrying out the operation. The cabinet approved the final plan on the 20 October and resolved not to tell the Americans until the operation began. Of all the decisions that the British government took during the Buraimi dispute, this one upset the Americans the most.

Chapter 16
Operation Bonaparte
The Buraimi Oasis, October–December 1955

The last time a military operation had been named Bonaparte was in 1944 when the British devised a scheme using Royal Navy gunboats to evacuate downed airmen from northern France.[1] The circumstances of the next Operation Bonaparte could not have been more different. On the evening of 23 October 1955 Bernard Burrows summoned Edward Henderson to the Residency in Bahrain. Henderson was the IPC liaison officer who had been seconded to the Foreign Office to assist with research into tribal allegiances. Burrows explained to him that, the Geneva arbitration talks having broken down, men of the Trucial Oman Levies led by British officers were about to occupy Hamasa. Henderson's task was to fly down to Buraimi in order to negotiate a settlement with the rebel sheikhs.[2]

The British had a plan for retaking the oasis. They aimed to surround the Saudi police camp, thus cutting off the water supply, and seize their wireless transmitter before Bin Nami could contact his Saudi masters in Dammam for instructions. They would also surround a house in Hamasa where another transmitter was suspected of being kept. The operation would be commanded by Colonel (formerly Major) Eric Johnson.[3]

Before dawn on 26 October two TOL squadrons left Kahil. At 5.10 a.m., Force A led by Captain John Rhodes and accompanied by Major Norman Smith drove into the Neutral Zone. They arrived at the Saudi police camp where they surprised its occupants just as they were getting ready for morning prayers. Major Smith was greeted quite normally by Abdullah bin Nami and, while they were talking, the Saudi policemen were being disarmed. They resisted at first, not by firing but by refusing to give up their weapons, which were eventually taken from them by force.[4]

According to Major Smith's account, Abdullah bin Nami entered into conversation with his clerk, then retired with him into his hut. Smith waited a few minutes before following them.[5] He caught Bin

Nami in the act of handing over a metal dispatch box to the clerk. Smith grasped the box but Bin Nami resisted and there was a three-way 'tug-of-war' to get it. Bin Nami presently released his grip to grab the tall and bulky Smith, pinning his arms to his sides and allowing the clerk to escape. In an effort to break free, Smith raised his knee sharply into Bin Nami's groin and threatened to shoot him if he did not let go. When there was no response, Smith pressed his revolver to the soft part of Bin Nami's thigh and fired. The bullet had the desired effect: Bin Nami fell backwards, leaving Smith free to pursue the clerk who was making off across the desert. A short distance later, he caught up with him and retrieved the dispatch box. On his return to camp, Smith gave Bin Nami an injection of morphine and treated his wound.

The Saudi soldiers were loaded on to a truck. Bin Nami was put into a car and Smith took the whole party to the airstrip. On arrival of the airplane, the doctor treated Bin Nami's wound and a head wound to one of the soldiers. 'I escorted Bin Nami to the plane,' concluded Smith, 'where after a touching goodbye and remarks about friends shooting each other, the plane took off.'

Meanwhile back at Hamasa much had happened. At 5.25 a.m., Force B commanded by Captain Tony Steggles and accompanied by Captain R.A. Laird had driven into the village from the north-west. On hearing the sound of their vehicles, some of the villagers came out of their houses to greet the convoy, thinking that Turki had returned. The levies entered Turki's house and occupied other buildings nearby. Any doubt in the villagers' minds about the levies' intentions was soon dispelled. As one officer later wrote 'The sight of Captain Steggles coming out of Bait Turki brandishing a Bren gun soon made things clear.'[6]

Hamasa erupted as Obaid bin Juma's men opened fire. The levies, now pinned down in the houses, returned fire but, as the sun climbed higher in the sky, their stock of ammunition ran low. Then, by an amazing stroke of luck, the levies found fresh ammunition hidden in the sacks of rice that the Saudis had smuggled in on their weekly supply flights. The levies inched forward, taking a few more houses, enlarging their foothold in the western end of the village. One of them reached a door and knocked hard. An old lady opened it, and told him to stop making so much noise and go away at once. After some discussion, the levies persuaded her to let them in. And yet, despite their success, the battle was finely balanced: the levies' progress was slow and they were still in a precarious situation, cut off from the main force while facing strong opposition in the eastern end of the village.

Meanwhile, an RAF Valetta had brought Edward Henderson to the oasis. He arrived expecting to find the peaceful surrender of 15 Saudi policemen but instead found a battle raging between the levies and 200 tribesmen loyal to the dissident sheikhs. Travelling from one sand dune to another, he caught up with Sheikhs Zayed and Hazza who were overlooking the battle from a safe distance.[7]

The crack of small-arms fire filled the air. At 11 a.m., the levy commander sent an ultimatum to Sheikhs Saqr, Rashid and Obaid in Hamasa. At 1 p.m. the gunfire from the village died down but an hour later the sheikhs sent a message refusing to surrender. Captain Clayton assembled the reserve troop, and in mid afternoon this force was driven in Land Rovers into the sand dunes south of the Hamasa wadi. They advanced on foot to the edge of the wadi, their objective a tower known as Burj al-Ajam about 500 metres away. Moving forward in open order, they came under sniper fire from a high tower in Hamasa. One section was detached to stifle the sniper while the remainder reached a large mound and set up a two-inch mortar aimed at the tower. However, due to the poor condition of the shells, the mortar could not reach its target and each shell landed with a loud bang in open country. The troop withdrew to the dunes and Clayton recalled the other section until sunset, when the sun would be in the sniper's eyes.[8]

After a brief lull, the troop re-entered the wadi at sunset and resumed their positions at the mound. When darkness fell, one section moved out to Bait Turki to reinforce the soldiers and the other made another attempt to take Burj al-Ajam. The levy sergeant reached the tower without incident and knocked on the door. A voice asked who was there. 'Soldiers' the sergeant replied. The shooting started again. Captain Steggles came careering out of the night from the direction of Bait Turki, driving a Land Rover without lights, drawing more rifle fire from the village. He exchanged reports with Captain Clayton and returned to Bait Turki to await developments.

The last ultimatum from TOL headquarters to the rebel sheikhs gave them the choice of going to Saudi Arabia or Muscat. Colonel Eric Johnson warned that the levies would mount a full attack in the night if the rebels did not surrender. Shortly before the attack was due to begin, Johnson received another message from the sheikhs saying that they were prepared to come in. A ceasefire was ordered at 10 p.m. after the sheikhs had confirmed that they were leaving the village.

We can picture, perhaps, the scene that now unfolds: a makeshift headquarters in the desert and a patch of light in the darkness, Sheikh Zayed, Henderson and Clayton scouring the night for signs of movement and, from the distance, the sound of a motor and the flash of headlights over the dunes. A battered old Ford appears from the desert carrying leading sheikhs of the Buraimi Oasis. They look troubled, crumpled and defeated as they step out of the car. They are brought before Colonel Johnson to make their surrender: the colonel asks them to choose between surrendering to the sultan of Oman or going into exile. The prospect of being incarcerated in the sultan's dreaded Jalali prison is likely to be preying on their minds, and they readily choose exile in Saudi Arabia.[9]

No doubt the sultan would have liked to deal with the sheikhs himself, but he was in no position to argue with this decision since his *wali* was still in transit. Although the sultan's representative, Pat Waterfield, was on the scene and did object, Henderson brushed him aside. With hindsight, the decision to allow the sheikhs to go into exile was unfortunate since they would continue to be a source of discontent for many years to come. But, at the time, the chance to avert a night attack and the great casualties it might bring was uppermost in Colonel Johnson's mind.[10]

The three sheikhs climbed into the back of a Land Rover. They were still armed with their *khanjars*, the last symbol of their former status, and Captain Clayton faced a delicate situation. With three armed sheikhs in the back and a soldier so cramped in the front that he could not raise his rifle, he risked having his throat slit as he drove along the desert tracks in the dark. So Clayton apologised to the sheikhs for any disrespect, took their *khanjars* and placed them down beside him. He later wrote: 'As we all knew each other this was accompanied with good grace, even Sheikh Obaid bin Juma, the most anti-British of the three, saw the humour of the situation.'[11]

The Saudi policemen were flown to Sharjah and put on HMS *Loch Alvie* heading for Bahrain and an onward passage to Dhahran. Back at Bait Turki, the levies seized sacks of rice and dates, many of which concealed hidden ammunition. But the metal dispatch box Major Smith had seized from the Saudis held the most shocking discovery of all. For when the political officers in Dubai opened the box, they found 150,000 rupees (£250,000 today) and an astonishing haul of secret communications, wireless signals, letters and other documents that had passed between the Saudi commander, Abdullah al-Qaraishi and Bin Jiluwi. It would take weeks for the vast amount of material to be translated but even the first few documents confirmed what the British had long suspected, that the Saudis had conducted a large-scale campaign of dispensing cash and smuggling guns from Hamasa.[12]

Like pieces in a gigantic jigsaw puzzle, the documents revealed the full picture of Saudi operations in Hamasa – and what a picture it was. They proved that Abdullah al-Qaraishi had lied to the Buraimi tribunal when he had denied that any payments had been made to anyone, and that Sheikh Yasin must have known he was lying. Other documents showed that the Saudis had been arming the imam and the Omani tribes for an uprising against the sultan. For the British, their decision to abandon the arbitration proceedings and take military action appeared to be fully vindicated.

But disclosure of these revelations would have to wait. The immediate problem facing Captain Clayton was the security of the rebel sheikhs. They were held in a small compound near the Al-Ain date gardens overnight and in the morning Captain Clayton put them on a plane to Sharjah, their *khanjars* restored to them. Saqr followed on a later flight, having been kept back to witness the surrender of the Hamasa and Buraimi tribesmen. The Buraimi men were allowed to keep their rifles but those of the Hamasa men were confiscated, 180 rifles in all.[13]

At three o'clock in the afternoon, soldiers of the sultan's army, the Muscat and Oman Field Force, arrived in the oasis, having been held back in order to avoid alerting the Saudi spies in the mountain passes that an attack was being planned. With Captain Clayton they went to Buraimi and approached Saqr's fort, which was reported to be manned by hostile tribesmen loyal to the sheikh. There was no Muscat flag flying from the battlements. Clayton went ahead to parley with the garrison and found that they had been ordered to defend the fort to the last man. They were unable to accept that Saqr had fled to Saudi Arabia, they were not moving, and they asked Clayton if he would kindly go away.

Standing on a causeway with a number of rifles pointing at him, Clayton was hardly in a position to argue. He did, however, get their agreement to leave if instructed to do so by Saqr's bailiff. After a trip into Buraimi to find the bailiff, Clayton returned with a message to the men that they were to leave the fort and come home. 'A few moments later,' wrote Clayton, 'the five men, with their rifles over their shoulders and their small sacks of belongings, filed out of the fort, crossed over the short causeway, exchanging compliments with me, and walked off in the direction of Buraimi and home.' On 31 October a Muscat *wali* arrived in the village and took up residence in the fort. Muscat flags flew everywhere.[14]

Hamasa and Buraimi were quiet now. The final casualties in the battle for Hamasa were two levies killed, three slightly wounded, two Saudis wounded and about ten tribesmen killed.[15] Bin Nami was taken to hospital in Sharjah for treatment to his leg wound. He refused to be parted from his sword and two heavy bundles that he carried with him. The political agent Peter Tripp managed to search these and extracted a sub-machine gun, a magazine and a bandolier of ammunition. When Tripp took Bin Nami on board the navy frigate that was to take him to Bahrain, and left him in the sick bay, he was 'looking very much restored in appearance and spirits.'[16]

On 2 November, at a jetty in Sharjah, a sad picture unfolded. Three dispirited old sheikhs and their retinues shuffled along a creaking gangplank to board a launch at the start of their journey to Dammam and a life in exile. Among those evicted from Hamasa was an 80-year-old blind *qadhi*, Abdullah bin Abdul Aziz al-Sulaiman. Despite his advanced years, the British considered him as a danger on the Trucial Coast, a fanatic who had allegedly been preaching a holy war and helping the Saudis by fanning the flames of hatred against the British. In truth, he had a wife in Sharjah, had been a *qadhi* in Hamasa for about 12 years and accepted as such by Turki when the Saudis had arrived in the village.[17]

The expulsion of the Saudis and declaration of a new boundary was good news for the oil company. No Oil Man's Land was no longer out of bounds, at least on the Abu Dhabi side of the Riyadh Line, and exploration could now start again in this area. Expulsion of the Saudis from Hamasa had also opened up the possibility of exploring the Dhahira plain.

On 2 November 1955, when the dust had settled over the Buraimi Oasis, a party of PDO geologists, which included Mike Morton, ventured from their camp in Ibri, 150 kilometres away, and headed north-west towards the rocky outline of Jebel Hafit and the Buraimi Oasis.

Thirty years before, when K. Washington Gray and George Lees had glimpsed, from a rocky scarp, the Dhahira plain and Buraimi in the distance, the area was strictly out-of-bounds. Now the geologists had the whole plain stretched out before them.[18]

On 3 November, the party arrived at Bait Turki in Hamasa village, now the headquarters of the Trucial Oman Levies. But their reception was cool and even Edward Henderson, the erstwhile IPC liaison officer, appeared ill at ease at their presence. The point was, of course, that the Foreign Office did not want the outside world to think that that the dispute was about oil. The geologists needed no second bidding and, making their exit from the house, they stayed only briefly in the area before returning to their camp in Ibri.[19]

* * * * *

Saudi anger was vented in a series of outpourings through the press and radio, with accusations and threats being made: the British were trying to make up for the loss of India; their attack on Hamasa was on a par with Japanese treachery at Pearl Harbor; and the Arab soldiers who fought under British command and killed their brother Arabs would be paid back in double measure.[20]

A storm of protest arose across the land. From Mecca, regular broadcasts directed to the Buraimi Oasis began. One of King Saud's brothers publicly volunteered to lead a Saudi army to take back Hamasa, a bold promise in the circumstances. Each day the local news-paper *Al-Bilad al-Saudiya* printed a page of telegrams from groups or individuals offering to serve king and country in a holy war against the British aggressors – although most of the telegrams came from tribal leaders and units of the Saudi army. Others pledged a share of their monthly salary to the armed forces. In one spectacular donation, a notable, whose generosity was celebrated at a beach party attended by the king himself, donated the sum of two million riyals (approximately £2.6 million today) to the war chest.

In an increasingly febrile Middle East, the outrage was widely felt. In Damascus, most newspapers condemned the British action. The general Arab view was that Britain had violated the Arbitration Agreement in order to gain oil deposits believed to be present in the area. *Manar*, the mouthpiece of the nationalist Muslim Brotherhood, saw the event as an attack on the Muslim holy land, while the left-wing press saw it as an example of imperialist aggression.[21]

On 27 October Prince Faisal was in Cairo to sign a mutual defence pact with Egypt and spared no time before condemning British actions.[22] Back in Riyadh, the king and his circle were angry, and supported the propaganda campaign. In explaining how the Saudi force had been evicted from Hamasa, the Saudi government alleged that hundreds of British troops with many aircraft and tanks had been used to round up a 'mere 15 Saudi policemen.' When a visiting ambassador told King Saud that he had only heard a brief account of the incident on Cairo Radio, the king proceeded to give him a lurid account of the operation 'not forgetting the usual emphasis on tanks and aircraft [being used] against defenceless women and children.'[23]

The Saudi government's statement, when it eventually appeared on 13 November, continued in this vein.[24] A British military force led by British officers, it claimed, had suddenly besieged the villages of Buraimi and Hamasa before dawn prayers and asked the inhabitants to surrender. However, they refused to obey and declared that they were followers of the house of Saud and still owed allegiance to His Majesty King Saud. The statement went on:

> The [tribal] chiefs confirmed that the British forces suffered loss of not less than 82 soldiers and a number of Arabs who were compelled by the British authorities to fight their brethren. Some of the Arabs who tried to avoid the clash with their fellow men of the territory were shot down by the British forces at the rear.

To add insult to injury, the captured sheikhs were subjected to 'Billingsgate language' – British officers had sworn at them.[25]

In the western towns of Saudi Arabia, reactions were subdued. The British ambassador reported from Jedda that the shopkeepers and workers of the town seemed more or less uninterested, but rumours were circulating in the *suq* that the government would soon clamp down on British trade and break off diplomatic relations. There had been few demonstrations of Saudi displeasure. 'A solitary poster affirming that Buraimi was Saudi was timidly handed to our doorkeeper and now graces one of the chancery offices,' he wrote.

One evening, at about midnight, a taxi-load of Arabs drove into the embassy compound, shouted a slogan 'War with the British!' and speedily drove out again.[26]

It was another story in the Eastern province. Here it seemed as though the people had risen up as one, united by fury at the British 'imperialists' and a desire for revenge. The three exiled sheikhs, a symbol of the dispossessed, provided a focus for their emotions. Bin Jiluwi was supposed to have met them on arrival at Dammam but had backache so sent a number of lesser notables in 40 vehicles in his place. Nonetheless, Bin Jiluwi provided the three sheikhs with all the necessary compensations. They went to pay a courtesy call on the king in Riyadh, whence they returned with handsome cash payments. But Sheikh Saqr, although happy to live in Saudi Arabia, was reported to be missing the fresh air of his homeland and the shade of a *ghaf* tree.[27]

Later in November, King Saud, travelling from Riyadh to Dammam by rail, made several stops and speeches along the way, declaring 'if the British remain [in Buraimi], then I will be the first soldier to go and sacrifice my life for yours.'[28]

To coincide with the king's visit, an official reception was laid on for the exiled sheikhs in Dammam. The townspeople greeted them as heroes, feting them as though they were returning from a victorious campaign. Crowds marched through the streets vowing *jihad* against the British. Press and radio demanded revenge. The British Bank closed as its Arab employees took to the streets to demonstrate their solidarity. There was a military parade past King Saud, including paratroopers wearing American helmets who were parachuted into its midst. The *mujahidin* made a wild-eyed appearance in a column of garish yellow trucks, shrieking and shooting their rifles in the air. A rendition of the *Arddh* followed, a rhythmic shuffling dance accompanied by a monotonous chant through the choking dust. When the king joined the dance brandishing a sword, 'the cheers of the populace rent the skies'.[29]

An enormous plywood tank perched on the back of a pick-up was rolled out, a gift from the town of Al-Khobar, its gun made of piping and its shape silhouetted in multi-coloured neon lights. The great and the good of Al-Khobar, the merchants and contractors who had paid for and built the tank, sat astride its turret. A banner proclaimed 'TO AL BURAIMI-VICTORY IS OURS' and, on its sides, 'AL KHOBAR – TOWN OF REDEMPTION AND SACRIFICE.'[30]

Anti-British feelings were running high. Bin Nami, having been treated for two days in the American hospital, declared to the press that Major Smith, his 'old friend', had deliberately shot him. A Palestinian doctor expelled from Hamasa arrived full of stories of British wickedness, telling the newspaper that British officers had treated him badly and given him 'hot tea mixed with poison' which made him sleep for 24 hours during his captivity.[31]

Meanwhile, the situation in western Abu Dhabi remained quiet. Owing to the lack of water and length of communication lines, it was not possible to maintain a large body of troops in the desert but the Trucial Oman Levies had occupied the most advanced posts in the west. From a base at Sila, where the oil company had a camp and air strip, daily patrols were conducted through Nakhla to the newly declared frontier and less frequently to the Udayd peninsula, and Lincoln bombers carried out daily reconnaissances of the area. Fears of a Saudi counter-attack failed to materialise: without massive Egyptian help, the Saudis were in no position to mount a large scale incursion, although they might have tried to seize the oil camp for reasons of prestige, but in the event nothing happened.[32]

A modern photograph of the ruins of Hamasa. (source: Latifa al-Haj)

In Hamasa, a simple truth prevailed. A symbol of the nineteenth-century Wahhabi occupation, the tower of Qasr al-Sudaira standing midway between Hamasa and Buraimi, was already a crumbling ruin. Now Turki's house, with its mud walls concealing untold number of spent bullets, and a levy wireless mast rising high above the village, stood as monuments to a more recent folly. Bin Nami's camp had been dismantled by the locals during the battle for Hamasa and the red flags of Muscat had replaced the green Saudi flags that had once flown so defiantly from the rooftops. The Wahhabis had departed.[33]

Chapter 17
The Road to Suez
Diplomacy, Oil Exploration and Oman, 1955–6

On 27 October 1955 Evelyn Shuckburgh received Hafiz Wahba at his office half-expecting him to break off diplomatic relations or even to declare war. Shuckburgh later described the meeting in his diary:

> In the end poor Hafiz Wahba had nothing to say and was quite friendly though sad, and at one point came out sharply, in reply to an intervention by Derek Riches, with the remark that 'the statement of the Prime Minister (in the House yesterday) is not the word of God.' He said he lamented that his country was getting so close to Egypt, but blamed us for it and said our action over Buraimi would push it further still.[1]

Shuckburgh was somewhat mystified by this relatively tame reaction. The following day he noted that 'the Saudis had protested rather politely about Buraimi but are clearly up to some mischief, perhaps involving the expulsion of British subjects from Saudi Arabia.'[2] The Saudis stopped short of breaking off relations – that would come a year later in the aftermath of the Suez crisis. The official Saudi response, when it did come, was a predictable diatribe against Britain.[3]

But there was another aspect to Saudi policy at this time, covert and dangerous. They intended to wage a clandestine war against those who were perceived to be the enemy, both at home and abroad. For example, they planned to undermine Sultan Said bin Taimur's rule and supported attempts to establish an imamate in central Oman.

Not for the first time, Aramco found itself in an awkward situation. Aramco vice-president, Terry Duce, took the view that the British had 'sabotaged' the arbitration proceedings. The danger of the company being sucked deeper into the dispute soon became apparent. In November 1955 Yusuf Yasin approached Aramco official Garry Owen with questions about the southern borders of the kingdom. He asked for any available information from the company's experts, technicians, drivers and guides about the borders because, he said, the government planned to take steps to prevent the British from 'pushing Aramco and the government around'. Company officials travelled to Jedda to discover exactly what Sheikh Yasin had in mind.[4]

In December 1955 two Aramco representatives, Homer Mueller and a colleague, had three lengthy meetings with Sheikh Yasin in Jedda. Abdullah al-Qaraishi, the former 'clerk' of the Saudi police post, attended the first meeting. An Egyptian army officer, the same Ali Khashabi who had secretly infiltrated Oman earlier in the year, joined subsequent meetings, as did an officer of the Saudi army. At first glance, the presence of an Egyptian Army officer at the meetings was unremarkable. The Saudis had recently signed the mutual defence pact with Egypt. The Saudi Arabian landscape was sprinkled with Egyptian administrators, schoolteachers, army officers and advisers in other key posts.

The meeting began innocently enough. Sheikh Yasin proposed a reconnaissance of the southern desert under the command of the Saudi army officer. He confirmed his request for information, adding that complete secrecy was necessary, especially with regard to the recon-naissance. But it soon dawned on Mueller that Khashabi's main interest was to establish contact with leaders in Oman who were unsympathetic to the sultan and the British – it will be recalled that Khashabi had visited the imam via Buraimi on his visit to the country in the spring of 1955. Khashabi asked questions about land routes to Nizwa, suitable places for aircraft landings in central Oman, and communications between Dammam and various places along the Gulf and southern Arabian coasts.

Sheikh Yasin intervened and tried to bring the discussion back to generalities in an attempt to disguise Khashabi's true designs but the Americans, sensing that Yasin had retaliation in mind, warned that any precipitate action might damage the US government's attempts to mediate between the Saudis and British.

Sheikh Yasin replied that his government only intended to establish border posts but it soon became clear that he was expecting more from Aramco than information. The Americans baulked, saying that they could not provide anything more. Yasin grew belligerent, announcing that he would rely on the Arabian Research Division for research, on Aramco bosses Davies and Ohliger for equipment and authority, and on Terry Duce for bombs. Yasin added that 'the British would know that they had been in a scrap next time they tried to take any Saudis into custody.'

This was Yasin at his worst, shrill and fanatical in his pursuit of the Saudi cause. For the Americans, it was an impossible task: lending vehicles with the company logo painted out was one thing, providing bombs quite another. Despite their support for the Saudi regime and the company's close connections with the CIA, the last thing Aramco wanted was to bomb the British out of Oman.

In his account of the meetings, Mueller did not disclose his reactions to Yasin's proposals but he must have appeared shocked when the full implications sank in. Whether the Aramcons saw this as another of Yasin's outbursts, something to be humoured but not acted upon, is not mentioned in his notes but, in any event, Terry Duce did not supply any bombs.

When Yasin got no satisfaction from Aramco, he looked elsewhere. Egypt stepped up and supplied some of the landmines that would be used to such lethal effect in central Oman in the late 1950s. Other landmines came from the Saudis' own stock. The American military attaché in Dhahran discovered that the serial numbers of mines used by rebel forces in Omani civil war matched those of mines supplied to the Saudis by the US government. To this end, Britain attempted to persuade the United States to stop supplying mines to Saudi Arabia. The US response was that the mines were supplied as part of a military assistance program and the manner in which they were used was of no concern to the supplier. American officials certainly had their own suspicions about Saudi efforts to supply the Omani rebels by sea.[5]

While Yasin was making plans to explore the southern desert, King Saud was on a state visit to India. Described as moose-tall (he was 6 ft. 6 in.), the 53-year-old Saud was accompanied by a party of 234, including nine royal princes and a dozen sheikhs, seven times larger than the contingent that had accompanied the Russian statesmen Bulganin and Khrushchev on their recent visit. Buraimi weighed heavily on the king's mind. Although he declared his desire for a peaceful settlement, he gave an ominous warning about using force if diplomatic means did not succeed.[6]

Shuckburgh's fears of Saudi mischief seemed to be realised a few days later when a group of Saudi army officers gathered in Dhahran, changed into civilian clothes, and held secret talks with Aramco and government officials. Aramco vehicles with the company logo painted out were provided. A party of 25 men left Dhahran in these vehicles on 16 December and returned on 5 January 1956. The convoy travelled though Selwah along the base of the Qatar peninsula, heading for the site of an Aramco deep test-drill. Then it mysteriously trundled off to carry reconnaissances in other parts of the desert.[7]

The appearance of Aramco field parties in areas close to, or believed to be within, concession areas belonging to the IPC group increased tensions. One day, surveyor Doug Manning, who was working for an IPC contractor, was laying down magnetometer and gravimeter lines on the edge of the Rub al-Khali when he was astonished to see through the eye-piece of his theodolite the outline of a drilling rig only a few hundred metres away. There was no doubt in his mind that the rig was within IPC's concession area and, taking his readings and returning to camp, he reported the matter to his party chief.[8] Other reports of Aramco incursions followed, leading to an incident in which a British officer commanding an Arab detachment of troops came upon an Aramco field party in the desert and ordered it at gunpoint to leave. They did so under protest, leaving their equipment behind.[9]

Occasions when oil company personnel bumped into each other in the desert were not always so fraught. In the same year PDTC had a survey party working near the Qatar border. Two members of the party were out on a reconnaissance when they came across an Aramco crew in what was supposedly Abu Dhabi territory. The meeting was polite and, indeed, the PDTC men invited the Americans to visit them later in the day. That evening, two of them came over the dunes to the PDTC camp and, as one of the PDTC surveyors later recalled, 'We gave them plenty of beer before they left.' By the time the Trucial Oman Levies arrived a few days later to investigate, the American crew had disappeared, having pulled back to Saudi Arabia.[10]

The political officers would surely have raised a disapproving eyebrow over this fraternising between rivals but, in the oil men's eyes, there was really no harm in sharing a few cold beers under the light of an Arabian moon.

* * * * *

A few days after the reoccupation of Buraimi, Deputy Secretary of State Herbert Hoover Jr. remonstrated with Sir Roger Makins, British ambassador to Washington about Britain's failure to notify the US

State Department in advance of Operation Bonaparte. 'We ought to have enough confidence in one another to be completely frank in exchanging information about our intentions and he [Hoover] hoped that we would be able to "play it together" from now on.'[11]

The attitude of Hoover's boss, John Foster Dulles, seemed slightly more relaxed. Harold Macmillan met him at a meeting of foreign ministers in Geneva. After Dulles had explained that the Buraimi dispute would make a lot of trouble and that his people in Washington were upset that the British had not given them prior notice of their plan, Macmillan replied that he wished to spare them from any accusation of complicity. 'Dulles took this all very calmly and, having ticked this off, did not press it. I did not regard it as much more than a formality.'[12]

On 3 November 1955, after the Saudis had threatened to take the dispute to the United Nations Security Council, Hoover informed Makins that the United States would not side with Britain if that happened. When Macmillan heard of this, he gave Hoover short shrift, reminding him that Britain had given its support to the United States over its intervention in Guatemala the previous year. 'The threat [to oppose Britain in the Security Council] will not cause us to alter our policy over Buraimi, which we consider to be entirely justified and from which we will not withdraw.' Dulles saw a return to arbitration as the best way to avoid the case coming before the Security Council.[13]

Meanwhile, events were coming to a head in Oman. In November 1955 the leading sheikhs of the Dhahira plain met at Dhank and swore allegiance to Sultan Said, leaving him free to confront the Imam Ghalib and his brother Talib. After years of indecision and self-imposed exile in his palm-fringed palace in Salalah, the sultan was suddenly galvanised into action and dispatched a British-led military force against the imam and his followers gathered in the area of Nizwa.

Whitehall was aware of the sultan's plans but decided to delay telling Washington in advance. Eden explained the rationale behind this decision in a minute: 'I agree about telling them before. But won't the State Department inevitably tell Aramco? I would have expected it. Shortest possible notice would be best.' As it happened, the American Embassy in London was informed three days before the sultan's troops were expected to reach Nizwa – too late for the Saudis to mount a military response in support of the imam.[14]

Anglo-American relations were now tense. On 7 December, Dulles sent two separate communiqués to London which caused a sharp reaction: 'Today we were thrown into a rage with the Americans upon receiving two notes,' wrote Shuckburgh. One message warned the British to return to arbitration on Buraimi otherwise the Saudis might take them to the Security Council; the other ordered them to call off Sultan Said's campaign against the imam, again to mollify the Saudis. 'Kirkpatrick [the British permanent under-secretary] is breathing fire and has sent for the US minister'.

According to the minister, Kirkpatrick at their meeting 'vigorously and somewhat emotionally professed British failure [to] comprehend United States policy towards Saudi Arabia [in] relation [to] Buraimi and Muscat'.[15]

The British were willing to take their chances at the Security Council, if it came to that. But while Hoover (a former oilman himself) was not disposed to support them, and leaned towards protecting American oil interests and Aramco, Eisenhower and Dulles were more sympathetic to the British cause. At one point, fearing that Hoover was forgetting that Britain was America's ally on the wider international stage, Dulles had to remind Hoover 'rather sharply' that Britain too was an American interest.[16]

Although Washington attached great importance to American interests and assets in Saudi Arabia – the Dhahran airbase and Saudi Arabian oil – they did not wish to undermine the British position in the Gulf. For the British it was a matter of oil and prestige: they refused to back down over Buraimi and threatened to make a major issue of the captured Saudi documents if the matter did go to the UN – which perhaps accounted for the Saudis' uncharacteristic silence at this time.[17]

Meanwhile, the sultan's forces pressed on. Nizwa was set in an oasis at the head of a mountain valley guarded by a massive circular fort. The advancing force under Lt-Col. Bill Cheeseman numbered 350 men with 43 vehicles, four old pack-guns and four 3-inch mortars. On 15 December, as the troops approached the town, they saw the sultan's red flag flying from the battlements. The imam, having failed to gain enough support to defend the town, had escaped from the fort at midnight by climbing down a rope and making off into the night.[18]

The imam's men surrendered without a fight and only a single shot was fired during the whole campaign. The sultan, having waited on

events, now decided the time had come to assert his authority in
Oman. In December 1955, in a convoy of seven Dodge Power Wagons
with red flags flying and dust billowing in its wake, he left Salalah with
his entourage for a tour of his realm. Driving along rough desert
tracks, they arrived at the PDO oil camp at Jebel Fahud where they
found a tall steel derrick being prepared for the start of drilling in a
few weeks' time.[19]

The climax of the tour was a festive meeting with Sheikh Shakhbut
and his brothers at the Buraimi Oasis: to the victors the spoils. Sheikh
Shakhbut with his humorous face and bushy eyebrows appeared in a
bright yellow finned Cadillac that came sweeping out of the desert. A
feast was laid out on a large carpet. The two rulers took their places
squatting at one end while various others arranged themselves on three
sides around them. Being anxious to follow the protocol of the rulers,
the guests waited for a lead before plunging their right hands into the
piles of rice, camel haunches and mutton that lay before them. Edward
Henderson, anxious to grab a warm handful of rice, found another

Left to right, Sheikhs Khaled and Shakhbut of Abu Dhabi, Sultan Said of Muscat and
Oman, and Sheikh Zayed of Abu Dhabi at their meeting in Buraimi, December 1955.
(source: *The Golden Bubble* by Roderic Owen, Faber & Faber)

hand trying to do exactly the same at the bottom of the pile. Sheikhly chatter mixed with munching and the sound of squelching as diners squeezed rice to remove the grease that dribbled to the floor. After it was finished, and the royal party had departed, a crowd fell like vultures on the remnants of the feast, devouring the leftovers in a frenzy that the royal diners had been unable to match.

The rulers climbed into their vehicles and drove with their respective convoys a short distance into Oman before Shakhbut's yellow Cadillac wheeled about and returned to Abu Dhabi. 'Our Yalta had apparently been a success,' wrote the journalist James Morris.[21]

At last, Oman was under the control of a single ruler. The sultan terminated the Treaty of Sib and abolished the office of imam. Suleiman bin Hamyar had already acknowledged the sultan's rule. Ghalib went to live quietly in his village of Bilad Sait while his brother Talib fled to Dammam and joined the Free Oman Army. All was peaceful in the country; at least that was how it seemed when calm returned to the Buraimi Oasis towards the end of 1955.

* * * * *

On 30 January 1956 Eden and his entourage arrived in Washington DC, their aircraft landing at the National Airport in drizzling rain. Homburg in hand, Eden listened carefully while Dulles welcomed the party: 'We meet here with a background – a tradition – of having worked together for freedom and a just peace.' Eden smiled: 'I am deeply grateful, Foster – if I may call you that. I am quite sure that we can make a serious and positive contribution to peace.'[22]

Beneath grey skies and scudding black clouds, the party sped off downtown for what the diplomats called a *tour d'horizon*, an overall review of common concerns. President Eisenhower welcomed Eden on the White House steps. When the visitor asked: 'How are you?' Ike, recovering from a recent heart attack and aware of eaves-dropping reporters, cupped his hand and jokingly whispered his reply. The talks took place around the octagonal table in the cabinet room, beneath a portrait of George Washington.

The British felt they held the trump card, the secret communications seized from the Saudi police post, which they had translated and shared with the Americans. The disclosure of these documents could not fail to make an impression, most of all on the Saudis themselves. A news correspondent in Washington noted that the Saudi Arabians had been showing themselves much more worried about the British case against them than the State Department had expected. 'There was a tendency in Washington to smile a little superciliously at the handfuls of captured documents [from the Saudi post], revealing Saudi complicity in bribery and in the slave trade that the British have been circulating.'[23]

But Washington would not come off the fence. In the American mind, the king's outstanding virtue was his staunch anti-communism. The British, on the other hand, felt quite the opposite: King Saud's autocratic and repressive regime was an excuse for a communist revolution. His regime could only survive while there was money to subsidise tribes and merchants, and bribe the Egyptians and Syrians. Eden feared that the Saudis aimed to supplant British influence in Jordan with subsidies, and hoped that the Americans might persuade the Saudis to regulate the use of their money in this regard.[24]

Anthony Eden (left) is welcomed to the USA by John Foster Dulles, 1 February 1956. (source: Ed Clark, Time & Life Pictures/Getty Images)

The Americans were prepared to make some compromises, however. At the Washington conference, Eisenhower dropped his demand that the parties return to arbitration, suggesting direct talks instead. Shuckburgh, who accompanied Eden, wrote:

> On Buraimi it soon became apparent that the president and Dulles were much nearer to us than Mr Hoover is. They pretty well accepted that we cannot go back to arbitration, and pressed us to agree to some sort of negotiation 'to save King Saud's face'. We stood on the offer to discuss 'minor modifications' of the frontier, but Ike wanted us to put a little more jam in this for the Saudis. We might be able to but not of course in Buraimi. We thought all this not at all bad.

Second, Eisenhower suggested arms sales to soak up Saudi money, diverting it from Egypt, Jordan and Syria. The official communiqué was bland but significant nonetheless: 'We reviewed the situation in Arabia and the Persian Gulf, with particular reference to current disputes and differences in the area. We believe that these differences can be resolved through friendly discussions.'[25]

Meanwhile, for Aramco, the death of Ibn Saud had brought more than a change of personality at the top; it had brought a difficult relationship with a new king. In 1954, against Aramco's wishes, Saud had negotiated with the Greek shipping magnate Aristotle Onassis an agreement to transport Saudi oil, thus ending Aramco's monopoly over oil resources in the kingdom – in the event, the deal collapsed. But there was a gradual drift away from the closeness that had once characterised the company's relations with the Saudi government, and the company quietly got on with its operations.

The squeezing of Aramco continued: in 1956 the company was paying the Saudi Arabian government $280 million (£2 billion today) for their share of the profits, and other sweeteners besides. Aramco executives were finding it difficult to divine what was in the king's mind. 'No longer can company officials, as in the past, go direct to the king with their problems', wrote one. In the Onassis affair, they had seen the Saudi Arabian government taking greater control of the means of oil production and distribution. Aramco's careful policies might have ensured the survival of the Al Saud but they could not avoid the company's eventual fate, its nationalisation in 1980.[26]

The British ambassador, Roderick Parkes, once remarked that 'if Calais was imprinted on Queen Mary's heart, Buraimi is certainly imprinted on mine.'[27] The same could have been said for King Saud. Although Saud did not have his father's gleam when talking about Buraimi, he was driven by a desire to recover the oasis by whatever means he could get away with. Pride rather than strategic or political considerations shaped his view: he had lost face in the eyes of his people and the world, and wanted to regain his honour.

Yet despite the rhetoric he appeared helpless to do anything about it. He was, according to a Foreign Office memorandum, 'unintelligent, weak and in the hands of his family and advisers.' These advisers, being 'exiles or refugees from their own countries, where they failed to achieve power [...] are more extreme and less responsible even than the ordinary Arab politician. They have no policy other than general hatred of the West and ambition for personal power.' The view among British diplomats of Saudi advisers as 'pinch-beck politicians' had not changed since Gilbert Clayton's day, indeed it had probably hardened.[28]

But the Saudis were in a weak position, and they knew it. King Saud had already promised not to take any action on Buraimi until the conclusion of the Eden-Eisenhower talks. Now, with those talks over, they agreed to sit down with the British.

The parties were a long way from making a breakthrough, however. Discussions in London had already ruled out the possibility of Khawr al-Udayd being offered to the Saudis – thus losing a valuable bargaining counter and leaving nothing on the table. The British were not going to make any concessions. 'If the talks take place and the Saudis raise Buraimi,' commented Foreign Secretary Selwyn Lloyd, 'the extent of our "discussions" would be to say that we stay exactly where we are now. If that caused the talks to terminate, so be it.'[29]

When Douglas Dodds-Parker, parliamentary under-secretary of state for foreign affairs, arrived in Jedda with a British delegation, the first signs looked good. They were received in public audience by the king and then entertained to a family supper of some 50 people in the 70-metre dining room of his new palace. But the British delegation was well aware that the formal courtesies and expressions of goodwill meant little in terms of progress. The serious business began when they left Jedda on 28 April and flew to Riyadh for discussions with the king and his advisers.[30]

They were entertained on a regal scale. Four air-conditioned Chryslers and Cadillacs were at the party's disposal throughout the day. In Jedda much had changed since the oil negotiations of 1933 when the Hamiltons and Twitchells had stayed at the Grand Hotel: the British delegation was offered four suites in the Kandara Palace Hotel. However, members chose instead to stay at the British Embassy and took a few meals at the hotel. In Riyadh they were accommodated at royal expense in the Riyadh Hotel, so newly built that wood shavings were still scattered on the floors. They stayed there for three days, leaving only for official calls and a couple of sight-seeing tours of the 'dusty dun-coloured' capital.

The talks soon stalled. The British stuck to the terms of Eden's statement of 26 October 1955, a stance that failed to impress the Saudis. Dodds-Parker mentioned the possibility of making minor corrections to the boundary – which might have led to a discussion of other issues – but it 'cast an evident chill on the meeting.' Faisal was adamant – he did not wish to discuss any other issue until the Buraimi dispute was resolved. In his view 'there was only one difference between us, whose solution would solve all other Anglo-Saudi issues'. The mission left with the promise of further talks but nothing more, and stalemate reigned once more.

But there was another way of looking at things. King Saud's real interest was in oil and money, and his attachment to the nationalism espoused by the Egyptian president, Gamel Nasser, was superficial at best. As Roderick Parkes noted: 'Today, the attraction of a ride on the Egyptian bandwagon has largely passed [...] and the king [...] would now gladly ease himself out of his link with Egypt.'[32] A Foreign Office official added that 'should we eliminate Nasser, Saud might thankfully put Buraimi into cold storage.'[33] With the support of the Americans, there was a real possibility that Eden might prise Saudi Arabia away from Egypt.[31]

It was not to be, however. In November 1956, the Anglo-French plan to invade Egypt – Operation Musketeer – was implemented. Its flimsy pretext, to protect the Suez Canal from warring Egyptian and Israeli forces, outraged the Arab world. Saudi Arabia broke off diplomatic relations with Britain, which put paid to any immediate prospect of detaching King Saud from President Nasser. It also meant that, in the medium term, a settlement of the Buraimi dispute would be impossible.

Colonel Nasser meets King Saud, 9 March 1956.
(source: AFP/Getty Images)

Paradoxically, King Saud may well have wanted a settlement of the Buraimi dispute. Behind the dark lenses and gold-plated smile was a generous man who liked to get on with his friends. But, even if he had been moved to strike a deal, he would have struggled against the views of his advisers. He was weak and indecisive, easily manipulated and boxed in by the hard-liners, most notably Crown Prince Faisal and the ever watchful emir of Al-Hasa, Saud Bin Jiluwi.[34]

One story illustrates this point. When the king sent an Amiri guide across the desert with a message for Sheikh Zayed of Abu Dhabi, Bin Jiluwi discovered the messenger's purpose and had him incarcerated for a month. Then, on releasing the poor soul, Bin Jiluwi threatened to cut out his tongue if he dared to return through his territory with a message from Zayed to the king. Some aspects of life in the kingdom never changed.[35]

Chapter 18
Rebels and Refugees
The Buraimi Oasis and Oman, 1956–72

After the protests had subsided, a new reality dawned. By the end of 1955 some 400 'Buraimi refugees' were living in the Dammam area.[1] From this group the Free Oman Army (or Oman Liberation Army) was formed, recruited by the Saudi Arabian Army and trained at the Dammam barracks under Talib bin Ali al-Hinai's supervision. All Talib's efforts were aimed at restoring an imamate to Oman. He visited Cairo to drum up support and spread his propaganda, and recruited more soldiers for his army from Omani refugees and labourers in the kingdom. It was estimated that, from July 1956 to May 1957, up to 500 Omani refugees were trained as a battalion.[2]

This was Talib's army. Although Saudi officers and NCOs served as instructors, it was reported that Talib was present nearly every day and that the group 'may have developed a personal loyalty' to him. The Omanis were trained with carbines, Beretta pistols and rocket launchers and instructed in guerrilla tactics. Two motor launches sold to Talib in August 1956 mysteriously disappeared from the coast of Al-Hasa and were believed to be in use along the Omani coast. In January 1957 Talib bought from the Dhahran NCO Club a two-engine fishing boat that was out of commission and half sunk. The boat was raised, had new engines fitted and likewise disappeared from view.[3]

From 1955 reports had been arriving in Muscat of night landings of illicit arms on the Batinah coast of Oman. Neil Innes, the sultan's foreign minister, decided to investigate a report of an arms cache found on a nearby island. Taking a detachment of troops, he spent a day cruising up and down looking at various islands and finding evidence of recent landings but no arms. Some Aramco maps, however, were picked up on the mainland shore. These showed Muscat as a small dot and a territory described as 'Independent Oman' stretching from the coast to the Saudi frontier. In October 1956 the Foreign Office reported the landing of several shipments of small arms by the Saudis at the Omani port of Sur.[4]

Back in Hamasa, the situation was dire. It was clear that reoccupation of the Buraimi Oasis had not brought overwhelming happiness to
the villagers since the departure of the Saudis had virtually destroyed
the local economy. For four years, the village had enjoyed Saudi
influence and money but now, with the principal players gone, the
village was a shadow of its former self.

The first effect of the military action, or 'British aggression' as the
Saudis would have it, had been to produce an exodus of people from
Hamasa and, to a lesser extent, from Buraimi. The principal sheikhs –
Rashid, Obaid and Saqr – had taken some 180 family members and
followers into exile with them. Another 150 people, possibly in fear of
the Muscat regime or expecting reward in Saudi Arabia, left a few days
later. Many others dispersed into the desert whence they had come.
The result was that, by early November 1955, the population of
Hamasa had shrunk from about 3,000 people in its Saudi heyday to
about 40 living on scraps.

Although most of the estimated £10,000 per month paid out by the
Saudis in subsidies and pensions had stayed in the sheikhs' coffers,
enough of it had filtered through to the villagers to have had a
significant impact on their living standards. The pro-Saudi villagers
lived on handouts, neglected their date palms and allowed their *aflaj* to
silt up and fall into disrepair. Those left behind after the exodus had
little to fall back on when the Saudis departed.

There were attempts to revive the local economy on both sides of
the border. However, while work proceeded in and around Al-Ain,
little was achieved on the Omani side. Edward Henderson was asked
to supervise the rebuilding of the crumbling *aflaj* but the sultan would
provide only 900 rupees (£1,500 today) for the work. Fortunately
Henderson had discovered Sheikh Saqr's secret hoard, five *lakhs*
(£830,000 today) of rupees in Kuwaiti chests at his fort in Buraimi. He
persuaded the new *wali* to use some of this money towards repairing
the *aflaj* and distribute some largesse of his own. As work progressed,
however, the sultan grew jealous of the partnership between Henderson and the *wali*. When Henderson left the oasis for a spell, the sultan
refused to provide any more money and all restoration of the Omani
aflaj came to a halt.[5]

The British government stepped in, agreeing to provide extra
money for the *aflaj* on the Abu Dhabi side of the oasis to be repaired.
There was some hope that the sultan might match the investment but

this was misplaced since he was 'not much interested in rehabilitation [...] or in our proposals for the future'. The sultan had a stern attitude towards the defeated villagers: he took the view that they had collaborated with the Saudis and should not expect preferential treatment over his loyal subjects.

These villagers were now set to discover the sultan's true feelings. He had an open and cheerful countenance when he visited them in December 1955 but he failed to distribute any largesse, leaving them disappointed. One of the Abu Dhabi sheikhs was heard to say, 'If the sultan continues with his tight-fisted policy in Dhahira and Oman, he will again be hated by his subjects. Rulers should always be generous.' As the political agent reported at the time, his remarks could have applied equally to Sheikh Shakhbut.[6]

This was a disaster in the making. Arguments over repairing the *aflaj*, clumsy attempts by the sultan's tax collectors to gather *zakat* in the area, the Muscat government's restrictions on trade, the sultan's miserliness and the general economic decline all combined to produce a disturbing contrast within the Buraimi Oasis between the villages of Oman and those of Abu Dhabi. When a political officer visited Buraimi in June 1956, he found that trade had forsaken Buraimi which was a dying community while the *suq* in Al-Ain was thriving. An old Omani asked him, 'How can I join forces with Sheikh Zayed? Here we are dying a slow death.'[7]

In a different era, the sultan might have escaped any public censure. But the world was changing and his indifference was not something that could be considered in isolation. If, as was quite possible, the UN Security Council decided to send a mission to the oasis, it could not fail to draw adverse conclusions about the sultan's treatment of his people. And once the report was published, Radio Cairo would no doubt ensure that those conclusions were broadcast to the Arab world in the shrillest tones.

* * * * *

In 1956 Salih bin Isa al-Harithi travelled to Cairo as the spokesman of the imamate of Oman, and imamate offices were opened in Cairo, Damascus, Riyadh and Beirut. In October Salih made an appeal to Arabs on Cairo Radio which amounted to little more than an anti-British rant: 'They [the British] seek your enslavement and exploitation. They aim only at sucking your blood [...] Britain is still as she had always been, treacherous and deceitful [...] She is an enemy of the Arabs.'[8]

It was stirring stuff and grist for the nationalist mill, but the real threat came from Talib. In June 1957 he landed at Al-Suwaiq on the Batinah coast with 100 men and headed for Bilad Sait, where he persuaded his brother Ghalib to come out of retirement and resume the title of imam. From his mountain fastness, Suleiman bin Hamyar decided to cast his lot with the rebels. Saudi land-mines were planted along the Semail Gap, an essential route linking the interior with Muscat. A short, brutal civil war followed, as rebels financed with Saudi money and supplied with Saudi arms took on the sultan's forces.[9]

Suddenly a crisis had enveloped the sultan, threatening to undo the gains of 1955. The sultan's army failed to take the rebels' mountain fortress on Jebel Akhdar. In December 1956 news came through to British intelligence staff in Bahrain that arms shipments were getting through to the rebels, some by Aramco trucks and others shipped by sea or overland by caravan. The RAF reported camels with suspiciously square loads moving through the Liwa region towards Oman, and bedouins said they had heard vehicles in remote places, an unusual occurrence in those days. The bedouin telegraph was humming.[10]

Most of these reports were rumours and without foundation. There were no confirmed sightings of Aramco trucks, and RAF reports of rebel encampments turned out to be sheikhly hunting parties; the camels loaded with ammunition turned out to be carrying salt; an armoured car was in fact a British Bedford lorry labouring across the desert. But it was clear that something was going on. Supplies were getting through: British officers could identify grenades captured from the rebels as American-made and, by implication, supplied by Saudi Arabia. These grenades, together with American-made land mines and rebel admissions that they had been trained in Saudi Arabia, would provide ample evidence of Saudi complicity.[11]

The ensuing conflict can be told briefly. The Saudis held back from direct involvement and in time, after a series of setbacks, the sultan with British support managed to suppress the rebels. In 1959 the *coup de grâce* was delivered when the SAS stormed the rebel stronghold of Jebel Akhdar. Talib, Imam Ghalib and Suleiman bin

Hamyar narrowly escaped from Oman by sea, fleeing to Dammam with the tattered remnants of the Free Oman Army. Here Ghalib struck a quiet figure, devout and thoughtful, still dreaming of an independent Oman under his imamate but unfamiliar with the ways of the wider world. 'He is kind and human,' wrote an interviewer, 'but hopelessly unaware of the intricacies of world politics. The more his thoughts are allowed to soar beyond Arabia and Islam, the more they sink into unfathomable darkness.' The imam remained well respected in Oman but lived a quiet life in Saudi Arabia until his death in 2009.[12]

The imamate was also slipping into obscurity. Over the next few years there were a few half-hearted attempts to find a solution to the Oman problem. In 1960 Suleiman bin Hamyar met British officials in Beirut, but after two further meetings their discussions came to an end. Arab supporters of the imamate pressed the United Nations to consider the situation in Oman, resulting in a motion to put it before the Security Council which was, however, narrowly defeated.

A combined patrol of Trucial Oman Scouts and Oman Gendarmerie in an operation on the border in 1962. Here a suspected mine smuggler is being questioned.
(source: M.F. Timmis)

* * * *

Life in Oman returned to its traditional ways, still uneasy, but largely undisturbed by the nationalism that was sweeping through the Middle East. The sultan was back in control.

There were a few moments of light relief. When the British Admiralty discovered that it did not have an up-to-date version of Oman's national anthem, officials made enquiries. The only version they could find was a B-flat clarinet score, which the Admiralty sent to the consul-general in Muscat for his comments.

The consul-general replied that the sultanate had not possessed a band since 1937. So far as he was aware, none of the sultan's subjects could read music, which the majority regarded as sinful. The manager of the British Bank of the Middle East was also consulted – he could read music but did not possess a clarinet. Even if he did, the dignitary who stood in for the sultan at ceremonial occasions and might have recognised the tune was somewhat deaf.

Nevertheless, Chauncy obtained a gramophone record that had a rendering by a British military band of the 'Salutation and March to His Highness the Sultan of Muscat and Oman.'[13] He observed:

> The first part of the tune, which was composed by the band-master of a cruiser in 1932, bears a close resemblance to a pianoforte rendering by the bank manager of the clarinet music enclosed with your lordship's dispatch. The only further testimony I can obtain of the correctness of this music is that it reminds a resident of longstanding of a tune once played by a long-defunct band of the now disbanded Muscat infantry, and known at the time to non-commissioned members of His Majesty's forces as (I quote the vernacular) 'Gawd Strike the Sultan Blind' [...] I am informed by the acting Minister of Foreign Affairs that there are now no occasions on which the Salutation is officially played. The last occasion on which it was known to have been played at all was on a gramophone at an evening reception given by the military secretary of the sultan, who inadvertently sat on the record afterwards and broke it.

An onlooker might have been forgiven for thinking that the consul-general had little to do apart from writing amusing letters and requesting manumission for the slaves who escaped from their owners and managed to clasp the British flagpole.[14]

There was of course a more serious legacy of the reoccupation of Hamasa. The plight of the refugees, those thousand-odd souls now living in exile in Dammam, remained unresolved. They lived in poor conditions, their houses crumbling, their main champion in the kingdom being Turki al-Otaishan who persistently lobbied officials to improve their lot. Shortly after the refugees arrived in Dammam, two Saudi businessmen approached Bernard Burrows in Bahrain saying that their government wished to return to arbitration or negotiation. 'The Saudis wanted to recover [the refugees'] homes or some compensation in order to prevent them feeling aggrieved and therefore acting as a constant reminder that the Saudis had lost this particular round.' But it was to no avail and the leading sheikhs were destined to end their days in Dammam, far from the palm trees and *aflaj* of their beloved oasis.[15]

It was not for lack of trying. At a diplomatic level, Saudi Arabia demanded the refugees' repatriation as a pre-condition of any talks over the future of the Buraimi Oasis. Neither Britain nor her allies were keen on this idea, since they considered that the sheikhs who had sworn allegiance to King Saud were likely to be malcontents and troublemakers if they returned to Hamasa. Only Sheikh Zayed seemed relaxed about the rebels' return, taking the view that they were a spent force in the area.[16]

In 1960 the United Nations appointed a mission led by Herbert de Ribbing to determine the exact number of refugees in Dammam. The Saudis told him there were 3,500, a figure that the British considered to be wildly inflated. According to one report, when de Ribbing visited Dammam, instead of finding a collection of poverty-ridden malnourished people, he found people well off, well fed and looking as if they had stepped out of a 'Hollywood studio'.[17]

Julian Walker, the political officer who had met Turki bin Abdullah al-Otaishan on the Cocatrix visit to Hamasa in July 1954, was appointed as the sultan's representative on the UN Team investigating the plight of the refugees. When the team visited Dhahran in the autumn of 1961, Turki was there to greet them. Turki had lost none of his *bonhomie*: he presented each member of the team with a Rolex watch. The fact that Turki was still distributing gifts might have seemed ironic in the context of the Buraimi dispute but, for Turki, this was simply good manners. The team went on to visit Crown Prince Faisal and King Saud in Riyadh, travelling on a special royal train, with two carriages for four people.[18]

Despite de Ribbing's efforts, the refugees – Sheikhs Rashid, Obaid and Saqr and their retainers – did not make it back to Hamasa. By the end of 1961 de Ribbing had sifted the cases of 320 heads of families who claimed to have fled from the oasis. However, a proposal to return them to the village was overruled by King Saud who demanded that the returning sheikhs should be allowed to retain their loyalty to him. The arguments went on but any hopes of reaching a settlement were evaporating away.[19]

By October 1962, de Ribbing's work was almost complete. The Saudis insisted on the establishment of an international body to oversee Buraimi. This was not acceptable to the sultan of Muscat and Oman since it threatened his sovereignty. The Saudi representative, Dr Azzam, kept reminding the UN secretary general that the next move was up to the British, but they dragged their feet, wishing to retain UN interest in the refugee issue while at the same time supporting the sultan's position and rejecting a settlement. Another stalemate was reached.[20]

The Oman question proved rather more durable. It became a regular feature of UN General Assembly sessions and numerous sub-committees. De Ribbing was pressed into service again in 1963, visiting Oman, Saudi Arabia and London on a fact-finding tour. He found that there had been no recent fighting in Oman, indeed no active warfare since January 1959 when the Jebel Akhdar rebels had been defeated. His mission tried to learn about the rebels but all those interviewed stated there were no rebels anywhere in Oman. There were indications, carefully and cautiously expressed, of a certain amount of criticism of the sultan. However, most respondents made comments like 'there is safety and security now' and 'before people were at each other's throats. Now there is peace.' De Ribbing concluded in his report that British officers had nothing to do with policy-making, and that Oman was an independent state free of colonial rule.[21]

The Arab nations were not satisfied. In response to their sustained pressure, the UN set up an ad hoc committee to report on the Oman question. Sultan Said, although agreeing to meet representatives on a visit to London, refused to allow them to visit Oman. Small wonder, then, that the committee should conclude Oman was a matter for international concern because of 'imperialistic policies and foreign intervention in Muscat and Oman'.[22] The UN General Assembly approved the committee's report and passed a resolution calling for British forces to be withdrawn and for self-determination in Oman. But no further action was taken and although the item was repeated on the General Assembly agenda for several years, nothing came of it. When Oman was admitted to the United Nations in 1971, the item finally became redundant.

The greatest danger to Oman was the sultan himself. After years of civil war in Dhofar, his only son Qaboos mounted a coup against his father. According to the Americans, the British knew of Qaboos' plans in advance, but they disclaimed any responsibility for the coup.[23] Sultan Said was removed from the throne and put on a plane to England.

Qaboos was a complete contrast to his father. Sandhurst-trained and having served with the British army, he had been under virtual house arrest in Salalah since 1964. When he stepped off the plane into the cauldron of Muscat in July 1970 at the age of 29, it was apparently the first time he had ever been to the capital city. Slim with a black beard, a dark gown over his white robe, wearing a red, blue and gold turban, he looked impossibly young for the throne. But it made no difference to the populace: drums, jubilant fusillades and waving red flags greeted his arrival.[24]

The old ministers were dismissed. Sultan Qaboos the moderniser, anxious to drag Oman out of the past and bring an end to the Dhofar war, proposed a general amnesty for rebels and exiles, many of whom returned to Oman. Even the imam's brother Talib was offered a post in the new government, which he refused, but other members of imamate families accepted, such as Sheikh Saud al-Khalili who became Minster of Education. Sheikh Saud went on to lay the foundations for a rapprochement with Saudi Arabia over Buraimi. In January 1971, as chairman of the Oman Friendship Committee, he visited Riyadh where he found a sympathetic ear. King Faisal was more concerned about left-wing revolutionaries like the Dhofar Liberation Front than in perpetuating a boundary dispute with Qaboos.[25]

The Arab League, having backed the imamate in the past, was now ready to recognise Qaboos as the legitimate ruler of Oman and to accept his application for membership. In the true spirit of Arab friendship, the League also tried reconciling the sultan with the Imam

Ghalib but this was no easy task. In August 1971 a meeting was held in Beirut between an official of the Arab League, the imam, his brother Talib and representatives of the sultan.

The talks ended in deadlock – not, according to the Beirut weekly *Al-Hawadith*, for an obvious reason. The Arab League representative had called on both sides to make their peace for the greater good of the Arab nation. The sultan's party assured the imam that he would receive the highest honours if he agreed to return to Oman. In reply, the imam declared that he had two conditions and, unless one of them was met, he would not renounce the imamate or his place at the Arab League: 'The first condition is that I get the agency for Pepsi Cola and my second, if that is impossible, is that I get the Shell agency for distribution of oil products.'[26] However bizarre that might have seemed, it was clear from the outcome of the meeting that hopes of an accommodation with the imam had been dashed.

In December 1971 Qaboos travelled to Riyadh for talks with King Faisal. While he appeared straight-faced at Faisal's side, television coverage showed him smiling and relaxed at functions. He made a good impression among the Saudis and even Faisal warmed to him, fondly recalling an occasion when he had stopped over in Muscat and Sultan Said had presented him with a camel. United by their concerns over the war in Dhofar, the two rulers discussed among other things the border and agreed on an interim settlement of the Buraimi dispute. As a result of Qaboos' visit, the Saudis lowered the tenor of their support for the imamate and, by implication, the level of their ambitions in Oman. Furthermore, Riyadh agreed to provide financial help for the sultan's military campaign in Dhofar.[27]

As well as British troops and advisers, the forces of several countries were now supporting Qaboos in Dhofar: Iran, India, Jordan, Pakistan and the United Arab Emirates. In 1973, with the arrival of an Iranian brigade, along with artillery and helicopters, the tide began turning in the sultan's favour. Omani and Iranian forces gradually wore down the guerrillas, pressing them back to the South Yemen border. By 1976 the province was peaceful again.

It was a far cry from the days of his father. When Sultan Said had arrived in England in 1970 to begin his life in exile, he seemed relieved. He went to live out his days at the Dorchester Hotel in London, settling easily into the style he had enjoyed on previous visits. Yet the pace of life had slackened: there were no more meetings, negotiations, politicians or soldiers beating a path to his door. In 1972 he decided to visit America but, as the liner was approaching New York, he suffered a severe heart attack on the staircase of the liner and returned to England, where he died.

Chapter 19
Shaybah Rising
Frontier Negotiations, 1956–present

The Eisenhower Doctrine, which the president launched in January 1956, was meant to represent a new world order. Designed to counter Soviet expansionism, it guaranteed the territorial integrity of a state from external aggression. However, Washington recognised Britain's special interest in Aden, Oman, Muscat and the Gulf sheikhdoms by excluding those areas from it. The doctrine marked a shift in the Middle Eastern pecking order, America filling the power vacuum left by the Suez debacle, but it largely proved to be a 'damp squib'.[1]

The decision of Prime Minister Anthony Eden not to inform the Americans in advance of Operation Musketeer, as the operation to retake the Suez Canal was code-named, had dealt a harsh blow to the special relationship. On 20 November 1956 the Australian ambassador to the United Nations reported a meeting with Hoover:

> I said I was greatly distressed by [the] atmosphere at [the] UN – the almost physical cleavage between the UK and US was one of the most distressing things I had ever experienced. Hoover said this cleavage had gone much deeper than people imagined. It had however started a long time ago even before Suez as far back as the Buraimi incident.[2]

But Hoover's comments represented only one strand of American diplomacy, and the underlying desire on both sides of the Atlantic was to repair relations. In the aftermath of the crisis, Washington acted quickly to restore oil supplies to Western Europe. At the Bermuda summit of April 1957 relations appeared to thaw. There was a good personal bond between Macmillan and Eisenhower, old wartime comrades and friends. Buraimi was mentioned only briefly: Eisenhower stressed the importance of maintaining friendly relations with Arab states in order to enjoy access to their supplies of oil, and asked Macmillan to be flexible over the Buraimi dispute. Macmillan said he would not betray his Gulf allies, a view that the president described as reasonable. With this came a tacit understanding that the British position in the Persian Gulf was worth preserving as a buffer against communism. Buraimi, it seemed, was no longer a major issue between the two countries.[3]

British relations with Saudi Arabia were not so easily mended. The Saudis, as we have seen, broke diplomatic relations with Britain in response to the Suez crisis, and it was not until 1963 that relations were restored. There were no celebrations and the most notable feature of the announcement was the silence that followed it, a clear indication that the Saudis were still unhappy about the unresolved dispute over Buraimi.[4]

Through the 1950s oil wealth rolled into Saudi Arabia and the royal family grew with the expanding state. King Saud had started his reign in the old fashioned way, visiting tribes and distributing largesse, but in the West he was seen as the caricature of an oil-enriched Arab, a white-robed figure in sunglasses wearing a gold Rolex watch.

Crown Prince Faisal found it difficult to watch from the sidelines while Saud squandered fortunes on his pleasures. Despite his efforts to rein in the royal budget, including a two-year austerity programme, Faisal was frustrated by Saud's extravagance. In 1964 he decided to act. He ordered the *ulema* to be convened and, while a *fatwa* was being drawn up, travelled slowly across the country in an outrageously flamboyant 400-car motorcade, making repeated stops to attract maximum attention. When news came through that he was to be king in place of Saud, Faisal professed astonishment but, after prayer and deep reflection, he accepted the *ulema's* call. Saud was deposed, eventually going into exile and dying in Athens in 1968.[5]

* * * * *

The situation in Abu Dhabi mirrored Saudi Arabia in one respect, the pledge that a parent had extracted from her sons. Sheikha Salaamah had the agreement of her sons not to kill each other, and her sons had kept their pledge, but Sheikhs Zayed and Hazza were chafing under Shakhbut's rule.

In 1958 the Anglo-French oil company, ADMA, had struck oil in Abu Dhabi territory in the Umm Shaif offshore field. This was followed in 1960 by the IPC subsidiary, PDTC, with an onshore strike

at Murban No. 3 well. In 1965 PDTC's successor, the Abu Dhabi
Petroleum Company (ADPC), signed a 50-50 oil-sharing agreement
with Sheikh Shakhbut. By 1966 Abu Dhabi was the fourth largest oil
producer in the Gulf and was expected to earn £25 million (worth
approximately £350 million today) in oil revenues. All this was good
news but, under Shakhbut, Abu Dhabi's 25,000 people saw little sign
of the wealth.[6]

As we have seen, Sheikh Shakhbut was a conservative ruler who
was unmoved by all this talk of progress. When he was aware that he
would soon become one of the richest men in the world, the oil
company asked him if he needed anything. Shakhbut replied that he
would like it very much if the company could possibly install a
telephone for him from his reception room to the palace gate and to
the harem. Such was the limit of his horizon at that time.[7]

But there was a serious side to this. The political agent, Archie
Lamb, took him for a flight over Abu Dhabi, hoping to persuade him
of the need to develop the country. Shakhbut enjoyed the flight but
announced that Abu Dhabi was beautiful as it was, and it would be a
shame to spoil it with more buildings. Foreign contractors and advisers
proposed roads, schools, power plants, harbours and sewage systems,
which Shakhbut always refused. Once he agreed to build a modern
hospital, but then refused to equip it. 'My people have lived here for a
thousand years in perfect health, why do they need a hospital?' he
remarked as the prefabricated building stood empty, gathering sand.[8]

For years, Zayed had tried to persuade his older brother to use the
oil wealth to develop the sheikhdom. Running out of patience,
members of the family plotted to remove Shakhbut but twice – in
1963 and 1965 – lost their nerve. In view of Zayed's pledge to his
mother not to kill his brother, and the family history of fratricide, it
was perhaps understandable that they were reluctant to risk a reprise
of the events of the 1920s. But in 1966 the Al Nahyan family finally
held its nerve, deposed Shakhbut and appointed Zayed as his
successor.[9]

On 6 August 1966, with the support of two squadrons of Trucial
Oman Scouts (formerly Levies), Shakhbut was removed from the
palace and went into exile. Zayed declared, 'Our priorities are many.
We need a deep-water port, an international airport, hospitals, schools
and town planning, plus some parks for the people. From now on, the
people will reap the fruits of our prosperity.'[10]

Sheikh Zayed's accession was greeted with relief in all parts of the country, although there were no public displays of jubilation. Many could not believe that Shakhbut had gone. Sheikha Salaamah was kept in the dark: in her eighties, crippled with arthritis, she was told that Shakhbut had gone away for treatment for his eyes.[11]

Yet, despite his unceremonious departure, Shakhbut remained on good terms with Zayed and returned from exile in December 1969. Of the 3–4000 people gathered at Abu Dhabi airport to greet him, the vast majority were of Shakhbut's generation. The bedouin appeared in their truckloads from Al-Ain and Liwa to pay their respects. It was an Abu Dhabian occasion, remarkably free of the foreigners and hangers-on who normally surrounded Sheikh Zayed.[12]

As he descended the steps from his aircraft, a frail Shakhbut was almost bowled over by the crowd that surged forward to meet him. A few officers from the Abu Dhabi Defence Force (ADDF) managed to form a cordon around the sheikh and escort him to the airport build-ings. As they moved slowly forward, several of the older bedouin knelt at Shakhbut's feet and others placed a garland around his neck. By the time he reached the VIP lounge, Shakhbut looked utterly exhausted. Once inside, the police tried to hold back the throng pressing against the door. In the confusion, a policeman punched a British diplomat in the stomach. Zayed retained his dignity, standing aside to allow the bedouin to greet Shakhbut. Indeed many people scarcely noticed that Zayed was there at all.

At a dinner that evening Shakhbut still looked tired but was full of curiosity about his old friends, both Arab and British. Next day, the bedouin dispersed and Shakhbut went to Al-Ain to live out his life in a palace specially built for him between the villages of Muwaiqi and Jimi. Zayed had no concerns about his people's affection for his brother and set off on a month's hunting in Pakistan, leaving the government in the hands of his son.

The frustrations of the Shakhbut years seemed a distant memory now. The oil wealth was rolling in, new roads were being built, buildings were springing up, and yet Shakhbut still retained the respect of his family and people. Michael Sterner, US Ambassador to the UAE, witnessed a touching scene in the 1970s when he attended a function at a newly built hotel in Al-Ain. There he found Shakhbut at his regal best, haughty and unbowed, standing at the top of stairs, receiving his cousins, Tahnoun, Mubarak, Hamdan, and others as they arrived. When each of them bent over to kiss him respectfully on the nose, Shakhbut moved not one inch towards them to make his nose more accessible. They may have deplored the old tyrant when he was in power, but he still held a commanding presence among them.[13]

Few of those who turned up to greet him had really wanted to turn the clock back. But, as Zayed himself was probably thinking at the time, old loyalties die hard.[14]

* * * * *

In 1965, without reference to Sheikh Shakhbut, King Faisal reached an agreement with the sheikh of Qatar over their countries' border, which would (in the absence of Abu Dhabi) have given the Saudis access to the lower Gulf through part of Khawr al-Udayd. This had done nothing to resolve other boundary disputes in the region. Following his accession, Sheikh Zayed visited Riyadh in April 1967 and had a frank, brotherly discussion with Faisal. However, the king and his advisers seemed to be wearying of the dispute. They were preoccupied with President Nasser of Egypt and the impact of his nationalist message on their own people. In fact, they seemed so obsessed with their domestic problems that they appeared to have no great energy left for anything else.[15]

The situation in the lower Gulf was about to change dramatically. In 1967 British forces were withdrawn from Aden, and the Gulf sheikhs, feeling nervous, looked to the British government for reassurance that Britain would stay in the region. In November, the minister of state at the Foreign Office, Goronwy Roberts, visited the Gulf rulers and delivered the necessary promises. In January, however, following a cabinet crisis over the devaluation of the pound, he was back with a completely different message: Britain would withdraw from the Gulf by the end of 1971. His words signalled the end of 150 years of peace based on British control of the Gulf, the so-called 'Pax Britannica'.[16]

The Gulf sheikhs felt betrayed and vulnerable. In the face of their pleas to Britain to remain – Sheikh Zayed even offered to pay the cost of a continuing military presence – Whitehall pressed on with its plan.

In 1970, much to the surprise of British officials, Faisal came up with a new proposal, trading his claim to Buraimi for territory east of Khawr al-Udayd and a newly-discovered oilfield. But the British were anxious to protect IPC's interests and persuaded Zayed not to discuss territorial issues with Faisal.

In May 1970 Zayed again travelled Riyadh in order to discuss Faisal's attitude towards the proposed federation of Gulf states. Faisal listened politely at first but then abruptly asked what proposals Zayed had brought to end the frontier dispute. True to his agreement with the British, Zayed declined to discuss the matter. Faisal repeated his demand for Khawr al-Udayd as a 'window on the Gulf', parts of the southern border and a plebiscite in the Buraimi Oasis. He also demanded that the Hamasa refugees living in Dammam should be allowed to return to their homes – and that IPC's associate company, ADPC, stop test-drilling the Shaybah–Zarrara oilfield.[17]

This brought a new factor into the equation. In 1968 ADPC had discovered the Zarrara oilfield, part of a super-giant oilfield that straddled both sides of the Riyadh Line. The southern end of the oilfield, in Saudi territory, known as Shaybah, had been discovered by Aramco. With oilfields aplenty, neither side was in any great hurry to develop the field: in fact Saudi Aramco, the nationalised successor to Aramco, did not start production there until 30 years later. But in 1968 it became embroiled in the great negotiation about the border. Zayed wished to assert his rights, but the British had different ideas.[18]

In the light of their impending withdrawal from the Gulf, and the vulnerability of the new federation, the United Arab Emirates, the British considered a different approach: Zayed should improve relations with the Saudis and Faisal should not be provoked. But then Faisal was unbending. Although Zayed agreed to suspend drilling at the site nearest to the Riyadh Line, Faisal insisted that all drilling on the oilfield should cease. When the Foreign Office suggested that the oil company should not recommence drilling in the Zarrara field until the boundary dispute was settled, the oilmen joined the argument.

IPC managing director, Christopher Dalley, contended that Zarrara was a major oilfield, as large as the Murban field, and was split almost equally between the two countries by the 1955 border line. In Dalley's view, Aramco had no interest in the Abu Dhabi part of the oilfield since it had more than enough oil already. ADPC would not stop drilling without specific instructions from Sheikh Zayed. With great reluctance, under diplomatic pressure, Zayed agreed to stop the drilling while allowing the oil company to leave a solitary oil rig standing on the field as a symbol of defiance.[19]

As their departure loomed, the British looked to resolving the boundary dispute before the deadline, but were becoming increasingly pessimistic about reaching a final settlement. There was always the possibility of doing a scuttle: 'It will not be a question of rights or wrongs but a *suq* bargain,' one official wrote. In truth, there was a complete stalemate: Faisal was ill disposed to compromise and Whitehall still had an eye on protecting ADPC's interests in the Zarrara oilfield.[20]

On the eve of Britain's departure from the Gulf in November 1971, the Iranians seized three small islands, Abu Musa and the Greater and Lesser Tunbs. Whitehall declined to intervene, thus confirming its commitment to withdrawal from the Gulf. Zayed did nothing about the seizure, being anxious to avoid confrontation and conflict with his more powerful neighbour.[21]

All this emphasised the perilous situation of the small Gulf states, flanked as they were by large and ambitious neighbours, Saudi Arabia and Iran. Internal bickering and dissent among the Trucial sheikhs made the situation worse, although the main territorial issues between them had already been settled.[22] Zayed, using all his persuasive skills, struggled to form a federation of the Trucial States, Qatar and Bahrain, against the resistance of two rulers in particular, Sheikh Saqr of Ras al-Khaima, who was described as a 'born plotter', and Sheikh Rashid of Dubai, a wealthy ruler in his own right, who did not have much affection for Zayed's grandiose schemes.[23] In the end, the rulers of the seven sheikhdoms of the lower Gulf agreed to enter a federation as the United Arab Emirates (UAE) while Bahrain and Qatar chose to go it alone.

Faisal bided his time. He voiced no objection to the idea of a federation, but refused to recognise it. In this, he held a bargaining counter in any future negotiations over the borders. For Faisal, like his father before him, stuck to the archaic notion that the rulers of the Trucial States were vassals 'squatting in Saudi territory', the Buraimi Oasis in particular.[24]

On 2 December 1971 the United Arab Emirates (UAE) was born into an uncertain world.[25] Virtually the first act of the new president, Sheikh Zayed, was to put his military forces on a state of alert, fearing that the Saudis were planning to attack Abu Dhabi. Hawker Hunter jets patrolled the western border twice a day, with numerous photographs being taken, and troops patrolled in the south near

Zarrara and Umm al-Zamul. In the event, Saudi troops did not materialise. Perhaps, as one observer noted, Zayed suddenly felt lonely without the British. In the same month, the British ambassador to Abu Dhabi, Jim Treadwell, wrote, 'So, I say, let both these independent states get on with it.'[26] And this is exactly what they did.

* * * * *

The first public sign that agreement had been reached over the border dispute came in a bland press release at the end of July, 1974. It was perhaps fitting that one of the first Westerners to hear the news was Michael Sterner. Sterner, it will be recalled, was a young Aramco employee working in Ras Tanura, Saudi Arabia, in August 1952 when Turki al-Otaishan disappeared to the Buraimi Oasis. Sterner was now the US ambassador to the UAE based in Abu Dhabi.

The town at this time was a massive building site with a host of construction cranes crowding the horizon. Foreign diplomats visiting the Foreign Ministry would have to step out of their cars onto a pavement and negotiate a small dune, their shoes filling with sand, to reach the entrance to the building.[27] Many government officials had left town to escape the sweltering heat. The minister of state for economy and industry, Muhammad Habroush al-Suweidi, was one of the few officials left in town.

At a meeting with Sterner, Habroush announced that a deal had been struck between the UAE and Saudi Arabia the day before. Sterner noted:

> The Saudis are given a corridor to the Gulf between Qatar and Abu Dhabi [...] In addition to a stretch of coastline of 50 kilometres or more, the Saudis would get a triangle in the south-western corner of Abu Dhabi and a long, thin triangle along Abu Dhabi's southern border. According to Habroush, [the agreement] will give the Saudis a larger portion of the Zarrara oilfield, but not all of it [...] In return for these territorial concessions, the Saudis agreed to waive their claim to Buraimi.[28]

This was historic news and a poignant moment for Sterner who, having been present at the start of the Buraimi dispute, was now seeing its conclusion. Even so, Habroush seemed strangely unmoved, adding that the conceded territory was of little value because there was no oil there and the land itself was mostly salt marsh; indeed he was puzzled why the Saudis had made such a fuss about it in the first place.

At a dinner that evening, Sterner told the UAE foreign minister, Ahmad bin Khalifa al-Suweidi, how pleasant it was to see the Buraimi dispute settled at last. The minister replied with a smile, 'I think your secretary of state has started something that is contagious'. He was referring to the Nobel Peace Prize awarded to the US secretary of state, Henry Kissinger, the year before.[29]

Although he was one of the most prominent officials in the UAE at the time, with good tribal connections, Ahmad bin Khalifa al-Suweidi was also a moderniser who believed the UAE should play an active role in the wider world. This was in contrast with the views of other important figures in the federation, but Sheikh Zayed respected his intelligence and integrity, and probably sympathised with him. However, Zayed was careful not to distance himself from his fellow sheikhs. Despite his political acumen and high status, al-Suwaidi was unable to disclose the exact terms of the border settlement to Sterner.[30]

The settlement, which became known as the 1974 Jedda Agreement, was not published at the time. In the opaque world of Arabian politics, this was unremarkable, but there were a few clues to be found elsewhere. Deputy prime minister of Saudi Arabia, Prince Fahd, told the US ambassador in Riyadh that initialling the border agreement with Abu Dhabi was the happy conclusion to six months' secret talks. He had avoided using pressure or any threat of force, drawing on his personal friendship with Zayed. Saudi Arabia had achieved its objectives in obtaining part of the Zarrara oilfield and a passageway to the Gulf, thus enhancing its position in the region.[31]

It was an intriguing statement, suggesting that territorial disputes were a thing of the past. Apparently, Zayed had said that boundary demarcation was a mere formality. There were 'no such things as boundaries on the Arabian Peninsula since all of the states were merely branches on the great tree of their Father Faisal'. This seemed to brush aside all the past difficulties of the Buraimi dispute. With history thus rewritten, it was little wonder that the British ambassador's face on hearing the news was said to be 'black'.[32]

But the US ambassador in Riyadh, James E. Akins, doubted that it was quite so clear-cut. Since Zayed's visit to Riyadh was only part of a grand tour of the Middle East, Akin observed, it could be seen as a pragmatic attempt to improve his country's standing in the Arab world:

> Zayed's upward-striving has been accompanied by the adoption of a policy of de facto rapprochement with the aspirations of the UAE's larger neighbours – Iran and Saudi Arabia – without whose cooperation the future stability of UAE would be in real doubt.[33]

That left the Saudi–Omani border issue to be resolved. In 1975 the Saudis asked the Omanis for a strip of territory that would give them access to the Arabian Sea through western Dhofar, cutting off Oman from the troublesome People's Democratic Republic of Yemen. The Omanis replied that they would not cede sovereignty over their territory in Dhofar but would 'cheerfully' agree to any Saudi facilities, such as a pipeline or a port.[34] They made a counter-proposal to move the UAE–Saudi border farther west and north, increasing Omani territory in order to take in a putative oilfield. In return, the Saudis would be compensated with a strip of desert territory in the south.[35]

For a moment, as the Omanis sought to redraw the UAE–Saudi border, it looked as though the 1974 Jedda Agreement might unravel. The UAE wanted none of it and, when the Saudis insisted that a large chunk of Omani territory should go to the UAE instead, Ahmad al-Suweidi told Michael Sterner: 'We don't want it. I told them we would prefer to let the old line stand.'[36]

The mystery about the details of the Jedda Agreement deepened in the summer of 1976 when Saudi guards halted an Abu Dhabi construction crew that was working on a road along the coast linking the UAE with Qatar, claiming that it had entered Saudi Arabian territory. Fresh talks ensued and a new agreement was reached the following year. The Saudi Ministry of Petroleum produced a map that showed the boundary starting some 30 kilometres west of the Sabkhat Matti and bearing an uncanny resemblance to the infamous Saudi 'Red Line', or 'Hamza Line', of 1935.

A month later, it was reported that the Saudis had paid the sum of $32 million to Abu Dhabi for an undisclosed purpose, possibly to pay for a road to be constructed across Saudi territory.[37] This appeared to conclude the boundary discussion with a new line, the 1977 line, drawn across the map, although officials said nothing about an agreement at that stage, preferring to keep their own counsel.

In March 1990 Saudi Arabia finally settled her borders with Oman in an agreement that also provided for shared grazing rights and use of water resources. There was speculation that the Omanis had granted the Saudis their wish to run a pipeline through Dhofar but this was never confirmed in public, and no such pipeline has been built to date. The exact details of the boundary were not disclosed, although the Saudis appear to have accepted a line that approximated to the modified Riyadh Line of 1937, as unilaterally declared by the British in October 1955.[38]

Details of the Jedda Agreement were finally disclosed in 1995. A public document was lodged with the United Nations confirming that all the oil and gas located in the Shaybah–Zarrara field belonged to Saudi Arabia. Article Three of the agreement stated that 'all hydrocarbons in the Shaybah–Zarrara field shall be considered as belonging to the Kingdom of Saudi Arabia,' and provided for the exploration and development of the whole field by Saudi Arabia.

Left to right, King Fahd of Saudi Arabia, Sheikh Zayed, president of the UAE, and Sultan Qaboos of Oman with other Gulf rulers at a meeting of the Gulf Cooperation Council (GCC), 21 December 1994. (source: Gamma-Rapho via Getty Images)

Article Four provided that Saudi Arabia and the UAE would:

> Each undertake to refrain from engaging in and from permitting the exploitation of hydrocarbons in that part of its territory to which the hydrocarbon fields primarily located in the territory of the other state extend.[39]

The agreement apparently defined the boundary line between the two states. It represented a retreat from the amended Riyadh Line as declared by the British in 1955, but was still a long way short of the original Saudi claim of 1949. The Saudis had abandoned their claim to the Buraimi Oasis and – to some diehards – sold out the Hamasa refugees in return for their long-cherished window on the Gulf and an oilfield. The Emiratis had lost an oilfield and gained the recognition of their neighbour. It seemed that a *suq* bargain had been struck after all.

* * * * *

By the end of an eventful century, it seemed that the ghosts of the Buraimi dispute had finally been laid to rest, the boundaries settled, the rebels defeated and the future of the Gulf sheikhs secured. But a few old ghosts still rattled their chains. In 2005 Omani security forces arrested more than 100 suspects, members of a group that called for the restoration of the imamate and seized a cargo of arms. The state security court found 31 defendants guilty of setting up a banned underground organisation and plotting to overthrow the regime and replacing it with an imamate. Sultan Qaboos bin Said ratified the sentences but later commuted them and granted a full pardon, just as he had done for those convicted in a similar plot in 1994.[40]

In the UAE, oil wealth brought fresh challenges and a new generation. Now that the old protagonists were gone – King Faisal killed by an assassin's bullet in 1975, Zayed dying from natural causes in 2004 and King Fahd in 2005 – the stage was set for the border dispute to be revived and fresh questions to be asked.

The catalyst was the Emirates' Dolphin gas project. This was a scheme to pipe gas from the enormous Qatari North Field to Abu Dhabi and Oman. Saudi Arabia had objected to a similar pipeline running to Kuwait because it would have crossed its territorial waters between Bahrain and Qatar. The UAE realised that, if the 1974 Jedda

Agreement was valid, Saudi Arabia could establish sovereignty to a strip of land between Abu Dhabi and Qatar – and block the pipeline or make a claim on its revenues.[41]

The flaws in the agreement were now exposed. Critics questioned its legality in international law on the basis that it had never been published or ratified by the UAE Federal National Council. They felt that it had been signed under duress, at a time when the UAE was especially vulnerable to pressure from her more powerful neighbour. The deal over the Shaybah–Zarrara oilfield still rankled, especially the thought that its 15 billion barrels of proven oil reserves and 25 trillion cubic feet of untapped gas reserves were going to Saudi Arabia.[42]

In 2005 it was reported that President Sheikh Khalifa, Zayed's eldest son and heir, had raised the border question with the Saudis on his first visit to Riyadh as a head of state. The Saudis for their part claimed that the issue had been settled under the Jedda Agreement.[43]

In June 2005 the UAE for the first time publicly stated 'its position, dating back 30 years, that there should be a review of the need for amendments to the 1974 provisional agreement signed between the two countries, but not formally ratified.' After the Saudi minister of the interior visited Abu Dhabi in the same month, Sheikh Hamdan bin Zayed, the UAE foreign minister, announced that a 'frank and transparent dialogue on certain boundary issues' had taken place, adding that:

> The UAE said that some parts of the 1974 boundary agreement can no longer be implemented. The UAE, therefore, presented fundamental amendments to these parts of the agreement [...] The [UAE's] stance in this respect is not new, since the UAE has been expressing the same position since 1975.

A smile and a brotherly embrace, pleasantries and a press release, these were the order of the day. The UAE Foreign Ministry reported that a negotiated solution to the issue, mainly the southern border close to the Zarrara oilfield, and Khawr al-Udaid in the west, was being actively sought.[44]

Who would have believed that, after all these years, ownership of Khawr al-Udayd was still a burning issue between the two countries? Improbable but true, it was reignited by a plan to build a causeway between Abu Dhabi and Qatar. The Saudi Arabian government, being sensitive about their perceived rights in the area, protested to their neighbours that the causeway would pass through Saudi territorial waters. Interior minister, Prince Nayef, repeated the claim that the Saudis owned maritime rights by virtue of their possession of Khawr al-Udayd. The design of the causeway was subsequently changed from 40 kilometres to 65 kilometres in length. In 2008 the cost of the project was estimated at £13bn.[45]

It became a battle of maps. The Saudi Ministry of Foreign Affairs published a map showing Buraimi in Saudi territory, together with several parts of neighbouring Oman and Yemen. This shape of Saudi Arabia was also represented in outline on the pages of Saudi passports.[46]

The UAE Ministry of Information and Culture became involved. In 2005 a map was published in the Map Room of the Ministry's website showing the boundaries as detailed in the Jedda Agreement. But in 2006 the map suddenly sprouted an extension of the Abu Dhabi frontier, bringing it to the boundary of Qatar and cutting off Saudi Arabia's access to the sea at Khawr al-Udayd.[47] Had the UAE suddenly regained its lost territory or was this was an unfortunate printer's error? Emirati officials had allegedly tipped off members of the local press, leaving them in little doubt that it was a deliberate ploy – there was no official disclaimer, which might have been forthcoming if the map had contained a simple mistake, it was claimed.[48]

A Saudi response soon followed. Since the Dolphin pipeline crossed Saudi offshore territory they argued, based on their maritime rights around Khawr al-Udayd, that their consent was required and had not been obtained. This was backed up by the Saudi Arabian government faxing a memo direct to the banks investing in the project stating, 'No construction may be undertaken [...] the kingdom will take all actions necessary to protect its sovereign rights and jurisdiction.'[49]

It sounded serious but came to nothing. Saudi objections to the route of the Dolphin pipeline made no significant impact on the project's implementation and did not affect its risk rating.[50] The Saudi move was interpreted as a warning shot for the UAE to deter it from renegotiating the Jedda Agreement. In July 2005 the pipeline was duly completed and gas production subsequently began.

But there was a lingering unease about the border. In the summer of 2009 Saudi border guards brought in a new fingerprint system and lengthy document checks at its border posts with Abu Dhabi, resulting

in traffic queues of 35 kilometres and delaying some lorries for a week
in the searing heat. The official explanation was that the checks had
been introduced to counter drug and alcohol smuggling. A Saudi
minister denied speculation that the problem was anything to do with
a decision to locate a new central bank in Riyadh instead of in Abu
Dhabi.[51]

Today, as in the past, the natural tendency is to keep disputes
between neighbours out of the public gaze, so it is all the more
surprising when an argument breaks into the public domain. In March
2010 the *Daily Telegraph* reported an incident in the Gulf in which the
UAE navy opened fire on a small Saudi patrol vessel and two Saudi
sailors were injured. 'It looks as though attempts were made to keep
this quiet, which is predictable given the important relationship
between the two countries and the strategic relationship with Iran,' a
Gulf-based diplomat said. 'But it does remind us of the simmering
rows that there are in this part of the Gulf.'[52]

These incidents are brief snapshots of relations between Saudi
Arabia and the UAE. They also represent how far these countries have
come in the space of two or three generations. Despite their recent
differences, Saudi Arabia and the UAE remain close. The two countries are members of the Gulf Co-operation Council and their pro-
Western policies are well co-ordinated. No doubt the close proximity
of the Islamic Republic of Iran and the rise of radical political Islam
have helped to concentrate minds and bring people together.

The days of annexation, when Turki al-Otaishan appeared in the
dusty village of Hamasa and raised the Saudi flag, are long gone.
Indeed, it is an age since Sheikh Shakhbut kept his country's wealth in
a shoebox beneath his bed, Sultan Said travelled in a Dodge Power
Wagon to meet the tribes of Oman and a glassy-eyed Ibn Saud pointed
in the direction of the Saudi oilfields saying to the British ambassador,
'*Ya ibni* [my son], that should all have been yours.'[53]

Epilogue

The Buraimi dispute has generated considerable interest among historians. John Barrett Kelly began the debate in 1964 with his book, *Eastern Arabian Frontiers*. Kelly had been a research fellow at the Institute of Commonwealth Studies at Oxford University under the guidance of Sir Reader Bullard. In 1957, with Bullard's encouragement, he visited the Gulf, befriended Sheikhs Shakhbut and Zayed and visited the Buraimi Oasis. As he developed an expertise on the tribes of Eastern Arabia, his advice was sought by the Foreign Office on the boundary problems of south-eastern Arabia. He later worked in Washington.[1]

Kelly took a pro-British stance. He argued that the Saudi occupations of the nineteenth century had been military incursions, not the periods of orderly and almost uninterrupted administration that were required under international law to establish sovereignty. Their occupations were by no means peaceful, for they were opposed and resisted by force. Indeed, Saudi communications between Al-Hasa and Buraimi had been largely by sea in order to avoid hostile inland tribes. After their occupation of Buraimi ended in 1869, the Saudis did not show an interest in the area until more than 50 years later when they sent tax collectors to the oasis. After that, their collection of *zakat* in the disputed areas was haphazard and irregular.

William Mulligan on the other hand took a pro-Aramco stance. 'The last thing Kelly's book can be called is a work of dispassionate scholarship,' he wrote. Mulligan, who had worked with George Rentz in researching the boundary dispute for Aramco, observed: 'Kelly chooses not only to gloss over the sneak dawn attack which established British control over the area in dispute, but finds not one error in the *UK Memorial* and hardly a sliver of evidence in support of Saudi Arabia's claim.' Kelly had dismissed large chunks of the *Saudi Memorial*, disregarded Saudi arguments against the boundary lines advanced by the British, and ignored the Saudis' willingness to settle the dispute by lawful rather than by forceful means. The dispute was a struggle between 'little' Saudi Arabia and 'powerful' Great Britain, Mulligan claimed.[2]

A more balanced approach came from Hussain Albaharna in *The Legal Status of the Arabian Gulf States* (1968). He concluded that the Saudi claim was weak because of their absence from the oasis between 1869 and 1952. However, the claims of the rulers of Abu Dhabi and Muscat were not particularly strong since they could not easily establish a better title over the disputed territory. It was doubtful that these rulers could rely on the forcible reoccupation of Hamasa to establish effective occupation under international law.

In *Arabia, the Gulf and the West* (1980), Kelly examined the Buraimi dispute in the wider context of regional conflicts. Britain's departure from the Gulf was an unnecessary abrogation of power: the Gulf sheikhs wanted her to remain and there was no significant opposition to her presence. On the border dispute, Kelly criticised British officials for trying to force through a settlement before they departed from the Gulf. His book highlighted the change of approach between the India Office of the 1930s and the Foreign Office of the 1960s, from a determination not to do a deal with Ibn Saud to an enthusiasm to do a deal at almost any price, a '*suq* bargain'.

In *Arabia's Frontiers: The Story of Britain's Boundary Drawing in the Desert* (1991), John Wilkinson brought a new perspective to the debate. Wilkinson, formerly an employee of IPC and Shell, had worked in the Gulf and Oman. He considered that the British case was based on a legal fiction since 'spheres of influence' meant nothing in international law, which recognised effective occupation as the key to sovereignty. Since the Anglo-Turkish Treaty of 1914 had been all about settling spheres of influence, relying on it was bound to fail in international law. The British nevertheless tried to use this fiction against the Saudis and, when their bluff failed, they had to resort to force.

Our knowledge of the Buraimi dispute has been considerably enhanced by archive editions. Jane Priestland's collection of primary source material from Foreign Office files, *Buraimi Dispute: Contemporary Documents 1950–1961* (1992), gives a comprehensive account of events as seen from the British perspective. This, together with Richard Schofield's work with others on Arabian boundaries (see bibliography), and the Buraimi *Memorials*, has certainly made the history of the dispute accessible to the researcher. However, the task of achieving a balanced approach is hampered by a lack of available documents from Saudi Arabian government for the period, although *Saudi Arabia: Secret Intelligence Records 1926–1939*, edited by Anita

Burdett, provides a fascinating snapshot of internal communications between Saudi officials, as do the communications seized from the Hamasa police post in October 1955.

One aspect that continues to intrigue observers is the Jedda Agreement of 1974, which Schofield has called a 'wholly bizarre boundary agreement'. Did it put an end to the Buraimi dispute? Publication of its provisions has done little to answer the question. Using new documents, Schofield was able to suggest that Faisal, Zayed and Qaboos had reached an agreement to end the Buraimi dispute at an Islamic Summit Conference at Lahore in February of that year. Perhaps this explains why there was no explicit mention of the dispute in the agreement struck between Fahd and Zayed a few months later.[3]

Some historians have looked at the Buraimi dispute in the context of Anglo-American relations in the mid-1950s. In *The Middle East between the Great Powers: Anglo-American Conflict and Co-operation, 1952–1957* (1992) Tore Petersen contended that the success of Operation Bonaparte encouraged the British to use military force more readily in the Middle East. In this respect, the dispute represented an important shift in British foreign policy. Conversely, Britain's intransigence so angered the Americans that they were prepared to act against her in the Suez crisis of the following year.[4]

In *Oil, God and Gold: The Story of Aramco and the Saudi Kings* (1999) Anthony Cave Brown made the sensational claim that Aramco's Arabian Research Division was part of a CIA-mounted plot to destabilise the British in Arabia. But the weight of evidence is against him, since the United States government favoured a British presence in the Gulf and tempered American support for the Saudis.

Nathan Citino in *From Arab Nationalism to OPEC: Eisenhower, King Saud, and the Making of US-Saudi Relations* (2002) argued that the Americans were supportive of the British in the defence of the 'post-war petroleum order' during this period, recognising that Britain's presence in the Gulf was vital to ensure a reliable supply of oil to Western Europe and the survival of Great Britain itself. Each country adopted different approaches which complicated their common objective to preserve the petroleum order, but they did not go so far as to fight a proxy war over oil resources.[5]

In *Separate Agendas: Churchill, Eisenhower, and Anglo-American Relations, 1953–1955* (2007) Daniel C. Williamson used the Buraimi dispute as a case study in Anglo-American relations. He concluded that the British decision to use military force against the wishes of the Americans was a demonstration of independent British power. The Americans valued their alliance with Great Britain over the risks to their friendship with Saudi Arabia. The Eisenhower administration backed a British presence in the Gulf as a bulwark against communism. Both Washington and London still saw Great Britain as a viable international power, capable of pursuing her own goals and defending her own interests at this time. The question was how far Washington could support the British without alienating the Saudis.

* * * * *

The enduring quality of the Buraimi dispute cannot be denied. It dominated Anglo-Saudi relations for more than 30 years, and still casts its shadow across the Gulf today. Yet before 1952, the Saudis did not have a conclusive claim to Buraimi, the extent of their realistic claim being the Red (Hamza) Line which fell some 160 kilometres short of the oasis. What happened after Turki al-Otaishan's arrival in Hamasa became obscured in fog of recrimination, allegations being made against the Saudis for bribery and gun-running, and against the British for wrecking the Buraimi tribunal.

A few facts emerge. Evidence culled from the secret communications seized from the Saudi police post in 1955, is compelling proof of serious Saudi misdoing. However, more recent evidence from Foreign Office files shows that the British, in recording a conversation with Dr Hasan, were not above some mischief of their own. It is clear that they deliberately threw the arbitration proceedings because they knew the tribunal was about to decide against them.

Were the British justified in doing this? The seeds of their dilemma were sown in the 1930s when they chose to rely on the dubious legality of the Blue Line. Ibn Saud might well have settled the dispute in 1935 had not the British taken this stand. After that, the Saudis pursued a course of brinkmanship, upping their claims when it suited them and, once Turki was ensconced in Hamasa, winning over the people of the oasis. They backed the British into a corner from which military action was the only equitable release, but it was a corner that the British had to some extent created for themselves.

At the heart of the matter was the disagreement over the Saudi use of cash payments, and whether they were 'bribery' or 'generosity'.

Any suggestion that this was simply a difference of interpretation, the result of a collision between Western and Arab values, is misconceived. The rulers of the Trucial Coast and Oman found the Saudi actions as unwelcome as the British did. They were not able to match the wealth of the Saudis, and it would have been wrong to award sovereignty to the highest bidder. Without their money, the Saudi claim was distinctly thin; with their money, the bona fide claims of the other rulers were undermined.

The history of the dispute says as much about the lack of clarity in British policy as it does for Saudi perseverance. The Foreign Office had twice received legal advice – in 1934 and again in 1950 – that its government's legal position was weak. Yet the British government still agreed to take the dispute to arbitration – something that was always going to be 'a leap in the dark', as one official put it.[6] The British delegation at Geneva then tried to play the Saudis at their own game by attempting to coach Sir Reader Bullard as their agent on their tribunal, a role that Bullard – quite properly – was not prepared to take. In the light of the secret communications subsequently seized, the British felt vindicated. But their tactics at the arbitration left an enduring sense in the Arab world that Britain had avoided an outcome on the issues.

The waning of British influence, particularly in Saudi Arabia, had an important impact on the Buraimi dispute. It had begun with the award of the Hasa oil concession to Socal in 1933, and gathered pace during the war years when Socal executives persuaded the Roosevelt administration to take a more pro-active role in US-Saudi relations. The financial demands of World War II took their toll, leading to a recognition that Britain could no longer be the global super-power it had once been. This decline coincided with a corresponding growth in American diplomatic influence in the region, spurred on by their need for oil during the war. The fact that Washington did not fully support the Saudis over Buraimi indicated that the Americans still considered the British presence in the Gulf an influence worth preserving. But there were limits to their forbearance and, in the Suez crisis, those limits were cruelly defined.

Evidence of this growing American influence came in October 1952 when pressure from Washington caused the British government to persuade the sultan of Oman to call off his march on Buraimi and later, to agree to arbitration. It was only when crucial national interests were engaged – such as oil – that the British demonstrated a measure of decisive, independent action. But Britain's use of military force was driven by several factors in addition to oil: Eden's impatience, the government's frustration over Saudi tactics and its need to dig itself out of the hole that the arbitration proceedings had brought. The role of the oil companies was secondary. Although Aramco assisted the Saudi Arabian government to prepare its case for arbitration and lobbied Washington at the highest level, US foreign policy was never fully squared with Saudi interests. IPC assisted the British government in preparing the *UK Memorial*, occasionally made representations, but took no part in policy decisions at government level.

In their twilight years in the Gulf, the British made ill-fated attempts to resolve the dispute but the final breakthrough only came after they had left the scene. In 1971 the Gulf sheikhs felt abandoned and vulnerable. Sheikh Zayed, as president of the newly formed UAE, felt particularly so because he was in charge of a fragile federation rather than a single state. His main priority was to create and maintain good relations with his two powerful neighbours, Saudi Arabia and Iran. With the Saudis, this meant agreeing in principle to most of what the Saudis wanted. But then Zayed, always the canny desert sheikh, never quite got round to confirming the specifics, which would have been hard for most Emiratis to swallow. The counterpart of this approach was, in the case of Iran, Zayed's quite passive reaction to the Shah's grab for the Tunbs and Abu Musa islands on the eve of the British withdrawal. Again, Zayed was trying to avoid confrontation and the possibility of conflict with his powerful neighbour. It was this motivation more than any other factor that led to a settlement of the Buraimi dispute.

Britain's withdrawal may have been hasty but, in the longer term, it has enabled her to develop relations with the Gulf states on a sounder footing, based on commercial affairs rather than the 'colonial' treaties of the past. Those relations remain amicable despite the rise of political Islam which, with all its stereotypes and radicalism, has replaced Arab nationalism as the driving force of anti-Western rhetoric in some parts of the Middle East. There is among the Gulf people a residual affection towards the British who, despite a reputation for perfidy, helped to keep the peace for more than 150 years.

* * * * *

Jebel Hafit to the south of the Buraimi Oasis is a steep and rock-littered hogback that pierces the sky high above the eastern desert. Taxis and tourist coaches make their way up a metalled road that twists and turns towards a glinting hotel on its summit. Nearby is a palace built for the ruling family to escape the oppressive heat and dust of the plain. Far below, the villages of the oasis appear as one, an urban sprawl dominated by the city of Al-Ain creeping out from its green heart where date plantations and mud walls still survive.

This is the Buraimi Oasis today, divided by the boundary that runs between Oman and the United Arab Emirates. The old forts and watch towers, symbols of a bygone age, now over-restored, their walls impossibly pristine, the stale smells of incarceration and decay banished forever, are still dotted around the oasis. More noticeable on the Emirati side are the shining artefacts of the oil age: the shiny limousine, the gated modern house, the businessman in his spotless white *thobe* wearing sunglasses and doing business in the Intercontinental Hotel. He wears a reminder of the bedouin way of life, a black *igall* bound around his head holding his white *ghutra* in place, its double cords symbolic of the ropes once used to hobble camels. As one drives through the city in an air-conditioned four-wheel-drive vehicle, modern life seems far removed from the 1950s. Even the few bedouin left in the desert are connected to the outside world with mobile phones and satellite dishes.

The contrast between Buraimi and Al-Ain is striking, the difference being between the quiet charm of the former and the bustling modernity of the latter. From a satellite view, the frontier line seems to wander randomly between Abu Dhabi and Oman. Until 2006 it was an open border, allowing people who found the rents in Al-Ain too high to settle in Buraimi. But fears about terrorism, drug smuggling and illegal immigrants have led the UAE government to build a fence and close the border, requiring visitors to apply for visas and cross at certain checkpoints.

Some of the ancient forts have been turned into museums. There is a keen interest in the history of the region but hardly anything is said about the Buraimi dispute. In a speech to the Emirates Centre for Strategic Studies and Research in Abu Dhabi in November 2008, the British foreign secretary, David Miliband, simply referred to it in passing as part of a positive story. It has been shadowed by more pressing concerns, such as international terrorism, the threat from Iran and pro-democracy movements, which unite rather than divide the Arabian governments. There is no appetite for raking over the coals of the past and, dare it be said, the outcome of the dispute has secured the futures of the UAE and Oman as independent states.

No oil has been found at Buraimi. In April 2008 Indago Petroleum drilling the Al Jariya-1 well under Jebel Hafit announced that the drill pipe had become stuck and that the drill-site would have to be abandoned. As the geologists of the early 1950s suspected, the big oil-fields lay to the west and south-east of the oasis. Whoever controlled Buraimi held the ring of south-eastern Arabia; if Buraimi had fallen to the Saudis, many of the oilfields in Abu Dhabi and Oman (and most, if not all, their territory) would probably belong to Saudi Arabia today.

The events of the past are easily forgotten. The oil wealth pours in, buildings spring up and the sunshine seems endless. The *aflaj*, many relying on pumped water, still bring water to the oases. In the distance, the mighty desert lives on, quietly covering fresh vehicle tracks in a fine dusting of wind-blown sand.

Maps

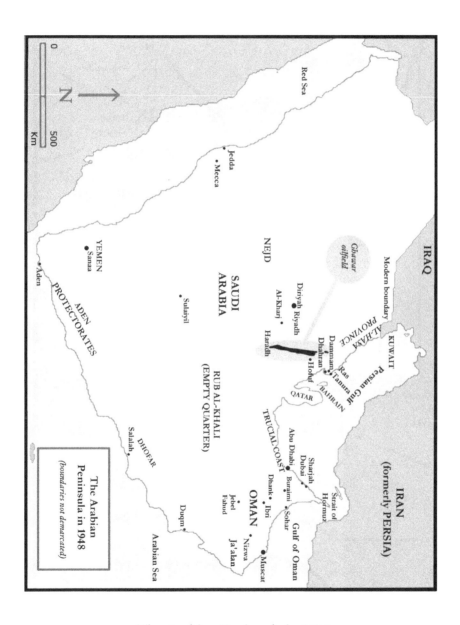

The Arabian Peninsula in 1948

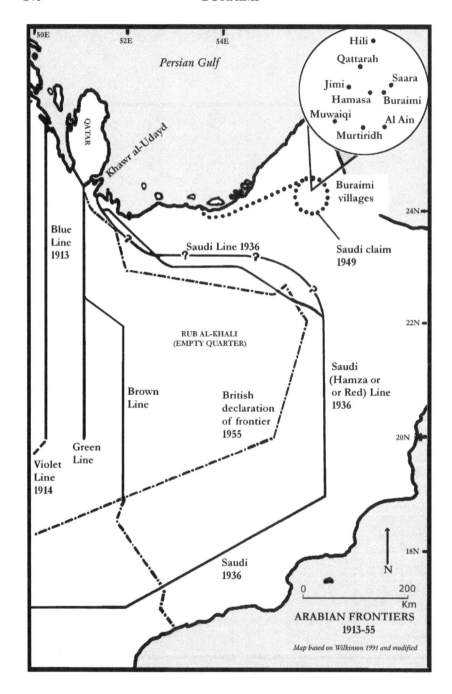

Boundary Proposals

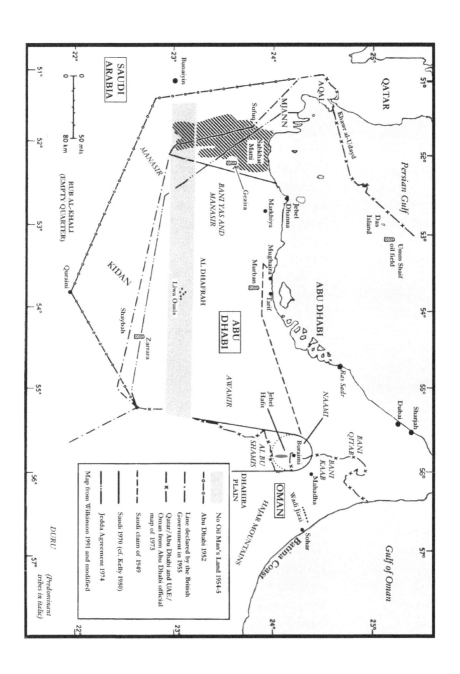

South-eastern Arabia

Glossary

Abba	Robe which serves as an overcoat.
Abeya	Long black robe worn by Arab women.
Aflaj (sing. *falaj*)	Water channels.
Ain	Spring.
Anticline	A convex fold in rock strata, typically in the form of an arch, with the oldest rocks at the core, and beds dipping away on either side.
Aramcons	Personnel of the Arabian American Oil Company, Aramco.
Arddh	Arabian sword dance.
Bait	House, settlement.
Baksheesh	Money.
Bani	The sons of (or tribe).
Barrasti	Bedouin dwelling constructed from palm branches and goat skins.
Bin	Son of.
Chargé d'affaires	Official placed in charge of diplomatic business during the temporary absence of the ambassador.
Cretaceous	Geological period 66–144 million years ago.
Diwan	Advisory body of ministers to the king.
Dhow	Arab sailing vessel.
Eid al Adha	'Feast of the Sacrifice' to honour the Abraham's willingness to sacrifice his first-born son to God, who put a lamb in his place.
Fatwa	Religious edict.
Ghutra	Headdress.
Hajj	The annual pilgrimage to Mecca.
Haji	Someone who has completed the *Haj*.
Hasawi	Someone from the province of Al-Hasa.
Igall	Cord worn around the *ghutra*.
Ikhwan	Wahhabis with the reputation of ruthless warriors.
Imam	Religious leader.
Imamate	Area ruled by an imam.
Ingleez	The English.

Jebel	Mountain or hilly land.
Jihad	Holy war.
Jurassic	Geological period 144–208 million years ago.
Khanjar	Highly decorated dagger, symbol of manhood in Oman.
Lakh	100,000 (usually referring to rupees).
Majlis	Meeting room, place where a ruler holds public audiences to hear petitions.
Marhaba	Welcome.
Markaz	Meeting place or military camp.
Muezzin	Crier who calls the faithful to prayer.
Mujahidin	Muslim warriors.
Nejd	The great desert of central Arabia.
Nejdi	A person from the Nejd.
Pirate Coast	The old name for the Trucial States, today's United Arab Emirates.
Political Agent	Senior British diplomatic representative. The Agent for the Trucial States was based in Sharjah until 1953, then in Dubai. In 1961, a separate political agent was appointed to Abu Dhabi.
Political Officer	Assistant to the political agent.
Political Resident (Persian Gulf)	The equivalent of the British ambassador in the Persian Gulf. Based in Bushire, Iran until 1946, then in Bahrain.
Qadhi	Judge ruling in accordance with *sharia* law.
Ras	Headland.
Rub al-Khali	The great sand desert of southern Arabia, the 'Empty Quarter'.
Sabkha	Salt flat, evaporation pan.
Salaam	Greeting.
Sangar	Small fortified position made of sandbags or rocks.
Shamal	Wind from the north.
Sharia Law	A body of law based on the Quran and the practice of the Prophet Muhammad. *Sharia* means 'the path to a watering hole'.
Spudding in	Term used to describe the start of drilling for oil.
Stratigraphy	Study of rock strata, especially the age, distribution, deposition and age of sedimentary rocks.
Suq	Market.

Tarifa	Representative.
Thamama	Geological term referring to a Cretaceous rock interval. The Upper Thamama, in offshore areas of Abu Dhabi, was found to be oil-bearing in 1958.
Thobe	Long shirt or robe.
Trucial Coast or Trucial States	The seven sheikhdoms of the lower Persian Gulf region: Abu Dhabi, Dubai, Ras al-Khaima, Sharjah, Fujairah, Ajman and Umm al Quwain. In the nineteenth century their rulers had entered into a truce with the British government to end piracy. In 1971 they became the United Arab Emirates (UAE).
Trucial Oman	Another name for the Trucial Coast.
Ulema	A body of Muslim scholars who were, and still are, an influential political force in Saudi Arabia. The Al Saud recognised the special religious position of the *ulema* and sought their approval on a wide range of issues.
Uruq	Sand ridges, derived from the Arabic word for 'vein'.
Wadi	Dried up river bed or valley.
Wali	A title derived from Ottoman times, a *wali* governed a *wilayah* (district).
Wazir	First minister to the sultan of Muscat and Oman.
Zakat	A religious tax.

References

Preliminary Pages
1. Parkes to Luce, 27 April 1966, FO 1016/737.

Note to the Reader
1. Vera Anstey, *The Economic Development of India* (New York, 1977), p. 383.
2. < http://www.bankofengland.co.uk/education/inflation/calculator > last accessed 27 April 2013.
3. Arthur N. Young, 'Financial Reforms in Saudi Arabia', *Middle East Journal*, Vol. 14, No. 4 (Spring, 1960), pp. 466–9.
4. < http://www.westegg.com/inflation > last accessed 27 April 2013.

Prologue
1. *The Buraimi Memorials* (Farnham Common, 1987) contain source material about the Wahhabis. For an account of the first Saudi state: Facey, William, *Dir'iyyah & the First Saudi State* (London, 1997).
2. For a history of Saudi occupations of Buraimi, see Albaharna, Hussain M., *The Legal Status of the Arabian Gulf States* (Manchester, 1968), pp. 208–18.
3. Davey. Charles E., *The Blood-red Arab Flag: an Investigation into Qasimi Piracy 1797–1820* (Exeter, 1997), pp. 91–128.
4. Philby, H. St John, TS draft of *More Arabian Days*, Philby Collection, Box 8, Middle East Centre Archive (MECA), St Antony's College, Oxford. GB165–0229.
5. Albaharna, *The Legal Status of the Arabian Gulf States*, pp. 25–30; and Heard-Bey, Frauke, *From Trucial States to United Arab Emirates* (Dubai, 2004), pp. 279–88.
6. Azzan ibn Qais to Pelly, Jumada 1, 1286/August 1869, India Office Secretary, Letters, Various, Vol. 15, quoted in Kelly, John B., *Eastern Arabian Frontiers* (London, 1964), p. 87; see also the *UK Memorial*, Vol. 1, p. 27.
7. Lorimer, John G., *Gazetteer of the Persian Gulf, Oman and Central Arabia* (Farnham Common, 1986), p. 264.
8. Lord Palmerston to Sir William Temple, 19 April 1833, *Cambridge History of British Foreign Policy*, Vol. 2, p. 162, as quoted in Leatherdale, Clive, *Britain and Saudi Arabia, 1925–1939, The Imperial Oasis* (London, 1983), p. 19.
9. Lacey, Robert, *Kingdom: Arabia and the House of Saud* (New York, 1982), pp. 79–82.
10. Cox to the Chiefs of Abu Dhabi, Debai, Shargah, Um-el-Kowein, Ajman and all the Trucial Chiefs, 22 April 1906, IOR R/15/1/556, quoted in Lacey, *Kingdom*, p. 81.
11. For an account of Britain's relations with Ibn Saud 1902–14, see Wilkinson, John C., *Arabia's Frontiers: The Story of Britain's Boundary Drawing in the Desert* (London, 1991), pp. 113–40.
12. Leatherdale, *Britain and Saudi Arabia*, p. 19.
13. Thomas, Bertram, *Alarms and Excursions* (London, 1931), pp. 174–5.
14. Letter dated 2 October 1929 from Muhammad bin Sultan to Sultan Said bin Taimur of Muscat and Oman FO 371/104278.

Chapter 1. Jedda Calling

1. C. Crane to B. Crane, 9 January 1927, Crane Collection, MECA. GB165–0067.
2. Ryan, Sir Andrew, TS of *Last of Dragomans*, Box 2 File 4, MECA. GB165–0248.
3. Lawrence, Thomas E., *Revolt in the Desert* (London, 1927), p. 1.
4. Ryan, TS of *Last of Dragomans*.
5. See Philby, Harry St J.B., *Arabian Oil Ventures* (Washington DC, 1964); Twitchell, Karl, *Saudi Arabia* (Princeton 1947); Longrigg, Stephen H., *Oil in the Middle East: Its Discovery and Development* 2nd ed. (Oxford, 1961).
6. Bell, Gertrude, *The Arab War* (London, 1940), p. 21.
7. Ryan, TS of *Last of Dragomans*.
8. 'Leading Personalities in Saudi Arabia', 9/7/46, FO 371/5283. Ibn Saud's later decline was apparent to diplomats who visited him: see van Der Meulen, Daniel, *The Wells of Ibn Saud* (London, 1957), pp. 229–30.
9. Longrigg to Skliros, 31 March 1933, PC 10A, BP Archive, Warwick University.
10. 'Jedda Report', April 1932 from the HM Legation, Jedda, Dispatch No. 312 of 29 May 1932, quoted in Niblock, Tim, *State, Society and Economy in Saudi Arabia* (Beckenham, Kent, 1982), p. 46.
11. 'Leading Personalities', 9/7/46, FO 371/52832.
12. Ibid.
13. 'Pinch-beck politicians': Clayton, Sir Gilbert, *An Arabian Diary* (Berkeley, 1969), p. 100.
14. Hodgkin, E.C. (ed.), *Two Kings in Arabia: Sir Reader Bullard's Letters from Jedda* (London, 1994), p. 191.
15. Burrows to Trott, 13 June 1948, FO 371/68777.
16. Philby, *Arabian Oil Ventures*, pp. 77–81.
17. Yergin, Daniel, *The Prize: The Epic Quest for Oil, Money and Power* (New York, 1991), p. 282.
18. Ryan to Warner, 15 March 1933, IOR/15/2/421.
19. Ibid.
20. Longrigg to Skliros, 14 March 1933, PC/10A, BP Archive.
21. 'Dead hand', Longrigg to Skliros, 18 April 1933, PC/10A, BP Archive.
22. Ryan to FO, 11 April 1933; Foreign Office Memorandum 'Oil Negotiations in Saudi Arabia', FO371/16871. The Americans struck oil with the Dammam No. 7 well in March 1938.
23. Skliros to Longrigg, 11 April 1933, PC/10A, BP Archive.
24. Yergin, *The Prize*, pp. 185–8; Longrigg, *Oil in the Middle East*, p. 70.
25. Longrigg, *Oil in the Middle East*, p. 70; Skliros to Longrigg, 9 May 1933, PC/10A BP Archive; Ward, Thomas E. *Negotiations for Oil Concessions in Bahrain, El Hasa (Saudi Arabia), the Neutral Zone, Qatar and Kuwait* (New York, 1965), p. 108.
26. Longrigg to Skliros, 12 March 1933, PC/10A BP Archive.
27. Philby, *Arabian Oil Ventures*, pp. 105–20.
28. Longrigg to Skliros, 16 April 1933, PC/10A, BP Archive.
29. Longrigg to Skliros, 9 May 1933, PC/10A, BP Archive.
30. Longrigg to Skliros, 15 May 1933, PC/10A, BP Archive.
31. Longrigg to Skliros, 14 May 23 May 1933; Skliros to Longrigg, 23 May 1933, PC/10A BP Archive.
32. Philby, *Arabian Oil Ventures*, p. 124.

33. Minister of finance to the king, 29 July 1933, Burdett, Anita, L.P. (ed.), *Saudi Arabia: Secret Intelligence Records 1926–1939*, Vol. 4 (Farnham Common, 2003).

34. As quoted in Kelly, *Eastern Arabian Frontiers*, p. 122.

35. The map shows the southern boundary of Saudi Arabia along the Blue and Violet Lines and the 'British Hinterland of Aden' (Chevron Archive, San Francisco).

Chapter 2. A Bend in the Wadi

1. Political Agent Kuwait to the Civil Commissioner Baghdad, 13 June 1920, IOR L/P&S/10/925, P6317/1920, citing Captain Shakespeare's 'unwritten desert law', C-62, 12 August 1912, cited in Lacey, *Kingdom*, p. 580; Kelly, *Eastern Arabian Frontiers*, pp. 18, 35, 126–7; Wilkinson, *Arabia's Frontiers*, pp. xvi–xvii, xxix–xxx, 259–67.

2. For descriptions of early Casoc surveys, see Barger, Thomas C., *Out in the Blue* (Vista CA, 2000).

3. Ibid., p. 28.

4. Ibid., p. 69.

5. Ibid., p. 24.

6. Thomas, Bertram, *Arabia Felix: Across the Empty Quarter* (London, 1938), pp. 281.

7. 'Business: Personal File', *Time*, 20 October 1961.

8. Barger, *Out in the Blue*, p. 56.

9. Ibid., p. 25.

10. B. 57, p. 77. Bahrain, C/376 of 11 June 1938, to the PRPG, cited in Priestland, Jane (ed.), *Buraimi Dispute: Contemporary Documents 1950–1961*, Vol. 1, p. 749.

11. Stegner, Wallace, *Discovery! The Search for Arabian Oil* (Vista CA, 2007), p. 118.

12. Ibid., pp. 138–9.

13. 'The King inspects Ras Tanura', 1 May 1939, Selwa Press website: < http://www.selwapress.com/video.php# > accessed 12 September 2010.

14. Speers, Peter C. 'Cave, Oil, God and Gold: The Story of Aramco and the Saudi Kings' (Review), *Middle East Policy Council Journal*, Vol. VII, October 1999, No. 1.

15. 'Middle East: Obliging Goliath', *Time*, 13 September 1963.

16. Iraq Petroleum Handbook, p. 26.

17. Philby, Harry St John, *The Heart of Arabia* (London, 1922), p. 71.

18. Tim Barger, email to the author, 25 July 2010.

19. 'Largest oilfield in the world': see Beydoun, Ziad R., *The Middle East: Regional Geology and Petroleum Resources* (Beaconsfield, 1988), p. 208.

Chapter 3. The Riyadh Line

1. Fowle to under secretary of state for colonies, 24 June 1933, IOR PS/12/2/213-0. For boundary negotiations, see Wilkinson, *Arabia's Frontiers*, pp. 186–221; Kelly, *Eastern Arabian Frontiers*, pp. 122–31; Muhammad Morsy Abdullah, *The United Arab Emirates: A Modern History* (London, 1978), pp. 159–99.

2. Correspondence in IOR L/PS/12/2/213–1; John B. Kelly, 'Arabian Frontiers and Anglo-American Relations', *Government and Opposition*, Vol. 27, issue 3, pages 368–9.

3. Telegram No. 233 from Ibrahim Aslam, Hasa, to the minister for finance, Mecca, 28 March 1935, Burdett, *Saudi Arabia: Secret Intelligence Records 1926–1939*, Vol. 5.

4. Fuad Hamza to Ryan, 20 June 1934, *UK Memorial*, Vol. 2, Annex D., No. 7.

5. Ryan, memorandum of 30 July 1934, E/5064/2429/25, quoted in Wilkinson, *Arabia's Frontiers*, p. 180.

6. Beckett, 29 August 1934, FO Confidential Print 15997, quoted in Wilkinson, *Arabia's Frontiers*, p. 182.

7. Kelly, *Eastern Arabian Frontiers*, p. 126. For a detailed analysis of Murrah and Manasir allegiances, see Wilkinson, *Arabia's Frontiers*. pp. 272–4.

8. Ryan to Simon, 11 March 1935, IOR PS/12/2/213–6.

9. At the Dammam Conference in 1952, for instance. See Kelly, *Eastern Arabian Frontiers*, p. 157.

10. For Ibn Saud's territorial ambitions, see *Saudi Memorial*, Vol. II, Annex 10, 'HM King Abdul Aziz to the Saudi Legation at London,' dated 7 October 1934, p. 31; 'if the Saudis always claimed' record of a discussion between Rendell and Yusuf Yasin, 19 March 1937, in the *UK Memorial*, Vol. II, Annex D, No. 14.

11. Rendell, personal interview with R. Lacey, London, January 1979, Lacey, *Kingdom*, p. 292.

12. Political resident Bushire to Walton, 20 February 1937, IOR/15/2/160.

13. Rendell to Laithwaite, 23 October 1934, IOR/15/1/63. See also Wilkinson, *Arabia's Frontiers*, pp. 189–90.

14. Loch, March 1937, IOR/15/2/160.

15. Neville Chamberlain, *Daily Sketch*, 1 October 1938.

16. Secretary of state for foreign affairs, telegram 18 February 1938, IOR/15/2/161.

17. Political resident Bushire, to Walton, 20 February 1937, IOR/15/2/160.

18. Annual Report for 1935, 21 March 1936, FO 371/20064; Bullard to Eden, 23 November 1936, IOR/15/2/160.

19. John Vale, email to the author, 25 May 2008.

20. IPC report prepared for the *UK Memorial*, paragraph D.9, 163974, BP Archive.

21. Political agent, Bahrain, to the political resident, Bushire, 19 February 1937, IOR/15/2/160.

22. Ryan to Eden, Annual Report for 1935, 29 February 1936, FO 371/20064; Bullard to secretary of state for foreign affairs, 31 December 1937, IOR/15/2/161.

23. Cox to Sheikh Zayed bin Khalifa, 1 December 1906, IOR/15/2/160.

24. Lansdowne to Monson, 19 March 1902, Persia and Arabia Confidential, IOR/15/1/475, quoted in Lacey, *The Kingdom*, p. 74; Leatherdale, *Britain and Saudi Arabia*, p. 248. For the political arrangements in the Persian Gulf, see Onley, James, *The Arabian Frontier of the British Raj: Merchants, Rulers, and the British in the Nineteenth Century Gulf* (New York, 2007).

25. Wilkinson, *Arabia's Frontiers*, pp. 218–21.

26. 'Historical Memorandum on the relations of the Wahhabi Amirs and Ibn Saud with Eastern Arabia and the British government 1800–1934', 26 September 1934, L/P & S/18/B437, referred to in Wilkinson, *Arabia's Frontiers*, p. 184.

27. Draft minutes of a meeting of the Committee of Imperial Defence, 19 July 1938, PRO CAB 24/278.

28. Political resident to political agent, Bahrain, 2 June 1939, IOR/15/2/161.

29. Burghardt, Andrew F., 'The Bases of Territorial Claims', *Geographical Review*, Vol. 63, No. 2 (April 1973), pp. 225–45.

Chapter 4. Lanterns in the Dark

1. Primary sources include *The Buraimi Memorials*, FO records at the National Archives, Kew and BP records at Warwick University.

2. Wilkinson, John C., 'The Oman Question: The Background to the Political Geography of South-eastern Arabia', *The Geographical Journal*, Vol. 137, No. 3 (September 1971), pp. 361–71.

3. Barger, *Out in the Blue*, p. 53.

4. Grey, W.G., 'Trade and Races of Oman, *Quarterly Journal of the Mythic Society*, Vol. 2, No. 2 (January 1911), p. 4, cited in Peterson, John E., 'Oman's Diverse Society: Northern Oman', *Middle East Journal*, Vol. 58, No. 5, p. 34.

5. Cox, Percy Z., 'Some Excursions in Oman', *Geographical Journal* Vol. 66, No. 3, September 1925, pp. 193–221.

6. Skeet, Ian, *Muscat and Oman, The End of an Era* (London, 1974), pp. 98–9. See also 'Treaty of Sib: brief for the UK delegation to the UN', 15 August 1957, FO 371/126886.

7. Albaharna, *The Legal Status of the Arabian Gulf States*, pp. 241–4.

8. Wilkinson, *Arabia's Frontiers*, pp. 353–4.

9. Rabi, Uzi, *The Emergence of States in a Tribal Society* (Portland, 2006), pp. 36–42.

10. For a detailed history of the imamate, see Wilkinson, John C., *The Imamate Tradition of Oman* (Cambridge, 1987).

11. Tuson, Penelope, Quick, Emma (eds), *Arabian Treaties, 1600–1960* (Farnham Common, 1993), Vol. 3, p. 247.

12. For an account of the expedition, see Julian Paxton, *History of PDO* (unpublished), chapter 1, pp. 2–5, GB165-0331, Middle East Archive Centre, St Antony's College, Oxford; Hope, Stanton, *Arabian Adventurer* (London, 1951), pp. 303–9; Lees, George M., and Gray, K. Washington, 'The Geology of Oman and adjoining portions of South Eastern Arabia', 1926, 130863, BP Archive.

13. Lees and Gray, 'The Geology of Oman'.

14. Phillips, Wendell, *Oman: A History* (London, 1967), p. 180.

15. Ibid., p. 247.

16. 'The Cabinet: Sultan Muskrat', *Time*, 14 March 1938.

17. Hope, *Arabian Adventurer*, p. 305.

18. Skeet, *Muscat and Oman*, pp. 169–96; C. Kutschera, 'Oman: The Death of the Last Feudal State', *Washington Post*, 27 December 1970 and D. Lamb, 'The Sultan of Oman,' *AFP Reporter*, Vol. 9 No. 3, 1986.

19. Bird to Lermitte, 15 March 1948, quoted in Paxton, chapter 2, p. 2.

20. Morton, D. Michael, Dhofar diary, 1948.

21. Middleton to Lloyd, 25 February 1959, FO 379/140.

22. Innes, Neil, *Minister in Oman* (New York 1987), pp. 11, 23.

23. Walker, Julian, *Tyro on the Trucial Coast* (Crook, 1999), p. 99.

24. Ibid.

25. Henderson, Edward, *This Strange Eventful History* (London 1988), p. 168.

26. 'Dhofar' was dropped from the title in 1950. For simplicity, Petroleum Development (Oman and Dhofar) has been shortened to PDO.

27. Sheikh Saqr to Sultan Said bin Taimur, 13 Ramadan 1357 (5 November 1938), letter from the Muscat archives, cited in the *UK Memorial*, Vol. 1, p. 39.

28. Thompson, 'Progress Report', 10 December 1938, PC/27A (84), BP Archive.

29. Paxton, *History of PDO*, chapter 2, pp. 1–4.

30. Henderson, *This Strange Eventful History*, p. 56.

31. Bird to Jackson, 17 April 1948, IOR R/15/2/599.

32. Henderson, *This Strange Eventful History*, p. 69.

33. Thesiger, Wilfred, 'Desert Borderlands of Oman', *The Geographical Journal*, Vol. 116, No. 4/6, October–December 1950), pp. 137–68.

34. Buckmaster, 5 January 1954, FO 371/104316.

35. Political agent, Sharjah to Pelly, 17 April 1949, IOR 15/12/599; see also Miers, Suzanne, *Slavery in the Twentieth Century*, pp. 308–9.

36. *IPC Exploration News*, February 1949.

37. Henderson, *This Strange Eventful History*, p. 59.

38. Lorimer, *Gazetteer*, IP 1063.

39. Bird, Report of 22 March 1949, IPC/27 part 5(5), BP Archive and Henderson, *This Strange Eventful History*, pp. 63–6.

40. Paxton, *History of PDO*, chapter 2, p. 3.

41. Thesiger, Wilfred, *Arabian Sands* (London 1959), p. 141.

42. Trott to Burrows, 13 June 1948, FO 371/68777.

43. Burrows to Trott, 28 June 1948, FO 371/68777.

44. Morton, Dhofar diary.

45. Thesiger, *Arabian Sands*, p. 81–2.

46. Ibid., p. 23.

47. Ibid., p. 294.

48. Ibid., p. 257.

49. Bird to Jackson, 17 April 1948, IOR R/15/2/599.

50. Bird, 'Note on Mr Thesiger', Box 5, File 6, Paxton Collection.

51. Ibid.

52. Note of Bird, 13 June 1948, attached to his letter to Longrigg, 14 January 1949, Box 5, File 6, the Paxton Collection.

53. Longrigg to Nuttall, 20 May 1949, PC/27 part 5 (157) BP Archive; see also Longrigg to Thesiger, 19 August 1948 (PC/27 part 4); 16 August 1949 (PC/27 part 5).

54. Rose to Hay 23 February 1950, FO 371/82123.

55. 'A Record of a Visit to Eastern Department by W. Thesiger on 12 April 1950', FO 371/82123.

56. Note by Bird of February 1953, Priestland, *Buraimi Dispute*, Vol. 3, p. 82.

57. Burrows to Trott, 11 October 1948, FO 371/68355.

Chapter 5. A Tale of Two Brothers

1. Primary sources include FO records at the National Archives, Kew and BP/IPC records at Warwick University; Priestland, *Buraimi Dispute*.

2. Thesiger, *Arabian Sands*, p. 269.

3. M. Buckmaster, 'Account of Events in Abu Dhabi', 6 May 1954, FO 371/109808.

4. Hillyard, Susan, *Before the Oil* (Bakewell, 2002), p. 170.

5. Wilkinson, *Arabia's Frontiers*, p. 286 and 395f.

6. S. Hillyard, *Before the Oil*, p. 61.

7. Walker, *Tyro on the Trucial Coast*, p. 144.

8. Wilkinson, *Arabia's Frontiers*, p. xxviii.

9. Al-Fahim, Mohammed, *From Rags to Riches* (London, 1995) p. 39.

10. Priestland, *Buraimi Dispute*, Vol. 1, p. 749; the Le Quesne report, 11 July 1954, FO 1016/265.

11. Article VI of the Treaty: Cmd. 2951 (1927), Treaty Series No. 25.

12. Note to the Saudi government, 30 November 1949, *UK Memorial*, Vol. II, Annex D, No. 27.

13. Priestland, *Buraimi Dispute*, p. 740.

14. B. 48, pp 23–4, Sharjah C/750-16/4 of 22 August 1937, letter to the political resident, Bahrain, Priestland, *Buraimi Dispute*, p. 740.

15. Barger, *Out in the Blue*, p. 10.

16. 'Leading Personalities in Saudi Arabia', received on 9/7/46, FO 371/52832.

17. Cheney, Michael S., *Big Oil Man from Arabia* (New York, 1958) p. 67.

18. 'One of the world's richest countries', 16th in the world for GDP per capita: < https://www.cia.gov/library/publications/the-world-factbook/geos/ae.html > last accessed 27 April 2013; 'had to eat their food raw', Hillyard, Before the Oil, p. 75.

19. For an account of early oil exploration in Abu Dhabi, see Owen, Edgar W., *Trek of the Oil Finders* (Tulsa, 1975), pp. 1343–7.

20. Elkington (APOC, Abadan) to London, 22 January 1936, 71730, BP Archive.

21. T.F. Williamson, quoted in Owen, *Trek of the Oil Finders*, p. 1344.

22. Ibid.

23. D. Hawley, *The Trucial States* (New York, 1970), p. 168.

24. Heard-Bey, *From Trucial States to United Arab Emirates*, p. 309.

25. Al-Fahim, *From Rags to Riches*, p. 52.

26. Heard-Bey, *From Trucial States to United Arab Emirates*, p. 206.

27. S. Hillyard, *Before the Oil*, pp. 61–2.

28. *The Times* obituary of 4 November 2004; 'Middle East: Sheik [*sic*] Jackpot', *Time*, 3 May 1963. See also Donald Hawley's reply to *The Times* obituary, 27 November 2004; Lamb, Archie, T., *A Long Way from Swansea* (Clunderwen, 2003), pp. 98–127.

29. T. Hillyard, 15 April 1954, 29990, BP Archive.

30. Owen, Roderic, *The Golden Bubble* (London, 1957), p. 101

31. T. Hillyard to J. Sutcliffe, 3 November 1954, 29990, BP Archive.

32. Ibid.; Julian Walker, *Tyro on the Trucial Coast*, p. 175.

33. T. Hillyard, 3 November 1954.

34. M.S. Weir to Sir Rupert Hay, 6 January 1953, FO 1016/224.

35. S. Hillyard, *Before the Oil*, p. 52.

36. Buckmaster, 6 May 1954, FO 371/109308.

37. Buckmaster, FO 371/104295.

38. Ibid.

39. *Two Glorious Years in the History of Abu Dhabi* (Abu Dhabi, 1968), pp. 46–8.

Chapter 6. Squeezing Aramco

1. Kunio Katakura, 'The Yokoyama Mission: Japanese Diplomacy for Oil, 1939', *The International History Review*, Vol. 8, No. 2 (May 1986), pp. 263–9.

2. 'Six Kingdoms of Oil: The Persian Gulf Strikes It Rich', *Time*, 3 March 1952.

3. 'The International Petroleum Cartel', report to the Federal Trade Commission, released through the Subcommittee on Monopoly of Select Committee on Small Business, US Senate, 83d Cong., 2 session (Washington, DC, 1952), Chapter 5, pp. 113–36.

4. Loomis to Messersmith, 25 April 1939, DS 124/90.f/8, quoted in DeNovo, John A., *American Interests and Policies in the Middle East* (Minneapolis, 1963), pp. 363, 362–5; Hart, Parker T., oral history transcript, Foreign Affairs Oral History Collection, Association for Diplomatic Studies and Training.

5. Miller, Aaron D., *Search for Security: Saudi Arabian Oil and American Foreign Policy 1939–1949* (Chapel Hill, NC, 1980), p. 34.

6. Roosevelt to Jones, 18 July 1941, *Foreign Relations of the United States (FRUS)*, *1941*, Vol. 3, p. 643.

7. Tinkle, Lon, *Mr De: A Biography of Everette Lee DeGolyer* (Boston, 1970), p. 258.

8. Ferris to Thornburg, 24 November 1941, 'A Study of the Foreign Oil Policy of the United States', quoted in Miller, *Search for Security*, p. 49.

9. DeGolyer, 'Preliminary Report of the Technical Oil Mission to the Middle East, 1944', Southern Methodist University, Texas Collection, box: 19 folder: 2315.

10. Miller, *Search for Security*, pp. 51, 60–1.

11. Shwadran, Benjamin, *The Middle East, Oil and the Great Powers* (Jerusalem, 1955), p. 308, quoted in Keating, *Mirage*, p. 510.

12. Miller, *Search for Security*, p. 102.

13. For an account of Lend-Lease, see Shwadran, *The Middle East*, pp. 301–7 and Yergin, *The Prize*, pp. 393–9.

14. Roosevelt to Ibn Saud, 5 April 1945: < http://avalon.law.yale.edu/20th_century/decad161.asp > last accessed 27 April 2013.

15. Truman to reporters, 12 April 1945: < http://www.whitehouse.gov/about/presidents/harrystruman > last accessed 27 April 2013.

16. Lacey, *Kingdom*, p. 274.

17. Cohen, Michael J., *Truman and Israel* (Berkeley, 1990), p. 219.

18. Pelham to Eden, 17 December 1952, FO 371/98828.

19. IPC Handbook, pp. 1–3.

20. Wall, Bennett H. and Gibb, George S., *Teagle of Jersey Standard* (New Orleans, 1974), p. 209.

21. Yergin, *The Prize*, pp. 413–19.

22. 'Oil: Share the Wealth', *Time*, 23 December 1946.

23. Ibid.

24. President H. S. Truman's address to a joint session of Congress on 12 March 1947. For the Truman Doctrine, see the Avalon Project at the Yale Law School at < http://avalon.law.yale.edu/20th_century/trudoc.asp > last accessed 27 April 2013.

25. President Truman to Ibn Saud, 31 October 1950, *FRUS, 1950,* Vol. 5, pp. 1190–1.

26. Cavendish, Richard, 'Death of Ibn Saud', *History Today*, Vol. 53, November 2003; Lacey, pp. 264, 302.

27. Ryan, Andrew, *Last of the Dragomans* (London, 1951), p. 277.

28. van der Meulen, *The Wells of Ibn Saud*, p. 190.

29. 'Middle East Oil', 11 September 1950, *FRUS, 1950,* Vol. 5 (1950), p. 83.

30. Quoted in Kelly, *Eastern Arabian Frontiers*, p. 122.

31. Hart, Parker T., *Saudi Arabia and the United States* (Bloomington, 1998), p. 56; Cheney, *Big Oil Man*, p. 152.

32. 'Foreign Trade: Half and Half', *Time*, 15 January 1951.

33. Brenchley, Frank, *Britain and the Middle East: an Economic History, 1945–87* (London 1991), pp. 58–9.

34. 'Field Parties Head South', *Arabian Sun and Flare*, 5 September 1951. See also Cheney, *Big Oil Man*, pp. 152–5.

35. Speers, Peter C., 'American Perspectives of Aramco, the Saudi-Arabian Oil-producing Company, 1930s to 1980s', oral history transcript, Bancroft Library, University of CA, Berkeley, 1995, pp. 487–90; Vitalis, Robert, *America's Kingdom* (Stanford, CA, 2007), pp, 201–3.

36. Michael Sterner, email to the author, 28 September 2009.

37. Lorimer, *Gazetteer*, p. 762.

38. Rentz, George, Mulligan, William E., 'The Zakah in Saudi Arabia', Tax Collecting, *The Eastern Reaches of Al Hasa Province* (1950),p. 3.

39. Henderson, 15 August 1974, FCO 8/2357; see also Abdullah, *The United Arab Emirates*, p. 207. Lorimer's *Gazetteer* was meant to be a secret document at this time.

40. Wilkinson, *Arabia's Frontiers*, p. 299.

41. Abdullah, *The United Arab Emirates*, p. 206f, p. 207.

42. Wilkinson, *Arabia's Frontiers*, p. 193.

43. Speers, oral history transcript, pp. 487–90.

44. Wilkinson, *Arabia's Frontiers*, p. 193.

45. 'The Tribal Situation and Ibn Saud', Thomas to the PRPG, 13 June 1927, IOR R/15/6/86.

Chapter 7. The Stobart Incident

1. Cheney, *Big Oil Man*, p. 153.

2. For a description of the Dukhan oilfield, see Beydoun, *The Middle East*, p. 203.

3. Hart, *Saudi Arabia and the United States*, p. 57.

4. Ibid., p. 56.

5. Longrigg to Nuttall, 3 May 1949, PC/27 part 5 (142), BP Archive).

6. Wilkinson, *Arabia's Frontiers*, p. 245.

7. Derham to Fields Manager, Dukhan, 2 March 1949, 16394, BP Archive.

8. Ibid.

9. Hopkinson to Lermitte, 12 April 1949, 16394, BP Archive.

10. Baker to the Managing Director, 4 May 1949, 163974, BP Archive.

11. Ibid.

12. 'Report of Movements of a Party from the South in Abu Dhabi Area', 4 April 1949, C.6 (AD) 163974 BP Archive.

13. Jedda 580/65/49, 15 August 1949, in Priestland, *Buraimi Dispute*, Vol. 1, p. 741.

14. *UK Memorial*, p. 89.

15. Lermitte to London, 20 April 1949, 163974, BP Archive.

16. 'A Report on a Visit by Road to the Western Area of the Abu Dhabi Sheikhdom', undated, C.7 (AD), 163974, BP Archive.

17. *UK Memorial*, Vol. 1, p. 93.

18. Longrigg to Nuttall, 3 May 1949 BP Archive PC27 30.

19. IPC *Handbook*, p. 2; Longrigg, *Oil in the Middle East*, p. 355.

20. Baker to Longrigg, letter dated 5 July 1949, BP Archive IPC 27 part 4.

21. Ibid.; IPC abandoned the well at a depth of 13,000 feet.

22. 'Frontier Negotiations with Saudi Arabia', Annex A, 'Legal Position', 26 August 1949, FO 371/82651.

23. Note of 30 November 1949, *UK Memorial*, Vol. II, Annex D, No. 27.

24. Tim Barger, email to the author, 13 December 2007; Hart, *Saudi Arabia*, p. 58; 'Jurisdictional Dispute of Saudi Arabia', *FRUS, 1950*, Vol. 5, p. 39.

25. 'The Tribal Situation and Ibn Saud', Thomas to the PRPG, 13 June 1927, IOR R/15/6/86.

26. Jackson (US chargé d'affaires to the UK) to Labouisse (Director of the Office of the British Commonwealth and Northern European Affairs), 10 January 1950, Paper of 29 April 1950, *FRUS, 1950*, Vol. 5, pp. 11, 40.

27. Memorandum of a conversation, 25 April 1950, *FRUS, 1950*, Vol. 5, pp. 41-7.

28. Childs, memorandum of 12 June 1950, *FRUS, 1950*, Vol. 5, pp. 53-5.

29. Hart, oral history transcript.

30. Kelly, *Eastern Arabian Frontiers*, p. 149.

31. Ibid., p. 158.

Chapter 8. Borderlands

1. Paxton, *History of PDO*, chapter 2, p. 1.

2. Qatar diary for February 1950 in Priestland, *Buraimi Dispute*, Vol. 1, p. 742.

3. Bird, 20 November 1950, paragraph B.22, 163974, BP Archive.

4. Wilkinson, *The Imamate Tradition*, p. 296; Morris, James, *Sultan in Oman* (London, 1957), p. 105; Suleiman bin Hamyar to Sir R. Hay, Priestland, *Buraimi Dispute*, Vol. 1, p. 698.

5. The Sultan (of Jebel Akhdar) talks to *Qafilah*, FO 1016/221.

6. Priestland, *Buraimi Dispute*, Vol. 1, p. 699.

7. *Saudi Memorial* (Annex 53), quoted in Kelly, *Eastern Arabian Frontiers*, p. 151.

8. Priestland, *Buraimi Dispute*, Vol. 1, p. 699.

9. Ibid.

10. Priestland, *Buraimi Dispute*, Vol. 1, p. 699.

11. Henderson, *This Strange Eventful History*, p. 91.

12. *Saudi Memorial*, Annex 54.

13. J. Wilton, Qatar and Sharjah, 1949–1952, R. Wilton's Esoterica at: < http://blogs.sun.com/racingsnake/entry/qatar_and_sharjah_1949_19526 > accessed 8 January 2010.

14. Wilton, letter to the author, 16 January 2010; Wilton's report of February 1952, FO 371/98370.

15. Bird, note of February 1953, FO371/104279.

16. Rashid bin Hamad to Ibn Saud, 14 June 1951, *Saudi Memorial* I, Ch. V, para. 83.

17. PRPG to FO, 28 September 1951, FO 1011/32/51, Priestland, *Buraimi Dispute*, Vol.1, p. 700.

18. FO 371/98370.

19. The US chargé d'affaires in Jedda to the Department of State, 14 May 1952, *FRUS, 1952-4*, Vol. 9, part 2 pp. 2468-70.

20. FO to Pelham, 7 April 1952, *UK Memorial*, Vol. II, Annex D., No. 39.

21. Kelly, *Eastern Arabian Frontiers*, p. 159.

22. Hay to FO, 23 August 1952, FO 371/98370.

23. Michael Sterner, email to the author, 26 September 2009.

Chapter 9. Turki and the Tribes

1. Pritzke, Herbert, *Bedouin Doctor* (London, 1957), pp. 236-45.

2. The origin of the name Buraimi is lost in time. One explanation is that it means 'the place of antelopes', which at one time were probably hunted in the area. Perhaps

the most convincing explanation is one that circulates among the older people of the oasis today: that it was named after a famous merchant known as Balbraimi who travelled in the region and was buried there. The practice of applying the name of one village to the whole oasis appears to be a European one, see Wilkinson, J.C., *Water and Tribal Settlement in South-East Arabia* (Oxford, 1977), p. 33 n.1.

3. Primary sources for this chapter are Walker, *Tyro on the Trucial Coast*, pp. 27–42 and 91–108, and his correspondence with the author; reports of British political and military officers in FO series 1016 and 371, which are annotated in the text, and Martin Buckmaster's report of 5 January 1954, FO 371/104316.

4. Henderson, *This Strange Eventful History*, p. 56.

5. Julian Walker, letter to the author, 8 September 2009.

6. Based on the author's conversation with Julian Walker, 24 August 2009; and the reports of Walker and Bustani of their visit to Hamasa, 6 July 1954, FO 371/109837; and biographical information in 'Notes on Turki bin Abdullah al-Otaishan', Box 2, Folder 1, Mulligan Papers, Georgetown University.

7. Michael Sterner, email to the author, 28 September 2009.

8. Dr A.T. Otaishan, conversation with the author, 16 March 2011.

9. Priestland, *Buraimi Dispute*, Vol.1 p. 743; see also a note of a private interview with Turki, 11 March 1973, in Lind, Gary, 'The Buraimi Oasis Dispute', PHD diss., American University of Beirut, 1973, p. 125 n40.

10. Mulligan, 7 February 1955, Box 2, Folder 50, Mulligan Papers.

11. *UK Memorial*, Vol.1, p. 44.

12. Quoted in Bierschenk, Thomas, 'Oil Interests and the Formation of Centralized government 1920–1970', *Orient*, 1989, Vol. 30, p. 216.

13. Political resident to FO, 10812/73/53 of 30 January 1953, Priestland, *Buraimi Dispute*, Vol. 1, p. 744.

14. Chauncy to Sultan Said bin Taimur, 26 September 1952, FO 371/98375.

15. Sultan Said bin Taimur to Chauncy, 27 September 1952, FO 371/98375.

16. Muscat to FO, 22 September 1952, FO 371/98372.

17. Chauncy to FO, 28 September 1952, FO 371/98373.

18. Kelly, 'Arabian Frontiers and Anglo-American Relations', p. 372.

19. The acting secretary of state to the US embassy London, 18 October 1952. *FRUS, 1952–4*, Vol. 9, part 2, 'Saudi Arabia', p. 2490.

20. 'Saudi Arabia', *FRUS, 1952–4*, Vol. 9, part 2, p. 2491.

21. Foreign Office to Bahrain, 10 October 1952, 371/98373.

22. Note by Bird of February 1953, FO 371/104279.

23. Ibid.

24. Chauncy to FO, 14 November 1952, FO371/98380.

25. Weir to Hay, 6 December 1952, FO 371/98388.

26. Weir to Hay, 28 January 1953, p. 6, FO 371/104278.

27. 'The Situation in Buraimi', Greenhill, 19 December 1952, FO371/98389; Burrows to FO, 17 September 1953, para. 4, FO 371/104304; Weir to Hay, 10 December 1952, FO 371/98388.

28. Weir to Chauncy, 14 November 1952, FO 1016/196.

29. Ibid.

30. 'The Sultan's continued confidence [...] is not shared by Hazza and Zayed', Weir to Hay, 10 December 1952, FO 371/98388.

31. Weir to Hay, 28 January 1953, FO 371/104278.
32. MEAF News Service, 'Combined Operation in Trucial Oman', FO 371/104279.
33. Weir to Hay, 28 January 1953, FO 371104278.
34. Weir to Hay, 25 March 1953, para. 7, FO 1016/229.
35. MEAF News Service, 'Combined Operation in Trucial Oman', FO 371/104279.

Chapter 10. Taking a Stand
1. 'Southern Arabian Frontier Dispute', 19 December 1952, PRO CAB 129/57.
2. 'British Policy in the Middle East', 12 July 1943, War Cabinet Paper No. 66, PRO; 'the basic British and American interest in the Near East is indivisible', Wilkins to Funkhouser, memorandum of 15 April 1950, *FRUS, 1950*, Vol. 5, p. 34.
3. Roosevelt, Elliott, *As He Saw It* (New York, 1946), p. 41.
4. Childs to the secretary of state, 10 July 1950, *FRUS, 1950*, Vol. 5, p. 62.
5. Foreign Office telegram to Washington, 16 December 1955, FO 371/114539.
6. Citino, Nathan J., *From Arab Nationalism to OPEC* (Bloomington, Indiana, University Press, 2002), pp. 8–9.
7. Burrows to Ross, 26 April 1953, FO 371/98828.
8. Memorandum of a conversation, 18 May 1953, *FRUS, 1952-4*, Vol. 9, part 1, pp. 99–105.
9. Bronson, Rachel, *Thicker than Oil: America's Uneasy Partnership with Saudi Arabia* (New York, 2006), p. 62.
10. Ibid., pp. 63–7; Kelly, 'Arabian Frontiers and Anglo-American Relations', p. 370.
11. Message from A. Dulles to J. F. Dulles, undated, *FRUS, 1955-7*, Vol. 13, p. 281.
12. Secretary of state to US embassy, Saudi Arabia, 2 April 1953; memorandum of Ca conversation, 3 April 1953, *FRUS, 1952-4*, Vol. 9, part 2, pp. 2531–2, 2533–5.
13. Eden, Sir Anthony, *Full Circle: the Memoirs of the Rt. Hon. Sir Anthony Eden K.G., P.C., M.C.* (London, 1960), p. 334. See also Kelly, John B., *Arabia, the Gulf and the West* (London, 1980), pp. 254–7.
14. J.F. Dulles: 'there was some degree of justice in the grievance felt by the Saudi Arabians'; A. Dulles: 'the Saudi Arabian government had acted with considerable moderation on the Buraimi problem'; Treasury secretary G.M. Humphrey: the dispute was simply about 'British prestige', meeting of the National Security Council, 27 May 1954, quoted in Bronson, *Thicker than Oil*, p. 67.
15. van der Meulen, *The Wells of Ibn Saud*, p. 228.
16. Ibid., p. 229–30.
17. Pelham to Eden, 14 May 1952, FO 371/98828.
18. Riches to Eden, 17 September 1952, FO 371/98372.
19. 'Sir Michael Weir', *The Telegraph*, 14 August 2006.
20. 'Sir Anthony Eden: The Man Who Waited', *Time*, 11 April 1955.
21. Eden to Eisenhower, 1 October 1956, PREM 11/1177 PRO.
22. Ibid., p. 342.
23. Burrows, Bernard, *Footnotes in the Sand: The Gulf in Transition, 1953-1958* (London, 1990), p. 104.
24. 'South Arabian Frontier Dispute', 4 November 1952, PRO CAB 129/56.
25. 'Saudi Arabian Frontier Dispute', 19 December 1952, PRO CAB 129/57.
26. 'Britain is Accused by Saudi Arabia', *New York Times*, 12 March 1953.
27. Weir to Hay, 25 March 1953, FO 1016/229.

28. Ibid.

29. Citino, *From Arab Nationalism to OPEC*, p. 46.

30. James, Robert Rhodes, *Anthony Eden* (London, 1986), *pp.* 362–4; see also Owen, Lord David, 'Diseased, Demented, Depressed: Serious Illness in Heads of State', *Quarterly Journal of Medicine*, 2003, 96: 325–36.

31. Churchill to Minster of State, 24 May 1953, PREM 11/698.

32. Eisenhower to Ibn Saud, 15 June 1953, *FRUS 1952–4*, Vol. 9, pp. 2540–2.

33. Colville, John C., *The Fringes of Power* (London, 2004), p. 627.

34. Cabinet notebook, 13 July 1953, PRO CAB 195/11.

35. Pelham to the secretary of state for foreign affairs, 28 April 1953, FO 1016/303.

Chapter 11. The Hamasa Blockade

1. 'The Nasty Affair at the Burami [sic] oasis', broadcast on 4 October 1956.

2. Weir to Le Quesne, 15 April 1953, FO 371/104292.

3. Hawley, p. 186.

4. 'Battle for Buraimi', Time, 27 April 1953.

5. For accounts of the blockade arrangements, see Burrows, telegram of 17 September 1953 and Pirie-Gordon to C. le Quesne, 3 May 1954, FO 371/109832; Clayton, Peter, *Two Alpha Lima* (London, 1994), pp. 33–4. For reports on the slave trade since the arrival of Turki, see Weir to Hay, 25 March 1953, para. 11, FO 1016/229; Weir to Hay, 28 January 1953, para. 17, FO 371/104278; Johnson to the Political agent, Trucial States, para. 1, 20 April 1955, FO 1016/407. For the estimate of £10, 000 a month, see Burrows to Samuel (undated), FO 371/114627.

6. Dr A.T. Otaishan, conversation with the author, 16 March 2011.

7. Weir to Le Quesne, 15 April 1953, FO 371/104292.

8. The British government referred to these activities as 'bribery', see the Marquess of Salisbury, *Hansard*, HL Deb 26 October 1955, Vol. 194, cc45–8. For the documents signed by the tribesmen, see the *Saudi Memorial*, Vol. II, Annexes 59–66, pp. 133–43.

9. 'Note on Saudi Documents Captured at Buraimi', para. 3, FO 371/120588.

10. Greenhill to Pelham, Riyadh, 19 February 1953, FO 371/104278.

11. Weir to Hay, 28 January 1953, paras. 9 and 10, FO 371/104278.

12. Ibid.

13. Weir to Le Quesne, 15 April 1953, FO 371/104292.

14. Weir to Le Quesne, 12 May 1953, FO 1016/232.

15. There are several accounts of this incident: Clayton, *Two Alpha Lima*, pp. 41–2; Mann, Michael *Trucial Oman Scouts* (Wilby, Norwich, 1994), pp. 37–41; Allfree, Philip, *Warlords of Oman* (London, 1967), p. 17; various reports in FO 371/104310.

16. Clayton, *Two Alpha Lima*, p. 41.

17. Burrows to FO, 17 September 1953, FO 371/104304.

18. Pirie-Gordon to Le Quesne, 22 June 1953, FO 1016/232.

19. Pirie-Gordon to Le Quesne, 2 August 1953; R. McGregor to Saiyid Ahmed bin Ibrahim, 4 August 1953, FO 371/1016/233.

20. *The Scotsman*, 24 September 1953.

21. Note of 18 September 1953, FO 371/104304.

22. 'Saudi Arabia Complains to the UN', *The Birmingham Post*, 24 September 1953, FO371/104304.

23. Sheikh Zayed to the political agent, 22 June 1953, FO 371/104301.

24. Walker, *Tyro on the Trucial Coast*, pp. 93–4.

25. Pirie-Gordon to Burrows, 21 May 1954, FO 371/109832.

26. Burrows to FO, telegram of 17 September 1953, FO 371/104304.

27. Pirie-Gordon to Le Quesne, 12 September 1953, FO 371/1016/234.

28. Pirie-Gordon to Burrows, 21 May 1954, FO 371/109832.

29. Sheikh Zayed to M. Weir, 24 May 1953 FO 371 /1016/ 232; 'ill advised', Bahrain to FO, 22 May 1953 FO 371/104295; 'aggressive military action', Jedda to FO, 25 May 1953 FO 371/104295.

30. Pirie-Gordon to Burrows, 21 May 1954, FO 371/109832.

31. Ibid.

32. Burrows, telegram to FO, 22 June 1954, Priestland, p. 526.

33. 'Saudi statement on Buraimi', Amman to FO, 25 May 1954, FO 371/109832; Yasin's initial communiqué to the British, Jedda to FO, 26 May 1954, FO 371/109831; 'Conditions in Hamasa: possible UK refusal to allow M. de Cocatrix to enter area', FO 371/109836.

34. See the reports of Walker (undated), Bustani (10 July 1954), FO 371/109837, and Walker, *Tyro on the Trucial Coast*, pp. 105–8.

Chapter 12. No Oil Man's Land

1. Telegram Foreign Office to Muscat, 7 January 1953 FO 371/104275.

2. J. Jones, 3 April 1954, Box 2, Folder 39, Mulligan Papers.

3. Gibson to Allen, 1 December 1953, FO 371/104402.

4. Jedda to FO, 3 December 1953, FO 371/104402.

5. Mulligan, 7 October 1953, Folder 33, Mulligan Papers; Bahrain to FO, 6 December 1953, FO 371/104402.

6. Record of a meeting, 11 November 1954, FO 371/109915.

7. Owen, *Trek of the Oil Finders*, p. 1345.

8. Brook, 'Saudi Arabia', 24 June 1954, FO 371/109836.

9. Eden to the cabinet, 7 January 1954, PREM 11/718; Kirkpatrick to Burrows, 29 January 1954, FO 371109828;

10. 'Saudi Arabia Frontier Dispute', undated; Department of State to Wadsworth, 16 February 1954, *FRUS, 1952–4*, Vol. 9, part 2, pp 2576–7, 2580; Burrows to Foreign Office, 2 May 1954, Fry to Beeley, 14 April 1954, FO 371/109831.

11. Davies, FO 371/109903; Davies to Dulles 12 April 1954, cited in Lind, p. 251.

12. Riches, 17 September 1952, FO 371/98372.

13. Pelham to Eden, 19 November 1952, FO 371/95828.

14. van der Meulen, *The Wells of Ibn Saud*, p. 186.

15. Pelham to FO, 16 April 1954, FO 371/109831.

16. 'Leading Personalities', FO 371/52832.

17. Shuckburgh, Evelyn, *Descent to Suez: Foreign Office Diaries, 1951–1956* (London, 1986), 9 June 1954, p. 218.

18. Phillips to Fry, Eastern Department, 18 March 1954, FO371/109830.

19. Pelham to Falla, 3 September 1953, FO 371/114617.

20. Jedda to FO 25 September 1953, FO 371/104305.

21. US chargé d'affaires to the State Department, 22 November 1953; memorandum of a conversation, 10 March 1954, *FRUS, 1952–4*, Vol. 9, part 2, pp. 2575–6, 2582–7.

22. Dated 5 October 1953, Shuckburgh, *Descent to Suez*, p. 105.

23. Holden and Johns, *The House of Saud*, p. 178; Lacey, *Kingdom*, p. 318

24. 'Leading Personalities', FO 371/52832.

25. Holden and Johns, *The House of Saud* pp. 177–80

26. Telegram Jedda to Foreign Office, 17 November 1953, FO 371/104312.

27. Memorandum, 3 April 1953, *FRUS, 1952–4*, Vol. 9, part 2, p. 2534.

28. 'Leading Personalities' FO 371/52832.

29. Holden and Johns, *The House of Saud*, pp. 202–3.

30. Quoted in Citino, *From Arab Nationalism to OPEC*, p. 74.

31. Secretary of state to the US embassy, Saudi Arabia, 2 April 1953, *FRUS, 1952–4*, Vol. 9, part 2, pp. 2531–2.

32. Memoranda of conversations by Plitt, 2 and 4 December 1952, *FRUS, 1952–4*, Vol. 9, pp. 2498–503.

33. Pelham, to Fry, 24 November 1953, FO 371/104312.

34. Pelham to Eden, 17 December 1952, FO/371/98828.

35. 'J.B. Kelly's Eastern Arabian Frontiers', Mulligan, 18 April 1964, Mulligan Papers.

36. For examples of early tensions, see Clarke, Angela, *Bahrain Oil and Development* (Boulder CO, 1990), pp. 118; Mylles, 9 July 1934, BP Archive 135500.

37. Riches, 11 October 1956, FO 371/120782.

38. Memorandum of a conversation, 25 April 1950, *FRUS, 1950*, Vol. 5, pp. 41–7.

39. Pelham to Eden, 31 July 1954, FO 371/109839.

40. Pelham to Fry, 18 March 1954, FO 109830.

41. Pelham to Eden, 22 May 1954, FO 371/109834.

42. Secretary of state to US embassy, London, 22 May 1954,; UK ambassador to the secretary of state, 24 May 1954, *FRUS, 1952–4*, Vol. 9, part 2, pp. 2606–8 and editorial notes, pp. 2608–9.

43. Telegram 347 to the US Embassy, Saudi Arabia, 7 June 1954, *FRUS, 1952–4*, Vol. 9, part 2, editorial note to p. 2612.

44. Shuckburgh, *Descent to Suez*, 3 June 1954, p. 217.

45. Walker, *Tyro on the Trucial Coast*, p. 103.

46. Shuckburgh, *Descent to Suez*, p. 217.

47. Walker, *Tyro on the Trucial Coast*, p. 102.

48. US Ambassador (Saudi Arabia) to Department of State, 6 June 1954, *FRUS, 1952–4*, Vol. 9, part 2, pp. 2611–12.

49. Mulligan to Cypher, 7 July 1954, Box 2, Folder 42, Mulligan Papers.

50. 'Prime Minister at the White House', *The Times*, 26 June 1954; 'Bright Pinpricks in the Gloom', *Time*, 5 July 1954.

51. Citino, *From Arab Nationalism to OPEC*, p. 73.

52. Arbitration Agreement, 30 July 1954, Jedda, HMSO Treaty series, 1954, No. 65; see also http://untreaty.un.org/unts/1_60000/5/35/00009703.pdf

53. For example see Riches file note, 21 October 1955, FO 371/120589.

Chapter 13. Make it a Red Fire

1. Primary sources are: Peter Clayton, notes of 9 February 2008 copied to the author; Clayton, *Two Alpha Lima* pp. 56–70; Julian Walker, correspondence with the author and *Tyro on the Trucial Coast* pp. 143–52; and FO files annotated in the text.

2. Burrows to Samuel, 19 August 1954, FO 371/109839.

3. Report from Buraimi, 28 August 1954, FO 371/109842.

4. Burrows to Eden, 24 September 1954, FO371/109841.

5. FO 1016/317; Priestland, *Buraimi Dispute*, Vol. 5, p. 577.

6. Clayton, notes of 9 February 2008.

7. Clayton, *Two Alpha Lima*, p. 57.

8. Clayton, notes of 9 February 2008.

9. Clayton, *Two Alpha Lima*, pp. 66–7.

10. Burrows to A.C.I. Samuel, 19 August 1954, FO 371/109839.

11. Dr A.T. al-Otaishan, conversation with the author, 16 March 2011.

12. Walker, p. 108.

13. Burrows to Samuel, 19 August 1954, FO 371/109839.

14. Report from Buraimi, Martin, 28 August 1954, Priestland, Vol. 5, p. 576, FO 1016/317; Burrows to A. Eden, 22 September 1954, FO 371/109841.

15. Note on Saudi documents captured at Buraimi (undated), FO 371/120588.

16. In-signal No. 5859 of 28 May 1955, FO 371/114633.

17. Kelly, *Eastern Arabian Frontiers*, pp. 181–2; note on captured documents, FO 371/ 120588

18. Pirie-Gordon to Richards, 6 April 1955, FO 1016/407.

19. Johnson, 20 April 1955, FO 1016/407

20. Bin Nami to Bin Jiluwi, 20 August 1954, FO 371/114633.

21. In-signal No. 7127 Bin Jiluwi to Bin Nami, undated, FO 371/114633.

22. Out-signal No. 61 Bin Nami to Bin Jiluwi, 9 November 1954, FO 371/114633.

23. Burrows to Eden, 24 September 1954, FO 371/109841.

24. Kelly, *Eastern Arabian Frontiers*, p. 178.

25. Walker, *Tyro on the Trucial Coast*, pp. 145–6.

26. Ibid., p. 148.

27. In-signal No. 3364 of 9 February 1955, FO 371/114633.

28. Kelly, *Eastern Arabian Frontiers*, pp. 178–9; note on captured documents, FO 371/120588; Bin Nami to Bin Jiluwi, 4 February 1955, FO 371/114633.

29. Out-signal No. 283, 23 December 1954, FO 371/114633.

30. Walker, *Tyro on the Trucial Coast*, pp. 143–4.

31. Walker, *Tyro on the Trucial Coast*, p. 144; Pirie-Gordon to Richards, 11 September 1954, FO 109841.

32. Walker, *Tyro on the Trucial Coast* p. 144.

33. Bullard, 24 January 1955, FO371/114608.

34. Ibid.

35. Sheridan, *Fahud*, p. 236.

36. Clayton, *Two Alpha Lima*, p. 64.

37. Morris, *Sultan in Oman*, p. 160.

38. Sheridan, *Fahud*, pp. 141–2.

39. In-signal No. 4514, 30 March 1955, FO 371/114633.

40. Johnson, 20 April 1955, FO 1016/407.

41. Clayton, *Two Alpha Lima*, pp. 68–9.

42. Statement of Sheikh Zayed, 3 March 1955, FO1016/407.

43. In-letter No. 5745, Bin Jiluwi to Sheikh Saqr bin Sultan, 25 May 1955, FO 371/114633.

44. In-signal No. 5557, 17 May 1955, FO 371/114633.

45. Clayton, *Two Alpha Lima*, pp. 64–5.

46. See the transcript of Clayton's evidence to the Arbitration Tribunal hearing, 11 September 1955, FO 371/114619.

47. Out-signal No. 797, 6 July 1955, FO 371/114633.

48. In-signal No. 104, 22 June 1955, FO 371/114633.

49. Out-signal No. 689, 11 June 1955, FO 371/114633.

50. Johnson, 13 July 1955, FO 1016/409.

51. Johnson, 20 April 1955, FO 1016/407.

52. Johnson, 13 July 1955, FO 1016/409.

53. Clayton, *Two Alpha Lima*, p. 69.

54. Evidence of Sheikh Zayed, transcript of the Arbitration Tribunal hearing, 11–15 September 1955, FO 371/114619; Smith, 22 August 1955, FO 1016/410.

55. Chauncy to Waterfield, 6 September 1955, FO 371/114620.

56. Kelly, p. 204; in-signal No. 406, undated, FO 371/114633; Simpson to FO, 16 September 1955, FO 371/114618.

Chapter 14. The Buraimi Arbitration Tribunal

1. Evidence of Sheikh Zayed and Abdullah al-Qaraishi, transcript of the Arbitration Tribunal hearing, 11–15 September 1955, FO 371/114619.

2. Ibid.

3. Shawcross, Sir Hartley, *Life Sentence* (London, 1995), p. 241.

4. Le Quesne to Richards, 1 September 1955, FO371/114617.

5. Clayton, notes of 9 February 2008.

6. Memorandum, 29 August 1955, FO 371/114617.

7. Biography of Sir Reader William Bullard by Hodgkin, Edward C., in the Oxford Dictionary of National Biography; see also Bullard, Sir Reader, *The Camels Must Go* (London, 1961).

8. Memos, Shuckburgh and Burrows, 9 and 26 August 1954, FO 371/109839.

9. Burrows to Shuckburgh, 20 March 1955, FO371/114610.

10. Buckmaster, 5 January 1954, FO 371/104316; Furlonge to Trott: 'arbitration must be a leap in the dark' 24 February 1950, FO 371/82651; Phillips to FO: 'the Saudi Arabian government is confident of winning', 30 March 1955; Fry, 'Saudi Arabia Frontier Dispute': 'arbitration is not ideal', 17 December 1953, FO 104316.

11. Burrows to Shuckburgh, 20 March 1955, FO371/114610.

12. Bullard, *The Camels Must Go*, p. 280.

13. 'Breakdown of Arbitration over Buraimi', *The Times*, 17 September 1955, also quoted in Kelly, *Eastern Arabian Frontiers*, p. 203; see also 'Buraimi', FO 371/114618

14. 'Sir Hartley Shawcross', Michael Beloff, Oxford Dictionary of National Biography; 'Lord Shawcross', James Morton, *The Independent*, 11 July 2003.

15. Shuckburgh to Burrows, 26 August 1954, FO 371/109839.

16. Shawcross, *Descent to Suez*, p. 240.

17. Pelham to Fry, 24 November 1953, FO 371/104312.

18. Clayton, notes of 9 February 2008.

19. Hart, *Saudi Arabia and the United States*, p. 67.

20. Primary sources for the Geneva hearings are: Clayton, notes of 9 February 2008, copied to the author; Shawcross, 'Report on the Buraimi Arbitration Tribunal', 17 September 1955, FO 371/114617; transcript of the hearing, FO 371/114619.

21. Simpson to Samuel, 5 September 1955, FO 371/114617.

22. Ibid.

23. Quoted in Kelly, *Eastern Arabian Frontiers*, p. 200.

24. Simpson, *op. cit.*; Bullard, 11 September 1955, FO 371/114620.

25. 'New Breach of Buraimi Pact', *The Times*, 14 September 1955.

26. Timetable of proceedings, FO 371/114619.

27. Shawcross, 'Report on the Buraimi Arbitration Tribunal', FO 371/114617.

28. For an analysis of Abdullah al-Qaraishi's testimony, see Kelly, *Eastern Arabian Frontiers*, pp. 201–3.

29. Kelly, *Eastern Arabian Frontiers*, p. 203.

30. Shawcross, 'Report on the Buraimi Arbitration Tribunal', FO 371/114617

31. Burrows to Shuckburgh, 20 March 1955, FO371/114610.

32. Shawcross, 'Report on the Buraimi Arbitration Tribunal', FO 371/114617.

33. Simpson to Samuel, 12 September 1955, FO 114/114620.

34. Ibid.

35. Ibid.

36. Shawcross, 'Report on the Buraimi Arbitration Tribunal', FO 371/114617.

37. Ibid.

38. Simpson to FO, 16 September 1955, FO 371/114618; Simpson, 23 September 1955, FO 371/114620.

39. Simpson, 23 September 1955, FO 371/114620.

40. Ibid.

41. Ibid.

42. Shuckburgh to Caccia, 17 September 1955, FO 371/114618.

43. For discussions about the press release, see Samuel, 24 September 1955; Broad, 10 October 1955, FO 371/114621.

44. 'Buraimi Tribunal Frustrated', *The Times*, 19 September 1955.

45. Shuckburgh, *Descent to Suez: Foreign Office Diaries, 1951–1956*, 7 October 1955, p. 289.

46. Shuckburgh to Fitzmaurice, 16 September 1955, FO 114/617.

47. Shawcross, 'Report on the Buraimi Arbitration Tribunal', FO 371/114617.

48. 'Arbitration Tribunal: Resignation of Dr de Visscher', FO 371/114621.

49. Telegram to the UK High Commission in Pakistan, 23 September 1955; Samuel, 7 October 1955, FO 371/114621; resignation of Ernesto di Dihigo, Clayton, *Two Alpha Lima*, p. 174; FO 371/114626, 114627.

50. Samuel, 'Buraimi', 24 September 1955; Gault to FO, 8 October 1955 and 13 October 1955, FO 371/114621.

51. Samuel, 20 September 1955, FO 371/114617.

52. 'Setting for an International Stage', *The Times*, 20 September 1955.

Chapter 15. Dust in Their Eyes

1. Shuckburgh, *Descent to Suez*, 21 September 1955, p. 278.

2. Burrows to FO, 24 September 1955, FO 371/114618; see also Samuel, 30 September 1955, FO 371/114621.

3. Burrows to FO, 24 September 1955, FO 371/114618; Bahrain to FO, 13 October 1955, FO 371/114621.

4. Burrows to FO, 24 September 1955, FO 371/114618.

5. Ibid.

6. Samuel, 'Buraimi', FO 371/114621.

7. Memorandum to the cabinet, 15 October 1955, PRO CAB 129/78, C(55)153.

8. 'United for Peace and Progress', *Conservative Party Manifesto: 1955*.

9. 'Cabinet Conclusions', 4 October 1955, CAB 128/29 PRO.

10. Broad, 10 October 1955, FO 371/114621.

11. Samuel, 'Buraimi', 22 September 1955, FO 371/114618.

12. Fitzmaurice to Samuel, 13 September 1955, FO 371/114621.

13. Manningham-Buller to Fitzmaurice, 24 October 1955, FO 371/114625.

14. 'Bribery by Saudi Arabia in Buraimi Oasis Dispute', *The Times*, 5 October 1955.

15. Shuckburgh, 6 October 1955, FO 371/114621.

16. FO to Washington, 21 October 1955, FO 371/114621.

17. E. Shuckburgh to Kirkpatrick, 11 October 1955.

18. 'Saudi Protest on Buraimi', *The Times*, 28 October 1955.

19. Samuel, 14 October 1955, FO 371/114625; Riches, 21 October 1955, FO 371/114621.

20. Ross, 19 October 1955, FO 371/114621.

21. Burrows to FO, 21 October 1955, FO 371/120589.

22. Riches, 21 October 1955, FO 371/114621; Samuel, 21 October 1955, FO 371/114625.

23. Memorandum by the secretary of state for foreign affairs, PRO CAB/129/78.

24. 'Cabinet Conclusions', 18 October 1955, para. 7, PRO CAB 128/29.

25. Ibid.

26. Ibid.

Chapter 16. Operation Bonaparte

1. *Air Force Escape and Evasion Society* (1992), pp. 71–3.

2. Henderson, *This Strange Eventful History*, p. 209.

3. Smith to the political agent, Dubai, 26 July 1955, FO 1016/409.

4. Clayton, *Two Lima Alpha*, p. 71.

5. Statement by Major N. Smith, 29 October 1955, FO 371/114627.

6. Clayton, notes of 9 February 2008, his correspondence with the author and *Two Lima Alpha*, pp. 71–2; Henderson, *This Strange Eventful History*; Col. E. Johnson, 'Operation Diary', 24 November 1955, FO 1016/420.

7. Henderson, *This Strange Eventful History*, p. 163.

8. Clayton, *Two Alpha Lima*, p. 73, and his notes to the author.

9. For differing accounts of the incident, see Henderson, pp. 166–7 and Clayton, p. 74; see also Burrows to Samuel, undated; Burrows to FO, 31 October 1955, FO 371/114624.

10 .Burrows to Samuel, para. 3, undated, FO 371/114627.

11. Clayton, *Two Lima Alpha*, p. 75.

12. Note on Saudi Documents captured at Buraimi, FO 371/120588.

13. Burrows to FO, 31 October 1955, FO 371/114624; Johnson, 'Operation Diary', FO 1016/420.

14. Clayton, *Two Lima Alpha*, p. 76; Burrows to Samuel, undated, FO 371/114624.

15. Burrows to Samuel, *ibid;* 'Buraimi', Riches, 27 October 1955, FO 371/114623.

16. Tripp to Burrows, 27 October 1955, FO1016/420.

17 Tripp to Richards, 2 November 1955, FO1016/421; Johnstone to Walmsley, 11 September 1961, FO 371/156682.

18. Morton, Michael Q., *In the Heart of the Desert* (Aylesford, 2006), pp. 176–80.

19. Sheridan, *Fahud*, p. 98.

20. Phillips to FO, 31 October 1955, FO 371/114624.

21. Phillips to FO, 10 November 1955, FO 1016/423; Jedda to FO, 26 November 1955, FO 371/114631; Damascus to FO, 28 October 1955, FO 114624.

22. 'Saudi Protest on Buraimi', *The Times*, 28 October 1955.

23. Phillips to Shuckburgh, 31 October 1955, FO 371/114877.

24. The Saudi Arabian government's statement on the Buraimi Dispute, 13 November 1955.

25. Billingsgate fish market in London was apparently known for the bad language of its traders, thus to 'talk Billingsgate' meant using coarse language.

26. Phillips to the Eastern Department, Foreign Office, 10 November 1955, FO 1016/423.

27. Bustani, 26 November 1955, FO1016/423.

28. British Embassy (Jedda) to FO, 26 November 1955, FO 371/114631.

29. Cheney, *Big Oil Man*, p. 252; quote from a local newspaper in Jedda to FO, 26 November 1955, FO 371/114631.

30. Cheney, *Big Oil Man*, p. 252.

31. Bustani, Report, 26 November 1955, FO 1016/423.

32. Burrows to Samuel, undated, FO 371/114624.

33. Burrows to FO, 31 October 1955, FO 371/114624.

Chapter 17. The Road to Suez

1. Shuckburgh, *Descent to Suez*, 27 October 1955, p. 294.

2. Ibid.

3. 'Saudi Protest on Buraimi', *The Times*, 28 October 1955.

4. Citino, *From Arab Nationalism to OPEC*, p. 84; James Terry Duce, 'Review of Oil and State in the Middle East', *Middle East Journal*, Summer 1960; 'Protection of Southern Borders', Homer Mueller, 7 February 1956, Box 2 Folder 50, Mulligan Papers.

5. Citino, *From Arab Nationalism to OPEC*, p. 130; Cumming to Hoover, 1 August 1957, *FRUS, 1955–7*, Vol. 13, pp. 234–5.

6. 'King Saud's Claim on Buraimi', *The Times*, 13 December 1955.

7. Mueller, 'Protection of Southern Borders'.

8. Doug Manning, email correspondence with the author, December 2008.

9. See Jim Ellis, 'Plain Tales from the Sands' in the *Journal of the British Yemeni Society*, July 2000; William Owen, oral history transcript, 'American Perspectives of Aramco, the Saudi-Arabian Oil-producing company, 1930s to 1980s', Bancroft Library, University of CA, Berkeley, 1995, pp. 328–9.

10. John Vale, email to the author of 25 May 2008.

11. Makins to Foreign Office, 27 October 1955, FO 371/114623.

12. Macmillan to FO, 28 October 1955, FO 371/114624.

13. Telegram to Washington 7 November 1955, FO 371/114626; Dulles to US Embassy, London, 23 November 1955, *FRUS, 1955–7*, Vol. 13, pp. 291–2.

14. Eden, Minute of 1 December 1955, FO 371/114559.

15. Shuckburgh, *Descent to Suez*, p. 311; US Embassy London to the State Department, 15 December 1955, *FRUS, 1955-7*, Vol. 13, pp. 223-5.

16. Shuckburgh, *Descent to Suez*, 20 January 1956, p. 323.

17. 'Buraimi', foreign secretary's memorandum, 9 January 1956, CAB/129/79; memorandum of a conversation, 13 January 1956, *FRUS, 1955-7*, Vol. 12, pp. 223-4.

18. 'A British Oil Venture in a Troubled Region', *Illustrated London News*, January 1956.

19. Morris, *Sultan in Oman*, pp. 70-85.

20. The court poet was Roderic Owen, author of *The Golden Bubble: Arabian Gulf Documentary* (London, 1957). See also Morris, *Sultan in Oman*, pp. 120-6.

21. Morris, *Sultan in Oman*, p. 127.

22. 'Tour of the Horizon', *Time*, 13 February 1956.

23. By a special correspondent, *American Aims in Middle East*, 12 February 1956. *The Observer*, retrieved 17 July 2009 from ProQuest Historical Newspapers.

24. Eden to Eisenhower, 16 January 1956, *FRUS, 1955-7*, Vol. 13, p. 313; Eden, *Full Circle*, p. 342.

25. Citino, *From Arab Nationalism to OPEC*, p. 195; memoranda of Eden Talks, 30-31 January 1956, *FRUS 1955-7*, Vol. 13, pp. 327-37 and editorial note on p. 338; Shuckburgh, *Descent to Suez*, p. 329.

26. Pendleton, Memorandum to the files, 30 December 1957, Box 2 Folder 57, Mulligan Papers. See also Lacey, *Kingdom*, pp. 303-7.

27. Parkes to Luce, 27 April 1966, FO 1016/737.

28. 'Conditions inside Saudi Arabia', 2 January 1956, FO 371/120582.

29. Lloyd as quoted in Al-Baho, Amer I.J., 'The Greatest Difference: Britain, the United States and the Buraimi Oasis Dispute, 1952-1957', PHD diss., London School of Economics and Political Science, December 1996 p. 208; see also FO to Jedda, 17 February 1956, FO 1016/474.

30. Dodds-Parker, 9 May 1956, FO 371/120768.

31. Operation Omega, see Citino, *From Arab Nationalism to OPEC*, p. 95

32. Parkes to Lloyd, 11 August 1956, FO 371/120759.

33. Pirie-Gordon, 30 August 1956, FO 371/120589.

34. Lacey, *Kingdom*, p. 302; Holden and Johns, *The House of Saud*, pp. 170-80.

35. Tripp, 10 November 1961, FO 371/156684.

Chapter 18. Rebels and Refugees

1. Mueller, 3 December 1955 Box 2, Folder 49, Mulligan Papers.

2. Cumming to Hoover, 1 August 1957, *FRUS, 1955-7*, Vol. 13, pp. 234-5.

3. Ibid.

4. Ibid.; Innes, *Minister in Oman*, pp. 113-14.

5. Gault to Lloyd, 10 July 1956, FO 371/120589; Henderson gives a lower figure for Saqr's hoard, 175,000 rupees: *This Strange Eventful History*, pp. 168-9.

6. Buckmaster to Tripp, 16 June 1956 and Gault to Lloyd, 10 July 1956, FO 371/120589.

7. Gault to Lloyd, *ibid*; see also Bahrain to FO, 29 October 1956, FO 371/120589.

8. 'An Appeal to the Arabs of Oman', transcript of a broadcast on Cairo Radio on 21 October 1956, FO 371/120543.

9. For accounts of the Jebel Akhdar War, see FO 371/126888; Smiley, David, with

Peter Kemp, *Arabian Assignment* (London, 1975), pp. 3–100; Allfree, *Warlords of Oman* pp. 58–125.

10. Shepherd, Anthony, *Arabian Adventure* (London, 1961), p. 79.

11. Cumming to Hoover, 1 August 1957, *FRUS, 1955–7,* Vol. 13, pp. 234–5; Smiley, *Arabian Assignment*, pp. 49–52; see also Burrows to FO, 29 November 1957, FO 371/126892. For arms smuggling, see Allfree, *Warlords of Oman*, pp. 92–5.

12. For an assessment of Talib's tactics, see Smiley, *Arabian Assignment*, p. 46; 'Interview with the Imam of Oman' by E. Salem, 7 January 1960, Box 2 Folder 64, Mulligan Papers. The imam died in exile on 29 November 2009.

13. 'Sultan's Salute', *Time*, 14 November 1960.

14. Slaves who escaped from their owners might gain their freedom by clasping the flagpole in the compound of the British Consulate. They were then issued with a certificate in English and Arabic and the sultan's agreement was sought before manumission, or release from slavery, was effected.

15. Dr A.T. Otaishan, conversation with the author, 16 March 2011; Burrows, *Footnotes in the Sand*, p. 104. The sheikhs all died in exile, the last one being Obaid bin Juma who passed away in 2010.

16. J.P. Tripp, 10 November 1961, FO 371/156684

17. Man to Walmsley, 1 October 1960, FO 371/149245.

18. Julian Walker, letter to the author, 19 August 2010.

19. FO to Bahrain, 1 November 1961, Priestland, pp. 752–8.

20. National Archives and Records Administration, RG 59, NEA/ARP Files: Lot 69 D 257, POL–Political Affairs & Rel., 1964, Middle East General, POL 3-a, US-UK Talks, January Position Papers, 29–30 January 1964.

21. Report of the Special Representative of the Secretary-General', New York 8 October 1963, A/5562 ('The de Ribbing Report').

22. Ad Hoc Committee report on Oman ('The Jiminez Report'), A/5846, p. 222.

23. Memorandum from Sisco to Rogers, 29 July 1970, US National Archives, RG 59, Central Files 1970–73, POL 15-1 OMAN. According to a telegram sent from the Department of State to London on 22 July, a variety of sources had indicated that 'something must be done' to get rid of Sultan Said bin Taimur.

24. Martin, Paul, 'Dhufar Rebellion's Eleventh Hour', *The Times*, 3 August 1970; 'Muscat and Oman: Family Coup', *Time*, 10 August 1970; Kutschera, Chris, 'Oman: The Death of the Last Feudal State', *Washington Post,* 27 December 1970.

25. Owtram, Francis, *A Modern History of Oman* (London, 2004), p. 140.

26. David Hirst, 'Imam's Pepsi Veneration', *The Guardian*, 4 September 1971. Retrieved 16 July 2009, from ProQuest Historical Newspapers (ID: 1125004002).

27. Telegram from Jedda to FCO, 14 December 1971, FCO 8/1616.

Chapter 19. Shaybah Rising

1. Citino, *From Arab Nationalism to OPEC*, pp. 117–43; special message to the Congress on the situation in the Middle East, 5 January 1957:
< http://www.presidency.ucsb.edu/ws/index.php?pid=11007&st=&st1= >
last accessed 27 April 2013; 'damp squib', Ashton, Nigel, review in *H-Diplo Roundtable Reviews*, Vol. XII, No. 14 (2011), last accessed 27 April 2013:
< http://www.h-net.org/ ~ diplo/roundtables/PDF/Roundtable-XII-14.pdf >

2. Australian Mission to the United Nations, 20 November 1956, FO 371/118916; see also Dulles with Cook, 28 February 1957, FO 371/12692.

3. Al-Baho, 'The Greatest Difference', pp. 241–4.

4. 'Arab Suspicion of British Moves', *The Times*, 21 January 1963.

5. 'A Brace of Kings', *Time*, 20 November 1964.

6. 'Abu Dhabi Ruler Deposed by his Family', *The Times*, 8 August 1966; 'World: Demise of a Midas', *Time*, 19 August 1966.

7. George Todd Collection, Middle East Centre Archive, St Antony's College, Oxford.

8. Lamb, Archie, *A Long Way from Swansea* (Clunderwen, 2003); Lamb, oral history transcript, 21 June 2000, British Diplomatic Oral History Programme.

9. ADPC press release, 21 September 1965; 'Report on Sheikh Shakhbut' (undated), FO 371/185527.

10. *Time*, 19 August 1966.

11. A.T. Lamb to H.G. Balfour-Paul, 14 August 1966,

12. A. Reeve to M.S. Weir, 20 December 1969, FCO 8/1276.

13. Michael Sterner, email to the author, 2 October 2009.

14. A. Reeve to M.S. Weir, 20 December 1969, FCO 8/1276.

15. Crawford, 18 April 1967, FCO 8/59; Schofield, Richard, 'The Crystallisation of a Complex Dispute: Britain and the Saudi–Abu Dhabi Borderland, 1966–71', *Journal of Arabian Studies*, 1:1, 27–51. The Saudi–Qatar agreement further entrenched positions: Britain and Abu Dhabi rejected it, Qatar refused to ratify it, while for King Faisal it simply confirmed that Khawr al-Udayd belonged to Saudi Arabia.

16. For an account of the British withdrawal from the Gulf, see Kelly, *Arabia, the Gulf and the West*, pp. 47–103; Wilkinson, *Arabia's Frontiers*, 336–40. For an American view, see the consulate general in Dhahran, 5 February 1969, Nixon Presidential Materials, NSC Files, Box 629, Country Files, Middle East, Saudi Arabia, Vol. I.

17. Kelly, *Arabia, the Gulf and the West*, pp. 74–8; Schofield, 'The Crystallisation of a Complex Dispute', p. 42.

18. Kelly, *Arabia, the Gulf and the West*, pp. 74, 78; Wilkinson, *Arabia's Frontiers*, pp. 338–40.

19. Record of a meeting held in FO, 15 May 1970, FCO 67/440; Kelly, *Arabia, the Gulf and the West*, p. 78.

20. Quote from Kelly, *Arabia, the Gulf and the West*, p. 85; Schofield, 'The Crystallisation of a Complex Dispute', p. 47.

21. M. Sterner, email to the author, 2 October 2009.

22. By 1963, the border issues between the Trucial sheikhdoms had been largely settled as a result of Julian Walker's work of mapping their boundaries.

23. Sterner to secretary of state, 30 July 1974, Washington, Central Foreign Policy Files, 1973–5, Record Group 59, General Records of the Department of State, 1974ABUDH01009.

24. Weir, 23 December 1966, FO 8/59.

25. With the exception of Ras al Khaima, which joined the UAE in February 1972.

26. Treadwell to Allen, Treadwell to Morris, 13 December 1971, FCO 8/1616.

27. Michael Sterner, email to the author, 2 October 2009.

28. Sterner to secretary of state, 30 July 1974, Washington, Central Foreign Policy Files, 1973–75, Record Group 59, General Records, 1974ABUDH01009.

29. Ibid.

30. Michael Sterner, email to the author, 2 October 2009.

31. Horan to secretary of state, 31 July 1974, Washington, Central Foreign Policy Files, 1973–75, Record Group 59, General Records of the Department of State, 1974 JIDDA04458.

32. Ibid.

33. Secretary of state to US embassy Tehran, 10 September 1974, Washington, Central Foreign Policy Files, 1973–5, Record Group 59, General Records of the Department of State, 1974STATE196907.

34. US Ambassador, London to secretary of state, 3 February 1975, Washington, Central Foreign Policy Files, 1973–75, Record Group 59, General Records of the Department of State, 1975LONDON01655.

35. Ibid.

36. Sterner to secretary of state, 15 October 1975, Washington, Central Foreign Policy Files, 1973–75, Record Group 59, General Records of the Department of State, 1975ABUDH02059.

37. See Kelly, *Arabia, the Gulf and the West*, pp. 210–12.

38. Schofield, Richard (ed.), *Arabian Boundary Disputes* (Farnham Common, 1992), Vol. 19, p. xxvi, 19.3.12.

39. *Middle East Economic Survey (MEES)*, 19 June 1995, D2.

40. BBC News, 2 May 2005: < http://news.bbc.co.uk/1/hi/world/middle_east/4505075.stmn > last accessed 27 April 2013.

41. Dargin, Justin, 'The Dolphin Project: The Development of a Gulf Gas Initiative, January 2008', pp. 23–8; 'Saudis Protest Pipeline Built by the Emirates', *International Herald Tribune*, 12 July 2006.

42. Dargin, p. 25.

43. Ibid.

44. The Permanent Mission of the UAE to the United Nations, 'The Foreign Policy of the United Arab Emirates', < http://www.un.int/uae/foreign.htm > accessed 19 December 2008.

45. 'UAE firm on sovereignty over waters of Al Adeed [*sic*]', *Al Khaleej Times*, 1 July 2005; *Middle East Economic Digest (MEED)*, 12 February 2008.

46. Henderson, Simon, 'Map Wars: The UAE Reclaims Lost Territory from Saudi Arabia', 26 January 2006, The Washington Institute for Near Eastern Policy, *Policy Watch* #1069.

47. < www.uaeinteract.com/uaeint_misc/pdf_2006/English_2006/eyb3.pdf > accessed 18 March 2008.

48. Henderson, 'Map Wars'.

49. 'Saudis Protest Pipeline Built by the Emirates', *International Herald Tribune*, 12 July 2006.

50. *MEES*, 17 July 2006.

51. *Gulf News*, 10, 15 June 2009.

52. Spencer, Richard, 'Naval Battle between UAE and Saudi Arabia Raises Fears for Gulf Security', *Telegraph*, 26 March 2010.

53. Phillips, Sir Horace, oral history transcript, 22 January 1997, British Diplomatic Oral History Programme.

Epilogue

1. 'Professor J.B. Kelly', *The Daily Telegraph*, 24 September 2009.

2. Mulligan, 'Comments on J.B. Kelly's Eastern Arabian Frontiers', Box 6, Folder 11, Mulligan Papers.

3. Schofield, Richard with Evans, Elizabeth (eds), *Arabian Boundaries: New Documents 1966–1975*, 16 vols (Farnham Common, 2009), Vol. 15, pp. viii–xv. Throughout the summer of 1974, the sultan of Oman was kept in the loop of negotiations, although not a party to the agreement that emerged. Sultan Qaboos was 'soothed by reassurances'.

4. Petersen, Tore T., *The Middle East between the Great Powers*, pp. 56, 74–5, discussed in Williamson, Daniel C., *Separate Agendas: Churchill, Eisenhower and Anglo-American Relations 1953–55* (Lanham, 2007), p. 98.

5. Brown, Anthony Cave, *Oil, God and Gold: the Story of Aramco and the Saudi Kings* (New York, 1999) pp. 213; Citino, *From Arab Nationalism to OPEC*, pp. 36–7.

6. Furlonge to Trott, 24 February 1950, FO 371/82651.

Bibliography

PRIMARY SOURCES

Archives and Collections

Association for Diplomatic Studies and Training, Library of Congress, Manuscript Division, Washington, D.C. 20540 USA, Oral Histories (Parker T. Hart): < http://memory.loc.gov/ammem/index.html > last accessed 27 April 2013.

BP Archive, Warwick University: BP and IPC records, 1945–1971.

Bancroft Library, University of California: Aramco Oral Histories: Peter C. Speers, W. Owen: < http://archive.org/details/aramcooilproduc00hickrich > last accessed 27 April 2013.

British Library, London, Asia, Pacific and Africa Collections: British and Saudi Memorials of 1955, India Office Records.

Chevron Archive, Dublin, California: Standard Oil Company of California files.

Churchill College, Cambridge: British Diplomatic History Programme, Archie T. Lamb, Sir Horace Phillips: < http://www.chu.cam.ac.uk/archives/collections/BDOHP > last accessed 27 April 2013.

D. M. Morton Collection: letters, diaries and papers in the possession of the author.

National Archives and Records Administration, College Park, Maryland: Policy Files Record Group 59, General Records of the Department of State.

Public Records Office, National Archive, Kew, London: Foreign and Cabinet Office files, namely series FO 371 (Eastern Department Correspondence, FO 1016 (Persian Gulf), FOCP (Foreign Office Confidential Prints), CAB 128/29. (Cabinet papers), records of the Prime Minister's Office (PREM) and records of the Ministry of Fuel and Power (POWE).

St Antony's College, Middle East Centre, Oxford: Private Papers Collection, notably those of George Todd, H. St J Philby, Andrew Ryan and Julian Paxton.

Southern Methodist University, Texas Collection: The Everette Lee DeGolyer, Sr. Papers.

State Department Archives, Foreign Relations of the United States *FRUS 1964–8*, < http://www.state.gov/www/about_state/history/vol_xxi > last accessed 27 April 2013.

The Avalon Project, Yale Law School: < http://avalon.law.yale.edu/20th_century/trudoc.asp > last accessed 27 April 2013.

University of Wisconsin Digital Collections Center, Foreign Relations United States (FRUS), 1940–58: < http://digital.library.wisc.edu/1711.dl/FRUS > last accessed 27 April 2013.

William E. Mulligan Papers, Special Collections, Georgetown University Library: Division, Lauinger Library, Georgetown University, Washington DC.

Published Primary Sources

Arabian American Oil Company, *Aramco Handbook*, 1960.

Burdett, A., ed., *Saudi Arabia: Secret Intelligence Records 1926–1939*, 8 vols (Farnham Common, 2003).

Hansard, *Parliamentary Debates*, 1952–1960.

Hodgkin, E.C. (ed.), *Two Kings in Arabia: Sir Reader Bullard's Letters from Jedda* (London: Ithaca Press, 1994).

Iraq Petroleum Company, *Handbook of the Territories which Form the Theatre of Operations of the Iraq Petroleum Company Limited and its Associated Companies* (London, 1948).

Permanent Mission of the UAE to the United Nations, 'The Foreign Policy of the United Arab Emirates', < http://www.un.int/uae/foreign.htm > accessed 19 December 2008.

Priestland, J. (ed.), *Buraimi Dispute: Contemporary Documents 1950–1961*, 10 vols (Farnham Common, 1992).

Schofield, Richard and Gerald Blake (eds), *Arabian Boundaries 1853–1960*, 30 vols (Farnham Common, 1988–92).

Schofield, Richard (ed.), *Arabian Boundaries 1961–1965*, 10 vols (Farnham Common, 1996).

Schofield, Richard with K.E. Evans (eds), *Arabian Boundaries: New Documents 1966–1975*, 16 vols (Farnham Common, 2009).

Tuson, Penelope, Quick, Emma (eds), *Arabian Treaties, 1600–1960*, 4 vols, (Farnham Common, 1993).

UAE Yearbooks, 2005 and 2006.

Periodicals

AFP Reporter

Arabian Sun and Flare

Aramco World

Al-Bilad al-Saudiya

Birmingham Post

Crescent (IPC) Magazine

Guardian

Gulf News

International Herald Tribune

IPC Newsletter

Al-Khaleej Times

Middle East Economic Digest

Middle East Economic Summary

New York Times

The Observer

Al-Qafilah

The Scotsman

Time

Times of London

Washington Post

Memoirs

Allfree, P. S., *Warlords of Oman* (London, 1967).

Barger, Thomas C., *Out in the Blue* (Vista: California, 2000).

Boustead, Colonel Sir Hugh, *The Wind of the Morning* (London, 1971).

Bullard, Reader Sir, *The Camels Must Go* (London, 1961).

Burrows, B.A.B., *Footnotes in the Sand* (London, 1990).

Butt, Gerald, *The Lion in the Sand* (London, 1995).

Cheney, Michael Sheldon, *Big Oil Man from Arabia* (New York, 1958).

Clayton, Sir Gilbert, *An Arabian Diary* (Berkeley, 1969).

Clayton, Peter, *Two Alpha Lima* (London, 1994).

Colville, J., *The Fringes of Power* (London, revised edition 2004).

Coriat, Percy, *Soldier in Oman* (London, 1960).

Cox, Percy, 'Some Excursions in Oman', *Geographical Journal*, Vol. 66, No. 3, September 1925.

Dickson, H.R.P., *Kuwait and Her Neighbours* (London, 1956).

Eddy, William A., *FDR Meets Ibn Saud* (New York, 1954).

Ellis, Jim, 'Plain Tales from the Sands' (*British Yemeni Journal*, July 2000).

Hart, Parker T., *Saudi Arabia and the United States* (Bloomington, 1998).

Hawley, Donald, *The Trucial States* (New York, 1970).

———*The Emirates: Witness to a Metamorphosis* (Norwich, 2007).

Henderson, E., Arabian Destiny: The Complete Autobiography (Dubai, 1999).

———*This Strange Eventful History* (London, 1988).

Hillyard, Susan, *Before the Oil, A Personal Memoir of Abu Dhabi 1954–58* (Bakewell, Derbyshire, 2002).

Innes, Neil M., *Minister in Oman* (New York, 1987).

Lamb, Sir Archie, *A Long Way from Swansea* (Clunderwen, 2003).

Lawrence, T.E., *Revolt in the Desert* (London, 1927).

Morris, James (now Jan), *Sultan in Oman* (London, 1957).

Owen, Roderic, *The Golden Bubble* (London, 1957).

Philby, H. St J. B., *Arabian Oil Ventures* (Washington DC, 1964).

Pritzke, Herbert, *Bedouin Doctor* (London, 1957).

Ryan, Sir Andrew, *Last of the Dragomans* (London, 1951).

Shawcross, Hartley Sir, *Life Sentence* (London:, 1995).

Shepherd, Anthony, *Arabian Adventure* (London, 1961).

Sheridan, Don, *Fahud – The Leopard Mountain* (Dublin, 2000).

Smiley, David, with Peter Kemp, *Arabian Assignment* (London, 1975).

Thesiger, Wilfred, *Arabian Sands* (London, 1959).

———'Desert Borderlands of Oman', *Geographical Journal*, Volume 116, nos. 4–6, October–December 1950, pages 137–168.

Thomas, Bertram, *Alarms and Excursions* (London, 1931).

———*Arabia Felix: Across the Empty Quarter* (London, 1938).

van Der Meulen, D., *The Wells of Ibn Saud* (London, 1957).

Walker, Julian, *Tyro on the Trucial Coast* (Crook, County Durham, 1999).

SECONDARY SOURCES

Unpublished Theses, Papers

Al-Baho, A.I.J., 'The Greatest Difference: Britain, the United States and the Buraimi Oasis Dispute, 1952–1957', PhD diss., London School of Economics and Political Science, December 1996.

Dargin, Justin, 'The Dolphin Project: The Development of a Gulf Gas Initiative, January 2008', Oxford Institute of Energy Studies.

Lind, Gary, 'The Buraimi Oasis Dispute', PhD diss., American University of Beirut, 1973.

Paxton, Julian, 'History of PDO', GB165-0331, Middle East Archive Centre, St Antony's College, Oxford.

Articles, Published Papers

Bierschenk, T., 'Oil Interests and the Formation of Centralized Government 1920–1970', *Orient*, 1989, Vol. 30, page 216.

Burghardt, Andrew F., 'The Bases of Territorial Claims', *Geographical Review*, Vol. 63, No. 2 (Apr., 1973), pp. 225–245.

Cavendish, Richard, 'Death of Ibn Saud', *History Today*, Vol. 53, November 2003.

DeGolyer, E.L., 'Preliminary Report of the Technical Oil Mission to the Middle East, 1944', Southern Methodist University Texas Collection, box 19, folder 2315.

———'Some Aspects of Oil in the Middle East', *The Near East & The Great Powers*, ed. Richard N. Frye, pp. 119–36 (Harvard University Press, 1951).

Duce, James Terry, 'Review of Oil in the Middle East', *Middle East Journal*, Summer 1960.

Grey, W.G, 'Trade and Races of Oman', *Quarterly Journal of the Mythical Society*, Vol. 2, No. 2 (January 1911).

Haworth, L., 'Persia and the Persian Gulf', *Journal of the Central Asian Society*, Vol. XVI, 1929, part IV, p. 501.

Henderson, Simon, 'Map Wars: The UAE Reclaims Lost Territory from Saudi Arabia', 26 January 2006, The Washington Institute for Near Eastern Policy, *Policy Watch* #1069.

Katakura, Kunio, 'The Yokoyama Mission: Japanese Diplomacy for Oil, 1939', *The International History Review*, Vol. 8, No. 2 (May 1986), pp. 263–269.

Kelly, J.B., 'Arabian Frontiers and Anglo-American Relations', *Government and Opposition*, Vol. 27, issue 3, pages 368–9.

Morton, D. Michael, 'The Geology of Oman', Proc. 5th World Petroleum Congress, Vol. 1, 272–93.

Morton, Michael Quentin, 'Narrowing the Gulf: Anglo-American Relations and Arabian Oil, 1928–74', *Liwa* journal of the National Center for Documentation and Research (UAE), Vol. 3, No. 6, Dec. 2011, pp. 38–54.

Owen, Lord David, 'Diseased, Demented, Depressed: Serious Illness in Heads of State', *Quarterly Journal of Medicine*, 2003, 96: 325–336.

Owen, P., 'The Rebellion in Dhofar – A Threat to Western Interests in the Gulf, The World', *Today*, June 1973.

Peterson, J.E., 'Oman's Diverse Society: Northern Oman', *Middle East Journal*, Vol. 58, No. 1 (Winter 2004), pp. 32–51.

Schofield, Richard (2011), 'The Crystallisation of a Complex Dispute: Britain and the Saudi–Abu Dhabi Borderland, 1966–71', *Journal of Arabian Studies*, 1:1, 27–51.

Wilkinson, J.C., 'The Oman Question: The Background to the Political Geography of South-eastern Arabia', *Geo. Journal*, Vol. 137, No. 3, Sept. 1971, pp. 361–71.

Books

Abdullah, Muhammad Morsy, *The United Arab Emirates: A Modern History* (London, 1978).

Abu Dhabi Documentation Centre, *Two Glorious Years in the History of Abu Dhabi*, 1968.

Albaharna, Hussain M., *The Legal Status of the Arabian Gulf States* (Manchester, 1968).

Allen, C., *God's Terrorists, The Wahhabi Cult and the Hidden Roots of Modern Terrorism* (London, 2006).

Anstey, Vera, *The Economic Development of India* (New York, 1977).

Asher, Michael, *Thesiger* (London, 1994).

Ashton, Nigel J. (ed.) *The Cold War in the Middle East: regional conflict and the superpowers, 1967–73* (London, 2007).

Belgrave, Sir Charles, *The Pirate Coast* (London, 1966).

Bell, Gertrude, *The Arab War* (London: 1940).

Beydoun, Ziad R, *The Middle East: Regional Geology and Petroleum Resources* (Beaconsfield, 1988).

Brenchley, Frank, *Britain and the Middle East: an Economic History, 1945–87* (London, 1991).

Bronson, Rachel, *Thicker than Oil: America's Uneasy Partnership with Saudi Arabia* (New York, 2006).

Brown, Anthony C., *Oil, God and Gold, The Story of Aramco and the Saudi Kings* (New York, 1999).

Citino, Nathan J., *From Arab Nationalism to OPEC* (Bloomington, 2002).

Clarke, Angela, Bahrain Oil and Development, 1929–1989 (Boulder, CO, 1990).

Davey, Charles E., *The Blood-red Arab Flag: An Investigation into Qasimi Piracy 1797–1820* (Exeter, 1997).

Davis, Simon, *Contested Space: Anglo-American Relations in the Persian Gulf, 1939–1947* (Leiden, Boston, 2009).

De Novo, A., *American Policies and Interests in the Middle East* (Minneapolis, 1963).

Dutton, David, *Eden: A Life and Reputation* (London, 1997).

Facey, William, Dir'iyyah and the First Saudi State (London, 1997).

Fain, W. Taylor, *American Ascendance and British Retreat in the Persian Gulf Region* (New York, 2008).

Gilbert, Martin, *Churchill: A Life* (London, 1992).

Gratz, Liesl, *The Omanis, Sentinels of the Gulf* (London, 1982).

Halliday, F., *Arabia Without Sultans* (New York, 1975).

Heard-Bey, Frauke, *From Trucial States to United Arab Emirates* (Dubai, 2004).

Holden, David, *Farewell to Arabia* (London, 1966).

Holden, David and Richard Johns, *The House of Saud* (London, 1981).

Hope, Stanton, *Arabian Adventurer* (London, 1951).

James, Robert Rhodes, *Anthony Eden* (London, 1986).

Keating, Aileen, *Mirage: Power, Politics and the Hidden History of Arabian Oil* (New York, 2005).

Kelly, John B., *Arabia, the Gulf and the West* (London, 1980).

———*Eastern Arabian Frontiers* (London, 1964).

Lacey, Robert, *Kingdom: Arabia and the House of Saud* (New York, 1982).

Leatherdale, Clive, *Britain and Saudi Arabia, 1925–1939, The Imperial Oasis* (London, 1983).

Longrigg, Stephen H., *Oil in the Middle East: Its Discovery and Development* 2 edition (Oxford, 1961).

Lorimer, John G., *Gazetteer of the Persian Gulf, Oman and Central Arabia*, 1908 & 1915 (Farnham Common, 1986).

Madawi Al-Rasheed, *A History of Saudi Arabia* (Cambridge, 2002).

Mann, Michael, *Trucial Oman Scouts: The Story of a Bedouin Force* (Wilby, 1994).

Miers, Suzanne, *Slavery in the Twentieth Century, the Evolution of a Global Pattern*, (Lanham, MD, 2003).

Miller, Aaron D., *Search for Security: Saudi Arabian Oil and American Foreign Policy* (Chapel Hill, NC, 1980).

Mohammed Al-Fahim, *From Rags to Riches: A Story of Abu Dhabi* (London, 1995).

Morton, Michael Quentin, *In the Heart of the Desert: the Story of an Exploration Geologist and the Search for Oil in the Middle East* (Aylesford, 2006).

Mulligan, William, George Rentz and F.S. Vidal, *Aramco Reports on Al-Hasa & Oman 1950–1955*, 4 vols (Farnham Common, 1990).

Nash, Gerald D., *United States Oil Policy 1890–1964* (Pittsburgh, 1968).

Niblock, Tim, *State, Society and Economy in Saudi Arabia* (Beckenham, Kent, 1982).

Onley, James, *The Arabian Frontier of the British Raj: Merchants, Rulers, and the British in the Nineteenth Century Gulf* (New York, 2007).

Owen, Edgar W., *Trek of the Oil Finders: A History of Exploration for Petroleum*, (Tulsa, Oklahoma, 1975).

Owtram, Francis, *A Modern History of Oman: Formation of the State since 1920* (London, 2004).

Petersen, Tore T., *The Middle East between the Great Powers: Anglo-American Conflict and Co-operation, 1952–1957* (Basingstoke, 2000).

Peterson, John. E., *Oman in the Twentieth Century: Political Foundations of an Emerging State* (London, 1978).

———*Oman's Insurgencies: The Sultanate's Struggle for Supremacy* (London, 2007).

Rabi, Uzi, *The Emergence of States in a Tribal Society* (Portland, Ore, 2006).

Roosevelt, Elliott, *As He Saw It* (New York, 1946).

Schofield, Richard (ed.), *Territorial Foundations of the Gulf States* (London, 1994).

Shwadran, Benjamin, *The Middle East, Oil and the Great Powers* (Jerusalem, 1955).

Skeet, Ian, *Muscat and Oman: The End of an Era* (London, 1974).

Stegner, Wallace, *Discovery! The Search for Arabian Oil* (Vista, California, 2007).

Thorpe, D.R., *Eden* (London, 2003).

Tinkle, Lon, *Mr De*, USA (Boston, 1970).

Townsend, John, *Oman: The Making of a Modern State* (London, 1977).

Vitalis, Robert, *America's Kingdom: Mythmaking on the Saudi Oil Frontier* (Stanford, California, 2007.

Wall, Bennett H. and Gibb, George S., *Teagle of Jersey Standard* (New Orleans, 1974).

Ward, Sir Adolphus W. and Ward, George, P. (eds), *The Cambridge History of British Foreign Policy 1783–1919*, 3 vols (Cambridge, 1923).

Ward, Thomas E. *Negotiations for Oil Concessions in Bahrain, El Hasa (Saudi Arabia), the Neutral Zone, Qatar and Kuwait* (New York, 1965).

Wilkinson, John C., *Arabia's Frontiers: The Story of Britain's Boundary Drawing in the Desert* (London, 1991).

———*The Imamate Tradition of Oman* (Cambridge, 1987).

———*Water and Tribal Settlement in South-East Arabia* (Oxford, 1977).

Williamson, Daniel C., *Separate Agendas: Churchill, Eisenhower and Anglo-American Relations 1953–55* (Lanham, 2007).

Yergin, Daniel, *The Prize: The Epic Quest for Oil, Money and Power* (New York, 1991).

Index

Page numbers in bold type indicate illustrations.

Abdul Aziz, king of Saudi Arabia, *see* Al
  Saud dynasty
Abqaiq, 76
Abu Dhabi, 16, 30, 31, 50–62, 98, 105–6,
  217–20, 223
  Defence Force (ADDF), 219
  discovery of oil in, 133, 217
  relations with Britain, 33, 39
  situation in (1955), 190
Abu Dhabi Marine Areas Ltd (ADMA),
  58, 217
Abu Dhabi Petroleum Company Ltd
  (ADPC), 218, 221
Abu Khiraiban, 78
Abu Musa, the Greater and Lesser
  Tunbs, 222, 236
Abu Sindah, 6, 40
Acheson, Dean, 103
Aflaj Ridge, 23
Afrika Korps, 95
Ain Haradh, 24
Ain Hisy, 24
Al-Ain, 4, 61, 62, 97, 102, 206, 207, 219,
  237
Albaharna, Hussain, 232
Al-Hasa province, Saudi Arabia, 5, 8, 12,
  18, 25, 34, 53, 76
Al-Kharj, 103
Al-Khobar, 189
Al-Suwaiq, 208
Anglo-Iranian Oil Company, 70
Anglo-Persian Oil Company, 13, 14, 26,
  36, 55
Aqal, territory of the Qubaisat tribe, 141
Aqil, Turki's assistant in Hamasa, 121
Arab League, 164, 213, 214
Arab Zone, 76
Arabian American Oil Company, *see*
  Aramco

Aramco, *see also* Saudi Aramco
  50-50 agreement, 70–1
  Arabian Research and Translation
    Division, 71–3, 133, 139, 233
  British suspicions about, 139
  and the CIA, 112
  discovery of the Shaybah oilfield,
    221
  discussions with Yusuf Yasin (1955),
    192–4
  expedition to the Mjann and Aqal
    (1954), 140–1
  exploration of the Rub al-Khali, 71,
    76
  formation, 25
  incursions into IPC concession areas,
    76–80, 195
  knowledge of Abu Dhabi oil strike,
    133
  opposition to a consortium with
    IPC, 135
  payments to the Saudi government,
    201
  and the Red Line Agreement, 66–7
  relations with Saudi Arabia, 69
  relations with the State Department,
    83, 197
  relationship with King Saud, 201
  terms of oil concession agreement
    (1948), 70
  view of Buraimi oil prospects, 134
Arbitration Agreement (1954), 142–4,
  167, 172, 173, 177, 179, 187, 259
  alleged breaches of, 149, 152, 153,
    158, 167
  appointment of arbitrator, 172
  British decision to denounce, 174,
    179
Azzam, Abdul Rahman, 153, 164, 166,
  168, 171, 212

Baba Gurgur, 11
Badi Palace, Riyadh, 113
Bahrain, 8, 25
Bait Aqil, 121
Bait Turki, 121, 131, 147, 182, 183, 184, 187
Baker, Norval, 77, 81
Bani Ghaith tribe, 150
Bani Ka'ab tribe, 107
Bani Qitab tribe, 105
Bani Riyam tribe, 88
Bani Yas tribe, 51, 53, 78
Barger, Thomas C., xiii, 18, 19, 20, 23, 24
Batin, 61
Batinah coast, 44, 205
Batinah plain, 35
Beirut, 214
Beit Baghdadi, Jedda, 11
Berg, Ernie, 24
Bilad Sait, 199, 208
Bin Qitami, 89
Bird, R.E.R. ('Dick'), xiii, 38, 41-2, 43, 44, 46, 47, 48, 86, 87, 104, 178
Blue Line, see Boundaries
Boundaries
    Blue Line, Anglo-Turkish boundary line, 26-8, 32, 82, 83, 234
    Brown Line, British proposal, 29
    Green Line, British proposal, 29
    Hamza Line, also known as the Red Line, 29, 84, 225, 234
    Red Line, see Hamza Line
    Riyadh Line, British proposal, 29-30, 178, 186, 221, 227
    Ryan Line, see Riyadh Line
    Saudi claim of 1949, 82-5
    Violet Line, Anglo-Turkish boundary line, 26, 82, 83
    Yellow Line, British proposal, 29
British Bank of the Middle East, 189, 210
British Petroleum (BP), 178
Brown, Anthony Cave, 233
Brown Line, see Boundaries
Buckmaster, Martin, 50, 61, 73, 162
Bulganin, Nikolay, 194

Bullard, Reader, xiv, 10, 153, 161, 162, 165, 169, 170, 171, 172, 176, 231
Buraimi Arbitration Tribunal, 153, 159-73
    British submissions (the UK Memorial), 164, 231
    Saudi submissions (the Saudi Arabian Memorial, 73, 160, 165
Buraimi Oasis, 43, **98**, 120-32, 154, 156
    aftermath of the Saudi withdrawal (1955-6), 206-7
    allegiances of the villagers in, 100
    arrival of Wilfred Thesiger, 46
    attempt by Bertram Thomas to visit (1927), 6
    in the early 1950s, 97-9
    influence of Sheikh Zayed bin Sultan in, 99
    influence of the Sultan and Imam in, 43
    influence of Zayed the Great in, 4
    IPC and, 50
    oil and gas prospects, 76, 134
    Saudi activities in (1954-5), 149, 155
    Saudi influence in, 87
    slave trade in, 43
    today, 237
    the villages of, 61
    visit of John Wilton (1949), 91-3
    and the Wahhabis, 2-6
Buraimi village
    execution in, 6
    influence of the Naimi tribe in, 4
    Sheikh Saqr's influence in, 40
    suq, 123, 126, **127**, 128
    surrender of Saqr's fort (1955), 185
Burj al-Ajam, 183
Burrows, Bernard, xiv, 133, 141, 161, 162, 168, 174, 178, 181, 211
Bustani, Ali, 129, 131, 132, 160

Cairo, 95
Cairo Radio, 207
California Arabian Standard Oil Company (Casoc), 25, 87, 140
    operations in the Rub al Khali, 17-20

Californian Texas Oil Company (Caltex), 20
Canning Award, 37
Central Intelligence Agency (CIA), 112, 233
Chamberlain, Neville, 30, 114
Chauncy, Major Leslie, 102, 104
Cheeseman, Lieut.-Col. Bill, 197
Childs, J. Rives, 83
Churchill, Winston, 110, 113, 114, 118, 141, 142
Citino, Nathan, 233
Clayton, Captain Peter, xiv, 144, 146, 147, 148, 155, 156, 157, 160, 164, 169, 170, 183, 184, 185
Cocatrix, Pierre de, 129–32
Committee of Imperial Defence, 32
Compagnie Française des Pétroles (CFP), 13, 67
Cousteau, Jacques, 58, 59, 75
Cox, Peter, geologist, 55
Cox, Sir Percy, 5, 26, 31, 34, 55, 56
Criddle, Captain C.W., 129

Dalley, Chris, 221
Dammam, 189, 199
    conference (1952), 84
    oilfield, 20
Davies, Fred, 70, 135, 193
DeGolyer, Everette Lee, 64
Derham, Jimmy, 76, 77, 78
Dhafrah (Zafrah), 79
Dhahira plain, 5, 36, 43, 44, 187
Dhahran, 21
    airbase, 111, 138, 197
Dhank, 40, 106, 150, 196
Dhawahir tribe, 2
Dhofar, 39, 225
Dhofar Liberation Front, 213
Dhofar War, see Oman
Dihaigo, Ernesto di, 165
Diriyah, 3
Dodds-Parker, Douglas, 202, 203
Dolphin gas project, 227, 229
Dubai, 52, 98
Duce, Terry, 112

Dulles, John Foster, xiv, 111–12, 142, 196, 197, 199, **200**, 201
Dunn, Robin, 164
Duru tribe, 35

East India Company, 3
Eccles, Captain G.J., 36
Eden, Anthony, xiv, 30, 110, 113, 114–19, 137, 142, 175, 179, 196, 199, **200**, 201, 203
Eisenhower Doctrine, 216
Eisenhower, Dwight D., 111, 112, 118, 197, 199, 201
Emirates Centre for Strategic Studies and Research, 237
Empty Quarter, see Rub al-Khali

Al Bu Falah, leading branch of the Bani Yas tribe, 51, 52
Farouk, king of Egypt, 95
Foster, John, 112, 142
Fowle, Trenchard, 26
Free Oman Army, 205, 209

Geneva, 173
geologists, work of, 19
Gezira, 134, 178
Ghafiri tribes, 35
Ghaghah Island, 78
Ghawar, oilfield, 25
Goon Show, 120
Gosum, Sheikh, 41
Government of India, 31
Gray, K. Washington, 36, 187
Green Line, see Boundaries
Gulbenkian, Calouste, 13, 67
Gulf Co-operation Council, 230
Great Britain, see United Kingdom
Gwadar, 39

Hail, 41, 150
Hajar Mountains, 34
Halifax, Lord, and Khawr al-Udayd, 33
Hamasa
    arrival of Turki bin Otaishan, 99–101
    battle for (1955), 181

Hamasa continued
blockade of, 117, 120–32
decline after Saudis' departure, 206–7
fire (July 1955), 157–8
Ibn Saud's influence in, 91
position in the Buraimi Oasis, 99
refugees, 211, 221
ruins, **190**
shooting incident, 125
slave trade, 43
visit of Pierre de Cocatrix, 129–32
visitors to, 105
water supply, 107
Hamilton, Lloyd, 11, 14, 15, 16
Hamza, Fuad, 10, 27, 28, 29, 53, 85, 135
Hamza Line, *see* Boundaries
Haradh, 24, 25
al-Hariq, Salim, 2
al-Harithi, Salih bin Isa, 207
Hasan, Dr Mahmoud, 165, 167, 169, 172, 176, 177
Hay, Sir Rupert, 85
Hayif, Emir, 79
Henderson, Edward, xiv, 73, 90, 160, 164, 181, 183, 184, 187
Hillyard, Tim, 60, 251
al-Hinai, Ghalib bin Ali, imam of Oman, xiv, **88**, 155, 185, 196, 197, 208, 213, 214
al-Hinai, Talib bin Ali, xvii, 196, 199, 205, 208, 213, 214
Hinawi tribes, 35
Holm, Don, 79
Hoover, Herbert Charles, 195, 197, 201, 216
Hotchkiss, Henry, 40
Hudson, Judge Manley O., 83, 165
Hugf Militia, *see* Muscat and Oman Field Force (MOFF)
Hume, Dr John Basil, 118

Ibadhi tribes, 35
Ibn Saud, *see* Al Saud dynasty
Ibrahim Pasha, 3
Ikhwan, 5
Imamate of Oman, *see* Oman
Indago Petroleum, 238

India Office, 32, 33, 115
Innes, Neil, 205
Institute of Commonwealth Studies, 161
Iran, 116
Iraq Petroleum Company (IPC)
50-50 agreement with Iraq, 70
Abu Dhabi oil concession, 57
American partners in, 81
attitude towards incursions, 80–1
attitude towards border (1955), 178
expedition to Jebel Fahud (1954), 154
interest in Al-Hasa, 8
monopoly of oil in the Middle East, 12
offer for Al-Hasa concession (1933), 14
oil strike at Baba Gurgur, 11
opposes giving Jebel Nakash to Ibn Saud, 30
plans for disputed territory, 134
and the Red Line Agreement, 66–7
relations with Wilfred Thesiger, 46–8
and the Zarrara oilfield, 221
Israel
US recognition of, 66

Jackson, Noel, 46
Jebel Akhdar, 35, 208
Jebel Akhdar War, *see* Oman
Jebel Dhanna, 56, 78
Jebel Dukhan, 76
Jebel Fahud, 43, 154, 198
Jebel Hafit, 47, 56, 76, 97, 99, 237, 238
Jebel Nakhsh, 29, 30
Jebel Natih, 43
Jedda, 202, 203, 258
oil negotiations in (1933), 7–15
Jiluwi, Abdullah bin, 4, 5, 54, 74
Jiluwi, Abdul Muhsin bin, 55
Jiluwi, Saud bin, xvi, **54**, 80, 84, 95, 100, 149, 150, 155, 185, 189, 204, 212
Jimi, **124**, 125
Johnson, Major later Colonel, Eric, xiv, 144, 181, 183, 184

al-Kaabi, Abdullah bin Salim, xiii, 108, 125, 126, 150, 151

al-Kaabi, Obaid bin Juma, xv, 90, **90**, 105, 107, 108, 125, 126, 147, 150–1, 182, 183, 184, 206
Kahil, 126, 151
Karim, Abdullah, 87
Kelly, John B., 231, 232
al-Khalili, Muhammad bin Abdullah, imam of Oman, xv, 35, 40, 101, 102, 104, 122
al-Khalili, Saud, 213
al-Kharusi, Salim bin Rashid, imam of Oman, 35
Khashabi, Ali, Lieut.-Col., 155, 193
Khatwa, 151
Khawatir tribe, 105
Khawr al-Udayd, 29, 76, 78, 79, 115, 140, 167, 178, 202, 221, 228, 229
    negotiations about (1930s), 31–3
Khrushchev, Nikita, 194
Khurnus, 108
Kirkpatrick, Ivonne, 197
Kitna, 150

Laird, Captain R. A., 182
Lansing, Robert, 112
Lawrence, T.E., 7
Layla, 18, 23, 24
Lees, George, 36, 187
Little, Major W.O., 155
Liwa Oasis, 19, 20, 51, 61, 83, 87, 102, 106, 178, 208
Lloyd, Selwyn, 202
Loch, Lieut.-Col. Gordon, 30
Longrigg, Stephen Hemsley, xv, 11, 12, 13, 14, 48, 80, 81
Loomis, Francis, 63
Lorimer, J.G. (*Gazetteer*), 44, 72

MacDonald, Major P., 132
Macmillan, Harold, 175, 178, 196, 216
Maghaira, 145, 148
Mahadha, 109, 125
    as an independent state (1953), 107–9
Makins, Sir Roger, 195
Al Maktoum dynasty:
    Rashid bin Saeed, ruler of Dubai and vice president of the UAE, 222

Al Maktoum hospital, Dubai, 99
Mana bin Muhammad, sheikh of the Dhawahir tribe, 160
Manasir tribe, 28, 53, 57, 97
Manning, Doug, 195
Manningham-Buller, Reginald, xv, 176, 179
Mansur, Muhammad bin, 24, 87, 116
Markaz al-Sarouj, 144, 147
Markhiya, 61
Marshall Plan, 111
Mazyad, 127
Mecca, 13
Meulen, Daniel van der, 68, 113, 136
Miles, Lieut.-Col. Samuel, 4
Miliband, David, 237
Mjann, 141
Monks, Noel, 120
Morris, James, 199
Morton, D.M. ('Mike'), 44, 154, 186
Mudarres, Sulaiman, 11
Mueller, Homer, 139, 193, 194
Mughira, 78
Mulayda, battle of, 1891, 4
Mulligan, William, 140
Murabba tower, 102
Murban
    No. 1 well, 133
    No. 3 well, 218
Murrah tribe, 6, 28, 29
Muscat, 34–5, 37, 210, 213
Muscat and Oman Field Force (MOFF), 39, 81, 185
Muslim Brotherhood, 95
Muttrah, 34
Muwaiqi, 50

Naamani, Dr, 129, 132
al-Nabhan, Suleiman bin Hamyar, xvi, 87–9, **88**, 155, 208, 209
Al Nahyan dynasty:
    Dhiyab bin Saqr, 152
    Hamdan bin Muhammad, 219
    Hamdan bin Zayed, 228
    Hazza bin Sultan, 50, 52, 58, 78, 79, 106, 152, 160, 167, 183, 217
    Khaled bin Sultan, 59, **198**

Al Nahyan dynasty continued
　Khalifa bin Zayed, ruler of Abu
　　Dhabi and president of the UAE,
　　228
　Mubarak bin Muhammad, 219
　Shakhbut bin Sultan, ruler of Abu
　　Dhabi, 20, 28, 31, 32, 33, 51, 52,
　　53, 55, 56, 57, **58**, 58–9, 59, 61,
　　78, 102, 105, 106, 152, **198**, 199,
　　207, 217–20, 230
　Tahnoun bin Muhammad, 219
　Zayed bin Khalifa, 'Zayed the
　　Great', 4, 31, 51
　Zayed bin Sultan, ruler of Abu
　　Dhabi and president of the UAE,
　　xvii, 47, 50–1, 52, 58, 60–2, **62**,
　　99, 101, 102, 122, 126–7, 128,
　　144, 149, 152, 155, 156, 158, 159–
　　60, 167, 169, 177, 183, **198**, 204,
　　211, 217, 218–9, 220–3, 224, 227,
　　226, 236
al-Naimi, Saqr bin Sultan, xvi, 6, 40–1,
　　42, 43, **89**, 91, 101, 104, 107, 109,
　　126, 127, 128, 149, 150, 151, 155,
　　157, 158, 183, 185, 189, 206
Naimi tribe, 2, 3, 4
Nakhla, 144, 190
Nami, Major Abdullah bin, xiii, 144,
　　145, **146**, 147, 149, 150, 151, 152,
　　155, 156, 157, 181, 182, 186, 190
Nasser, Colonel Gamel, 114, 115, 154,
　　203, **204**, 220
Near East Development Corporation, 13
Nixon, Richard, 142
Nizwa, 158, 197
No Oil Man's Land, 142, 178, 186

Ohliger, Floyd W., 193
oil
　origin of petroleum, 19
　origin of petroleum in the Middle
　　East, 75–6
　reserves in the Middle East in 1943,
　　64
　reserves in the USA, 11
Oman
　arms smuggling into, 205

arms traffic into, 151
borderlands, 16
chieftainship in, 42
Dhofar War, 213, 214
early difficulties of oil exploration,
　39, 41, 46
early history, 34
Free Oman Army, 199
Friendship Committee, 213
geography, 34
imamate, 154, 207, 209, 214, 227
Jebel Akhdar War (1957–9), 207–9
reaction to expulsion of Saudis from
　Hamasa, 196
reaction to Saudi occupation of
　Hamasa, 103
rebels, 205, 212
relations with Great Britain, 33, 39
Saudi ambitions towards, 96
sultan's campaign against the imam
　(1955), 196–8
tribes, 35
and the United Nations, 212–13
Wahhabi attacks on, 2
Onassis, Aristotle, 201
Operation Bonaparte, 181–4, 233
Operation Boxer, 116
Operation Musketeer, *see* Suez Crisis
Organisation of Petroleum Exporting
　Countries (OPEC), 71
al-Otaishan, Turki bin Abdullah, xvii,
　94, 95, 96, 97, 99–101, **100**, 107,
　113, 121, 123, 128, 129, 131, 132,
　137, 142, 147–8, 148, 149, 211,
　223, 230
Ottoman Empire, 26
Owen, Garry, 192

Palestine
　British withdrawal from (1948), 66
　link with Arabian boundaries issue,
　　30
　US–Saudi differences over, 65
Partex, 13
Pearl Harbor, 1941, 25
Pelham, George, 103, 134
Pelly, Colonel Lewis, 3

PDRY, People's Democratic Republic of
    Yemen, 225
Persia, 273
Persian Gulf, 30, 273
    British withdrawal from, 220
    strategic importance to the West, 64,
        111, 217
Petersen, Tore T., 233
Petroleum Development (Oman and
    Dhofar), 44
Petroleum Development (Qatar), 26, 76
Petroleum Development (Trucial Coast
    Ltd (PDTC), 57
Philby, Harry St John, xv, 10–11, 14, 23,
    122
pilgrims to Mecca, 9
Political Residency, transfer from
    Bushire to Bahrain, 57
Priestland, Jane, 232
Pritzke, Herbert, 95, 96, 97

Qais, Azzan ibn, ruler of Muscat and
    Oman, 3
al-Qaraishi, Abdullah, xiii, 145–6, 149,
    155, 157, 158, 159, 167, 168, 185,
    193
Al Qasimi dynasty:
    Saqr bin Mohammad, ruler of Ras al-
        Khaima, 222
Qasr al-Hosn, 58
Qasr al-Sudaira, 191
Qatar, 26, 29, 31, 87
    discovery of oil in, 76
Qatar North Field, offshore gas field,
    227
Qatar Petroleum Company, 26
Qawasim tribe, 2
    and piracy, 3
Qubaisat tribe, 31, 78, 141
al-Qubaisi, Salaamah bint Butti, 52, 59,
    61, 133, 217, 219

Rabia, 150
Ras al-Hamra, 78
Ras al-Khaima, 51
Ras Sadr, 78, 81

Ras Tanura, 21, 96
    opening the oil terminal at (1939), 21
Al Rashid tribe, 5
Red Line (1935), see Boundaries
Red Line Agreement (1928), operating
    framework of the IPC group of
    companies, 66
Rendell, George, 30
Rentz, Dr George, xv, 71, 72, 78, 133,
    139, 160, 164
Rhodes, Captain John, 181
de Ribbing, Herbert, 211, 212
Riches, Derek, 103, 140, 192
Riyadh, 45, 140, 189, 202, 203
Riyadh Line, see Boundaries
Robert Ray Geophysical Company Ltd,
    79
Roberts, Goronwy, 220
Roosevelt, Franklin D., 64, 65, 110
Royal Dutch Shell Ltd ('Shell'), 13, 14,
    178
Rub al-Khali, 8, 11, 15, 16, 18, 19, 23, 26,
    29, 30, 34, 45, 48, 76
Ryan, Sir Andrew, xvi, 7, 12, 14, 27, 28,
    29
Ryan Line, see Boundaries

Saara, 99
    influence of the Naimi tribe in, 4
Sabkhat Matti, 20, 34, 78, 225
Al Bu Said dynasty:
    Qaboos bin Said, sultan of Oman,
        213–14, 213, **226**, 227
    Said bin Taimur, sultan of Muscat
        and Oman, xvi, 37–9, **38**, 40, 43,
        45, 51, 86, 102, 104, 109, 157,
        174, 192, 196, **198**, 212, 214, 230
    Taimur bin Faisal, sultan of Muscat
        and Oman, 35, 36
Salalah, 38, 39, 196
Salih, Muhammad, 121
Al Saud dynasty:
    Abdul Aziz ibn Abdur Rahman, 'Ibn
        Saud', king of Saudi Arabia, xiii,
        4–6, **8**, 8–9, 10, 11, 12, 13, 15, 18,
        21, **22**, 23, 26, 27, 29, 32, 33, 39,
        40, 43, 45, 53, 63, 67, 68, 70, 73,

Abdul Aziz continued
74, 86–7, 90, 91, 92, 96, 103, 111,
113, 114, 115, 116, 119, 137,
201, 230
Abdullah ibn Faisal, 3
Abdullah ibn Saud, imam, 3
Fahd ibn Abdul Aziz, crown prince
and king of Saudi Arabia, xiv,
224, **226**, 227, 233
Faisal ibn Abdul Aziz, crown prince
and king of Saudi Arabia, xiv, 84,
85, 116, **117**, 137, 138, 178, 188,
203, 204, 213, 214, 217, 220, 221,
222, 224, 227
Saud ibn Abdul al-Aziz, crown
prince and king of Saudi Arabia,
xvi, 68, 111, 137, 140, 149, 150,
156, 157, 189, 194, 201, 202, 203,
204, 217
Muhammad ibn Saud, 1
Nayef bin Abdul-Aziz, crown
prince, 229
Al Saud history, 1–6
Saudi Arabia, 66
50-50 agreement, 70–1
decline of British influence in, 65
Dodds-Parker Mission to (1956), 202
financial position, 68, 217
largest oil producer in the world, 12
oil concessions, 69
reaction to expulsion from Hamasa,
188–90, 192
relations with Aramco, 69
relations with the UK, 3, 111, 217
relations with the USA, 63–6, 65,
67–8, 111
Saudi Aramco, *see also* Aramco
production at Shaybah begins, 221
Sbaat, 151
Schofield, Richard, 232
Selwah, 76, 77
Semail Gap, 208
Al Bu Shamis tribe, 90, 91, 107
al-Shamsi, Muhammad bin Salimin, 90,
105, 157
al-Shamsi, Rashid bin Hamad, xv, 43, 91,
92, 93, 94, 101, 106, 107, 121,

129, 132, 147, 149, 150, 156, 158,
183, 206
sharia law, 23
Sharjah, 77, 98
Sharm, 108
Shawcross, Sir Hartley, 160, **163**, 164,
166, 167, 169, 170, 171, 172
Shaybah–Zarrara oilfield, 221–2, 223,
226–7, 228
Shuckburgh, Evelyn, xvi, 137, 141, 161,
164, 171, 174, 175, 177, 178, 192,
194, 197, 201
Sila, 190
Simpson, John L., 165, 169
Skliros, John, 13, 14
slave trade, 22, 43, 120
Smith, Major Norman, 181, 184
Sohar, 102, 103, 104
Standard Oil of California (Socal), 8, 11,
12, 15, 17, 26, 39
Standard Oil of New Jersey, 66, 70, 81
Standard Oil of New York (Socony), 66
Standstill Agreement (1952), 104, 115
Status Quo Agreement (1950), 84, 102
Steggles, Captain A.R., 182, 183
Steineke, Max, 133
Sterner, Michael, xvi, 94, 219, 223, 224,
267
Stobart incident, 75–80
Stobart, Patrick, 78, 79, 80, 82
Suez Crisis, 203, 235
Operation Musketeer, 203, 216
Sufuq, 79
Sufuq Wells, 29, 30
al-Sulaiman, Abdullah bin Abdul Aziz,
qadhi of Hamasa, 186
Sulaiyil, 18, 24, 49
Suleiman, Abdullah, finance minister,
xiii, 9, 13, 14, 15, 68, **69**, 70
Sultan bin Surur, sheikh of the
Dhawahir tribe, 160
al-Suweidi, Ahmad bin Khalifa, 224, 225
al-Suweidi, Muhammad Habroush, 223,
224

Tapline, 66
Tarif, 93, 116

Al Thani dynasty:
  Ali bin Abdullah, ruler of Qatar, 105
Thesiger, Wilfred, 42, 43, 45–9, **47**, 50,
      81, 164
  relations with IPC, 46–8
Thomas, Bertram, 6, 8, 11, 18, 74
Thomson, Lester, 40
Thwaites, Major Otto, 123
Treaties
  Anglo-Turkish Treaty (1914), 166,
      232
  General Treaty of Peace (1820), 3
  Jedda Agreement (1974), 224–6, 226,
      227, 228, 229, 233
  Jedda Treaty (1927), 53, 82
  Maritime Truce (1835), 3
  Perpetual Maritime Truce (1853), 3,
      31
  Treaty of Sib (1920), 35, 89, 199
Tripp, Peter, 186
Trucial Coast, 51, 97, 116
  conditions in 1950, 98
  influence of Ibn Saud in, 53, 81
  suppression of piracy along, 3
Trucial Oman Levies, 81, 93, 102, 108,
      116, 122, 123, 182
Truman Doctrine, 1947, 67
Truman, Harry, 65, 67
Tuwaiq Mountains, 24
Twitchell, Karl, 11, 12, 15, 71

ulema, 23, 217, 244
Umm al-Zamul, 223
Umm Shaif, 217
United Arab Emirates (UAE)
  after the death of Sheikh Zayed, 227
  Federal Council, 228
  formation, 221, 222
  relations with Iran, 236
  relations with Saudi Arabia, 236
  support for Oman in the Dhofar
      war, 214
United Kingdom
  accuses Saudi Arabia of bribery, 176
  and arbitration of the Buraimi
      dispute, 142, 162, 177
  attitude to the Hamasa refugees, 211

  early relations with Abu Dhabi, 33,
      39
  early relations with Oman, 33, 39
  early relations with the sheikhs of
      the Trucial Coast, 3
  and the Eisenhower Doctrine, 216
  oil interests in the Middle East, 179
  position in the Persian Gulf, 197
  as a post-war global power, 234
  and the post-war petroleum order,
      233
  recognition of Nejd and Al-Hasa, 5
  relations with Saudi Arabia, 53, 111,
      217
  relations with the USA, 111, 197,
      199–201, 216–17
  and the sterling area of the Middle
      East, 111
  and the UN Security Council, 196
  withdrawal from the Gulf, 220
United Nations, 116
  ad hoc committee on Oman, 212
  admission of Oman (1971), 213
  Charter, 165
  de Ribbing mission (1960), 211
  de Ribbing report (1963), 212
  resolution on Oman, 213
  Saudi delegation, 125
  Security Council, 175, 196, 197, 207,
      209
United States
  attitude towards the British position
      in the Persian Gulf, 197
  attitude towards the British
      reoccupation of Hamasa, 196
  attitude towards the Saudi
      occupation of Hamasa, 103
  and Lend-Lease, 65
  oil reserves in the USA, 64
  policy towards Israel and Palestine,
      65
  and the post-war petroleum order,
      233
  relations with Saudi Arabia, 63–6,
      65, 67–8, 111
  relations with the UK, 111, 197,
      199–201, 216–17

Upper Thamama rock interval, 134
Uqair, conference of 1922, 26

Violet Line, *see* Boundaries
Visscher, Charles de, 165

Wabar, 23
Wadi al-Qaur, 108
Wadi Jizzi, 44, 151
Wadi Sahba, 24, 25
Wadsworth, George, 136
Wahba, Hafiz, xvii, 10, 136, 137, 138,
    177, 178, 192
al-Wahhab, Muhammad ibn Abdul, xv,
    1, 23
Wahhabis, 1–6, 18, 24, 51, 166
Waldock, Humphrey, 163
Walker, Julian, 129, 131, 141, 211
Wasit, 150
Wasuth, 41
Waterfield, Pat, 184

Weir, Michael, 114
Wellings, F.E., 43, 154
Wilkinson, John C., 232
Williamson, Daniel C., 233
Williamson, William 'Haji', 36, 55, 56
Wilson, Woodrow, 112
Wilton, John, 91, 92, 93, 98

Yamama, 24
Yanqul, 36
Yasin, Yusuf, xvii, 10, 128, 135–6, **135**,
    140, 149, 153, 161, 162, 164, 165,
    167, 168, 170, 171, 172, 176, 185,
    192, 193, 194
Yellow Line, *see* Boundaries
Young, Richard, 112, 153, 164

zakat, 3, 27, 53, 72, 73–4, 83, 87, 116,
    117, 207
Zekrit Zone, *see* the Arab Zone